THE $30,000 BEQUEST

and Other Stories

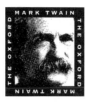

THE OXFORD MARK TWAIN

Shelley Fisher Fishkin, Editor

The
$30,000 Bequest
and Other Stories

Mark Twain

FOREWORD

SHELLEY FISHER FISHKIN

INTRODUCTION

FREDERICK BUSCH

AFTERWORD

JUDITH YAROSS LEE

New York   Oxford

OXFORD UNIVERSITY PRESS

1996

OXFORD UNIVERSITY PRESS

Oxford   New York

Athens, Auckland, Bangkok, Bogotá, Bombay

Buenos Aires, Calcutta, Cape Town, Dar es Salaam

Delhi, Florence, Hong Kong, Istanbul, Karachi

Kuala Lumpur, Madras, Madrid, Melbourne

Mexico City, Nairobi, Paris, Singapore

Taipei, Tokyo, Toronto

and associated companies in

Berlin, Ibadan

Copyright © 1996 by

Oxford University Press, Inc.

Introduction © 1996 by Frederick Busch

Afterword © 1996 by Judith Yaross Lee

A Note on the Illustrations © 1996 by Ray Sapirstein

Text design by Richard Hendel

Composition: David Thorne

Published by

Oxford University Press, Inc.

198 Madison Avenue, New York,

New York 10016

Oxford is a registered trademark of

Oxford University Press

Library of Congress

Cataloging-in-Publication Data

Twain, Mark, 1835–1910.

The $30,000 bequest and other stories / by Mark

Twain; with an introduction by Frederick Busch and

an afterword by Judith Yaross Lee.

p. cm. — (The Oxford Mark Twain)

1. United States—Social life and customs—Fiction.

2. Humorous stories, American. I. Title. II. Series:

Twain, Mark, 1835–1910. Works. 1996.

PS1322.T4 1996

813'.4—dc20

96-14730

CIP

ISBN 0-19-510146-4 (trade ed.)

ISBN 0-19-511423-x (lib. ed.)

ISBN 0-19-509088-8 (trade ed. set)

ISBN 0-19-511345-4 (lib. ed. set)

9 8 7 6 5 4 3 2 1

Printed in the United States of America

on acid-free paper

FRONTISPIECE

Albert Bigelow Paine photographed Samuel L.

Clemens in Dublin, New Hampshire, in 1906, the

year Clemens published *The $30,000 Bequest and

Other Stories*. (The Mark Twain House, Hartford,

Connecticut)

CONTENTS

EDITOR'S NOTE

The Oxford Mark Twain consists of twenty-nine volumes of facsimiles of the first American editions of Mark Twain's works, with an editor's foreword, new introductions, afterwords, notes on the texts, and essays on the illustrations in volumes with artwork. The facsimiles have been reproduced from the originals unaltered, except that blank pages in the front and back of the books have been omitted, and any seriously damaged or missing pages have been replaced by pages from other first editions (as indicated in the notes on the texts).

In the foreword, introduction, afterword, and essays on the illustrations, the titles of Mark Twain's works have been capitalized according to modern conventions, as have the names of characters (except where otherwise indicated). In the case of discrepancies between the title of a short story, essay, or sketch as it appears in the original table of contents and as it appears on its own title page, the title page has been followed. The parenthetical numbers in the introduction, afterwords, and illustration essays are page references to the facsimiles.

FOREWORD

Shelley Fisher Fishkin

Samuel Clemens entered the world and left it with Halley's Comet, little dreaming that generations hence Halley's Comet would be less famous than Mark Twain. He has been called the American Cervantes, our Homer, our Tolstoy, our Shakespeare, our Rabelais. Ernest Hemingway maintained that "all modern American literature comes from one book by Mark Twain called *Huckleberry Finn*." President Franklin Delano Roosevelt got the phrase "New Deal" from *A Connecticut Yankee in King Arthur's Court*. *The Gilded Age* gave an entire era its name. "The future historian of America," wrote George Bernard Shaw to Samuel Clemens, "will find your works as indispensable to him as a French historian finds the political tracts of Voltaire."[1]

There is a Mark Twain Bank in St. Louis, a Mark Twain Diner in Jackson Heights, New York, a Mark Twain Smoke Shop in Lakeland, Florida. There are Mark Twain Elementary Schools in Albuquerque, Dayton, Seattle, and Sioux Falls. Mark Twain's image peers at us from advertisements for Bass Ale (his drink of choice was Scotch), for a gas company in Tennessee, a hotel in the nation's capital, a cemetery in California.

Ubiquitous though his name and image may be, Mark Twain is in no danger of becoming a petrified icon. On the contrary: Mark Twain lives. *Huckleberry Finn* is "the most taught novel, most taught long work, and most taught piece of American literature" in American schools from junior high to the graduate level.[2] Hundreds of Twain impersonators appear in theaters, trade shows, and shopping centers in every region of the country.[3] Scholars publish hundreds of articles as well as books about Twain every year, and he is the subject of daily exchanges on the Internet. A journalist somewhere in the world finds a reason to quote Twain just about every day. Television series such as *Bonanza, Star Trek: The Next Generation,* and *Cheers* broadcast episodes that feature Mark Twain as a character. Hollywood screenwriters regularly produce movies inspired by his works, and writers of mysteries and science fiction continue to weave him into their plots.[4]

A century after the American Revolution sent shock waves throughout Europe, it took Mark Twain to explain to Europeans and to his countrymen alike what that revolution had wrought. He probed the significance of this new land and its new citizens, and identified what it was in the Old World that America abolished and rejected. The founding fathers had thought through the political dimensions of making a new society; Mark Twain took on the challenge of interpreting the social and cultural life of the United States for those outside its borders as well as for those who were living the changes he discerned.

Americans may have constructed a new society in the eighteenth century, but they articulated what they had done in voices that were largely inter-changeable with those of Englishmen until well into the nineteenth century. Mark Twain became the voice of the new land, the leading translator of what and who the "American" was — and, to a large extent, is. Frances Trollope's *Domestic Manners of the Americans,* a best-seller in England, Hector St. John de Crèvecoeur's *Letters from an American Farmer,* and Tocqueville's *Democracy in America* all tried to explain America to Europeans. But Twain did more than that: he allowed European readers to *experience* this strange "new world." And he gave his countrymen the tools to do two things they had not quite had the confidence to do before. He helped them stand before the cultural icons of the Old World unembarrassed, unashamed of America's lack of palaces and shrines, proud of its brash practicality and bold inventiveness, unafraid to reject European models of "civilization" as tainted or corrupt. And he also helped them recognize their own insularity, boorishness, arrogance, or ignorance, and laugh at it — the first step toward transcending it and becoming more "civilized," in the best European sense of the word.

Twain often strikes us as more a creature of our time than of his. He appreciated the importance and the complexity of mass tourism and public relations, fields that would come into their own in the twentieth century but were only fledgling enterprises in the nineteenth. He explored the liberating potential of humor and the dynamics of friendship, parenting, and marriage. He narrowed the gap between "popular" and "high" culture, and he meditated on the enigmas of personal and national identity. Indeed, it would be difficult to find an issue on the horizon today that Twain did not touch on somewhere in his work. Heredity versus environment? Animal rights? The boundaries of gender? The place of black voices in the cultural heritage of the United States? Twain was there.

With startling prescience and characteristic grace and wit, he zeroed in on many of the key challenges — political, social, and technological — that would face his country and the world for the next hundred years: the challenge of race relations in a society founded on both chattel slavery and ideals of equality, and the intractable problem of racism in American life; the potential of new technologies to transform our lives in ways that can be both exhilarating and terrifying — as well as unpredictable; the problem of imperialism and the difficulties entailed in getting rid of it. But he never lost sight of the most basic challenge of all: each man or woman's struggle for integrity in the face of the seductions of power, status, and material things.

Mark Twain's unerring sense of the right word and not its second cousin taught people to pay attention when he spoke, in person or in print. He said things that were smart and things that were wise, and he said them incomparably well. He defined the rhythms of our prose and the contours of our moral map. He saw our best and our worst, our extravagant promise and our stunning failures, our comic foibles and our tragic flaws. Throughout the world he is viewed as the most distinctively American of American authors — and as one of the most universal. He is assigned in classrooms in Naples, Riyadh, Belfast, and Beijing, and has been a major influence on twentieth-century writers from Argentina to Nigeria to Japan. The Oxford Mark Twain celebrates the versatility and vitality of this remarkable writer.

The Oxford Mark Twain reproduces the first American editions of Mark Twain's books published during his lifetime.[5] By encountering Twain's works in their original format — typography, layout, order of contents, and illustrations — readers today can come a few steps closer to the literary arti-facts that entranced and excited readers when the books first appeared. Twain approved of and to a greater or lesser degree supervised the publica-tion of all of this material.[6] The Mark Twain House in Hartford, Connecticut, generously loaned us its originals.[7] When more than one copy of a first American edition was available, Robert H. Hirst, general editor of the Mark Twain Project, in cooperation with Marianne Curling, curator of the Mark Twain House (and Jeffrey Kaimowitz, head of Rare Books for the Watkinson Library of Trinity College, Hartford, where the Mark Twain House collection is kept), guided our decision about which one to use.[8] As a set, the volumes also contain more than eighty essays commissioned especially for The Oxford Mark Twain, in which distinguished contributors reassess Twain's achievement as a writer and his place in the cultural conversation that he did so much to shape.

Each volume of The Oxford Mark Twain is introduced by a leading American, Canadian, or British writer who responds to Twain — often in a very personal way — as a fellow writer. Novelists, journalists, humorists, columnists, fabulists, poets, playwrights — these writers tell us what Twain taught them and what in his work continues to speak to them. Reading Twain's books, both famous and obscure, they reflect on the genesis of his art and the characteristics of his style, the themes he illuminated, and the aes-thetic strategies he pioneered. Individually and collectively their contribu-tions testify to the place Mark Twain holds in the hearts of readers of all kinds and temperaments.

Scholars whose work has shaped our view of Twain in the academy today have written afterwords to each volume, with suggestions for further reading. Their essays give us a sense of what was going on in Twain's life when he wrote the book at hand, and of how that book fits into his career. They explore how each book reflects and refracts contemporary events, and they show Twain responding to literary and social currents of the day, variously accepting, amplifying, modifying, and challenging prevailing paradigms. Sometimes they argue that works previously dismissed as quirky or eccentric departures actually address themes at the heart of Twain's work from the start. And as they bring new perspectives to Twain's composition strategies in familiar texts, several scholars see experiments in form where others saw only formlessness, method where prior critics saw only madness. In addition to elucidating the work's historical and cultural context, the afterwords provide an overview of responses to each book from its first appearance to the present.

Most of Mark Twain's books involved more than Mark Twain's words: unique illustrations. The parodic visual send-ups of "high culture" that Twain himself drew for *A Tramp Abroad*, the sketch of financial manipulator Jay Gould as a greedy and sadistic "Slave Driver" in *A Connecticut Yankee in King Arthur's Court*, and the memorable drawings of Eve in *Eve's Diary* all helped Twain's books to be sold, read, discussed, and preserved. In their essays for each volume that contains artwork, Beverly R. David and Ray Sapirstein highlight the significance of the sketches, engravings, and photographs in the first American editions of Mark Twain's works, and tell us what is known about the public response to them.

The Oxford Mark Twain invites us to read some relatively neglected works by Twain in the company of some of the most engaging literary figures of our time. Roy Blount Jr., for example, riffs in a deliciously Twain-like manner on "An Item Which the Editor Himself Could Not Understand," which may well rank as one of the least-known pieces Twain ever published. Bobbie Ann Mason celebrates the "mad energy" of Twain's most obscure comic novel, *The American Claimant*, in which the humor "hurtles beyond tall tale into simon-pure absurdity."[9] Garry Wills finds that *Christian Science* "gets us very close to the heart of American culture." Lee Smith reads "Political Economy" as a sharp and funny essay on language. Walter Mosley sees "The Stolen White Elephant," a story "reduced to a series of ridiculous telegrams related by an untrustworthy narrator caught up in an adventure that is as impossible as it is ludicrous," as a stunningly compact and economical satire of a world we still recognize as our own. Anne Bernays returns to "The Private History of a Campaign That Failed" and finds "an antiwar manifesto that is also con-

XVI : SHELLEY FISHER FISHKIN

fession, dramatic monologue, a plea for understanding and absolution, and a romp that gradually turns into atrocity even as we watch." After revisiting Captain Stormfield's heaven, Frederik Pohl finds that there "is no imaginable place more pleasant to spend eternity." Indeed, Pohl writes, "one would almost be willing to die to enter it."

While less familiar works receive fresh attention in The Oxford Mark Twain, new light is cast on the best-known works as well. Judith Martin ("Miss Manners") points out that it is by reading a court etiquette book that Twain's pauper learns how to behave as a proper prince. As important as etiquette may be in the palace, Martin notes, it is even more important in the slums.

> That etiquette is a sorer point with the ruffians in the street than with the proud dignitaries of the prince's court may surprise some readers. As in our own streets, etiquette is always a more volatile subject among those who cannot count on being treated with respect than among those who have the power to command deference.

And taking a fresh look at *Adventures of Huckleberry Finn,* Toni Morrison writes,

> much of the novel's genius lies in its quiescence, the silences that pervade it and give it a porous quality that is by turns brooding and soothing. It lies in ... the subdued images in which the repetition of a simple word, such as "lonesome," tolls like an evening bell; the moments when nothing is said, when scenes and incidents swell the heart unbearably precisely because unarticulated, and force an act of imagination almost against the will.

Engaging Mark Twain as one writer to another, several contributors to The Oxford Mark Twain offer new insights into the processes by which his books came to be. Russell Banks, for example, reads *A Tramp Abroad* as "an important revision of Twain's incomplete first draft of *Huckleberry Finn,* a second draft, if you will, which in turn made possible the third and final draft." Erica Jong suggests that *1601,* a freewheeling parody of Elizabethan manners and mores, written during the same summer Twain began *Huckleberry Finn*, served as "a warm-up for his creative process" and "primed the pump for other sorts of freedom of expression." And Justin Kaplan suggests that "one of the transcendent figures standing behind and shaping" *Joan of Arc* was Ulysses S. Grant, whose memoirs Twain had recently published, and who, like Joan, had risen unpredictably "from humble and obscure origins" to become a "military genius" endowed with "the gift of command, a natural eloquence, and an equally natural reserve."

As a number of contributors note, Twain was a man ahead of his times. *The Gilded Age* was the first "Washington novel," Ward Just tells us, because "Twain was the first to see the possibilities that had eluded so many others." Commenting on *The Tragedy of Pudd'nhead Wilson*, Sherley Anne Williams observes that "Twain's argument about the power of environment in shaping character runs directly counter to prevailing sentiment where the negro was concerned." Twain's fictional technology, wildly fanciful by the standards of his day, predicts developments we take for granted in ours. DNA cloning, fax machines, and photocopiers are all prefigured, Bobbie Ann Mason tells us, in *The American Claimant*. Cynthia Ozick points out that the "telelectrophonoscope" we meet in "From the 'London Times' of 1904" is suspiciously like what we know as "television." And Malcolm Bradbury suggests that in the "phrenophones" of "Mental Telegraphy" "the Internet was born."

Twain turns out to have been remarkably prescient about political affairs as well. Kurt Vonnegut sees in *A Connecticut Yankee* a chilling foreshadowing (or perhaps a projection from the Civil War) of "all the high-tech atrocities which followed, and which follow still." Cynthia Ozick suggests that "The Man That Corrupted Hadleyburg," along with some of the other pieces collected under that title — many of them written when Twain lived in a Vienna ruled by Karl Lueger, a demagogue Adolf Hitler would later idolize — shoot up moral flares that shed an eerie light on the insidious corruption, prejudice, and hatred that reached bitter fruition under the Third Reich. And Twain's portrait in this book of "the dissolving Austria-Hungary of the 1890s," in Ozick's view, presages not only the Sarajevo that would erupt in 1914 but also "the disintegrated components of the former Yugoslavia" and "the *fin-de-siècle* Sarajevo of our own moment."

Despite their admiration for Twain's ambitious reach and scope, contributors to The Oxford Mark Twain also recognize his limitations. Mordecai Richler, for example, thinks that "the early pages of *Innocents Abroad* suffer from being a tad broad, proffering more burlesque than inspired satire," perhaps because Twain was "trying too hard for knee-slappers." Charles Johnson notes that the Young Man in Twain's philosophical dialogue about free will and determinism (*What Is Man?*) "caves in far too soon," failing to challenge what through late-twentieth-century eyes looks like "pseudoscience" and suspect essentialism in the Old Man's arguments.

Some contributors revisit their first encounters with Twain's works, recalling what surprised or intrigued them. When David Bradley came across "Fenimore Cooper's Literary Offences" in his college library, he "did not at first realize that Twain was being his usual ironic self with all this business about the 'nineteen rules governing literary art in the domain of romantic fiction,' but by the time I figured out there was no such list outside Twain's own head, I had decided that the rules made *sense*. . . . It seemed to me they were a pretty good blueprint for writing — Negro writing included." Sherley Anne Williams remembers that part of what attracted her to *Pudd'nhead Wilson* when she first read it thirty years ago was "that Twain, writing at the end of the nineteenth century, could imagine negroes as characters, albeit white ones, who actually thought for and of themselves, whose actions were the product of their thinking rather than the spontaneous ephemera of physical instincts that stereotype assigned to blacks." Frederik Pohl recalls his first reading of *Huckleberry Finn* as "a watershed event" in his life, the first book he read as a child in which "bad people" ceased to exercise a monopoly on doing "bad things." In *Huckleberry Finn* "some seriously bad things — things like the possession and mistreatment of black slaves, like stealing and lying, even like killing other people in duels — were quite often done by people who not only thought of themselves as exemplarily moral but, by any other standards I knew how to apply, actually *were* admirable citizens." The world that

Tom and Huck lived in, Pohl writes, "was filled with complexities and contradictions," and resembled "the world I appeared to be living in myself."

Other contributors explore their more recent encounters with Twain, explaining why they have revised their initial responses to his work. For Toni Morrison, parts of *Huckleberry Finn* that she "once took to be deliberate evasions, stumbles even, or a writer's impatience with his or her material," now strike her "as otherwise: as entrances, crevices, gaps, seductive invitations flashing the possibility of meaning. Unarticulated eddies that encourage diving into the novel's undertow — the real place where writer captures reader." One such "eddy" is the imprisonment of Jim on the Phelps farm. Instead of dismissing this portion of the book as authorial bungling, as she once did, Morrison now reads it as Twain's commentary on the 1880s, a period that "saw the collapse of civil rights for blacks," a time when "the nation, as well as Tom Sawyer, was deferring Jim's freedom in agonizing play." Morrison believes that Americans in the 1880s were attempting "to bury the combustible issues Twain raised in his novel," and that those who try to kick Huck Finn out of school in the 1990s are doing the same: "The cyclical attempts to remove the novel from classrooms extend Jim's captivity on into each generation of readers."

Although imitation-Hemingway and imitation-Faulkner writing contests draw hundreds of entries annually, no one has ever tried to mount a faux-Twain competition. Why? Perhaps because Mark Twain's voice is too much a part of who we are and how we speak even today. Roy Blount Jr. suggests that it is impossible, "at least for an American writer, to parody Mark Twain. It would be like doing an impression of your father or mother: he or she is already there in your voice."

Twain's style is examined and celebrated in The Oxford Mark Twain by fellow writers who themselves have struggled with the nuances of words, the structure of sentences, the subtleties of point of view, and the trickiness of opening lines. Bobbie Ann Mason observes, for example, that "Twain loved the sound of words and he knew how to string them by sound, like different shades of one color: 'The earl's barbaric eye,' 'the Usurping Earl,' 'a double-dyed humbug.'" Twain "relied on the punch of plain words" to show writers how to move beyond the "wordy romantic rubbish" so prevalent in nineteenth-century fiction, Mason says; he "was one of the first writers in America to deflower literary language." Lee Smith believes that "American writers have benefited as much from the way Mark Twain opened up the possibilities of first-person narration as we have from his use of vernacular language." (She feels that "the ghost of Mark Twain was hovering someplace in the background" when she decided to write her novel *Oral History* from the standpoint of multiple first-person narrators.) Frederick Busch maintains that "A Dog's Tale" "boasts one of the great opening sentences" of all time: "My father was a St. Bernard, my mother was a collie, but I am a Presbyterian." And Ursula Le Guin marvels at the ingenuity of the following sentence that she encounters in *Extracts from Adam's Diary*.

> . . . This made her sorry for the creatures which live in there, which she calls fish, for she continues to fasten names on to things that don't need them and don't come when they are called by them, which is a matter of no consequence to her, as she is such a numskull anyway; so she got a lot of them out and brought them in last night and put them in my bed to keep warm, but I have noticed them now and then all day, and I don't see that they are any happier there than they were before, only quieter.[10]

Le Guin responds,

> Now, that is a pure Mark-Twain-tour-de-force sentence, covering an immense amount of territory in an effortless, aimless ramble that seems to be heading nowhere in particular and ends up with breathtaking accuracy at the gold mine. Any sensible child would find that funny, perhaps not following all its divagations but delighted by the swing of it, by the word "numskull," by the idea of putting fish in the bed; and as that child grew older and reread it, its reward would only grow; and if that grown-up child had to write an essay on the piece and therefore earnestly studied and pored over this sentence, she would end up in unmitigated admiration of its vocabulary, syntax, pacing, sense, and rhythm, above all the beautiful

timing of the last two words; and she would, and she does, still find it funny.

The fish surface again in a passage that Gore Vidal calls to our attention, from *Following the Equator*: "'The Whites always mean well when they take human fish out of the ocean and try to make them dry and warm and happy and comfortable in a chicken coop,' which is how, through civilization, they did away with many of the original inhabitants. Lack of empathy is a principal theme in Twain's meditations on race and empire."

Indeed, empathy — and its lack — is a principal theme in virtually all of Twain's work, as contributors frequently note. Nat Hentoff quotes the following thoughts from Huck in *Tom Sawyer Abroad*:

> I see a bird setting on a dead limb of a high tree, singing with its head tilt- ed back and its mouth open, and before I thought I fired, and his song stopped and he fell straight down from the limb, all limp like a rag, and I run and picked him up and he was dead, and his body was warm in my hand, and his head rolled about this way and that, like his neck was broke, and there was a little white skin over his eyes, and one little drop of blood on the side of his head; and laws! I could n't see nothing more for the tears; and I hain't never murdered no creature since that war n't doing me no harm, and I ain't going to.[11]

"The Humane Society," Hentoff writes, "has yet to say anything as powerful — and lasting."

Readers of The Oxford Mark Twain will have the pleasure of revisiting Twain's Mississippi landmarks alongside Willie Morris, whose own lower Mississippi Valley boyhood gives him a special sense of connection to Twain. Morris knows firsthand the mosquitoes described in *Life on the Mississippi* — so colossal that "two of them could whip a dog" and "four of them could hold a man down"; in Morris's own hometown they were so large during the flood season that "local wags said they wore wristwatches." Morris's Yazoo City and Twain's Hannibal shared a "rough-hewn democracy . . . complicated by all the visible textures of caste and class, . . . harmless boyhood fun and mischief right along with . . . rank hypocrisies, churchgoing sanctimonies, racial hatred, entrenched and unrepentant greed."

For the West of Mark Twain's *Roughing It*, readers will have George Plimpton as their guide. "What a group these newspapermen were!" Plimpton writes about Twain and his friends Dan De Quille and Joe Goodman in Virginia City, Nevada. "Their roisterous carryings-on bring to mind the kind of frat-house enthusiasm one associates with college humor magazines like the *Harvard Lampoon*." Malcolm Bradbury examines Twain as "a living example of what made the American so different from the European." And Hal Holbrook, who has interpreted Mark Twain on stage for some forty years, describes how Twain "played" during the civil rights movement, during the Vietnam War, during the Gulf War, and in Prague on the eve of the demise of Communism.

Why do we continue to read Mark Twain? What draws us to him? His wit? His compassion? His humor? His bravura? His humility? His understanding of who and what we are in those parts of our being that we rarely open to view? Our sense that he knows we can do better than we do? Our sense that he knows we can't? E. L. Doctorow tells us that children are attracted to *Tom Sawyer* because in this book "the young reader confirms his own hope that no matter how troubled his relations with his elders may be, beneath all their disapproval is their underlying love for him, constant and steadfast." Readers in general, Arthur Miller writes, value Twain's "insights into America's always uncertain moral life and its shifting but everlasting hypocrisies"; we appreciate the fact that he "is not using his alienation from the public illusions of his hour in order to reject the country implicitly as though he could live without it, but manifestly in order to correct it." Perhaps we keep reading Mark Twain because, in Miller's words, he "wrote much more like a father than a son. He doesn't seem to be sitting in class taunting the teacher but standing at the head of it challenging his students to acknowledge their own humanity, that is, their immemorial attraction to the untrue."

Mark Twain entered the public eye at a time when many of his countrymen considered "American culture" an oxymoron; he died four years before a world conflagration that would lead many to question whether the contradiction in terms was not "European civilization" instead. In between he worked in journalism, printing, steamboating, mining, lecturing, publishing, and editing, in virtually every region of the country. He tried his hand at humorous sketches, social satire, historical novels, children's books, poetry, drama, science fiction, mysteries, romance, philosophy, travelogue, memoir, polemic, and several genres no one had ever seen before or has ever seen since. He invented a self-pasting scrapbook, a history game, a vest strap, and a gizmo for keeping bed sheets tucked in; he invested in machines and processes designed to revolutionize typesetting and engraving, and in a food supplement called "Plasmon." Along the way he cheerfully impersonated himself and prior versions of himself for doting publics on five continents while playing out a charming rags-to-riches story followed by a devastating riches-to-rags story followed by yet another great American comeback. He had a long-running real-life engagement in a sumptuous comedy of manners, and then in a real-life tragedy not of his own design: during the last fourteen years of his life almost everyone he ever loved was taken from him by disease and death.

Mark Twain has indelibly shaped our views of who and what the United States is as a nation and of who and what we might become. He understood the nostalgia for a "simpler" past that increased as that past receded — and he saw through the nostalgia to a past that was just as complex as the present. He recognized better than we did ourselves our potential for greatness and our potential for disaster. His fictions brilliantly illuminated the world in which he lived, changing it — and us — in the process. He knew that our feet often danced to tunes that had somehow remained beyond our hearing; with perfect pitch he played them back to us.

My mother read *Tom Sawyer* to me as a bedtime story when I was eleven. I thought Huck and Tom could be a lot of fun, but I dismissed Becky Thatcher as a bore. When I was twelve I invested a nickel at a local garage sale in a book that contained short pieces by Mark Twain. That was where I met Twain's Eve. Now, *that's* more like it, I decided, pleased to meet a female character I could identify *with* instead of against. Eve had spunk. Even if she got a lot wrong, you had to give her credit for trying. "The Man That Corrupted

XXIV : SHELLEY FISHER FISHKIN

Hadleyburg" left me giddy with satisfaction: none of my adolescent reveries of getting even with my enemies were half as neat as the plot of the man who got back at that town. "How I Edited an Agricultural Paper" set me off in uncontrollable giggles.

People sometimes told me that I looked like Huck Finn. "It's the freckles," they'd explain — not explaining anything at all. I didn't read *Huckleberry Finn* until junior year in high school in my English class. It was the fall of 1965. I was living in a small town in Connecticut. I expected a sequel to *Tom Sawyer*. So when the teacher handed out the books and announced our assignment, my jaw dropped: "Write a paper on how Mark Twain used irony to attack racism in *Huckleberry Finn*."

The year before, the bodies of three young men who had gone to Mississippi to help blacks register to vote — James Chaney, Andrew Goodman, and Michael Schwerner — had been found in a shallow grave; a group of white segregationists (the county sheriff among them) had been arrested in connection with the murders. America's inner cities were simmering with pent-up rage that began to explode in the summer of 1965, when riots in Watts left thirty-four people dead. None of this made any sense to me. I was confused, angry, certain that there was something missing from the news stories I read each day: the why. Then I met Pap Finn. And the Phelpses.

Pap Finn, Huck tells us, "had been drunk over in town" and "was just all mud." He erupts into a drunken tirade about "a free nigger . . . from Ohio — a mulatter, most as white as a white man," with "the whitest shirt on you ever see, too, and the shiniest hat; and there ain't a man in town that's got as fine clothes as what he had."

> . . . they said he was a p'fessor in a college, and could talk all kinds of languages, and knowed everything. And that ain't the wust. They said he could *vote*, when he was at home. Well, that let me out. Thinks I, what is the country a-coming to? It was 'lection day, and I was just about to go and vote, myself, if I warn't too drunk to get there; but when they told me there was a State in this country where they'd let that nigger vote, I drawed out. I says I'll never vote agin. Them's the very words I said. . . . And to see the

cool way of that nigger — why, he wouldn't a give me the road if I hadn't shoved him out o' the way.[12]

Later on in the novel, when the runaway slave Jim gives up his freedom to nurse a wounded Tom Sawyer, a white doctor testifies to the stunning altruism of his actions. The Phelpses and their neighbors, all fine, upstanding, well-meaning, churchgoing folk,

> agreed that Jim had acted very well, and was deserving to have some notice took of it, and reward. So every one of them promised, right out and hearty, that they wouldn't curse him no more.
>
> Then they come out and locked him up. I hoped they was going to say he could have one or two of the chains took off, because they was rotten heavy, or could have meat and greens with his bread and water, but they didn't think of it.[13]

Why did the behavior of these people tell me more about why Watts burned than anything I had read in the daily paper? And why did a drunk Pap Finn railing against a black college professor from Ohio whose vote was as good as his own tell me more about white anxiety over black political power than anything I had seen on the evening news? Mark Twain knew that there was nothing, absolutely *nothing*, a black man could do — including selflessly sacrificing his freedom, the only thing of value he had — that would make white society see beyond the color of his skin. And Mark Twain knew that depicting racists with chilling accuracy would expose the viciousness of their world view like nothing else could. It was an insight echoed some eighty years after Mark Twain penned Pap Finn's rantings about the black professor, when Malcolm X famously asked, "Do you know what white racists call black Ph.D.'s?" and answered, " '*Nigger!*' "[14]

Mark Twain taught me things I needed to know. He taught me to understand the raw racism that lay behind what I saw on the evening news. He taught me that the most well-meaning people can be hurtful and myopic. He taught me to recognize the supreme irony of a country founded in freedom that continued to deny freedom to so many of its citizens. Every time I hear of another effort to kick Huck Finn out of school somewhere, I recall everything that Mark Twain taught *this* high school junior, and I find myself jumping into the fray.[15] I remember the black high school student who called CNN during the phone-in portion of a 1985 debate between Dr. John Wallace, a black educator spearheading efforts to ban the book, and myself. She accused Dr. Wallace of insulting her and all black high school students by suggesting they weren't smart enough to understand Mark Twain's irony. And I recall the black cameraman on the *CBS Morning News* who came up to me after he finished shooting another debate between Dr. Wallace and myself. He said he had never read the book by Mark Twain that we had been arguing about — but now he really wanted to. One thing that puzzled him, though, was why a white woman was defending it and a black man was attacking it, because as far as he could see from what we'd been saying, the book made whites look pretty bad.

As I came to understand *Huckleberry Finn* and *Pudd'nhead Wilson* as commentaries on the era now known as the nadir of American race relations, those books pointed me toward the world recorded in nineteenth-century black newspapers and periodicals and in fiction by Mark Twain's black contemporaries. My investigation of the role black voices and traditions played in shaping Mark Twain's art helped make me aware of their role in shaping all of American culture.[16] My research underlined for me the importance of changing the stories we tell about who we are to reflect the realities of what we've been.[17]

Ever since our encounter in high school English, Mark Twain has shown me the potential of American literature and American history to illuminate each other. Rarely have I found a contradiction or complexity we grapple with as a nation that Mark Twain had not puzzled over as well. He insisted on taking America seriously. And he insisted on *not* taking America seriously: "I think that there is but a single specialty with us, only one thing that can be called by the wide name 'American,'" he once wrote. "That is the national devotion to ice-water."[18]

Mark Twain threw back at us our dreams and our denial of those dreams, our greed, our goodness, our ambition, and our laziness, all rattling around together in that vast echo chamber of our talk — that sharp, spunky American talk that Mark Twain figured out how to write down without robbing it of its energy and immediacy. Talk shaped by voices that the official arbiters of "culture" deemed of no importance — voices of children, voices of slaves, voices of servants, voices of ordinary people. Mark Twain listened. And he made us listen. To the stories he told us, and to the truths they conveyed. He still has a lot to say that we need to hear.

Mark Twain lives — in our libraries, classrooms, homes, theaters, movie houses, streets, and most of all in our speech. His optimism energizes us, his despair sobers us, and his willingness to keep wrestling with the hilarious and horrendous complexities of it all keeps us coming back for more. As the twenty-first century approaches, may he continue to goad us, chasten us, delight us, berate us, and cause us to erupt in unrestrained laughter in unexpected places.

NOTES

1. Ernest Hemingway, *Green Hills of Africa* (New York: Charles Scribner's Sons, 1935), 22. George Bernard Shaw to Samuel L. Clemens, July 3, 1907, quoted in Albert Bigelow Paine, *Mark Twain: A Biography* (New York: Harper and Brothers, 1912), 3:1398.

2. Allen Carey-Webb, "Racism and *Huckleberry Finn*: Censorship, Dialogue and Change," *English Journal* 82, no. 7 (November 1993):22.

3. See Louis J. Budd, "Impersonators," in J. R. LeMaster and James D. Wilson, eds., *The Mark Twain Encyclopedia* (New York: Garland Publishing Company, 1993), 389–91.

4. See Shelley Fisher Fishkin, "Ripples and Reverberations," part 3 of *Lighting Out for the Territory: Reflections on Mark Twain and American Culture* (New York: Oxford University Press, 1996).

5. There are two exceptions. Twain published chapters from his autobiography in the *North American Review* in 1906 and 1907, but this material was not published in book form in Twain's lifetime; our volume reproduces the material as it appeared in the *North American Review*. The other exception is our final volume, *Mark Twain's Speeches*, which appeared two months after Twain's death in 1910.

An unauthorized handful of copies of *1601* was privately printed by an Alexander Gunn of Cleveland at the instigation of Twain's friend John Hay in 1880. The first American edition authorized by Mark Twain, however, was printed at the United States Military Academy at West Point in 1882; that is the edition reproduced here.

It should further be noted that four volumes — *The Stolen White Elephant and Other Detective Stories, Following the Equator and Anti-imperialist Essays, The Diaries of Adam and Eve,* and *1601, and Is Shakespeare Dead?* — bind together material originally published separately. In each case the first American edition of the material is the version that has been reproduced, always in its entirety. Because Twain constantly recycled and repackaged previously published works in his collections of short pieces, a certain amount of duplication is unavoidable. We have selected volumes with an eye toward keeping this duplication to a minimum.

Even the twenty-nine-volume Oxford Mark Twain has had to leave much out. No edition of Twain can ever claim to be "complete," for the man was too prolix, and the file drawers of both ephemera and as yet unpublished texts are deep.

6. With the possible exception of *Mark Twain's Speeches.* Some scholars suspect Twain knew about this book and may have helped shape it, although no hard evidence to that effect has yet surfaced. Twain's involvement in the production process varied greatly from book to book. For a fuller sense of authorial intention, scholars will continue to rely on the superb definitive editions of Twain's works produced by the Mark Twain Project at the University of California at Berkeley as they become available. Dense with annotation documenting textual emendation and related issues, these editions add immeasurably to our understanding of Mark Twain and the genesis of his works.

7. Except for a few titles that were not in its collection. The American Antiquarian Society in Worcester, Massachusetts, provided the first edition of *King Leopold's Soliloquy;* the Elmer Holmes Bobst Library of New York University furnished the 1906–7 volumes of the *North American Review* in which *Chapters from My Autobiography* first appeared; the Harry Ransom Humanities Research Center at the University of Texas at Austin made their copy of the West Point edition of *1601* available; and the Mark Twain Project provided the first edition of *Extract from Captain Stormfield's Visit to Heaven.*

8. The specific copy photographed for Oxford's facsimile edition is indicated in a note on the text at the end of each volume.

9. All quotations from contemporary writers in this essay are taken from their introductions to the volumes of The Oxford Mark Twain, and the quotations from Mark Twain's works are taken from the texts reproduced in The Oxford Mark Twain.

10. *The Diaries of Adam and Eve,* The Oxford Mark Twain [hereafter OMT] (New York: Oxford University Press, 1996), p. 33.

11. *Tom Sawyer Abroad,* OMT, p. 74.

12. *Adventures of Huckleberry Finn,* OMT, p. 49–50.

13. Ibid., p. 358.

14. Malcolm X, *The Autobiography of Malcolm X,* with the assistance of Alex Haley (New York: Grove Press, 1965), p. 284.

15. I do not mean to minimize the challenge of teaching this difficult novel, a challenge for which all teachers may not feel themselves prepared. Elsewhere I have developed some concrete strategies for approaching the book in the classroom, including teaching it in the context of the history of American race relations and alongside books by black writers. See Shelley Fisher Fishkin, "Teaching *Huckleberry Finn*," in James S. Leonard, ed., *Making Mark Twain Work in the Classroom* (Durham: Duke University Press, forthcoming). See also Shelley Fisher Fishkin, *Was Huck Black? Mark Twain and African-American Voices* (New York: Oxford University Press, 1993), pp. 106–8, and a curriculum kit in preparation at the Mark Twain House in Hartford, containing teaching suggestions from myself, David Bradley, Jocelyn Chadwick-Joshua, James Miller, and David E. E. Sloane.

16. See Fishkin, *Was Huck Black?* See also Fishkin, "Interrogating 'Whiteness,' Complicating 'Blackness': Remapping American Culture," in Henry Wonham, ed., *Criticism and the Color Line: Desegregating American Literary Studies* (New Brunswick: Rutgers UP, 1996, pp. 251–90 and in shortened form in *American Quarterly* 47, no. 3 (September 1995):428–66.

17. I explore the roots of my interest in Mark Twain and race at greater length in an essay entitled "Changing the Story," in Jeffrey Rubin-Dorsky and Shelley Fisher Fishkin, eds., *People of the Book: Thirty Scholars Reflect on Their Jewish Identity* (Madison: U of Wisconsin Press, 1996), pp. 47–63.

18. "What Paul Bourget Thinks of Us," *How to Tell a Story and Other Essays*, OMT, p. 197.

INTRODUCTION
Actual Clemens, True Twain
Frederick Busch

In discussing matters of authorship in an essay he calls "An Entertaining Article," Mark Twain says, "If any man doubts my word now, I will kill him. No, I will not kill him; I will win his money" (225). It does not seem strange that the profession of letters and a concern for authenticity and honesty, as well as matters of life and death, are joined for Twain as he equates death with losing money. For this is in many ways a book about the acquisition of money, the retention of money, the loss of money, and the cost of getting it. One reason Twain remains crucial to us is his alertness to wealth and its distribution. That sensitivity was as alive as ever when he assembled the stories and essays before us. Most were written when Twain's great work was done, and their sum is therefore a miscellany of what crossed a fine writer's mind and desk when he was waiting for what might become a major effort. Because Twain was involved, and in need of money, its contents are often enough sentimental, harsh, tutelary, and financial. And, often enough, its contents are true.

The book starts with a story that takes as its subject money more than the people who win or lose it, and the book concludes with a story that not only imitates Conan Doyle but shamelessly appropriates Doyle's creation as Twain engages in what seems his obsessive pursuit: chasing down dollars.

Even in one of his most sentimental pieces, "Saint Joan of Arc," Twain focuses not only on the courage and sacrifices of St. Joan, but on unfair taxation; he uses money to create an index of corruption by which Joan's struggle can be measured. And describing her speech, he praises a "moving beauty and simple grace it would *bankrupt* the arts of language to surpass" (147, my italics). In "A Monument to Adam," Twain emphasizes the venery of bankers and the cost of the monument — $25,000 — and in "A Humane Word from Satan" he has Satan point out that "there isn't a rich man in your vast city who doesn't perjure himself every year before the tax board" (238). In "Edward Mills and George Benton: A Tale," the Cain-and-Abel parable demonstrates Twain's tight focus; it is not on his prose, which is slack — "While all these things were going on . . ." Twain writes (136) — but on misspent money (his arithmetic is precise).

So a good and often great writer's handling of central myths — Adam, Satan, Abel and Cain — and topics of the day, as well as his management of his own talent, is affected, and often diminished, by the economic concern that Emerson subsumed with the word "things"; in this book, they *are* in the saddle, they *do* ride.

The title story, although it becomes predictable, remains interesting. During the time of the making of this book, Twain circled about the writing of his autobiography and his own obituary — he was concerned with determining how a future world would regard him — and he circled about the idea of the last will and testament. Not only is that document a convenient source of formulaic stories, those that come perhaps too easily to the writer who isn't galvanized by something larger and more original; it seemed to be a real concern for Twain — he thinks much about death in this book, and a will is that document which gives people of power their only hope of exerting it in a world from which they will have disappeared.

The story's gender switchings are more superficial, less about sexuality, than those of, say, Woolf's *Orlando* or Hemingway's *The Garden of Eden.* Twain has fun with what were considered "male" and "female" characteristics — for example, such revolutionary matters as a wife's being more capable with finances than her husband. If expectations are not overturned, they here, anyway, wobble.

What seems far more interesting about "The $30,000 Bequest," the story of a hoax about money and a couple's temptation-unto-insanity by the idea of making money with money they never got hold of, is how Sally and Aleck, in dramatic dialogue, demonstrate the dynamics of a domestic relationship. While they do not generate the sexual tension of Daisy Buchanan and Jay Gatsby about money and what it buys, they do show how a couple's intercourse becomes linguistic, numerical, and, at last, pure chimera; they merge perfectly in a *folie à deux*. That coupled madness is, of course, a fiction, which they construct day by day, minute by minute, detail by detail. Their lifetime together is an imaginative story, and they "write" well. As ever, when Twain is submerged in a persona, in a voice — and here it is that of the fictional couple his fictional couple creates — his language is at least efficient, brisk, and sometimes stimulated, usually persuasive.

Like Franklin in his diaries, like Gatsby in Fitzgerald's novel, Aleck and Sally create themselves. They are the American story, enacting as they do the self-generated enfleshment of the dream about going from poverty to powerful wealth. Although Twain's language is not superb in this story, it is frequently alive, attentive not only to the homily or cliché, but to the specific physical object, through which life in fiction flows. Of the phony bequeather, a journalist who knew him says, in a moment of killing disclosure for Aleck and Sally, "He hadn't anything to leave but a wheelbarrow, and he left that to me. It hadn't any wheel, and wasn't any good" (47–48). The image works in a manner not unlike the "red wheel/barrow" in Dr. Williams' poem; it is a living sermon on the power of the specific. We see a structure designed for nothing but functioning with a wheel, its shape moving the eye from hand grasp to wheel rim, and we see in the image not only the barrow's gaping failure to function, but the bequeather's falsehood. The life his victims built has become as functionless as the only bequest he left. We hear Twain, having made the barrow's uselessness clear with "It hadn't any wheel," add "and wasn't any good"; it is tempting to believe that Twain was so taken over by the story, and by the journalist's voice, that he added the unnecessary four words not for any sense, since none is required there, but for the sake of the rhythm of the prose. (Try saying the first half of the balanced sentence without the second; Twain and his journalist repair the barrow by adding the clause.)

"A Dog's Tale," with its punning title, boasts one of the great opening sentences: "'My father was a St. Bernard, my mother was a collie, but I am a Presbyterian" (50). Ostensibly a story told by a dog about her life of devotion, and how cruelly mankind has repaid her — as with so much of his sentimentality, Twain reposes it in a female point of view — the "Tale" keeps the reader returning to notions of slavery. We see a generous and noble being, willing to sacrifice herself for her mistress and the mistress's child, often mistreated, bred with cold scientism by a stern father-of-the-household, and finally betrayed. The characterization of the owners is based on what the dog overhears; Twain taps the political hierarchy of servant and slave stories as destiny is interpreted by the powerless through fragments of eavesdropped talk.

If one accepts the donnée, this story of a dog who addresses us with even her dying breaths threatens to be moving. Sophisticated readers tend to stay *en garde*, and the dog's description of her puppy — "I ran at once to my little darling, and snuggled close to it where it lay, and licked the blood, and it put its head against mine, whimpering softly, and I knew in my heart it was a comfort to it in its pain and trouble to feel its mother's touch" (65) — will signal them to gauge how reminiscent this passage, with its clunking repetition of "it," is to the worst of bad Dickens. The reader will then recall Oscar Wilde's dictum that one must have a heart of stone not to laugh at the death of Little Nell, and Twain's spell, even for unregenerate dog lovers, will fail. But the reader will have been reminded, too, of the depth of Twain's sentimentality, and how that emotional softness resides beside the same hard genius that portrayed Huck's pap.

Twain, so influenced by African-American language, and so concerned with the inhumanity of slavery, echoes the implicit condemnation in "A Dog's Tale" with his "General Washington's Negro Body-Servant." The poor fellow's death is constantly reported, and as Twain points out, his age increases with each report, until, at last, by Twain's calculations, he dies at such an astonishing age as to have been too old to have lived on earth as a human being. Twain, in this genuinely funny essay, may be jollying journalists and, through such chivvying, the appetites, the force of commerce, behind newspaper work — even perhaps the force behind his own. But it seems to me that his less noisy and unhumorous point may be how, once more, an African American is appropriated — in his death, even, in the corruption of his flesh and the powdering of his bones — for the casual purposes of white folks.

In the soft and homiletic "Was it Heaven? Or Hell?" — in which once again strong sentiment is reposed for us in women — Twain asserts his strengths, if not in characterization or storytelling, surely then in bitter, memorable commentary. The two old women who are to be taught about truth and lying are described like this: "They had completed the human being's first duty — which is to think about himself until he has exhausted the subject, then he is in a condition to take up minor interests and think of other people" (80). Twain lays siege to the world's Pecksniffs in this Victorian melodrama of mother-daughter love. Each is afflicted by typhoid, and neither must be told of the other's grave condition. The old ladies learn to lie in order to save others. Truth, they are taught, is relative to need. "You are like all the rest of the moral moles: you lie from morning till night," the doctor tells them, "but because you don't do it with your mouths, but only with your lying eyes, your lying inflections, your deceptively misplaced emphasis, and your misleading gestures, you turn up your complacent noses and parade before God and the world as saintly and unsmirched Truth-Speakers" (82).

The dramatic structure of the story, maudlin and unpeopled as it is, cannot support this sort of speechmaking. While the speech demonstrates Twain's anger, and while his anger generates a powerful sermon, there are no actual characters through whom we can locate our attention and emotions. They are shadows over whom Mark Twain shouts. Such bathos as is offered in this story ought to have signaled Twain to excise it from his book. That he chose to include it suggests a keen knowledge of the marketplace and a need to speak the truth about Truth-Speakers that outweighs a writer's sense of literary tact.

The neighboring story, "The Californian's Tale," which gives us a good description of California's post–Gold Rush wasteland — "hard, cheerless, materialistic desolation" (105) — and of a soul starved for art, is also freighted with melodrama: a miner is maddened by loneliness and his need to not face the fact of his young wife's death. He is observed and described by a first-person narrator who tells us how much he is moved, but who is a bystander, not a dramatic persona, and not an integral part of the story's action. We are told, here, of certain late-nineteenth- and early-twentieth-century immutabil-ities — men's comradely affection, the beauty and light generated by sylphlike young wives, the constancy of lovers, and the decency of men such as the nar-rator — but we read contemporary stories about ambiguity and uncertainty, stories with shifting surfaces that examine the frailty of love. No doubt, the older story is tempting, a haven in a time of dark portrayals when little is sure. Comparing this story with anything recent and serious — Charles Baxter's "How I Found My Brother," say, which probes our reassurances about fami-ly and brotherhood — we would, I suggest, find ourselves unable to opt for the comforting, if sad, older story.[*] We cannot believe in Twain's verities. In such stories as this one, Twain sought to demonstrate that he did so believe — or he demonstrated that he believed his readers did, anyway.

"The Californian's Tale" could be fiction and it could be a tale collected in a frontier bar and given the verisimilitude of a first-person narrator. The "I" who addresses us — depending on whether the market was a magazine or newspaper in search of colorful reporting, or a more literary venue — could be a nameless narrator or the celebrated Mark Twain. Most of the stories in this book are in that fashion chameleons, and surely that is true of "A Helpless Situation," patently an essay by the famous Mark Twain, but narra-tively no different from the first-person tale of California that precedes it.

Here, Twain receives a letter from an inept woman who wishes his help in being published. Her request is as greedy and stupid as most such letters re-ceived by most writers, and we learn nothing new. From Twain's reply, how-ever, we learn of his conception of a writer: "He has talent and knows it, and he goes into his fight eagerly and with energy and determination — all alone,

---

[*] Baxter's narrator writes, "The universe is vast, you cannot predict it. From the great resources of anger I pulled my fund, my honest share. But I do not remember how, or exactly why, I said something terrible and hit my brother. . . . My soul ached. My soul was lying face down. . . . I had lost my wife, and now I had lost him, too."

preferring to be alone." Often enough, writers complain of their loneliness, and here Twain celebrates his preference for the solitary grind. (Was it not Twain who said, "Be good and you will be lonesome"?) We also learn something about publishing practices. Twain characterizes a Mr. H., a publisher — Mr. Harper? — as he responds to Twain's correspondent's fear that her work will be ignored because she is unknown: "Why, what we are here *for* is to examine books — anybody's book that comes along. It's our *business*. Why should we turn away a book unexamined because it's a stranger's? It would be foolish. No publisher does it" (120). If Twain ridicules the publishing practices of the day, he speaks the same language any present-day writer would speak of any publishing house. If the description he gives is happily true of his times in any measure at all, the statement, we note, is radically untrue for today's writers, who know that publishers read no unsolicited manuscript whatsoever, and precious few that may be called solicited. We must not forget that Twain can speak with accuracy as writer *and* publisher. Like so many writers, he helped to bankrupt a publishing house (his own); like so few, he labored to save it.

He was different in so may ways from so many contemporary writers. He worked in the hard and actual trades of his time; he piloted riverboats and experienced firsthand the rough camps of the American Gold Rush. He worked at mining, at recording, editing, printing, and performing what he had learned; and he wrote memorable and even great reports from the interior, the bright and the dark aspects of the nation's, and of Europe's, soul. One would be hard pressed to find a writer whose life is comparable.

He was sufficiently talented, and he was welcomed by the paying public, to write what he wanted to write. The stories of Tom Sawyer and Huck Finn and Pudd'nhead Wilson had to be written; so did the stories about the boyhood and youth of Samuel Clemens, for these are driven by the language of the world the boy inhabited, and the early relishing of dialect and rhythm and idiosyncratic diction gave birth, in a way, to the great characters — Huck, Tom, and Jim — who will speak to us as long as the shoals of publishing and the curious need of the semiliterate to censor what they do not understand are navigable.

Moreover, Twain learned, as he published and as he lectured, that the performance of the one had much to do with the performance of the other. Writers are, I think, actors on the page; in their personae they can strut and fuss and parade, as well as slink and dodge and commit depravities. Their license is the approval of their audience, which expresses its acceptance of the authorial disguises by paying cash money for tickets to the show or for the purchase of a book. As I have said elsewhere,[*] one of our great examples of writers who did not receive money — the return mail that might have replied to the fiction they sent off like a letter to unknown readers whose approval they sought — was Herman Melville. In one of his famous exchanges with Hawthorne (conducted by mail), Melville writes of Agatha Hatch Robertson, who waited seventeen years for mail from her absent husband; of her mailbox, Melville says, "As her hopes gradually decay in her, so does the post itself and the little box decay." That rot is what Melville succumbed to, I believe, and it is what every writer seeks to avoid.

Twain knew how to do it. He sent out the mail, and he stimulated mail in return — anger, praise, laughter, sorrow, and American currency. He kept himself viable not only as an entrepreneur but as a writing person. "The Danger of Lying in Bed," a clever little essay on the hazards of not going abroad — this, from the adventurer who also preached the sacredness of home and hearth — is not only a smart column. It is also Twain's way of talking about his death, which must surely be one of his commonest topics, while reminding himself and us that he lives. It is a kind of prayer in disguise, then, a way of controlling huge circumstance with accurate language. And it is also a way of stimulating laughter. It is far more dangerous to lie abed, he says, than to venture abroad. The essay is funny. It is also concerned to some small degree with money — Twain's refusal to buy travel insurance when purchasing a ticket — because it was probably written to earn money for the dual purpose I've suggested: for economic reasons, and for the crucial psychic one. I am

---

[*] In the introduction to the Penguin Classics *Billy Budd and Other Stories* (New York, 1986). Reprinted in *When People Publish: Essays on Writers and Writing* (Iowa City: University of Iowa Press, 1986).

alive, the essay says to Twain's readers; kindly tell me that you're half as pleased as I am.

As with almost every moment of his life, or so it seems to me, Twain was of two minds. In the distinguished autumnal years of his career, both praised to the point of tears (as during his return to Hannibal) and decried for his anti-missionary writing (still a sign of his public importance), he wrote sneeringly of public opinion that it "is held in reverence. . . . Some think it the Voice of God" ("Corn Pone Opinions"). But he courted it hard.

Whether he was only cynical, whether he was frightened about finances or angry about and jealous of Arthur Conan Doyle's great success with Sherlock Holmes, Twain produced "A Double-Barrelled Detective Story," the longest piece in this book. Its plot is not only labyrinthine, it is often unfollowable, even to the Minotaur, I would suspect. It is a story of revenge as exacted by a terribly wronged woman through the agency of her beloved son, and it is difficult to believe that Twain felt much when he wrote it. It starts by recounting a wedding "between a handsome young man of slender means and a rich young girl — a case of love at first sight . . . bitterly opposed" by the girl's father (449). It would be hard to cram more clichés into twenty-two words.

Twain's psychosexual interests are perhaps suggested by the next two pages of the novella, in which for three months the young wife is subjected to sadism and sexual slavery. Her reappearance at the edge of civilization is as a version of Hester Prynne: "She did her own work, she discouraged acquaintanceships, and had none. The butcher, the baker, and the others that served her could tell the villagers nothing about her. . . ." Even her son's query — "Mamma, am I different from other children?" (453) — recalls Hester's Pearl.

The boy grows up with a singular talent: he can *smell* where people have been, and he can see in the dark — he is a kind of hunting animal, and whether Twain means to spoof Holmesian stories of pursuit or *The Hound of the Baskervilles* or the detectivizing bloodhound Holmes himself, the result is a tale not many sophisticated readers can take seriously. As Twain's female protagonist charges her son with his mission, she speaks a bitter, satirical truth amid the fluff she must say: "In this world one must be like everybody else if he doesn't want to provoke scorn or envy or jealousy" (455). This is nothing new for Twain, but it suggests, at least, that he retains his senses as he writes — in which case, the nonsense that he also writes must suggest that his motives for generating it go beyond the literary, or that he feels a special urgency; he needs or wants his readers' response.

Unless, of course, his primary concern is to wreak a kind of vengeance on Conan Doyle. For he goes on to appropriate Doyle's Sherlock Holmes by writing him into his double-barreled story. The question remains: At whom does he discharge the barrels?

The mother aims her son, like a weapon, at Denver, Colorado, where the villain lives. She tells him, "You will drive him from that place; you will hunt him down and drive him again; and yet again, and again, and again, persistently, relentlessly, poisoning his life, filling it with mysterious terrors. . . ." The son, like a parody of horror-story monsters, intones, "I will obey, mother" (458).

Whether from boredom or the desire to make metafictional mischief, Twain incorporates in chapter 4 a letter to the editor that purports to question the use of the word "oesophagus" in the story. But of course he has a fine time in pointing out the dreadfully purple language in the text to which the letter refers. This passage tells us that Twain is aware of his authorial malfeasances and that they are as hard on him as they are on us. It suggests, too, that Twain is doing what writers often do: he is toiling at the shovel for his bread, and he is using a very broad shovel indeed.

Enter, soon enough, Sherlock Holmes, "the Extraordinary Man who had filled the world with the fame of his more than human ingenuities." As a bystander observes, "And look at that frown — that's *deep* thinking — away down, down, forty fathom into the bowels of things" (490). Twain's tongue is so far in his cheek that he is in danger of choking. Soon enough, we suffer through double and triple switches of identity, and we experience a Holmesian disquisition on guilt, but in a dusty frontier tavern instead of an English sitting room. As Holmes speaks, Twain impales him again and again on the seeming admiration of his auditors: "(*Buzz of admiration; muttered remark, 'By George, but he's deep!'*)."

So Twain has his fun, and perhaps his jealousy, but he also — using Holmes to attract readers, perhaps — gets to eat his cake. He has not written a brilliant detective novella. He proved earlier, with *Tom Sawyer, Detective*, that he could write a bad detective story. But he has enjoyed himself, and presumably so have many of his readers.

Some emotions we ought not try to write. Because we are writers, though, we hardly hesitate. So with "In Memoriam," Twain's poem for his dead daughter. It is signed "S.L.C.," so the mask is off: the father's naked emotion, the man — not the writing persona — speaks directly. Note, as ever, the need to speak that Clemens (in this case) cannot deny. The poem is doggerel — "They stand, yet where erst they stood/Speechless in that dim morning long ago" (352) — artless, because the writer is beyond art; he lives in pain and seeks to communicate its longitude and latitude, and he cannot. But his inability speaks as powerfully in this collection as any of its more artful companion pieces, and we feel, reading through the occasional essays, the potboilers, and the skillful and effective work, that we have come upon the actual man.

The same is true for "Eve's Diary," which of course portrays her as perceptive, delicate, and intelligent — Adam is usually none of these — and which is sometimes heavy-handed in its denials of perception and intelligence: "But I am only a girl, and the first that has examined this matter, and it may turn out that in my ignorance and inexperience I have not got it right" (310).

Eve's closing line is "I am the first wife; and in the last wife I shall be repeated" (310). Reminded thus that Twain wants us to believe that all wives carry Eve's polarities — delicacy, dedication, wit — we run into this final sentence, spoken not by Eve but by Adam, at her grave: "Wheresoever she was, *there* was Eden" (310). And once more we feel the man himself inside the language. We feel the strength of his emotion and the possibility that here, within the brilliance and cleverness, beneath the glittering evocations of the Gilded Age and under the angers, the observations, the expressions of need, we have come for an instant upon the actual Clemens, true Twain.

THE $30,000 BEQUEST

and Other Stories

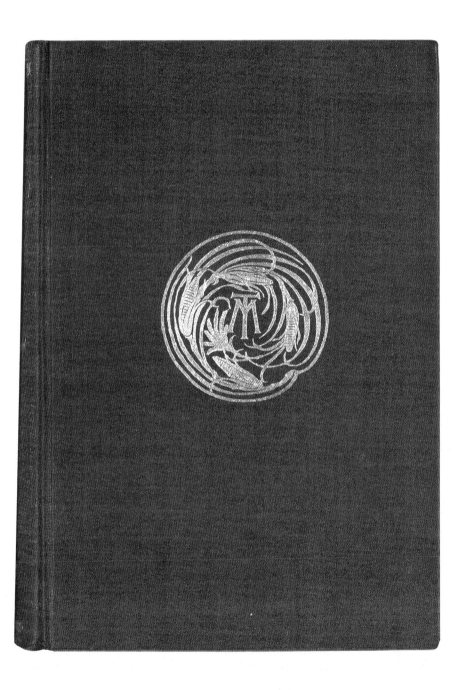

MARK TWAIN AT HIS 70TH BIRTHDAY

THE $30,000 BEQUEST

AND OTHER STORIES

BY

MARK TWAIN

ILLUSTRATED

NEW YORK AND LONDON
HARPER & BROTHERS PUBLISHERS
1906

CONTENTS

iv   Contents

ILLUSTRATIONS

THE $30,000 BEQUEST

THE $30,000 BEQUEST

I

LAKESIDE was a pleasant little town of five or six thousand inhabitants, and a rather pretty one, too, as towns go in the Far West. It had church accommodations for 35,000, which is the way of the Far West and the South, where everybody is religious, and where each of the Protestant sects is represented and has a plant of its own. Rank was unknown in Lakeside — unconfessed, anyway; everybody knew everybody and his dog, and a sociable friendliness was the prevailing atmosphere.

Saladin Foster was book-keeper in the principal store, and the only high-salaried man of his profession in Lakeside. He was thirty-five years old, now; he had served that store for fourteen years; he had begun in his marriage-week at four hundred dollars a year, and had climbed steadily up, a hundred dollars a year, for four years; from that time forth his wage had remained eight hundred — a handsome figure indeed, and everybody conceded that he was worth it.

His wife, Electra, was a capable helpmeet, although —like himself—a dreamer of dreams and a private dabbler in romance. The first thing she did, after her marriage—child as she was, aged only nineteen— was to buy an acre of ground on the edge of the town, and pay down the cash for it—twenty-five dollars, all her fortune. Saladin had less, by fifteen. She instituted a vegetable garden there, got it farmed on shares by the nearest neighbor, and made it pay her a hundred per cent. a year. Out of Saladin's first year's wage she put thirty dollars in the savings-bank, sixty out of his second, a hundred out of his third, a hundred and fifty out of his fourth. His wage went to eight hundred a year, then, and meantime two children had arrived and increased the expenses, but she banked two hundred a year from the salary, nevertheless, thenceforth. When she had been married seven years she built and furnished a pretty and comfortable two-thousand-dollar house in the midst of her garden-acre, paid half of the money down and moved her family in. Seven years later she was out of debt and had several hundred dollars out earning its living.

Earning it by the rise in landed estate; for she had long ago bought another acre or two and sold the most of it at a profit to pleasant people who were willing to build, and would be good neighbors and furnish a general comradeship for herself and her growing family. She had an independent income from safe investments of about a hundred dollars a year; her children were growing in years and grace; and she was a pleased and happy woman. Happy in her husband, happy in her children, and the husband and the children were happy in her. It is at this point that this history begins.

The youngest girl, Clytemnestra—called Clytie for short—was eleven; her sister, Gwendolen—called Gwen for short—was thirteen; nice girls, and comely. The names betray the latent romance-tinge in the parental blood, the parents' names indicate that the tinge was an inheritance. It was an affectionate family, hence all four of its members had pet names. Saladin's was a curious and unsexing one—Sally; and so was Electra's—Aleck. All day long Sally was a good and diligent book-keeper and salesman; all day long Aleck was a good and faithful mother and house-wife, and thoughtful and calculating business-woman; but in the cosey living-room at night they put the plodding world away, and lived in another and a fairer, reading romances to each other, dreaming dreams, comrading with kings and princes and stately lords and ladies in the flash and stir and splendor of noble palaces and grim and ancient castles.

II

Now came great news! Stunning news — joyous news, in fact. It came from a neighboring State, where the family's only surviving relative lived. It was Sally's relative—a sort of vague and indefinite uncle or second or third cousin by the name of Tilbury Foster, seventy and a bachelor, reputed well-off and correspondingly sour and crusty. Sally had tried to make up to him once, by letter, in a by-gone time, and had not made that mistake again. Tilbury now wrote to Sally, saying he should shortly die, and should leave him thirty thousand dollars, cash; not for love, but because money had given him most of his troubles and exasperations, and he wished to place it where there was good hope that it would continue its malignant work. The bequest would be found in his will, and would be paid over. *Provided*, that Sally should be able to prove to the executors that he had *taken no notice of the gift by spoken word or by letter, had made no inquiries concerning the moribund's progress towards the everlasting tropics, and had not attended the funeral.*

As soon as Aleck had partially recovered from the tremendous emotions created by the letter, she sent to the relative's habitat and subscribed for the local paper.

Man and wife entered into a solemn compact, now, to never mention the great news to any one while the relative lived, lest some ignorant person carry the fact to the death-bed and distort it and make it appear that they were disobediently thankful for the bequest, and just the same as confessing it and publishing it, right in the face of the prohibition.

For the rest of the day Sally made havoc and confusion with his books, and Aleck could not keep her mind on her affairs, nor even take up a flower-pot or book or a stick of wood without forgetting what she had intended to do with it. For both were dreaming.

"Thir-ty thousand dollars!"

All day long the music of those inspiring words sang through those people's heads.

From his marriage-day forth, Aleck's grip had been upon the purse, and Sally had seldom known what it was to be privileged to squander a dime on non-necessities.

"Thir-ty thousand dollars!" the song went on and on. A vast sum, an unthinkable sum!

All day long Aleck was absorbed in planning how to invest it, Sally in planning how to spend it.

There was no romance-reading that night. The children took themselves away early, for the parents were silent, distraught, and strangely unentertaining. The good-night kisses might as well have been impressed upon vacancy, for all the response they got; the parents were not aware of the kisses, and the

children had been gone an hour before their absence
was noticed. Two pencils had been busy during that
hour — note-making; in the way of plans. It was
Sally who broke the stillness at last. He said, with
exultation—

"Ah, it 'll be grand, Aleck! Out of the first thousand we'll have a horse and a buggy for summer, and
a cutter and a skin lap-robe for winter."

Aleck responded with decision and composure—

"Out of the *capital?* Nothing of the kind. Not
if it was a million!"

Sally was deeply disappointed; the glow went out
of his face.

"Oh, Aleck!" he said, reproachfully. "We've always worked so hard and been so scrimped; and now
that we are rich, it does seem—"

He did not finish, for he saw her eye soften; his
supplication had touched her. She said, with gentle
persuasiveness—

"We must not spend the capital, dear, it would not
be wise. Out of the income from it—"

"That will answer, that will answer, Aleck! How
dear and good you are! There will be a noble income,
and if we can spend that—"

"Not *all* of it, dear, not all of it, but you can spend
a part of it. That is, a reasonable part. But the
whole of the capital—every penny of it—must be put
right to work, and kept at it. You see the reasona-
bleness of that, don't you?"

"Why, ye-s. Yes, of course. But we'll have to

wait so long. Six months before the first interest falls due."

"Yes—maybe longer."

"Longer, Aleck? Why? Don't they pay half-yearly?"

"*That* kind of an investment—yes; but I sha'n't invest in that way."

"What way then?"

"For big returns."

"Big. That's good. Go on, Aleck. What is it?"

"Coal. The new mines. Cannel. I mean to put in ten thousand. Ground floor. When we organize, we'll get three shares for one."

"By George, but it sounds good, Aleck! Then the shares will be worth—how much? And when?"

"About a year. They'll pay ten per cent. half-yearly, and be worth thirty thousand. I know all about it; the advertisement is in the Cincinnati paper here."

"Land, thirty thousand for ten—in a year! Let's jam in the whole capital and pull out ninety! I'll write and subscribe right now—to-morrow it may be too late."

He was flying to the writing-desk, but Aleck stopped him and put him back in his chair. She said:

"Don't lose your head so. We mustn't subscribe till we've got the money; don't you know that?"

Sally's excitement went down a degree or two, but he was not wholly appeased.

"Why, Aleck, we'll *have* it, you know—and so soon,

too. He's probably out of his troubles before this, it's a hundred to nothing he's selecting his brimstone-shovel this very minute. Now, I think—"

Aleck shuddered, and said:

"How *can* you, Sally! Don't talk in that way, it is perfectly scandalous."

"Oh well, make it a halo, if you like, *I* don't care for his outfit, I was only just talking. Can't you let a person talk?"

"But why should you *want* to talk in that dreadful way? How would you like to have people talk so about *you*, and you not cold yet?"

"Not likely to be, for *one* while, I reckon, if my last act was giving away money for the sake of doing somebody a harm with it. But never mind about Tilbury, Aleck, let's talk about something worldly. It does seem to me that that mine is the place for the whole thirty. What's the objection?"

"All the eggs in one basket—that's the objection."

"All right, if you say so. What about the other twenty? What do you mean to do with that?"

"There is no hurry; I am going to look around before I do anything with it."

"All right, if your mind's made up," sighed Sally. He was deep in thought awhile, then he said:

"There'll be twenty thousand profit coming from the ten a year from now. We can spend that, can't we, Aleck?"

Aleck shook her head.

"No, dear," she said, "it won't sell high till we've

had the first semi-annual dividend. You can spend part of that."

"Shucks, only *that*—and a whole year to wait! Confound it, I—"

"Oh, do be patient! It might even be declared in three months—it's quite within the possibilities."

"Oh, jolly! oh, thanks!" and Sally jumped up and kissed his wife in gratitude. "It 'll be three thousand —three whole thousand! how much of it can we spend, Aleck? Make it liberal—do, dear, that's a good fellow."

Aleck was pleased; so pleased that she yielded to the pressure and conceded a sum which her judgment told her was a foolish extravagance—a thousand dollars. Sally kissed her half a dozen times and even in that way could not express all his joy and thankfulness. This new access of gratitude and affection carried Aleck quite beyond the bounds of prudence, and before she could restrain herself she had made her darling another grant—a couple of thousand out of the fifty or sixty which she meant to clear within a year out of the twenty which still remained of the bequest. The happy tears sprang to Sally's eyes, and he said:

"Oh, I want to hug you!" And he did it. Then he got his notes and sat down and began to check off, for first purchase, the luxuries which he should earliest wish to secure. "Horse—buggy—cutter—lap-robe— patent-leathers—dog—plug hat—church-pew—stem-winder—new teeth—*say*, Aleck!"

2

"Well?"

"Ciphering away, aren't you? That's right. Have you got the twenty thousand invested yet?"

"No, there's no hurry about that; I must look around first, and think."

"But you are ciphering; what's it about?"

"Why, I have to find work for the thirty thousand that comes out of the coal, haven't I?"

"Scott, what a head! I never thought of that. How are you getting along? Where have you arrived?"

"Not very far—two years or three. I've turned it over twice; once in oil and once in wheat."

"Why, Aleck, it's splendid! How does it aggregate?"

"I think—well, to be on the safe side, about a hundred and eighty thousand clear, though it will probably be more."

"My! isn't it wonderful? By gracious! luck has come our way at last, after all the hard sledding. Aleck!"

"Well?"

"I'm going to cash-in a whole three hundred on the missionaries—what real right have we to care for expenses!"

"You couldn't do a nobler thing, dear; and it's just like your generous nature, you unselfish boy."

The praise made Sally poignantly happy, but he was fair and just enough to say it was rightfully due to Aleck rather than to himself, since but for her he should never have had the money.

Then they went up to bed, and in their delirium of
bliss they forgot and left the candle burning in the
parlor. They did not remember until they were un-
dressed; then Sally was for letting it burn; he said
they could afford it, if it was a thousand. But Aleck
went down and put it out.

A good job, too; for on her way back she hit on a
scheme that would turn the hundred and eighty thousand into half a million before it had had time to get
cold.

III

THE little newspaper which Aleck had subscribe for was a Thursday sheet; it would make the trip of five hundred miles from Tilbury's village and arrive on Saturday. Tilbury's letter had started on Friday, more than a day too late for the benefactor to die and get into that week's issue, but in plenty of time to make connection for the next output. Thus the Fosters had to wait almost a complete week to find out whether anything of a satisfactory nature had happened to him or not. It was a long, long week, and the strain was a heavy one. The pair could hardly have borne it if their minds had not had the relief of wholesome diversion. We have seen that they had that. The woman was piling up fortunes right along, the man was spending them—spending all his wife would give him a chance at, at any rate.

At last the Saturday came, and the *Weekly Sagamore* arrived. Mrs. Eversly Bennett was present. She was the Presbyterian parson's wife, and was working the Fosters for a charity. Talk now died a sudden death—on the Foster side. Mrs. Bennett presently discovered that her hosts were not hearing a word she was saying; so she got up, wondering and indignant, and went away. The moment she was out of the house, Aleck eagerly tore the wrapper from the paper, and her eyes and Sally's swept the columns for the death notices. Disappointment! Tilbury was not anywhere mentioned. Aleck was a Christian from the cradle, and duty and the force of habit required her to go through the motions. She pulled herself together and said, with a pious two-per-cent. trade joyousness:

"Let us be humbly thankful that he has been spared; and—"

"Damn his treacherous hide, I wish—"

"Sally! For shame!"

"I don't care!" retorted the angry man. "It's the way *you* feel, and if you weren't so immorally pious you'd be honest and say so."

Aleck said, with wounded dignity:

"I do not see how you can say such unkind and unjust things. There is no such thing as immoral piety."

Sally felt a pang, but tried to conceal it under a shuffling attempt to save his case by changing the form of it—as if changing the form while retaining the juice could deceive the expert he was trying to placate. He said:

"I didn't mean so bad as that, Aleck; I didn't really mean immoral piety, I only meant — meant — well, conventional piety, you know; er—shop piety; the— the—why, *you* know what I mean, Aleck—the—well, where you put up the plated article and play it for solid, you know, without intending anything improper

but just out of trade habit, ancient policy, petrified
custom, loyalty to—to—hang it, I can't find the right
words, but *you* know what I mean, Aleck, and that
there isn't any harm in it. I'll try again. You see,
it's this way. If a person—"

"You have said quite enough," said Aleck, coldly;
let the subject be dropped."

"*I'm* willing," fervently responded Sally, wiping
the sweat from his forehead and looking the thankfulness he had no words for. Then, musingly, he apologized to himself. "I certainly held threes—I *know*
it—but I drew and didn't fill. That's where I'm so
often weak in the game. If I had stood pat—but I
didn't. I never do. I don't know enough."

Confessedly defeated, he was properly tame now
and subdued. Aleck forgave him with her eyes.

The grand interest, the supreme interest, came
instantly to the front again; nothing could keep it in
the background many minutes on a stretch. The
couple took up the puzzle of the absence of Tilbury's
death notice. They discussed it every which way,
more or less hopefully, but they had to finish where
they began, and concede that the only really sane
explanation of the absence of the notice must be—
and without doubt was—that Tilbury was not dead.
There was something sad about it, something even
a little unfair, maybe, but there it was, and had to be
put up with. They were agreed as to that. To Sally
it seemed a strangely inscrutable dispensation; more
inscrutable than usual, he thought; one of the most

unnecessarily inscrutable he could call to mind, in fact—and said so, with some feeling; but if he was hoping to draw Aleck he failed; she reserved her opinion, if she had one; she had not the habit of taking injudicious risks in any market, worldly or other.

The pair must wait for next week's paper—Tilbury had evidently postponed. That was their thought and their decision. So they put the subject away, and went about their affairs again with as good heart as they could.

Now, if they had but known it, they had been wronging Tilbury all the time. Tilbury had kept faith, kept it to the letter; he was dead, he had died to schedule. He was dead more than four days now and used to it; entirely dead, perfectly dead, as dead as any other new person in the cemetery; dead in abundant time to get into that week's *Sagamore*, too, and only shut out by an accident; an accident which could not happen to a metropolitan journal, but which happens easily to a poor little village rag like the *Sagamore*. On this occasion, just as the editorial page was being locked up, a gratis quart of strawberry water-ice arrived from Hostetter's Ladies' and Gents' Ice-Cream Parlors, and the stickful of rather chilly regret over Tilbury's translation got crowded out to make room for the editor's frantic gratitude.

On its way to the standing-galley Tilbury's notice got pied. Otherwise it would have gone into some future edition, for *Weekly Sagamores* do not waste "live" matter, and in their galleys "live" matter is immortal, unless a pi accident intervenes. But a thing that gets pied is dead, and for such there is no resurrection; its chance of seeing print is gone, forever and ever. And so, let Tilbury like it or not, let him rave in his grave to his fill, no matter—no mention of his death would ever see the light in the *Weekly Sagamore*.

IV

Five weeks drifted tediously along. The *Sagamore* arrived regularly on the Saturdays, but never once contained a mention of Tilbury Foster. Sally's patience broke down at this point, and he said, resentfully:

"Damn his livers, he's immortal!"

Aleck gave him a very severe rebuke, and added, with icy solemnity:

"How would you feel if you were suddenly cut off just after such an awful remark had escaped out of you?"

Without sufficient reflection Sally responded:

"I'd feel I was lucky I hadn't got caught with it *in* me."

Pride had forced him to say something, and as he could not think of any rational thing to say he flung that out. Then he stole a base—as he called it—that is, slipped from the presence, to keep from getting brayed in his wife's discussion-mortar.

Six months came and went. The *Sagamore* was still silent about Tilbury. Meantime, Sally had several times thrown out a feeler—that is, a hint that he would like to know. Aleck had ignored the hints. Sally now resolved to brace up and risk a frontal

attack. So he squarely proposed to disguise himself
and go to Tilbury's village and surreptitiously find
out as to the prospects. Aleck put her foot on the
dangerous project with energy and decision. She
said:

"What can you be thinking of? You do keep my
hands full! You have to be watched all the time,
like a little child, to keep you from walking into the
fire. You'll stay right were you are!"

"Why, Aleck, I could do it and not be found out—
I'm certain of it."

"Sally Foster, don't you know you would have to
inquire around?"

"Of course, but what of it? Nobody would suspect who I was."

"Oh, listen to the man! Some day you've got to
prove to the executors that you never inquired.
What then?"

He had forgotten that detail. He didn't reply;
there wasn't anything to say. Aleck added:

"Now then, drop that notion out of your mind,
and don't ever meddle with it again. Tilbury set
that trap for you. Don't you know it's a trap? He
is on the watch, and fully expecting you to blunder
into it. Well, he is going to be disappointed—at
least while I am on deck. Sally!"

"Well?"

"As long as you live, if it's a hundred years, don't
you ever make an inquiry. Promise!"

"All right," with a sigh and reluctantly.

Then Aleck softened and said:

"Don't be impatient. We are prospering; we can wait; there is no hurry. Our small dead-certain income increases all the time; and as to futures, I have not made a mistake yet—they are piling up by the thousands and the tens of thousands. There is not another family in the State with such prospects as ours. Already we are beginning to roll in eventual wealth. You know that, don't you?"

"Yes, Aleck, it's certainly so."

"Then be grateful for what God is doing for us, and stop worrying. You do not believe we could have achieved these prodigious results without His special help and guidance, do you?"

Hesitatingly, "N-no, I suppose not." Then, with feeling and admiration, "And yet, when it comes to judiciousness in watering a stock or putting up a hand to skin Wall Street I don't give in that *you* need any outside amateur help, if I do I wish I—"

"Oh, *do* shut up! I know you do not mean any harm or any irreverence, poor boy, but you can't seem to open your mouth without letting out things to make a person shudder. You keep me in constant dread. For you and for all of us. Once I had no fear of the thunder, but now when I hear it I—"

Her voice broke, and she began to cry, and could not finish. The sight of this smote Sally to the heart and he took her in his arms and petted her and comforted her and promised better conduct, and upbraided himself and remorsefully pleaded for forgiveness.

And he was in earnest, and sorry for what he had
done and ready for any sacrifice that could make up
for it.

And so, in privacy, he thought long and deeply over
the matter, resolving to do what should seem best.
It was easy to *promise* reform; indeed he had already
promised it. But would that do any real good, any
permanent good? No, it would be but temporary—
he knew his weakness, and confessed it to himself with
sorrow—he could not keep the promise. Something
surer and better must be devised; and he devised it.
At cost of precious money which he had long been
saving up, shilling by shilling, he put a lightning-rod
on the house.

At a subsequent time he relapsed.

What miracles habit can do! and how quickly and
how easily habits are acquired—both trifling habits
and habits which profoundly change us. If by accident we wake at two in the morning a couple of nights
in succession, we have need to be uneasy, for another
repetition can turn the accident into a habit; and a
month's dallying with whiskey—but we all know these
commonplace facts.

The castle-building habit, the day-dreaming habit
—how it grows! what a luxury it becomes; how we
fly to its enchantments at every idle moment, how we
revel in them, steep our souls in them, intoxicate
ourselves with their beguiling fantasies—oh yes, and
how soon and how easily our dream-life and our
material life become so intermingled and so fused

together that we can't quite tell which is which, any
more.

By-and-by Aleck subscribed for a Chicago daily
and for the *Wall Street Pointer*.   With an eye single
to finance she studied these as diligently all the week
as she studied her Bible Sundays.   Sally was lost in
admiration, to note with what swift and sure strides
her genius and judgment developed and expanded in
the forecasting and handling of the securities of both
the material and spiritual markets.   He was proud
of her nerve and daring in exploiting worldly stocks,
and just as proud of her conservative caution in working her spiritual deals.   He noted that she never lost
her head in either case; that with a splendid courage
she often went short on worldly futures, but heedfully
drew the line there—she was always long on the
others.   Her policy was quite sane and simple, as
she explained it to him: what she put into earthly
futures was for speculation, what she put into spiritual futures was for investment; she was willing to
go into the one on a margin, and take chances, but
in the case of the other, "margin her no margins"
—she wanted to cash-in a hundred cents per dollar's-worth, and have the stock transferred on the
books.

It took but a very few months to educate Aleck's
imagination and Sally's.   Each day's training added
something to the spread and effectiveness of the two
machines.   As a consequence, Aleck made imaginary
money much faster than at first she had dreamed of

making it, and Sally's competency in spending the overflow of it kept pace with the strain put upon it, right along. In the beginning, Aleck had given the coal speculation a twelvemonth in which to materialize, and had been loath to grant that this term might possibly be shortened by nine months. But that was the feeble work, the nursery work, of a financial fancy that had had no teaching, no experience, no practice. These aids soon came, then that nine months vanished, and the imaginary ten-thousand-dollar investment came marching home with three hundred per cent. profit on its back!

It was a great day for the pair of Fosters. They were speechless for joy. Also speechless for another reason: after much watching of the market, Aleck had lately, with fear and trembling, made her first flyer on a "margin," using the remaining twenty thousand of the bequest in this risk. In her mind's eye she had seen it climb, point by point—always with a chance that the market would break—until at last her anxieties were too great for further endurance—she being new to the margin-business and unhardened, as yet—and she gave her imaginary broker an imaginary order by imaginary telegraph to sell. She said forty thousand dollars profit was enough. The sale was made on the very day that the coal-venture had returned with its rich freight. As I have said, the couple were speechless. They sat dazed and blissful that night, trying to realize the immense fact, the overwhelming fact, that they were actually worth a hundred thousand dollars in clean, imaginary cash. Yet so it was.

It was the last time that ever Aleck was afraid of a margin; at least afraid enough to let it break her sleep and pale her cheek to the extent that this first experience in that line had done.

Indeed it was a memorable night. Gradually the realization that they were rich sank securely home into the souls of the pair, then they began to place the money. If we could have looked out through the eyes of these dreamers, we should have seen their tidy little wooden house disappear, and a two-story brick with a cast-iron fence in front of it take its place; we should have seen a three-globed gas-chandelier grow down from the parlor ceiling; we should have seen the homely rag carpet turn to noble Brussels, a dollar and a half a yard; we should have seen the plebeian fireplace vanish away and a recherché, big base-burner with isinglass windows take position and spread awe around. And we should have seen other things, too; among them the buggy, the lap-robe, the stove-pipe hat, and so on.

From that time forth, although the daughters and the neighbors saw only the same old wooden house there, it was a two-story brick to Aleck and Sally; and not a night went by that Aleck did not worry about the imaginary gas-bills, and get for all comfort Sally's reckless retort, "What of it? we can afford it."

Before the couple went to bed, that first night that

they were rich, they had decided that they must celebrate. They must give a party—that was the idea.
But how to explain it—to the daughters and the
neighbors? They could not expose the fact that they
were rich. Sally was willing, even anxious, to do it;
but Aleck kept her head and would not allow it. She
said that although the money was as good as in, it
would be as well to wait until it was actually in. On
that policy she took her stand, and would not budge.
The great secret must be kept, she said—kept from
the daughters and everybody else.

The pair were puzzled. They must celebrate, they
were determined to celebrate, but since the secret
must be kept, what could they celebrate? No birth-
days were due for three months. Tilbury wasn't
available, evidently he was going to live forever;
what the nation *could* they celebrate? That was
Sally's way of putting it; and he was getting impatient, too, and harassed. But at last he hit it—just
by sheer inspiration, as it seemed to him—and all
their troubles were gone in a moment; they would
celebrate the Discovery of America. A splendid idea!

Aleck was almost too proud of Sally for words—
she said *she* never would have thought of it. But
Sally, although he was bursting with delight in the
compliment and with wonder at himself, tried not to
let on, and said it wasn't really anything, anybody
could have done it. Whereat Aleck, with a prideful
toss of her happy head, said:

"Oh, certainly! Anybody could—oh, anybody!

Hosannah Dilkins, for instance! Or maybe Adelbert Peanut—oh, *dear*—yes! Well, I'd like to see them try it, that's all. Dear-me-suz, if they could think of the discovery of a forty-acre island it's more than *I* believe they could; and as for a whole continent, why, Sally Foster, you know perfectly well it would strain the livers and lights out of them and *then* they couldn't!"

The dear woman, she knew he had talent; and if affection made her over-estimate the size of it a little, surely it was a sweet and gentle crime, and forgive-able for its source's sake.

3

V

THE celebration went off well. The friends were all present, both the young and the old. Among the young were Flossie and Gracie Peanut and their brother Adelbert, who was a rising young journeyman tinner, also Hosannah Dilkins, Jr., journeyman plasterer, just out of his apprenticeship. For many months Adelbert and Hosannah had been showing interest in Gwendolen and Clytemnestra Foster, and the parents of the girls had noticed this with private satisfaction. But they suddenly realized now that that feeling had passed. They recognized that the changed financial conditions had raised up a social bar between their daughters and the young mechanics. The daughters could now look higher—and must. Yes, must. They need marry nothing below the grade of lawyer or merchant; poppa and momma would take care of this; there must be no mésalliances.

However, these thinkings and projects of theirs were private, and did not show on the surface, and therefore threw no shadow upon the celebration. What showed upon the surface was a serene and lofty contentment and a dignity of carriage and gravity of deportment which compelled the admiration and likewise the wonder of the company. All noticed it, all commented upon it, but none was able to divine the secret of it. It was a marvel and a mystery. Three several persons remarked, without suspecting what clever shots they were making:

"It's as if they'd come into property."

That was just it, indeed.

Most mothers would have taken hold of the matrimonial matter in the old regulation way; they would have given the girls a talking to, of a solemn sort and untactful—a lecture calculated to defeat its own purpose, by producing tears and secret rebellion; and the said mothers would have further damaged the business by requesting the young mechanics to discontinue their attentions. But this mother was different. She was practical. She said nothing to any of the young people concerned, nor to any one else except Sally. He listened to her and understood; understood and admired. He said:

"I get the idea. Instead of finding fault with the samples on view, thus hurting feelings and obstructing trade without occasion, you merely offer a higher class of goods for the money, and leave nature to take her course. It's wisdom, Aleck, solid wisdom, and sound as a nut. Who's your fish? Have you nominated him yet?"

"No, she hadn't. They must look the market over —which they did. To start with, they considered and discussed Bradish, rising young lawyer, and Fulton, rising young dentist. Sally must invite them to dinner. But not right away; there was no hurry, Aleck said. Keep an eye on the pair, and wait; nothing would be lost by going slowly in so important a matter.

It turned out that this was wisdom, too; for inside of three weeks Aleck made a wonderful strike which swelled her imaginary hundred thousand to four hundred thousand of the same quality. She and Sally were in the clouds that evening. For the first time they introduced champagne at dinner. Not real champagne, but plenty real enough for the amount of imagination expended on it. It was Sally that did it, and Aleck weakly submitted. At bottom both were troubled and ashamed, for he was a high-up Son of Temperance, and at funerals wore an apron which no dog could look upon and retain his reason and his opinion; and she was a W. C. T. U., with all that that implies of boiler-iron virtue and unendurable holiness. But there it was; the pride of riches was beginning its disintegrating work. They had lived to prove, once more, a sad truth which had been proven many times before in the world: that whereas principle is a great and noble protection against showy and degrading vanities and vices, poverty is worth six of it. More than four hundred thousand dollars to the good! They took up the matrimonial matter again. Neither the dentist nor the lawyer was mentioned; there was no occasion, they were out of the running. Disqualified. They discussed the son of the pork-packer and the son of the village banker. But finally, as in the previous case, they concluded to wait and think, and go cautiously and sure.

Luck came their way again. Aleck, ever watchful, saw a great and risky chance, and took a daring flyer. A time of trembling, of doubt, of awful uneasiness followed, for non-success meant absolute ruin and nothing short of it. Then came the result, and Aleck, faint with joy, could hardly control her voice when she said:

"The suspense is over, Sally—and we are worth a cold million!"

Sally wept for gratitude, and said:

"Oh, Electra, jewel of women, darling of my heart, we are free at last, we roll in wealth, we need never scrimp again. It's a case for Veuve Cliquot!" and he got out a pint of spruce-beer and made sacrifice, he saying "Damn the expense," and she rebuking him gently with reproachful but humid and happy eyes.

They shelved the pork-packer's son and the banker's son, and sat down to consider the Governor's son and the son of the Congressman.

VI

It were a weariness to follow in detail the leaps and bounds the Foster fictitious finances took from this time forth. It was marvellous, it was dizzying, it was dazzling. Everything Aleck touched turned to fairy gold, and heaped itself glittering towards the firmament. Millions upon millions poured in, and still the mighty stream flowed thundering along, still its vast volume increased. Five millions—ten millions—twenty—thirty—was there never to be an end?

Two years swept by in a splendid delirium, the intoxicated Fosters scarcely noticing the flight of time. They were now worth three hundred million dollars; they were in every board of directors of every prodigious combine in the country; and still, as time drifted along, the millions went on piling up, five at a time, ten at a time, as fast as they could tally them off, almost. The three hundred doubled itself —then doubled again—and yet again—and yet once more.

Twenty-four hundred millions!

The business was getting a little confused. It was necessary to take an account of stock, and straighten it out. The Fosters knew it, they felt it, they realized that it was imperative; but they also knew that to do

it properly and perfectly the task must be carried to
a finish without a break when once it was begun.   A
ten-hours' job; and where could *they* find ten leisure
hours in a bunch?   Sally was selling pins and sugar
and calico all day and every day; Aleck was cooking
and washing dishes and sweeping and making beds
all day and every day, with none to help, for the
daughters were being saved up for high society.   The
Fosters knew there was one way to get the ten hours,
and only one.   Both were ashamed to name it; each
waited for the other to do it.   Finally Sally said:

"Somebody's got to give in.   It's up to me.   Consider that I've named it—never mind pronouncing it
out loud."

Aleck colored, but was grateful.   Without further
remark, they fell.   Fell, and—broke the Sabbath.
For that was their only free ten-hour stretch.   It was
but another step in the downward path.   Others
would follow.   Vast wealth has temptations which
fatally and surely undermine the moral structure of
persons not habituated to its possession.

They pulled down the shades and broke the Sabbath.   With hard and patient labor they overhauled
their holdings and listed them.   And a long-drawn
procession of formidable names it was!   Starting
with the Railway Systems, Steamer Lines, Standard
Oil, Ocean Cables, Diluted Telegraph, and all the rest,
and winding up with Klondike, De Beers, Tammany
Graft, and Shady Privileges in the Post-office Department.

Twenty-four hundred millions, and all safely planted in Good Things, gilt-edged and interest-bearing.
Income, $120,000 000 a year.   Aleck fetched a long
purr of soft delight, and said:

"Is it enough?"

"It is, Aleck."

"What shall we do?"

"Stand pat."

"Retire from business?"

"That's it."

"I am agreed.   The good work is finished; we will
take a long rest and enjoy the money."

"Good!   Aleck!"

"Yes, dear?"

"How much of the income can we spend?"

"The whole of it."

It seemed to her husband that a ton of chains fell
from his limbs.   He did not say a word; he was
happy beyond the power of speech.

After that, they broke the Sabbaths right along,
as fast as they turned up.   It is the first wrong steps
that count.   Every Sunday they put in the whole
day, after morning service, on inventions—inventions of ways to spend the money.   They got to con-
tinuing this delicious dissipation until past midnight;
and at every séance Aleck lavished millions upon
great charities and religious enterprises, and Sally
lavished like sums upon matters to which (at first)
he gave definite names.   Only at first.   Later the
names gradually lost sharpness of outline, and

eventually faded into "sundries," thus becoming entirely—but safely—undescriptive. For Sally was crumbling. The placing of these millions added seriously and most uncomfortably to the family expenses—in tallow candles. For a while Aleck was worried. Then, after a little, she ceased to worry, for the occasion of it was gone. She was pained, she was grieved, she was ashamed; but she said nothing, and so became an accessory. Sally was taking candles; he was robbing the store. It is ever thus. Vast wealth, to the person unaccustomed to it, is a bane; it eats into the flesh and bone of his morals. When the Fosters were poor, they could have been trusted with untold candles. But now they—but let us not dwell upon it. From candles to apples is but a step: Sally got to taking apples; then soap; then maple-sugar; then canned-goods; then crockery. How easy it is to go from bad to worse, when once we have started upon a downward course!

Meantime, other effects had been milestoning the course of the Fosters' splendid financial march. The fictitious brick-dwelling had given place to an imaginary granite one with a checker-board mansard roof; in time this one disappeared and gave place to a still grander home—and so on and so on. Mansion after mansion, made of air, rose, higher, broader, finer, and each in its turn vanished away; until now, in these latter great days, our dreamers were in fancy housed, in a distant region, in a sumptuous vast palace which looked out from a leafy summit upon a noble prospect of vale and river and receding hills steeped in tinted mists—and all private, all the property of the dreamers; a palace swarming with liveried servants, and populous with guests of fame and power, hailing from all the world's capitals, foreign and domestic.

This palace was far, far away towards the rising sun, immeasurably remote, astronomically remote, in Newport, Rhode Island, Holy Land of High Society, ineffable Domain of the American Aristocracy. As a rule, they spent a part of every Sabbath—after morning service—in this sumptuous home, the rest of it they spent in Europe, or in dawdling around in their private yacht. Six days of sordid and plodding Fact-life at home on the ragged edge of Lakeside and straitened means, the seventh in Fairyland—such had become their programme and their habit.

In their sternly restricted Fact-life they remained as of old — plodding, diligent, careful, practical, economical. They stuck loyally to the little Presbyterian Church, and labored faithfully in its interests and stood by its high and tough doctrines with all their mental and spiritual energies. But in their Dream-life they obeyed the invitations of their fancies, whatever they might be, and howsoever the fancies might change. Aleck's fancies were not very capricious, and not frequent, but Sally's scattered a good deal. Aleck, in her dream-life, went over to the Episcopal camp, on account of its large official titles; next she became High-church on account of the candles and shows; and next she naturally changed to Rome, where there were cardinals and more candles. But these excursions were as nothing to Sally's. His Dream-life was a glowing and continuous and persistent excitement, and he kept every part of it fresh and sparkling by frequent changes, the religious part along with the rest. He worked his religions hard, and changed them with his shirt.

The liberal spendings of the Fosters upon their fancies began early in their prosperities, and grew in prodigality step by step with their advancing fortunes. In time they became truly enormous. Aleck built a university or two per Sunday; also a hospital or two; also a Rowton hotel or so; also a batch of churches; now and then a cathedral; and once, with untimely and ill-chosen playfulness, Sally said, "It was a cold day when she didn't ship a cargo of missionaries to persuade unreflecting Chinamen to trade off twenty-four carat Confucianism for counterfeit Christianity."

This rude and unfeeling language hurt Aleck to the heart, and she went from the presence crying. That spectacle went to his own heart, and in his pain and shame he would have given worlds to have those unkind words back. She had uttered no syllable of reproach—and that cut him. Not one suggestion that he look at his own record—and she could have made, oh, so many, and such blistering ones! Her generous silence brought a swift revenge, for it turned

his thoughts upon himself, it summoned before him
a spectral procession, a moving vision of his life as
he had been leading it these past few years of limitless prosperity, and as he sat there reviewing it his
cheeks burned and his soul was steeped in humiliation.   Look at her life—how fair it was, and tending
ever upward; and look at his own—how frivolous,
how charged with mean vanities, how selfish, how
empty, how ignoble!   And its trend—never upward,
but downward, ever downward!

He instituted comparisons between her record and
his own.   He had found fault with her—so he mused
—*he!*   And what could he say for himself?   When
she built her first church what was he doing?   Gathering other blasé multimillionaires into a Poker
Club; defiling his own palace with it; losing hundreds
of thousands to it at every sitting, and sillily vain of
the admiring notoriety it made for him.   When she
was building her first university, what was he doing?
Polluting himself with a gay and dissipated secret
life in the company of other fast bloods, multimillionaires in money and paupers in character.   When
she was building her first foundling asylum, what
was he doing?   Alas!   When she was projecting her
noble Society for the Purifying of the Sex, what was
he doing?   Ah, what, indeed!   When she and the
W. C. T. U. and the Woman with the Hatchet, moving with resistless march, were sweeping the fatal
bottle from the land, what was he doing?   Getting
drunk three times a day.   When she, builder of a

hundred cathedrals, was being gratefully welcomed
and blest in papal Rome and decorated with the
Golden Rose which she had so honorably earned,
what was he doing? Breaking the bank at Monte
Carlo.

He stopped. He could go no farther; he could not
bear the rest. He rose up, with a great resolution
upon his lips: this secret life should be revealed, and
confessed; no longer would he live it clandestinely;
he would go and tell her All.

And that is what he did. He told her All; and
wept upon her bosom; wept, and moaned, and
begged for her forgiveness. It was a profound
shock, and she staggered under the blow, but he was
her own, the core of her heart, the blessing of her
eyes, her all in all, she could deny him nothing, and
she forgave him. She felt that he could never again
be quite to her what he had been before; she knew
that he could only repent, and not reform; yet all
morally defaced and decayed as he was, was he not
her own, her very own, the idol of her deathless worship? She said she was his serf, his slave, and she
opened her yearning heart and took him in.

VII

ONE Sunday afternoon some time after this they were sailing the summer seas in their dream-yacht, and reclining in lazy luxury under the awning of the after-deck. There was silence, for each was busy with his own thoughts. These seasons of silence had insensibly been growing more and more frequent of late; the old nearness and cordiality were waning. Sally's terrible revelation had done its work; Aleck had tried hard to drive the memory of it out of her mind, but it would not go, and the shame and bitterness of it were poisoning her gracious dream-life. She could see now (on Sundays) that her husband was becoming a bloated and repulsive Thing. She could not close her eyes to this, and in these days she no longer looked at him, Sundays, when she could help it.

But she—was she herself without blemish? Alas, she knew she was not. She was keeping a secret from him, she was acting dishonorably towards him, and many a pang it was costing her. *She was breaking the compact, and concealing it from him.* Under strong temptation she had gone into business again; she had risked their whole fortune in a purchase of all the railway systems and coal and steel companies in the country on a margin, and she was now trembling, every Sabbath hour, lest through some chance word of hers he find it out. In her misery and remorse for this treachery she could not keep her heart from going out to him in pity; she was filled with compunctions to see him lying there, drunk and content, and never suspecting. Never suspecting—trusting her with a perfect and pathetic trust, and she holding over him by a thread a possible calamity of so devastating a—

"*Say*—Aleck?"

The interrupting words brought her suddenly to herself. She was grateful to have that persecuting subject from her thoughts, and she answered, with much of the old-time tenderness in her tone:

"Yes, dear."

"Do you know, Aleck, I think we are making a mistake—that is, you are. I mean about the marriage business." He sat up, fat and froggy and benevolent, like a bronze Buddha, and grew earnest. "Consider—it's more than five years. You've continued the same policy from the start: with every rise, always holding on for five points higher. Always when I think we are going to have some weddings, you see a bigger thing ahead, and I undergo another disappointment. *I* think you are too hard to please. Some day we'll get left. First, we turned down the dentist and the lawyer. That was all right—it was sound. Next, we turned down the banker's son and the pork-butcher's heir— right again, and sound. Next, we turned down the Congressman's son and the Governor's—right as a trivet, I confess it. Next, the Senator's son and the son of the Vice-President of the United States—perfectly right, there's no permanency about those little distinctions. Then you went for the aristocracy; and I thought we had struck oil at last—yes. We would make a plunge at the Four Hundred, and pull in some ancient lineage, venerable, holy, ineffable, mellow with the antiquity of a hundred and fifty years, disinfected of the ancestral odors of salt cod and pelts all of a century ago, and unsmirched by a day's work since; and then! why, then the marriages, of course. But no, along comes a pair of real aristocrats from Europe, and straightway you throw over the half-breeds. It was awfully discouraging, Aleck! Since then, what a procession! You turned down the baronets for a pair of barons; you turned down the barons for a pair of viscounts; the viscounts for a pair of earls; the earls for a pair of marquises; the marquises for a brace of dukes. *Now*, Aleck, cash-in!—you've played the limit. You've got a job lot of four dukes under the hammer; of four nationalities; all sound in wind and limb and pedigree, all bankrupt and in debt up to the ears. They come high, but we can afford it. Come, Aleck, don't delay any longer, don't keep up the suspense: take the whole lay-out, and leave the girls to choose!"

Aleck had been smiling blandly and contentedly all through this arraignment of her marriage-policy;

a pleasant light, as of triumph with perhaps a nice surprise peeping out through it, rose in her eyes, and she said, as calmly as she could:

"Sally, what would you say to—*royalty?*"

Prodigious! Poor man, it knocked him silly, and he fell over the garboard-strake and barked his shin on the cat-heads. He was dizzy for a moment, then he gathered himself up and limped over and sat down by his wife and beamed his old-time admiration and affection upon her in floods, out of his bleary eyes.

"By George!" he said, fervently, "Aleck, you *are* great—the greatest woman in the whole earth! I can't ever learn the whole size of you. I can't ever learn the immeasurable deeps of you. Here I've been considering myself qualified to criticise your game. *I!* Why, if I had stopped to think, I'd have known you had a lone hand up your sleeve. Now, dear heart, I'm all red-hot impatience—tell me about it!"

The flattered and happy woman put her lips to his ear and whispered a princely name. It made him catch his breath, it lit his face with exultation.

"Land!" he said, "it's a stunning catch! He's got a gambling-hell, and a graveyard, and a bishop, and a cathedral—all his very own. And all gilt-edged five-hundred-per-cent. stock, every detail of it; the tidiest little property in Europe. And that graveyard—it's the selectest in the world: none but suicides admitted; *yes*, sir, and the free-list suspended,

4

too, *all* the time. There isn't much land in the principality, but there's enough: eight hundred acres in the graveyard and forty - two outside. It's a *sovereignty*—that's the main thing; *land's* nothing. There's plenty land, Sahara's drugged with it."

Aleck glowed; she was profoundly happy. She said:

"Think of it, Sally—it is a family that has never married outside the Royal and Imperial Houses of Europe: our grandchildren will sit upon thrones!"

"True as you live, Aleck—and bear sceptres, too; and handle them as naturally and nonchalantly as I handle a yardstick. It's a grand catch, Aleck. He's corralled, is he? Can't get away? You didn't take him on a margin?"

"No. Trust me for that. He's not a liability, he's an asset. So is the other one."

"Who is it, Aleck?"

"His Royal Highness Sigismund-Siegfried-Lauenfeld-Dinkelspiel-Schwartzenberg Blutwurst, Hereditary Grand Duke of Katzenyammer."

"No! You can't mean it!"

"It's as true as I'm sitting here, I give you my word," she answered.

His cup was full, and he hugged her to his heart with rapture, saying:

"How wonderful it all seems, and how beautiful! It's one of the oldest and noblest of the three hundred and sixty-four ancient German principalities, and one of the few that was allowed to retain its

royal estate when Bismarck got done trimming them.
I know that farm, I've been there. It's got a rope-walk and a candle-factory and an army. Standing
army. Infantry and cavalry. Three soldiers and a
horse. Aleck, it's been a long wait, and full of
heartbreak and hope deferred, but God knows I am
happy now. Happy, and grateful to you, my own,
who have done it all. When is it to be?"

"Next Sunday."

"Good. And we'll want to do these weddings up
in the very regalest style that's going. It's properly
due to the royal quality of the parties of the first
part. Now as I understand it, there is only one
kind of marriage that is sacred to royalty, exclusive
to royalty: it's the morganatic."

"What do they call it that for, Sally?"

"I don't know; but anyway it's royal, and royal
only."

"Then we will insist upon it. More—I will compel it. It is morganatic marriage or none."

"That settles it!" said Sally, rubbing his hands
with delight. "And it will be the very first in
America. Aleck, it will make Newport sick."

Then they fell silent, and drifted away upon their
dream-wings to the far regions of the earth to invite
all the crowned heads and their families and provide
gratis transportation for them.

VIII

DURING three days the couple walked upon air, with their heads in the clouds. They were but vaguely conscious of their surroundings; they saw all things dimly, as through a veil; they were steeped in dreams, often they did not hear when they were spoken to; they often did not understand when they heard; they answered confusedly or at random; Sally sold molasses by weight, sugar by the yard, and furnished soap when asked for candles, and Aleck put the cat in the wash and fed milk to the soiled linen. Everybody was stunned and amazed, and went about muttering, "What *can* be the matter with the Fosters?"

Three days. Then came events! Things had taken a happy turn, and for forty-eight hours Aleck's imaginary corner had been booming. Up—up—still up! Cost-point was passed. Still up—and up—and up! Five points above cost—then ten—fifteen—twenty! Twenty points cold profit on the vast venture, now, and Aleck's imaginary brokers were shouting frantically by imaginary long-distance, "Sell! sell! for Heaven's sake *sell!*"

She broke the splendid news to Sally, and he, too, said, "Sell! sell—oh, don't make a blunder, now, you own the earth!—sell, sell!" But she set her iron will and lashed it amidships, and said she would hold on for five points more if she died for it.

It was a fatal resolve. The very next day came the historic crash, the record crash, the devastating crash, when the bottom fell out of Wall Street, and the whole body of gilt-edged stocks dropped ninety-five points in five hours, and the multimillionaire was seen begging his bread in the Bowery. Aleck sternly held her grip and "put up" as long as she could, but at last there came a call which she was powerless to meet, and her imaginary brokers sold her out. Then, and not till then, the man in her was vanquished, and the woman in her resumed sway. She put her arms about her husband's neck and wept, saying:

"I am to blame, do not forgive me, I cannot bear it. We are paupers! Paupers, and I am so miserable. The weddings will never come off; all that is past; we could not even buy the dentist, now."

A bitter reproach was on Sally's tongue: "I *begged* you to sell, but you—" He did not say it; he had not the heart to add a hurt to that broken and repentant spirit. A nobler thought came to him and he said:

"Bear up, my Aleck, all is not lost! You really never invested a penny of my uncle's bequest, but only its unmaterialized future; what we have lost was only the increment harvested from that future by your incomparable financial judgment and sagacity.

Cheer up, banish these griefs; we still have the thirty thousand untouched; and with the experience which you have acquired, think what you will be able to do with it in a couple of years! The marriages are not off, they are only postponed."

These were blessed words. Aleck saw how true they were, and their influence was electric; her tears ceased to flow, and her great spirit rose to its full stature again. With flashing eye and grateful heart, and with hand uplifted in pledge and prophecy, she said:

"Now and here I proclaim—"

But she was interrupted by a visitor. It was the editor and proprietor of the *Sagamore*. He had happened into Lakeside to pay a duty-call upon an obscure grandmother of his who was nearing the end of her pilgrimage, and with the idea of combining business with grief he had looked up the Fosters, who had been so absorbed in other things for the past four years that they had neglected to pay up their subscription. Six dollars due. No visitor could have been more welcome. He would know all about Uncle Tilbury and what his chances might be getting to be, cemeterywards. They could, of course, ask no questions, for that would squelch the bequest, but they could nibble around on the edge of the subject and hope for results. The scheme did not work. The obtuse editor did not know he was being nibbled at; but at last, chance accomplished what art had failed in. In illustration of something under discussion which required the help of metaphor, the editor said:

"Land, it's as tough as Tilbury Foster!—as *we* say."

It was sudden, and it made the Fosters jump. The editor noticed it, and said, apologetically:

"No harm intended, I assure you. It's just a saying; just a joke, you know—nothing in it. Relation of yours?"

Sally crowded his burning eagerness down, and answered with all the indifference he could assume:

"I—well, not that I know of, but we've heard of him." The editor was thankful, and resumed his composure. Sally added: "Is he—is he—well?"

"Is he *well?* Why, bless you he's in Sheol these five years!"

The Fosters were trembling with grief, though it felt like joy. Sally said, non-committally — and tentatively:

"Ah, well, such is life, and none can escape—not even the rich are spared."

The editor laughed.

"If you are including Tilbury," said he, "it don't apply. *He* hadn't a cent; the town had to bury him."

The Fosters sat petrified for two minutes; petrified and cold. Then, white-faced and weak-voiced, Sally asked:

"Is it true? Do you *know* it to be true?"

"Well, I should say! I was one of the executors. He hadn't anything to leave but a wheelbarrow, and

he left that to me. It hadn't any wheel, and wasn't
any good. Still, it was something, and so, to square
up, I scribbled off a sort of a little obituarial send-off
for him, but it got crowded out."

The Fosters were not listening—their cup was full,
it could contain no more. They sat with bowed
heads, dead to all things but the ache at their hearts.

An hour later. Still they sat there, bowed, motionless, silent, the visitor long ago gone, they unaware.

Then they stirred, and lifted their heads wearily,
and gazed at each other wistfully, dreamily, dazed;
then presently began to twaddle to each other in a
wandering and childish way. At intervals they
lapsed into silences, leaving a sentence unfinished,
seemingly either unaware of it or losing their way.
Sometimes, when they woke out of these silences
they had a dim and transient consciousness that
something had happened to their minds; then with a
dumb and yearning solicitude they would softly
caress each other's hands in mutual compassion and
support, as if they would say: "I am near you, I will
not forsake you, we will bear it together; somewhere
there is release and forgetfulness, somewhere there is
a grave and peace; be patient, it will not be long."

They lived yet two years, in mental night, always
brooding, steeped in vague regrets and melancholy
dreams, never speaking; then release came to both
on the same day.

Towards the end the darkness lifted from Sally's ruined mind for a moment, and he said:

"Vast wealth, acquired by sudden and unwholesome means, is a snare. It did us no good, transient were its feverish pleasures; yet for its sake we threw away our sweet and simple and happy life—let others take warning by us."

He lay silent awhile, with closed eyes; then as the chill of death crept upward towards his heart, and consciousness was fading from his brain, he muttered:

"Money had brought him misery, and he took his revenge upon us, who had done him no harm. He had his desire: with base and cunning calculation he left us but thirty thousand, knowing we would try to increase it, and ruin our life and break our hearts. Without added expense he could have left us far above desire of increase, far above the temptation to speculate, and a kinder soul would have done it; but in him was no generous spirit, no pity, no—"

A DOG'S TALE

I

M Y father was a St. Bernard, my mother was a
collie, but I am a Presbyterian. This is what
my mother told me; I do not know these nice distinctions myself. To me they are only fine large
words meaning nothing. My mother had a fondness
for such; she liked to say them, and see other dogs
look surprised and envious, as wondering how she
got so much education. But, indeed, it was not real
education; it was only show: she got the words by
listening in the dining-room and drawing-room when
there was company, and by going with the children
to Sunday-school and listening there; and whenever
she heard a large word she said it over to herself
many times, and so was able to keep it until there
was a dogmatic gathering in the neighborhood, then
she would get it off, and surprise and distress them
all, from pocket-pup to mastiff, which rewarded her
for all her trouble. If there was a stranger he was
nearly sure to be suspicious, and when he got his
breath again he would ask her what it meant. And

she always told him. He was never expecting this, but thought he would catch her; so when she told him, he was the one that looked ashamed, whereas he had thought it was going to be she. The others were always waiting for this, and glad of it and proud of her, for they knew what was going to happen, because they had had experience. When she told the meaning of a big word they were all so taken up with admiration that it never occurred to any dog to doubt if it was the right one; and that was natural, because, for one thing, she answered up so promptly that it seemed like a dictionary speaking, and for another thing, where could they find out whether it was right or not? for she was the only cultivated dog there was. By-and-by, when I was older, she brought home the word Unintellectual, one time, and worked it pretty hard all the week at different gatherings, making much unhappiness and despondency; and it was at this time that I noticed that during that week she was asked for the meaning at eight different assemblages, and flashed out a fresh definition every time, which showed me that she had more presence of mind than culture, though I said nothing, of course. She had one word which she always kept on hand, and ready, like a life-preserver, a kind of emergency word to strap on when she was likely to get washed overboard in a sudden way —that was the word Synonymous. When she happened to fetch out a long word which had had its day weeks before and its prepared meanings gone to her dump-pile, if there was a stranger there of course it knocked him groggy for a couple of minutes, then he would come to, and by that time she would be away down the wind on another tack, and not expecting anything; so when he'd hail and ask her to cash in, I (the only dog on the inside of her game) could see her canvas flicker a moment—but only just a moment—then it would belly out taut and full, and she would say, as calm as a summer's day, "It's synonymous with supererogation," or some godless long reptile of a word like that, and go placidly about and skim away on the next tack, perfectly comfortable, you know, and leave that stranger looking profane and embarrassed, and the initiated slatting the floor with their tails in unison and their faces transfigured with a holy joy.

And it was the same with phrases. She would drag home a whole phrase, if it had a grand sound, and play it six nights and two matinées, and explain it a new way every time—which she had to, for all she cared for was the phrase; she wasn't interested in what it meant, and knew those dogs hadn't wit enough to catch her, anyway. Yes, she was a daisy! She got so she wasn't afraid of anything, she had such confidence in the ignorance of those creatures. She even brought anecdotes that she had heard the family and the dinner guests laugh and shout over; and as a rule she got the nub of one chestnut hitched onto another chestnut, where, of course, it didn't fit and hadn't any point; and when she delivered the nub she fell over and rolled on the floor and laughed and barked in the most insane way, while I could see that she was wondering to herself why it didn't seem as funny as it did when she first heard it. But no harm was done; the others rolled and barked too, privately ashamed of themselves for not seeing the point, and never suspecting that the fault was not with them and there wasn't any to see.

You can see by these things that she was of a rather vain and frivolous character; still, she had virtues, and enough to make up, I think. She had a kind heart and gentle ways, and never harbored resentments for injuries done her, but put them easily out of her mind and forgot them; and she taught her children her kindly way, and from her we learned also to be brave and prompt in time of danger, and not to run away, but face the peril that threatened friend or stranger, and help him the best we could without stopping to think what the cost might be to us. And she taught us not by words only, but by example, and that is the best way and the surest and the most lasting. Why, the brave things she did, the splendid things! she was just a soldier; and so modest about it—well, you couldn't help admiring her, and you couldn't help imitating her; not even a King Charles spaniel could remain entirely despicable in her society. So, as you see, there was more to her than her education.

II

WHEN I was well grown, at last, I was sold and taken away, and I never saw her again. She was broken-hearted, and so was I, and we cried; but she comforted me as well as she could, and said we were sent into this world for a wise and good purpose, and must do our duties without repining, take our life as we might find it, live it for the best good of others, and never mind about the results; they were not our affair. She said men who did like this would have a noble and beautiful reward by-and-by in another world, and although we animals would not go there, to do well and right without reward would give to our brief lives a worthiness and dignity which in itself would be a reward. She had gathered these things from time to time when she had gone to the Sunday-school with the children, and had laid them up in her memory more carefully than she had done with those other words and phrases; and she had studied them deeply, for her good and ours. One may see by this that she had a wise and thoughtful head, for all there was so much lightness and vanity in it.

So we said our farewells, and looked our last upon each other through our tears; and the last thing she said—keeping it for the last to make me remember it the better, I think — was, "In memory of me, when there is a time of danger to another do not think of yourself, think of your mother, and do as she would do."

Do you think I could rorget that? No.

III

It was such a charming home!—my new one; a
fine great house, with pictures, and delicate decorations, and rich furniture, and no gloom anywhere,
but all the wilderness of dainty colors lit up with
flooding sunshine; and the spacious grounds around
it, and the great garden—oh, greensward, and noble
trees, and flowers, no end! And I was the same as a
member of the family; and they loved me, and petted
me, and did not give me a new name, but called me
by my old one that was dear to me because my
mother had given it me—Aileen Mavourneen. She
got it out of a song; and the Grays knew that song,
and said it was a beautiful name.

Mrs. Gray was thirty, and so sweet and so lovely,
you cannot imagine it; and Sadie was ten, and just
like her mother, just a darling slender little copy of
her, with auburn tails down her back, and short
frocks; and the baby was a year old, and plump and
dimpled, and fond of me, and never could get enough
of hauling on my tail, and hugging me, and laughing
out its innocent happiness; and Mr. Gray was thirty-
eight, and tall and slender and handsome, a little
bald in front, alert, quick in his movements, business-

like, prompt, decided, unsentimental, and with that kind of trim-chiselled face that just seems to glint and sparkle with frosty intellectuality! He was a renowned scientist. I do not know what the word means, but my mother would know how to use it and get effects. She would know how to depress a rat-terrier with it and make a lap-dog look sorry he came. But that is not the best one; the best one was Laboratory. My mother could organize a Trust on that one that would skin the tax-collars off the whole herd. The laboratory was not a book, or a picture, or a place to wash your hands in, as the college president's dog said—no, that is the lavatory; the laboratory is quite different, and is filled with jars, and bottles, and electrics, and wires, and strange machines; and every week other scientists came there and sat in the place, and used the machines, and discussed, and made what they called experiments and discoveries; and often I came, too, and stood around and listened, and tried to learn, for the sake of my mother, and in loving memory of her, although it was a pain to me, as realizing what she was losing out of her life and I gaining nothing at all; for try as I might, I was never able to make anything out of it at all.

Other times I lay on the floor in the mistress's work-room and slept, she gently using me for a foot-stool, knowing it pleased me, for it was a caress; other times I spent an hour in the nursery, and got well tousled and made happy; other times I watched

5

by the crib there, when the baby was asleep and the nurse out for a few minutes on the baby's affairs; other times I romped and raced through the grounds and the garden with Sadie till we were tired out, then slumbered on the grass in the shade of a tree while she read her book; other times I went visiting among the neighbor dogs—for there were some most pleasant ones not far away, and one very handsome and courteous and graceful one, a curly-haired Irish setter by the name of Robin Adair, who was a Presbyterian like me, and belonged to the Scotch minister.

The servants in our house were all kind to me and were fond of me, and so, as you see, mine was a pleasant life. There could not be a happier dog than I was, nor a gratefuler one. I will say this for myself, for it is only the truth: I tried in all ways to do well and right, and honor my mother's memory and her teachings, and earn the happiness that had come to me, as best I could.

By-and-by came my little puppy, and then my cup was full, my happiness was perfect. It was the dearest little waddling thing, and so smooth and soft and velvety, and had such cunning little awkward paws, and such affectionate eyes, and such a sweet and innocent face; and it made me so proud to see how the children and their mother adored it, and fondled it, and exclaimed over every little wonderful thing it did. It did seem to me that life was just too lovely to—

Then came the winter.   One day I was standing a
watch in the nursery.   That is to say, I was asleep
on the bed.   The baby was asleep in the crib, which
was alongside the bed, on the side next the fireplace.
It was the kind of crib that has a lofty tent over it
made of a gauzy stuff that you can see through.
The nurse was out, and we two sleepers were alone.
A spark from the wood-fire was shot out, and it lit
on the slope of the tent.   I suppose a quiet interval
followed, then a scream from the baby woke me, and
there was that tent flaming up towards the ceiling!
Before I could think, I sprang to the floor in my
fright, and in a second was half-way to the door; but
in the next half-second my mother's farewell was
sounding in my ears, and I was back on the bed
again.   I reached my head through the flames and
dragged the baby out by the waistband, and tugged
it along, and we fell to the floor together in a cloud
of smoke; I snatched a new hold, and dragged the
screaming little creature along and out at the door
and around the bend of the hall, and was still tugging away, all excited and happy and proud, when
the master's voice shouted:

"Begone, you cursed beast!" and I jumped to
save myself; but he was wonderfully quick, and
chased me up, striking furiously at me with his cane,
I dodging this way and that, in terror, and at last a
strong blow fell upon my left foreleg, which made
me shriek and fall, for the moment, helpless; the
cane went up for another blow, but never descended,

for the nurse's voice rang wildly out, "The nursery's on fire!" and the master rushed away in that direction, and my other bones were saved.

The pain was cruel, but, no matter, I must not lose any time; he might come back at any moment; so I limped on three legs to the other end of the hall, where there was a dark little stairway leading up into a garret where old boxes and such things were kept, as I had heard say, and where people seldom went. I managed to climb up there, then I searched my way through the dark among the piles of things, and hid in the secretest place I could find. It was foolish to be afraid there, yet still I was; so afraid that I held in and hardly even whimpered, though it would have been such a comfort to whimper, because that eases the pain, you know. But I could lick my leg, and that did me some good.

For half an hour there was a commotion downstairs, and shoutings, and rushing footsteps, and then there was quiet again. Quiet for some minutes, and that was grateful to my spirit, for then my fears began to go down; and fears are worse than pains— oh, much worse. Then came a sound that froze me. They were calling me—calling me by name—hunting for me!

It was muffled by distance, but that could not take the terror out of it, and it was the most dreadful sound to me that I had ever heard. It went all about, everywhere, down there: along the halls, through all the rooms, in both stories, and in the basement and the cellar; then outside, and farther and farther away — then back, and all about the house again, and I thought it would never, never stop. But at last it did, hours and hours after the vague twilight of the garret had long ago been blotted out by black darkness.

Then in that blessed stillness my terrors fell little by little away, and I was at peace and slept. It was a good rest I had, but I woke before the twilight had come again. I was feeling fairly comfortable, and I could think out a plan now. I made a very good one; which was, to creep down, all the way down the back stairs, and hide behind the cellar door, and slip out and escape when the iceman came at dawn, while he was inside filling the refrigerator; then I would hide all day, and start on my journey when night came; my journey to—well, anywhere where they would not know me and betray me to the master. I was feeling almost cheerful now; then suddenly I thought: Why, what would life be without my puppy!

That was despair. There was no plan for me; I saw that; I must stay where I was; stay, and wait, and take what might come—it was not my affair; that was what life is—my mother had said it. Then —well, then the calling began again! All my sorrows came back. I said to myself, the master will never forgive. I did not know what I had done to make him so bitter and so unforgiving, yet I judged it was something a dog could not understand, but which was clear to a man and dreadful.

They called and called—days and nights, it seemed to me. So long that the hunger and thirst near drove me mad, and I recognized that I was getting very weak. When you are this way you sleep a great deal, and I did. Once I woke in an awful fright—it seemed to me that the calling was right there in the garret! And so it was: it was Sadie's voice, and she was crying; my name was falling from her lips all broken, poor thing, and I could not believe my ears for the joy of it when I heard her say:

"Come back to us—oh, come back to us, and forgive—it is all so sad without our—"

I broke in with *such* a grateful little yelp, and the next moment Sadie was plunging and stumbling through the darkness and the lumber and shouting for the family to hear, "She's found, she's found!"

The days that followed—well, they were wonderful. The mother and Sadie and the servants—why, they just seemed to worship me. They couldn't seem to make me a bed that was fine enough; and as for food, they couldn't be satisfied with anything but game and delicacies that were out of season; and every day the friends and neighbors flocked in to hear about my heroism—that was the name they called it by, and it means agriculture. I remember my mother pulling it on a kennel once, and explaining it that way, but didn't say what agriculture was, except that it was synonymous with intramural in-candescence; and a dozen times a day Mrs. Gray and Sadie would tell the tale to new-comers, and say I risked my life to save the baby's, and both of us had burns to prove it, and then the company would pass me around and pet me and exclaim about me, and you could see the pride in the eyes of Sadie and her mother; and when the people wanted to know what made me limp, they looked ashamed and changed the subject, and sometimes when people hunted them this way and that way with questions about it, it looked to me as if they were going to cry.

And this was not all the glory; no, the master's friends came, a whole twenty of the most distin-guished people, and had me in the laboratory, and discussed me as if I was a kind of discovery; and some of them said it was wonderful in a dumb beast, the finest exhibition of instinct they could call to mind; but the master said, with vehemence, "It's far above instinct; it's *reason*, and many a man, privileged to be saved and go with you and me to a better world by right of its possession, has less of it than this poor silly quadruped that's foreordained to perish;" and then he laughed, and said: "Why, look at me—I'm a sarcasm! bless you, with all my grand intelligence, the only thing I inferred was that the dog had gone mad and was destroying the child, whereas but for the beast's intelligence—it's *reason*, I tell you!—the child would have perished!"

They disputed and disputed, and *I* was the very

centre and subject of it all, and I wished my mother could know that this grand honor had come to me; it would have made her proud.

Then they discussed optics, as they called it, and whether a certain injury to the brain would produce blindness or not, but they could not agree about it, and said they must test it by experiment by-and-by; and next they discussed plants, and that interested me, because in the summer Sadie and I had planted seeds—I helped her dig the holes, you know—and after days and days a little shrub or a flower came up there, and it was a wonder how that could happen; but it did, and I wished I could talk—I would have told those people about it and shown them how much I knew, and been all alive with the subject; but I didn't care for the optics; it was dull, and when they came back to it again it bored me, and I went to sleep.

Pretty soon it was spring, and sunny and pleasant and lovely, and the sweet mother and the children patted me and the puppy good-bye, and went away on a journey and a visit to their kin, and the master wasn't any company for us, but we played together and had good times, and the servants were kind and friendly, so we got along quite happily and counted the days and waited for the family.

And one day those men came again, and said, now for the test, and they took the puppy to the laboratory, and I limped three-leggedly along, too, feeling proud, for any attention shown the puppy was a pleasure to me, of course. They discussed and experimented, and then suddenly the puppy shrieked, and they set him on the floor, and he went staggering around, with his head all bloody, and the master clapped his hands and shouted:

"There, I've won—confess it! He's as blind as a bat!"

And they all said:

"It's so—you've proved your theory, and suffering humanity owes you a great debt from henceforth," and they crowded around him, and wrung his hand cordially and thankfully, and praised him.

But I hardly saw or heard these things, for I ran at once to my little darling, and snuggled close to it where it lay, and licked the blood, and it put its head against mine, whimpering softly, and I knew in my heart it was a comfort to it in its pain and trouble to feel its mother's touch, though it could not see me. Then it dropped down, presently, and its little velvet nose rested upon the floor, and it was still, and did not move any more.

Soon the master stopped discussing a moment, and rang in the footman, and said, "Bury it in the far corner of the garden," and then went on with the discussion, and I trotted after the footman, very happy and grateful, for I knew the puppy was out of its pain now, because it was asleep. We went far down the garden to the farthest end, where the children and the nurse and the puppy and I used to play in the summer in the shade of a great elm, and there the footman dug a hole, and I saw he was going to plant the puppy, and I was glad, because it would grow and come up a fine handsome dog, like Robin Adair, and be a beautiful surprise for the family when they came home; so I tried to help him dig, but my lame leg was no good, being stiff, you know, and you have to have two, or it is no use. When the footman had finished and covered little Robin up, he patted my head, and there were tears in his eyes, and he said: "Poor little doggie, you SAVED *his* child."

I have watched two whole weeks, and he doesn't come up! This last week a fright has been stealing upon me. I think there is something terrible about this. I do not know what it is, but the fear makes me sick, and I cannot eat, though the servants bring me the best of food; and they pet me so, and even come in the night, and cry, and say, "Poor doggie—do give it up and come home; *don't* break our hearts!" and all this terrifies me the more, and makes me sure something has happened. And I am so weak; since yesterday I cannot stand on my feet any more. And within this hour the servants, looking towards the sun where it was sinking out of sight and the night chill coming on, said things I could not understand, but they carried something cold to my heart.

"Those poor creatures! They do not suspect They will come home in the morning, and eagerly

" POOR LITTLE DOGGIE, YOU *SAVED HIS* CHILD "

ask for the little doggie that did the brave deed, and who of us will be strong enough to say the truth to them: 'The humble little friend is gone where go the beasts that perish.'"

WAS IT HEAVEN? OR HELL?

I

"YOU told a *lie?*"

"You confess it — you actually confess it — you told a lie!"

II

THE family consisted of four persons: Margaret Lester, widow, aged thirty-six; Helen Lester, her daughter, aged sixteen; Mrs. Lester's maiden aunts, Hannah and Hester Gray, twins, aged sixty-seven. Waking and sleeping, the three women spent their days and nights in adoring the young girl; in watching the movements of her sweet spirit in the mirror of her face; in refreshing their souls with the vision of her bloom and beauty; in listening to the music of her voice; in gratefully recognizing how rich and fair for them was the world with this presence in it; in shuddering to think how desolate it would be with this light gone out of it.

By nature—and inside—the aged aunts were utterly dear and lovable and good, but in the matter of morals and conduct their training had been so uncompromisingly strict that it had made them exteriorly austere, not to say stern. Their influence was effective in the house; so effective that the mother and the daughter conformed to its moral and religious requirements cheerfully, contentedly, happily, unquestionably. To do this was become second nature to them. And so in this peaceful heaven there were no clashings, no irritations, no fault-findings, no heart-burnings.

In it a lie had no place. In it a lie was unthinkable. In it speech was restricted to absolute truth,
iron-bound truth, implacable and uncompromising
truth, let the resulting consequences be what they
might. At last, one day, under stress of circumstances, the darling of the house sullied her lips with
a lie—and confessed it, with tears and self-upbraid-
ings. There are not any words that can paint the
consternation of the aunts. It was as if the sky had
crumpled up and collapsed and the earth had tum-
bled to ruin with a crash. They sat side by side,
white and stern, gazing speechless upon the culprit,
who was on her knees before them with her face
buried first in one lap and then the other, moaning
and sobbing, and appealing for sympathy and forgiveness and getting no response, humbly kissing the
hand of the one, then of the other, only to see it with-
drawn as suffering defilement by those soiled lips.

Twice, at intervals, Aunt Hester said, in frozen
amazement:

"You told a *lie?*"

Twice, at intervals, Aunt Hannah followed with the
muttered and amazed ejaculation:

"You confess it—you actually confess it—you told
a lie!"

It was all they could say. The situation was new,
unheard-of, incredible; they could not understand it,
they did not know how to take hold of it, it approximately paralyzed speech.

At length it was decided that the erring child must

be taken to her mother, who was ill, and who ought to know what had happened. Helen begged, besought, implored that she might be spared this further disgrace, and that her mother might be spared the grief and pain of it; but this could not be: duty required this sacrifice, duty takes precedence of all things, nothing can absolve one from a duty, with a duty no compromise is possible.

Helen still begged, and said the sin was her own, her mother had had no hand in it—why must she be made to suffer for it?

But the aunts were obdurate in their righteousness, and said the law that visited the sins of the parent upon the child was by all right and reason reversible; and therefore it was but just that the innocent mother of a sinning child should suffer her rightful share of the grief and pain and shame which were the allotted wages of the sin.

The three moved towards the sick-room.

At this time the doctor was approaching the house. He was still a good distance away, however. He was a good doctor and a good man, and he had a good heart, but one had to know him a year to get over hating him, two years to learn to endure him, three to learn to like him, and four or five to learn to love him. It was a slow and trying education, but it paid. He was of great stature; he had a leonine head, a leonine face, a rough voice, and an eye which was sometimes a pirate's and sometimes a woman's, ac-

cording to the mood. He knew nothing about etiquette, and cared nothing about it; in speech, manner, carriage, and conduct he was the reverse of
conventional. He was frank, to the limit; he had
opinions on all subjects; they were always on tap
and ready for delivery, and he cared not a farthing
whether his listener liked them or didn't. Whom he
loved he loved, and manifested it; whom he didn't
love he hated, and published it from the house-tops.
In his young days he had been a sailor, and the salt
airs of all the seas blew from him yet. He was a
sturdy and loyal Christian, and believed he was the
best one in the land, and the only one whose Christianity was perfectly sound, healthy, full - charged
with common-sense, and had no decayed places in it.
People who had an axe to grind, or people who for
any reason wanted to get on the soft side of him,
called him The Christian—a phrase whose delicate
flattery was music to his ears, and whose capital T
was such an enchanting and vivid object to him that
he could *see* it when it fell out of a person's mouth
even in the dark. Many who were fond of him stood
on their consciences with both feet and brazenly
called him by that large title habitually, because it
was a pleasure to them to do anything that would
please him; and with eager and cordial malice his
extensive and diligently cultivated crop of enemies
gilded it, beflowered it, expanded it to "The *Only*
Christian." Of these two titles, the latter had the
wider currency; the enemy, being greatly in the

majority, attended to that. Whatever the doctor
believed, he believed with all his heart, and would
fight for it whenever he got the chance; and if the
intervals between chances grew to be irksomely wide,
he would invent ways of shortening them himself.
He was severely conscientious, according to his rather
independent lights, and whatever he took to be a
duty he performed, no matter whether the judgment
of the professional moralists agreed with his own or
not. At sea, in his young days, he had used profanity
freely, but as soon as he was converted he made a rule,
which he rigidly stuck to ever afterwards, never to
use it except on the rarest occasions, and then only
when duty commanded. He had been a hard drinker
at sea, but after his conversion he became a firm and
outspoken teetotaler, in order to be an example to
the young, and from that time forth he seldom drank;
never, indeed, except when it seemed to him to be a
duty—a condition which sometimes occurred a couple
of times a year, but never as many as five times.

Necessarily, such a man is impressionable, impulsive, emotional. This one was, and had no gift at
hiding his feelings; or if he had it he took no trouble
to exercise it. He carried his soul's prevailing
weather in his face, and when he entered a room the
parasols or the umbrellas went up—figuratively speaking—according to the indications. When the soft
light was in his eye it meant approval, and delivered
a benediction; when he came with a frown he lowered
the temperature ten degrees. He was a well-beloved

man in the house of his friends, but sometimes a
dreaded one.

He had a deep affection for the Lester household,
and its several members returned this feeling with
interest.   They mourned over his kind of Christianity,
and he frankly scoffed at theirs; but both parties went
on loving each other just the same.

He was approaching the house—out of the distance;
the aunts and the culprit were moving towards the
sick-chamber.

III

THE three last named stood by the bed; the aunts austere, the transgressor softly sobbing. The mother turned her head on the pillow; her tired eyes flamed up instantly with sympathy and passionate mother-love when they fell upon her child, and she opened the refuge and shelter of her arms.

"Wait!" said Aunt Hannah, and put out her hand and stayed the girl from leaping into them.

"Helen," said the other aunt, impressively, "tell your mother all. Purge your soul; leave nothing unconfessed."

Standing stricken and forlorn before her judges, the young girl mourned her sorrowful tale through to the end, then in a passion of appeal cried out:

"Oh, mother, can't you forgive me? won't you forgive me?—I am so desolate!"

"Forgive you, my darling? Oh, come to my arms! —there, lay your head upon my breast, and be at peace. If you had told a thousand lies—"

There was a sound—a warning—the clearing of a throat. The aunts glanced up, and withered in their clothes—there stood the doctor, his face a thunder-cloud. Mother and child knew nothing of his presence; they lay locked together, heart to heart, steeped in immeasurable content, dead to all things else. The physician stood many moments glaring and glooming upon the scene before him; studying it, analyzing it, searching out its genesis; then he put up his hand and beckoned to the aunts. They came trembling to him, and stood humbly before him and waited. He bent down and whispered:

"Didn't I tell you this patient must be protected from all excitement? What the hell have you been doing? Clear out of the place!"

They obeyed. Half an hour later he appeared in the parlor, serene, cheery, clothed in sunshine, conducting Helen, with his arm about her waist, petting her, and saying gentle and playful things to her; and she also was her sunny and happy self again.

"Now, then," he said, "good-bye, dear. Go to your room, and keep away from your mother, and behave yourself. But wait—put out your tongue. There, that will do—you're as sound as a nut!" He patted her cheek and added, "Run along now; I want to talk to these aunts."

She went from the presence. His face clouded over again at once; and as he sat down he said:

"You two have been doing a lot of damage—and maybe some good. Some good, yes—such as it is. That woman's disease is typhoid! You've brought it to a show-up, I think, with your insanities, and that's a service—such as it is. I hadn't been able to determine what it was before."

With one impulse the old ladies sprang to their feet, quaking with terror.

"Sit down! What are you proposing to do?"

"Do? We must fly to her. We—"

"You'll do nothing of the kind; you've done enough harm for one day. Do you want to squander all your capital of crimes and follies on a single deal? Sit down, I tell you. I have arranged for her to sleep; she needs it; if you disturb her without my orders, I'll brain you—if you've got the materials for it."

They sat down, distressed and indignant, but obedient, under compulsion. He proceeded:

"Now, then, I want this case explained. *They* wanted to explain it to me—as if there hadn't been emotion and excitement enough already. You knew my orders; how did you dare to go in there and get up that riot?"

Hester looked appealingly at Hannah; Hannah returned a beseeching look at Hester—neither wanted to dance to this unsympathetic orchestra. The doctor came to their help. He said:

"Begin, Hester."

Fingering at the fringes of her shawl, and with lowered eyes, Hester said, timidly:

"We should not have disobeyed for any ordinary cause, but this was vital. This was a duty. With a duty one has no choice; one must put all lighter considerations aside and perform it. We were obliged to arraign her before her mother. She had told a lie."

The doctor glowered upon the woman a moment, and seemed to be trying to work up in his mind an understanding of a wholly incomprehensible proposition; then he stormed out:

"She told a lie! *Did* she? God bless my soul! I tell a million a day! And so does every doctor. And so does everybody—including you—for that matter. And *that* was the important thing that authorized you to venture to disobey my orders and imperil that woman's life! Look here, Hester Gray, this is pure lunacy; that girl *couldn't* tell a lie that was intended to injure a person. The thing is impossible —absolutely impossible. You know it yourselves— both of you; you know it perfectly well."

Hannah came to her sister's rescue:

"Hester didn't mean that it was that kind of a lie, and it wasn't. But it was a lie."

"Well, upon my word, I never heard such nonsense! Haven't you got sense enough to discriminate between lies? Don't you know the difference between a lie that helps and a lie that hurts?"

"*All* lies are sinful," said Hannah, setting her lips together like a vise; "all lies are forbidden."

The Only Christian fidgeted impatiently in his chair. He wanted to attack this proposition, but he did not quite know how or\where to begin. Finally he made a venture:

"Hester, wouldn't you tell a lie to shield a person from an undeserved injury or shame?"

"No."

"Not even a friend?"

"No."

"Not even your dearest friend?"

"No. I would not."

The doctor struggled in silence awhile with this situation; then he asked:

"Not even to save him from bitter pain and misery and grief?"

"No. Not even to save his life."

Another pause. Then:

"Nor his soul."

There was a hush — a silence which endured a measurable interval — then Hester answered, in a low voice, but with decision:

"Nor his soul."

No one spoke for a while; then the doctor said:

"Is it with you the same, Hannah?"

"Yes," she answered.

"I ask you both—why?"

"Because to tell such a lie, or any lie, is a sin, and could cost us the loss of our own souls—*would*, indeed, if we died without time to repent."

"Strange . . . strange . . . it is past belief." Then he asked, roughly: "Is such a soul as that *worth* saving?" He rose up, mumbling and grumbling, and started for the door, stumping vigorously along. At the threshold he turned and rasped out an admonition: "Reform! Drop this mean and sordid and selfish devotion to the saving of your shabby little souls, and hunt up something to do that's got some

dignity to it! *Risk* your souls! risk them in good
causes; then if you lose them, why should you care?
Reform!"

The good old gentlewomen sat paralyzed, pul-
verized, outraged, insulted, and brooded in bitterness and indignation over these blasphemies. They
were hurt to the heart, poor old ladies, and said they
could never forgive these injuries.

"Reform!"

They kept repeating that word resentfully. "Reform—and learn to tell lies!"

Time slipped along, and in due course a change
came over their spirits. They had completed the
human being's first duty—which is to think about
himself until he has exhausted the subject, then he
is in a condition to take up minor interests and
think of other people. This changes the complexion
of his spirits—generally wholesomely. The minds of
the two old ladies reverted to their beloved niece and
the fearful disease which had smitten her; instantly
they forgot the hurts their self-love had received, and
a passionate desire rose in their hearts to go to the
help of the sufferer and comfort her with their love,
and minister to her, and labor for her the best they
could with their weak hands, and joyfully and affectionately wear out their poor old bodies in her dear
service if only they might have the privilege.

"And we shall have it!" said Hester, with the
tears running down her face. "There are no nurses
comparable to us, for there are no others that will

stand their watch by that bed till they drop and die, and God knows we would do that."

"Amen," said Hannah, smiling approval and endorsement through the mist of moisture that blurred her glasses. "The doctor knows us, and knows we will not disobey again; and he will call no others. He will not dare!"

"Dare?" said Hester, with temper, and dashing the water from her eyes; "he will dare anything— that Christian devil! But it will do no good for him to try it this time—but, laws! Hannah! after all's said and done, he is gifted and wise and good, and he would not think of such a thing. . . . It is surely time for one of us to go to that room. What is keeping him? Why doesn't he come and say so?"

They caught the sound of his approaching step. He entered, sat down, and began to talk.

"Margaret is a sick woman," he said. "She is still sleeping, but she will wake presently; then one of you must go to her. She will be worse before she is better. Pretty soon a night-and-day watch must be set. How much of it can you two undertake?"

"All of it!" burst from both ladies at once.

The doctor's eyes flashed, and he said, with energy:

"You *do* ring true, you brave old relics! And you *shall* do all of the nursing you can, for there's none to match you in that divine office in this town; but you can't do all of it, and it would be a crime to let you." It was grand praise, golden praise, coming from such a source, and it took nearly all the resentment out of the aged twins' hearts. "Your Tilly and my old Nancy shall do the rest—good nurses both, white souls with black skins, watchful, loving, tender—just perfect nurses!—and competent liars from the cradle. . . . Look you! keep a little watch on Helen; she is sick, and is going to be sicker."

The ladies looked a little surprised, and not credulous; and Hester said:

"How is that? It isn't an hour since you said she was as sound as a nut."

The doctor answered, tranquilly:

"It was a lie."

The ladies turned upon him indignantly, and Hannah said:

"How can you make an odious confession like that, in so indifferent a tone, when you know how we feel about all forms of—"

"Hush! You are as ignorant as cats, both of you, and you don't know what you are talking about. You are like all the rest of the moral moles: you lie from morning till night, but because you don't do it with your mouths, but only with your lying eyes, your lying inflections, your deceptively misplaced emphasis, and your misleading gestures, you turn up your complacent noses and parade before God and the world as saintly and unsmirched Truth-Speakers, in whose cold-storage souls a lie would freeze to death if it got there! Why will you humbug yourselves with that foolish notion that no lie is a lie ex-

cept a spoken one? What is the difference between
lying with your eyes and lying with your mouth?
There is none; and if you would reflect a moment
you would see that it is so. There isn't a human
being that doesn't tell a gross of lies every day of his
life; and you—why, between you, you tell thirty
thousand; yet you flare up here in a lurid hypocritical
horror because I tell that child a benevolent and sinless lie to protect her from her imagination, which
would get to work and warm up her blood to a fever
in an hour, if I were disloyal enough to my duty to
let it. Which I should probably do if I were interested in saving my soul by such disreputable
means.

"Come, let us reason together. Let us examine
details. When you two were in the sick-room raising
that riot, what would you have done if you had
known I was coming?"

"Well, what?"

"You would have slipped out and carried Helen
with you—wouldn't you?"

The ladies were silent.

"What would be your object and intention?"

"Well, what?"

"To keep me from finding out your guilt; to beguile me to infer that Margaret's excitement proceeded from some cause not known to you. In a
word, to tell me a lie—a silent lie. Moreover, a possibly harmful one."

The twins colored, but did not speak.

"You not only tell myriads of silent lies, but you tell lies with your mouths—you two."

"*That* is not so!"

"It is so. But only harmless ones. You never dream of uttering a harmful one. Do you know that that is a concession—and a confession?"

"How do you mean?"

"It is an unconscious concession that harmless lies are not criminal; it is a confession that you constantly *make* that discrimination. For instance, you declined old Mrs. Foster's invitation last week to meet those odious Higbies at supper—in a polite note in which you expressed regret and said you were very sorry you could not go. It was a lie. It was as unmitigated a lie as was ever uttered. Deny it, Hester—with another lie."

Hester replied with a toss of her head.

"That will not do. Answer. Was it a lie, or wasn't it?"

The color stole into the cheeks of both women, and with a struggle and an effort they got out their confession:

"It was a lie."

"Good—the reform is beginning; there is hope for you yet; you will not tell a lie to save your dearest friend's soul, but you will spew out one without a scruple to save yourself the discomfort of telling an unpleasant truth."

He rose. Hester, speaking for both, said, coldly:

"We have lied; we perceive it; it will occur no

more. To lie is a sin. We shall never tell another one of any kind whatsoever, even lies of courtesy or benevolence, to save any one a pang or a sorrow decreed for him by God."

"Ah, how soon you will fall! In fact, you have fallen already; for what you have just uttered is a lie. Good-bye. Reform! One of you go to the sick-room now."

IV

Twelve days later.

Mother and child were lingering in the grip of the hideous disease. Of hope for either there was little. The aged sisters looked white and worn, but they would not give up their posts. Their hearts were breaking, poor old things, but their grit was steadfast and indestructible. All the twelve days the mother had pined for the child, and the child for the mother, but both knew that the prayer of these longings could not be granted. When the mother was told—on the first day—that her disease was typhoid, she was frightened, and asked if there was danger that Helen could have contracted it the day before, when she was in the sick-chamber on that confession visit. Hester told her the doctor had poo-pooed the idea. It troubled Hester to say it, although it was true, for she had not believed the doctor; but when she saw the mother's joy in the news, the pain in her conscience lost something of its force—a result which made her ashamed of the constructive deception which she had practised, though not ashamed enough to make her distinctly and definitely wish she had refrained from it. From that moment the sick woman understood that her daughter must remain away, and she said she would reconcile herself to the separation the best she could, for she would rather suffer death than have her child's health imperilled. That afternoon Helen had to take to her bed, ill. She grew worse during the night. In the morning her mother asked after her:

"Is she well?"

Hester turned cold; she opened her lips, but the words refused to come. The mother lay languidly looking, musing, waiting; suddenly she turned white and gasped out:

"Oh, my God! what is it? is she sick?"

Then the poor aunt's tortured heart rose in rebellion, and words came:

"No—be comforted; she is well."

The sick woman put all her happy heart in her gratitude:

"Thank God for those dear words! Kiss me. How I worship you for saying them!"

Hester told this incident to Hannah, who received it with a rebuking look, and said, coldly:

"Sister, it was a lie."

Hester's lips trembled piteously; she choked down a sob, and said:

"Oh, Hannah, it was a sin, but I could not help it; I could not endure the fright and the misery that were in her face."

"No matter. It was a lie. God will hold you to account for it."

"Oh, I know it, I know it," cried Hester, wringing

her hands, "but even if it were now, I could not help it. I know I should do it again."

"Then take my place with Helen in the morning. I will make the report myself."

Hester clung to her sister, begging and imploring:

"Don't, Hannah, oh, don't—you will kill her."

"I will at least speak the truth."

In the morning she had a cruel report to bear to the mother, and she braced herself for the trial. When she returned from her mission, Hester was waiting, pale and trembling, in the hall. She whispered:

"Oh, how did she take it—that poor, desolate mother?"

Hannah's eyes were swimming in tears. She said:

"God forgive me, I told her the child was well!"

Hester gathered her to her heart, with a grateful "God bless you, Hannah!" and poured out her thankfulness in an inundation of worshipping praises.

After that, the two knew the limit of their strength, and accepted their fate. They surrendered humbly, and abandoned themselves to the hard requirements of the situation. Daily they told the morning lie, and confessed their sin in prayer; not asking forgiveness, as not being worthy of it, but only wishing to make record that they realized their wickedness and were not desiring to hide it or excuse it.

Daily, as the fair young idol of the house sank lower and lower, the sorrowful old aunts painted her glowing bloom and her fresh young beauty to the

wan mother, and winced under the stabs her ecstasies
of joy and gratitude gave them.

In the first days, while the child had strength to
hold a pencil, she wrote fond little love-notes to her
mother, in which she concealed her illness; and these
the mother read and re-read through happy eyes wet
with thankful tears, and kissed them over and over
again, and treasured them as precious things under
her pillow.

Then came a day when the strength was gone from
the hand, and the mind wandered, and the tongue
babbled pathetic incoherences. This was a sore di-
lemma for the poor aunts. There were no love-notes
for the mother. They did not know what to do.
Hester began a carefully studied and plausible explanation, but lost the track of it and grew confused;
suspicion began to show in the mother's face, then
alarm. Hester saw it, recognized the imminence of
the danger, and descended to the emergency, pulling
herself resolutely together and plucking victory from
the open jaws of defeat. In a placid and convincing
voice she said:

"I thought it might distress you to know it, but
Helen spent the night at the Sloanes'. There was a
little party there, and although she did not want to
go, and you so sick, we persuaded her, she being young
and needing the innocent pastimes of youth, and we
believing you would approve. Be sure she will write
the moment she comes."

"How good you are, and how dear and thoughtful

for us both! Approve? Why, I thank you with all my heart. My poor little exile! Tell her I want her to have every pleasure she can—I would not rob her of one. Only let her keep her health, that is all I ask. Don't let that suffer; I could not bear it. How thankful I am that she escaped this infection—and what a narrow risk she ran, Aunt Hester! Think of that lovely face all dulled and burned with fever. I can't bear the thought of it. Keep her health. Keep her bloom! I can see her now, the dainty creature— with the big, blue, earnest eyes; and sweet, oh, so sweet and gentle and winning! Is she as beautiful as ever, dear Aunt Hester?"

"Oh, more beautiful and bright and charming than ever she was before, if such a thing can be"—and Hester turned away and fumbled with the medicine-bottles, to hide her shame and grief.

V

AFTER a little, both aunts were laboring upon a
difficult and baffling work in Helen's chamber. Patiently and earnestly, with their stiff old fingers, they
were trying to forge the required note. They made
failure after failure, but they improved little by little
all the time. The pity of it all, the pathetic humor
of it, there was none to see; they themselves were
unconscious of it. Often their tears fell upon the
notes and spoiled them; sometimes a single mis-
formed word made a note risky which could have
been ventured but for that; but at last Hannah produced one whose script was a good enough imitation
of Helen's to pass any but a suspicious eye, and
bountifully enriched it with the petting phrases and
loving nicknames that had been familiar on the
child's lips from her nursery days. She carried it to
the mother, who took it with avidity, and kissed it,
and fondled it, reading its precious words over and
over again, and dwelling with deep contentment upon
its closing paragraph:

"Mousie darling, if I could only see you, and kiss
your eyes, and feel your arms about me! I am so
glad my practising does not disturb you. Get well

soon. Everybody is good to me, but I am so lonesome without you, dear mamma."

"The poor child, I know just how she feels. She cannot be quite happy without me; and I—oh, I live in the light of her eyes! Tell her she must practise all she pleases; and, Aunt Hannah—tell her I can't hear the piano this far, nor her dear voice when she sings: God knows I wish I could. No one knows how sweet that voice is to me; and to think—some day it will be silent! What are you crying for?"

"Only because—because—it was just a memory. When I came away she was singing, 'Loch Lomond.' The pathos of it! It always moves me so when she sings that."

"And me, too. How heart-breakingly beautiful it is when some youthful sorrow is brooding in her breast and she sings it for the mystic healing it brings. . . . Aunt Hannah?"

"Dear Margaret?"

"I am very ill. Sometimes it comes over me that I shall never hear that dear voice again."

"Oh, don't—don't, Margaret! I can't bear it!"

Margaret was moved and distressed, and said, gently:

"There—there—let me put my arms around you. Don't cry. There—put your cheek to mine. Be comforted. I wish to live. I will live if I can. Ah, what could she do without me! . . . Does she often speak of me?—but I know she does."

"Oh, all the time—all the time!"

"My sweet child! She wrote the note the moment she came home?"

"Yes—the first moment. She would not wait to take off her things."

"I knew it. It is her dear, impulsive, affectionate way. I knew it without asking, but I wanted to hear you say it. The petted wife knows she is loved, but she makes her husband tell her so every day, just for the joy of hearing it. . . . She used the pen this time. That is better; the pencil-marks could rub out, and I should grieve for that. Did you suggest that she use the pen?"

"Y-no—she—it was her own idea."

The mother looked her pleasure, and said:

"I was hoping you would say that. There was never such a dear and thoughtful child! . . . Aunt Hannah?"

"Dear Margaret?"

"Go and tell her I think of her all the time, and worship her. Why—you are crying again. Don't be so worried about me, dear; I think there is nothing to fear, yet."

The grieving messenger carried her message, and piously delivered it to unheeding ears. The girl babbled on unaware; looking up at her with wondering and startled eyes flaming with fever, eyes in which was no light of recognition:

"Are you—no, you are not my mother. I want her—oh, I want her! She was here a minute ago—I did not see her go. Will she come? will she come quickly? will she come now?... There are so many houses ... and they oppress me so ... and everything whirls and turns and whirls ... oh, my head, my head!"—and so she wandered on and on, in her pain, flitting from one torturing fancy to another, and tossing her arms about in a weary and ceaseless persecution of unrest.

Poor old Hannah wetted the parched lips and softly stroked the hot brow, murmuring endearing and pitying words, and thanking the Father of all that the mother was happy and did not know.

VI

DAILY the child sank lower and steadily lower towards the grave, and daily the sorrowing old watchers carried gilded tidings of her radiant health and loveliness to the happy mother, whose pilgrimage was also now nearing its end. And daily they forged loving and cheery notes in the child's hand, and stood by with remorseful consciences and bleeding hearts, and wept to see the grateful mother devour them and adore them and treasure them away as things beyond price, because of their sweet source, and sacred because her child's hand had touched them.

At last came that kindly friend who brings healing and peace to all. The lights were burning low. In the solemn hush which precedes the dawn vague figures flitted soundless along the dim hall and gathered silent and awed in Helen's chamber, and grouped themselves about her bed, for a warning had gone forth, and they knew. The dying girl lay with closed lids, and unconscious, the drapery upon her breast faintly rising and falling as her wasting life ebbed away. At intervals a sigh or a muffled sob broke upon the stillness. The same haunting thought was in all minds there: the pity of this death, the going out into the great darkness, and the mother not here to help and hearten and bless.

Helen stirred; her hands began to grope wistfully about as if they sought something—she had been blind some hours. The end was come; all knew it. With a great sob Hester gathered her to her breast, crying, "Oh, my child, my darling!" A rapturous light broke in the dying girl's face, for it was mercifully vouchsafed her to mistake those sheltering arms for another's; and she went to her rest murmuring, "Oh, mamma, I am so happy—I so longed for you— now I can die."

Two hours later Hester made her report. The mother asked.

"How is it with the child?"

"She is well."

VII

A SHEAF of white crape and black was hung upon
the door of the house, and there it swayed and
rustled in the wind and whispered its tidings. At
noon the preparation of the dead was finished, and
in the coffin lay the fair young form, beautiful, and
in the sweet face a great peace. Two mourners sat
by it, grieving and worshipping—Hannah and the
black woman Tilly. Hester came, and she was trembling, for a great trouble was upon her spirit. She
said:

"She asks for a note."

Hannah's face blanched. She had not thought of
this; it had seemed that that pathetic service was
ended. But she realized now that that could not be.
For a little while the two women stood looking into
each other's face, with vacant eyes; then Hannah
said:

"There is no way out of it—she must have it; she
will suspect, else."

"And she would find out."

"Yes. It would break her heart." She looked at
the dead face, and her eyes filled. "I will write it,"
she said.

Hester carried it. The closing line said:

"Darling Mousie, dear sweet mother, we shall soon be together again. Is not that good news? And it is true; they all say it is true."

The mother mourned, saying:

"Poor child, how will she bear it when she knows? I shall never see her again in life. It is hard, so hard. She does not suspect? You guard her from that?"

"She thinks you will soon be well."

"How good you are, and careful, dear Aunt Hester! None goes near her who could carry the infection?"

"It would be a crime."

"But you *see* her?"

"With a distance between—yes."

"That is so good. Others one could not trust; but you two guardian angels—steel is not so true as you. Others would be unfaithful; and many would deceive, and lie."

Hester's eyes fell, and her poor old lips trembled.

"Let me kiss you for her, Aunt Hester; and when I am gone, and the danger is past, place the kiss upon her dear lips some day, and say her mother sent it, and all her mother's broken heart is in it."

Within the hour, Hester, raining tears upon the dead face, performed her pathetic mission.

VIII

ANOTHER day dawned, and grew, and spread its sunshine in the earth. Aunt Hannah brought comforting news to the failing mother, and a happy note, which said again, "We have but a little time to wait, darling mother, then we shall be together."

The deep note of a bell came moaning down the wind.

"Aunt Hannah, it is tolling. Some poor soul is at rest. As I shall be soon. You will not let her forget me?"

"Oh, God knows she never will!"

"Do not you hear strange noises, Aunt Hannah? It sounds like the shuffling of many feet."

"We hoped you would not hear it, dear. It is a little company gathering, for—for Helen's sake, poor little prisoner. There will be music—and she loves it so. We thought you would not mind."

"Mind? Oh no, no—oh, give her everything her dear heart can desire. How good you two are to her, and how good to me! God bless you both, always!"

After a listening pause:

"How lovely! It is her organ. Is she playing it herself, do you think?" Faint and rich and inspiring the chords floated to her ears on the still air. "Yes, it is her touch, dear heart, I recognize it. They are singing. Why—it is a hymn! and the sacredest of all, the most touching, the most consoling. . . . It seems to open the gates of paradise to me. . . . If I could die now. . . ."

Faint and far the words rose out of the stillness:

> Nearer, my God, to Thee,
> Nearer to Thee,
> E'en though it be a cross
> That raiseth me.

With the closing of the hymn another soul passed to its rest, and they that had been one in life were not sundered in death. The sisters, mourning and rejoicing, said:

"How blessed it was that she never knew!"

IX

At midnight they sat together, grieving, and the angel of the Lord appeared in the midst transfigured with a radiance not of earth; and speaking, said:

"For liars a place is appointed. There they burn in the fires of hell from everlasting unto everlasting. Repent!"

The bereaved fell upon their knees before him and clasped their hands and bowed their gray heads, adoring. But their tongues clove to the roof of their mouths, and they were dumb.

"Speak! that I may bear the message to the chancery of heaven and bring again the decree from which there is no appeal."

Then they bowed their heads yet lower, and one said:

"Our sin is great, and we suffer shame; but only perfect and final repentance can make us whole; and we are poor creatures who have learned our human weakness, and we know that if we were in those hard straits again our hearts would fail again, and we should sin as before. The strong could prevail, and so be saved, but we are lost."

They lifted their heads in supplication. The angel was gone. While they marvelled and wept he came again; and bending low, he whispered the decree.

X

Was it Heaven?   Or Hell?

THE CALIFORNIAN'S TALE

THIRTY-FIVE years ago I was out prospecting on the Stanislaus, tramping all day long with pick and pan and horn, and washing a hatful of dirt here and there, always expecting to make a rich strike, and never doing it. It was a lovely region, woodsy, balmy, delicious, and had once been populous, long years before, but now the people had vanished and the charming paradise was a solitude. They went away when the surface diggings gave out. In one place, where a busy little city with banks and newspapers and fire companies and a mayor and aldermen had been, was nothing but a wide expanse of emerald turf, with not even the faintest sign that human life had ever been present there. This was down towards Tuttletown. In the country neighborhood thereabouts, along the dusty roads, one found at intervals the prettiest little cottage homes, snug and cosey, and so cobwebbed with vines snowed thick with roses that the doors and windows were wholly hidden from sight — sign that these were deserted homes, forsaken years ago by defeated and disappointed families who could neither sell them nor give

them away.   Now and then, half an hour apart, one
came across solitary log cabins of the earliest mining
days, built by the first gold-miners, the predecessors
of the cottage-builders.   In some few cases these
cabins were still occupied; and when this was so, you
could depend upon it that the occupant was the very
pioneer who had built the cabin; and you could depend on another thing, too—that he was there because he had once had his opportunity to go home to
the States rich, and had not done it; had later lost
his wealth, and had then in his humiliation resolved
to sever all communication with his home relatives
and friends, and be to them thenceforth as one dead.
Round about California in that day were scattered a
host of these living dead men—pride-smitten poor
fellows, grizzled and old at forty, whose secret
thoughts were made all of regrets and longings—regrets for their wasted lives, and longings to be out of
the struggle and done with it all.

It was a lonesome land!   Not a sound in all those
peaceful expanses of grass and woods but the drowsy
hum of insects; no glimpse of man or beast; nothing
to keep up your spirits and make you glad to be
alive.   And so, at last, in the early part of the afternoon, when I caught sight of a human creature, I
felt a most grateful uplift.   This person was a man
about forty-five years old, and he was standing at
the gate of one of those cosey little rose-clad cottages
of the sort already referred to.   However, this one
hadn't a deserted look; it had the look of being lived

in and petted and cared for and looked after; and so had its front yard, which was a garden of flowers, abundant, gay, and flourishing. I was invited in, of course, and required to make myself at home—it was the custom of the country.

It was delightful to be in such a place, after long weeks of daily and nightly familiarity with miners' cabins — with all which this implies of dirt floor, never-made beds, tin plates and cups, bacon and beans and black coffee, and nothing of ornament but war pictures from the Eastern illustrated papers tacked to the log walls. That was all hard, cheerless, materialistic desolation, but here was a nest which had aspects to rest the tired eye and refresh that something in one's nature which, after long fasting, recognizes, when confronted by the belongings of art, howsoever cheap and modest they may be, that it has unconsciously been famishing and now has found nourishment. I could not have believed that a rag carpet could feast me so, and so content me; or that there could be such solace to the soul in wall-paper and framed lithographs, and bright-colored tidies and lamp-mats, and Windsor chairs, and varnished whatnots, with sea-shells and books and china vases on them, and the score of little unclassifiable tricks and touches that a woman's hand distributes about a home, which one sees without knowing he sees them, yet would miss in a moment if they were taken away. The delight that was in my heart showed in my face, and the man

8

saw it and was pleased; saw it so plainly that he answered it as if it had been spoken.

"All her work," he said, caressingly; "she did it all herself—every bit," and he took the room in with a glance which was full of affectionate worship. One of those soft Japanese fabrics with which women drape with careful negligence the upper part of a picture-frame was out of adjustment. He noticed it, and rearranged it with cautious pains, stepping back several times to gauge the effect before he got it to suit him. Then he gave it a light finishing pat or two with his hand, and said: "She always does that. You can't tell just what it lacks, but it does lack something until you've done that—you can see it yourself after it's done, but that is all you know; you can't find out the law of it. It's like the finishing pats a mother gives the child's hair after she's got it combed and brushed, I reckon. I've seen her fix all these things so much that I can do them all just her way, though I don't know the law of any of them. But she knows the law. She knows the why and the how both; but I don't know the why; I only know the how."

He took me into a bedroom so that I might wash my hands; such a bedroom as I had not seen for years: white counterpane, white pillows, carpeted floor, papered walls, pictures, dressing-table, with mirror and pin-cushion and dainty toilet things; and in the corner a wash-stand, with real china-ware bowl and pitcher, and with soap in a china dish, and on a rack more than a dozen towels—towels too clean and white for one out of practice to use without some vague sense of profanation. So my face spoke again, and he answered with gratified words:

"All her work; she did it all herself—every bit. Nothing here that hasn't felt the touch of her hand. Now you would think— But I mustn't talk so much."

By this time I was wiping my hands and glancing from detail to detail of the room's belongings, as one is apt to do when he is in a new place, where everything he sees is a comfort to his eye and his spirit; and I became conscious, in one of those unaccountable ways, you know, that there was something there somewhere that the man wanted me to discover for myself. I knew it perfectly, and I knew he was trying to help me by furtive indications with his eye, so I tried hard to get on the right track, being eager to gratify him. I failed several times, as I could see out of the corner of my eye without being told; but at last I knew I must be looking straight at the thing—knew it from the pleasure issuing in invisible waves from him. He broke into a happy laugh, and rubbed his hands together, and cried out:

"That's it! You've found it. I knew you would. It's her picture."

I went to the little black-walnut bracket on the farther wall, and did find there what I had not yet noticed — a daguerreotype-case. It contained the sweetest girlish face, and the most beautiful, as it seemed to me, that I had ever seen. The man drank the admiration from my face, and was fully satisfied.

"Nineteen her last birthday," he said, as he put the picture back; "and that was the day we were married. When you see her—ah, just wait till you see her!"

"Where is she? When will she be in?"

"Oh, she's away now. She's gone to see her people. They live forty or fifty miles from here. She's been gone two weeks to-day."

"When do you expect her back?"

"This is Wednesday. She'll be back Saturday, in the evening—about nine o'clock, likely."

I felt a sharp sense of disappointment.

"I'm sorry, because I'll be gone then," I said, regretfully.

"Gone? No—why should you go? Don't go. She'll be so disappointed."

She would be disappointed—that beautiful creature! If she had said the words herself they could hardly have blessed me more. I was feeling a deep, strong longing to see her—a longing so supplicating, so insistent, that it made me afraid. I said to myself: "I will go straight away from this place, for my peace of mind's sake."

"You see, she likes to have people come and stop with us—people who know things, and can talk—people like you. She delights in it; for she knows— oh, she knows nearly everything herself, and can talk, oh, like a bird—and the books she reads, why, you would be astonished. Don't go; it's only a little while, you know, and she'll be so disappointed."

I heard the words, but hardly noticed them, I was so deep in my thinkings and strugglings. He left me, but I didn't know it. Presently he was back, with the picture-case in his hand, and he held it open before me and said:

"There, now, tell her to her face you could have stayed to see her, and you wouldn't."

That second glimpse broke down my good resolution. I would stay and take the risk. That night we smoked the tranquil pipe, and talked till late about various things, but mainly about her; and certainly I had had no such pleasant and restful time for many a day. The Thursday followed and slipped comfortably away. Towards twilight a big miner from three miles away came—one of the grizzled, stranded pioneers—-and gave us warm salutation, clothed in grave and sober speech. Then he said:

"I only just dropped over to ask about the little madam, and when is she coming home. Any news from her?"

"Oh yes, a letter. Would you like to hear it Tom?"

"Well, I should think I would, if you don't mind, Henry!"

Henry got the letter out of his wallet, and said he would skip some of the private phrases, if we were willing; then he went on and read the bulk of it—a loving, sedate, and altogether charming and gracious

piece of handiwork, with a postscript full of affectionate regards and messages to Tom, and Joe, and
Charley, and other close friends and neighbors.

As the reader finished, he glanced at Tom, and
cried out:

"Oho, you're at it again! Take your hands
away, and let me see your eyes. You always do
that when I read a letter from her. I will write and
tell her."

"Oh no, you mustn't, Henry. I'm getting old,
you know, and any little disappointment makes me
want to cry. I thought she'd be here herself, and
now you've got only a letter."

"Well, now, what put that in your head? I
thought everybody knew she wasn't coming till
Saturday."

"Saturday! Why, come to think, I did know it.
I wonder what's the matter with me lately? Certainly I knew it. Ain't we all getting ready for her?
Well, I must be going now. But I'll be on hand
when she comes, old man!"

Late Friday afternoon another gray veteran
tramped over from his cabin a mile or so away, and
said the boys wanted to have a little gayety and a
good time Saturday night, if Henry thought she
wouldn't be too tired after her journey to be kept up.

"Tired? She tired! Oh, hear the man! Joe,
you know she'd sit up six weeks to please any one of
you!"

When Joe heard that there was a letter, he asked

to have it read, and the loving messages in it for him
broke the old fellow all up; but he said he was such
an old wreck that *that* would happen to him if she
only just mentioned his name. "Lord, we miss her
so!" he said.

Saturday afternoon I found I was taking out my
watch pretty often. Henry noticed it, and said,
with a startled look:

"You don't think she ought to be here so soon, do
you?"

I felt caught, and a little embarrassed; but I
laughed, and said it was a habit of mine when I was
in a state of expectancy. But he didn't seem quite
satisfied; and from that time on he began to show
uneasiness. Four times he walked me up the road
to a point whence we could see a long distance; and
there he would stand, shading his eyes with his
hand, and looking. Several times he said:

"I'm getting worried, I'm getting right down worried. I know she's not due till about nine o'clock,
and yet something seems to be trying to warn me
that something's happened. You don't think anything has happened, do you?"

I began to get pretty thoroughly ashamed of him
for his childishness; and at last, when he repeated
that imploring question still another time, I lost my
patience for the moment, and spoke pretty brutally
to him. It seemed to shrivel him up and cow him;
and he looked so wounded and so humble after that,
that I detested myself for having done the cruel and

unnecessary thing. And so I was glad when Charley, another veteran, arrived towards the edge of the evening, and nestled up to Henry to hear the letter read, and talked over the preparations for the welcome. Charley fetched out one hearty speech after another, and did his best to drive away his friend's bodings and apprehensions.

"Anything *happened* to her? Henry, that's pure nonsense. There isn't anything going to happen to her; just make your mind easy as to that. What did the letter say? Said she was well, didn't it? And said she'd be here by nine o'clock, didn't it? Did you ever know her to fail of her word? Why, you know you never did. Well, then, don't you fret; she'll *be* here, and that's absolutely certain, and as sure as you are born. Come, now, let's get to decorating—not much time left."

Pretty soon Tom and Joe arrived, and then all hands set about adorning the house with flowers. Towards nine the three miners said that as they had brought their instruments they might as well tune up, for the boys and girls would soon be arriving now, and hungry for a good, old-fashioned breakdown. A fiddle, a banjo, and a clarinet—these were the instruments. The trio took their places side by side, and began to play some rattling dance-music, and beat time with their big boots.

It was getting very close to nine. Henry was standing in the door with his eyes directed up the road, his body swaying to the torture of his mental distress. He had been made to drink his wife's health and safety several times, and now Tom shouted:

"All hands stand by! One more drink, and she's here!"

Joe brought the glasses on a waiter, and served the party. I reached for one of the two remaining glasses, but Joe growled, under his breath:

"Drop that! Take the other."

Which I did. Henry was served last. He had hardly swallowed his drink when the clock began to strike. He listened till it finished, his face growing pale and paler; then he said:

"Boys, I'm sick with fear. Help me—I want to lie down!"

They helped him to the sofa. He began to nestle and drowse, but presently spoke like one talking in his sleep, and said: "Did I hear horses' feet? Have they come?"

One of the veterans answered, close to his ear: "It was Jimmy Parrish come to say the party got delayed, but they're right up the road a piece, and coming along. Her horse is lame, but she'll be here in half an hour."

"Oh, I'm *so* thankful nothing has happened!"

He was asleep almost before the words were out of his mouth. In a moment those handy men had his clothes off, and had tucked him into his bed in the chamber where I had washed my hands. They closed the door and came back. Then they seemed preparing to leave; but I said: "Please don't go, gentlemen. She won't know me; I am a stranger."

They glanced at each other. Then Joe said:

"She? Poor thing, she's been dead nineteen years!"

"Dead?"

"That or worse. She went to see her folks half a year after she was married, and on her way back, on a Saturday evening, the Indians captured her within five miles of this place, and she's never been heard of since."

"And he lost his mind in consequence?"

"Never has been sane an hour since. But he only gets bad when that time of the year comes round. Then we begin to drop in here, three days before she's due, to encourage him up, and ask if he's heard from her, and Saturday we all come and fix up the house with flowers, and get everything ready for a dance. We've done it every year for nineteen years. The first Saturday there was twenty-seven of us, without counting the girls; there's only three of us now, and the girls are all gone. We drug him to sleep, or he would go wild; then he's all right for another year—thinks she's with him till the last three or four days come round; then he begins to look for her, and gets out his poor old letter, and we come and ask him to read it to us. Lord, she was a darling!"

A HELPLESS SITUATION

ONCE or twice a year I get a letter of a certain pattern, a pattern that never materially changes, in form and substance, yet I cannot get used to that letter—it always astonishes me. It affects me as the locomotive always affects me: I say to myself, "I have seen you a thousand times, you always look the same way, yet you are always a wonder, and you are always impossible; to contrive you is clearly beyond human genius—you can't exist, you don't exist, yet here you are!"

I have a letter of that kind by me, a very old one. I yearn to print it, and where is the harm? The writer of it is dead years ago, no doubt, and if I conceal her name and address—her this-world address— I am sure her shade will not mind. And with it I wish to print the answer which I wrote at the time but probably did not send. If it went—which is not likely—it went in the form of a copy, for I find the original still here, pigeon-holed with the said letter. To that kind of letters we all write answers which we do not send, fearing to hurt where we have no desire to hurt; I have done it many a time, and this is doubtless a case of the sort.

THE LETTER

X——., CALIFORNIA, *June 3, 1879.*
Mr. S. L. Clemens, Hartford, Conn.:

DEAR SIR,—You will doubtless be surprised to know who has presumed to write and ask a favor of you. Let your memory go back to your days in the Humboldt mines—'62–'63. You will remember, you and Clagett and Oliver and the old blacksmith Tillou lived in a lean-to which was half-way up the gulch, and there were six log cabins in the camp—strung pretty well separated up the gulch from its mouth at the desert to where the last claim was, at the divide. The lean-to you lived in was the one with a canvas roof that the cow fell down through one night, as told about by you in *Roughing It*—my uncle Simmons remembers it very well. He lived in the principal cabin, half-way up the divide, along with Dixon and Parker and Smith. It had two rooms, one for kitchen and the other for bunks, and was the only one that had. You and your party were there on the great night, the time they had dried-apple-pie, Uncle Simmons often speaks of it. It seems curious that dried-apple-pie should have seemed such a great thing, but it was, and it shows how far Humboldt was out of the world and difficult to get to, and how slim the regular bill of fare was.

Sixteen years ago—it is a long time. I was a little girl then, only fourteen. I never saw you, I lived in Washoe. But Uncle Simmons ran across you every now and then, all during those weeks that you and party were there working your claim which was like the rest. The camp played out long and long ago, there wasn't silver enough in it to make a button. You never saw my husband, but he was there after you left, *and lived in that very lean-to*, a bachelor then but married to me now. He often wishes there had been a photographer there in those days, he would have taken the lean-to. He got hurt in the old Hal Clayton claim that was abandoned like the others, putting in a blast and not climbing out quick enough, though he scrambled the best he could. It landed him clear down on the trail and hit a Piute. For weeks they thought he would not get over it but he did, and is all right, now. Has been ever since. This is a long introduction but it is the only way I can make myself known. The favor I ask I feel assured your generous heart will grant: Give me some advice about a book I have written. I do not claim anything for it only it is mostly true and as interesting as most of the books of the times. I am unknown in the literary world and you know what that means unless one has some one of influence (like yourself) to help you by speaking a good word for you. I would like to place the book on royalty basis plan with any one you would suggest.

This is a secret from my husband and family. I intend it as a surprise in case I get it published.

Feeling you will take an interest in this and if possible write me a letter to some publisher, or, better still, if you could see them for me and then let me hear.

I appeal to you to grant me this favor. With deepest gratitude I thank you for your attention.

One knows, without inquiring, that the twin of that embarrassing letter is forever and ever flying in this and that and the other direction across the continent in the mails, daily, nightly, hourly, unceasingly, unrestingly. It goes to every well-known merchant, and railway official, and manufacturer, and capitalist, and Mayor, and Congressman, and Governor, and editor, and publisher, and author, and broker, and banker—in a word, to every person who is supposed to have "influence." It always follows the one pattern: "You do not know me, *but you once knew a relative of mine*," etc., etc. We should all like to help the applicants, we should all be glad to do it, we should all like to return the sort of answer that is desired, but— Well, there is not a thing we can do that would be a help, for not in any instance does that letter ever come from any one who *can* be helped. The struggler whom you *could* help does his own helping; it would not occur to him to apply to you, a stranger. He has talent and knows it, and he goes into his fight eagerly and with energy and determination — all alone, preferring to be alone. That pathetic letter which comes to you from the incapable, the unhelpable—how do you who are familiar with it answer it? What do you find to say? You do not want to inflict a wound; you hunt ways to avoid that. What do you find? How do you get out of your hard place with a contented conscience? Do you try to explain? The old reply of mine to such a letter shows that I tried that once. Was I satisfied with the result? Possibly; and possibly not; probably not; almost certainly not. I have long ago forgotten all about it. But, anyway, I append my effort:

THE REPLY

I know Mr. H., and I will go to him, dear madam, if upon reflection you find you still desire it. There will be a conversation. I know the form it will take. It will be like this:

Mr. H. How do her books strike you?
Mr. Clemens. I am not acquainted with them.
H. Who has been her publisher?
C. I don't know.
H. She *has* one, I suppose?
C. I—I think not.
H. Ah. You think this is her first book?
C. Yes—I suppose so. I think so.
H. What is it about? What is the character of it?

C. I believe I do not know.

H. Have you seen it?

C. Well—no, I haven't.

H. Ah-h.   How long have you known her?

C. I don't know her.

H. Don't know her?

C. No.

H. Ah-h.   How did you come to be interested in her book, then?

C. Well, she—she wrote and asked me to find a publisher for her, and mentioned you.

H. Why should she apply to you instead of to me?

C. She wished me to use my influence.

H. Dear me, what has *influence* to do with such a matter?

C. Well, I think she thought you would be more likely to examine her book if you were influenced.

H. Why, what we are here *for* is to examine books —anybody's book that comes along.   It's our *business*.   Why should we turn away a book unexamined because it's a stranger's?   It would be foolish. No publisher does it.   On what ground did she request your influence, since you do not know her? She must have thought you knew her literature and could speak for it.   Is that it?

C. No; she knew I didn't.

H. Well, what then?   She had a reason of *some* sort for believing you competent to recommend her literature, and also under obligations to do it?

C. Yes, I—I knew her uncle.

H. Knew her *uncle?*

C. Yes.

H. Upon my word! So, you knew her uncle; her uncle knows her literature; he endorses it to you; the chain is complete, nothing further needed; you are satisfied, and therefore—

C. No, that isn't all, there are other ties. I knew the cabin her uncle lived in, in the mines; I knew his partners, too; also I came near knowing her husband before she married him, and I *did* know the abandoned shaft where a premature blast went off and he went flying through the air and clear down to the trail and hit an Indian in the back with almost fatal consequences.

H. To *him*, or to the Indian?

C. She didn't say which it was.

H. (*With a sigh.*) It certainly beats the band! You don't know *her*, you don't know her literature, you don't know who got hurt when the blast went off, you don't know a single thing for us to build an estimate of her book upon, so far as I—

C. I knew her uncle. You are forgetting her uncle.

H. Oh, what use is *he?* Did you know him long? How long was it?

C. Well, I don't know that I really knew him, but I must have met him, anyway. I think it was that way; you can't tell about these things, you know, except when they are recent.

H. Recent? When was all this?

9

C. Sixteen years ago.

H. What a basis to judge a book upon! At first you said you knew him, and now you don't know whether you did or not.

C. Oh yes, I knew him; anyway, I think I thought I did; I'm perfectly certain of it.

H. What makes you think you thought you knew him?

C. Why, she says I did, herself.

H. She says so!

C. Yes, she does, and I *did* know him, too, though I don't remember it now.

H. Come—how can you know it when you don't remember it.

C. I don't know. That is, I don't know the process, but I *do* know lots of things that I don't remember, and remember lots of things that I don't know. It's so with every educated person.

H. (*After a pause.*) Is your time valuable?

C. No—well, not very.

H. Mine is.

So I came away then, because he was looking tired. Overwork, I reckon; I never do that; I have seen the evil effects of it. My mother was always afraid I would overwork myself, but I never did.

Dear madam, you see how it would happen if I went there. He would ask me those questions, and I would try to answer them to suit him, and he would hunt me here and there and yonder and get me embarrassed more and more all the time, and at last he would look tired on account of overwork, and there it would end and nothing done. I wish I could be useful to you, but, you see, they do not care for uncles or any of those things; it doesn't move them, it doesn't have the least effect, they don't care for anything but the literature itself, and they as good as despise influence. But they do care for books, and are eager to get them and examine them, no matter whence they come, nor from whose pen. If you will send yours to a publisher—any publisher —he will certainly examine it, I can assure you of that.

A TELEPHONIC CONVERSATION

CONSIDER that a conversation by telephone—when you are simply sitting by and not taking any part in that conversation—is one of the solemnest curiosities of this modern life. Yesterday I was writing a deep article on a sublime philosophical subject while such a conversation was going on in the room. I notice that one can always write best when somebody is talking through a telephone close by. Well, the thing began in this way. A member of our household came in and asked me to have our house put into communication with Mr. Bagley's, down-town. I have observed, in many cities, that the sex always shrink from calling up the central office themselves. I don't know why, but they do. So I touched the bell, and this talk ensued:

Central Office. (*Gruffly.*) Hello!

I. Is it the Central Office?

C. O. Of course it is. What do you want?

I. Will you switch me on to the Bagleys, please?

C. O. All right. Just keep your ear to the telephone.

Then I heard, *k-look, k-look, k'look—klook-klook-klook-look-look!* then a horrible "gritting" of teeth, and finally a piping female voice: Y-e-s?   (*Rising inflection.*)   Did you wish to speak to me?

Without answering, I handed the telephone to the applicant, and sat down.   Then followed that queerest of all the queer things in this world—a conversation with only one end to it.   You hear questions asked; you don't hear the answer.   You hear invitations given; you hear no thanks in return.   You have listening pauses of dead silence, followed by apparently irrelevant and unjustifiable exclamations of glad surprise or sorrow or dismay.   You can't make head or tail of the talk, because you never hear anything that the person at the other end of the wire says.   Well, I heard the following remarkable series of observations, all from the one tongue, and all shouted—for you can't ever persuade the sex to speak gently into a telephone:

Yes?   Why, how did *that* happen?

Pause.

What did you say?

Pause.

Oh no, I don't think it was.

Pause.

No!   Oh no, I didn't mean *that.*   I meant, put it in while it is still boiling—or just before it *comes* to a boil.

Pause.

WHAT?

Pause.

I turned it over with a backstitch on the selvage edge.

Pause.

Yes, I like that way, too; but I think it's better to baste it on with Valenciennes or bombazine, or something of that sort. It gives it such an air— and attracts so much notice.

Pause.

It's forty - ninth Deuteronomy, sixty - fourth to ninety-seventh inclusive. I think we ought all to read it often.

Pause.

Perhaps so; I generally use a hair-pin.

Pause.

What did you say? (*Aside.*) Children, do be quiet!

Pause.

Oh! B *flat!* Dear me, I thought you said it was the cat!

Pause.

Since *when ?*

Pause.

Why, *I* never heard of it.

Pause.

You astound me! It seems utterly impossible!

Pause.

Who did?

Pause.

Good-ness gracious!

Pause.

Well, what *is* this world coming to? Was it right in *church ?*

Pause.

And was her *mother* there?

Pause.

Why, Mrs. Bagley, I should have died of humiliation! What did they *do?*

Long pause.

I can't be perfectly sure, because I haven't the
notes by me; but I think it goes something like this:
te-rolly-loll-loll, loll lolly-loll-loll, O tolly-loll-loll-*lee-*
ly-li-i-do! And then *repeat*, you know.

Pause.

Yes, I think it *is* very sweet—and very solemn
and impressive, if you get the andantino and the
pianissimo right.

Pause.

Oh, gum-drops, gum-drops! But I never allow
them to eat striped candy. And of course they
can't, till they get their teeth, anyway.

Pause.

What?

Pause.

Oh, not in the least—go right on. He's here
writing—it doesn't bother *him.*

Pause.

Very well, I'll come if I can. (*Aside.*) Dear me,
how it does tire a person's arm to hold this thing up
so long! I wish she'd—

Pause.

Oh no, not at all; I *like* to talk—but I'm afraid
I'm keeping you from your affairs.

Pause.

Visitors?

Pause.

No, we never use butter on them.

Pause.

Yes, that is a very good way; but all the cook-books say they are very unhealthy when they are out of season. And *he* doesn't like them, anyway—especially canned.

Pause.

Oh, I think that is too high for them; we have never paid over fifty cents a bunch.

Pause.

Must you go?   Well, *good*-bye.

Pause.

Yes, I think so.   *Good*-bye.

Pause.

Four o'clock, then—I'll be ready.   *Good*-bye.

Pause.

Thank you ever so much.   *Good*-bye.

Pause.

Oh, not at all!—just as fresh— *Which?* Oh, I'm glad to hear you say that.   *Good*-bye.

(Hangs up the telephone and says, "Oh, it *does* tire a person's arm so!")

A man delivers a single brutal "Good-bye," and that is the end of it.   Not so with the gentle sex—I say it in their praise; they cannot abide abruptness.

EDWARD MILLS AND GEORGE BEN-TON: A TALE

THESE two were distantly related to each other —seventh cousins, or something of that sort. While still babies they became orphans, and were adopted by the Brants, a childless couple, who quickly grew very fond of them. The Brants were always saying: "Be pure, honest, sober, industrious, and considerate of others, and success in life is assured." The children heard this repeated some thousands of times before they understood it; they could repeat it themselves long before they could say the Lord's Prayer; it was painted over the nursery door, and was about the first thing they learned to read. It was destined to become the unswerving rule of Edward Mills's life. Sometimes the Brants changed the wording a little, and said: "Be pure, honest, sober, industrious, considerate, and you will never lack friends."

Baby Mills was a comfort to everybody about him. When he wanted candy and could not have it, he listened to reason, and contented himself without it. When Baby Benton wanted candy, he cried for it

until he got it. Baby Mills took care of his toys;
Baby Benton always destroyed his in a very brief
time, and then made himself so insistently disagreeable that, in order to have peace in the house, little
Edward was persuaded to yield up his playthings to
him.

When the children were a little older, Georgie became a heavy expense in one respect: he took no
care of his clothes; consequently, he shone frequently in new ones, which was not the case with
Eddie. The boys grew apace. Eddie was an increasing comfort, Georgie an increasing solicitude.
It was always sufficient to say, in answer to Eddie's
petitions, "I would rather you would not do it"—
meaning swimming, skating, picnicking, berrying,
circusing, and all sorts of things which boys delight
in. But *no* answer was sufficient for Georgie; he
had to be humored in his desires, or he would carry
them with a high hand. Naturally, no boy got more
swimming, skating, berrying, and so forth than he;
no boy ever had a better time. The good Brants did
not allow the boys to play out after nine in summer
evenings; they were sent to bed at that hour; Eddie
honorably remained, but Georgie usually slipped out
of the window towards ten, and enjoyed himself till
midnight. It seemed impossible to break Georgie of
this bad habit, but the Brants managed it at last by
hiring him, with apples and marbles, to stay in. The
good Brants gave all their time and attention to vain
endeavors to regulate Georgie; they said, with grate-

ful tears in their eyes, that Eddie needed no efforts of theirs, he was so good, so considerate, and in all ways so perfect.

By-and-by the boys were big enough to work, so they were apprenticed to a trade: Edward went voluntarily; George was coaxed and bribed. Edward worked hard and faithfully, and ceased to be an expense to the good Brants; they praised him, so did his master; but George ran away, and it cost Mr. Brant both money and trouble to hunt him up and get him back. By-and-by he ran away again—more money and more trouble. He ran away a third time — and stole a few little things to carry with him. Trouble and expense for Mr. Brant once more; and, besides, it was with the greatest difficulty that he succeeded in persuading the master to let the youth go unprosecuted for the theft.

Edward worked steadily along, and in time became a full partner in his master's business. George did not improve; he kept the loving hearts of his aged benefactors full of trouble, and their hands full of inventive activities to protect him from ruin. Edward, as a boy, had interested himself in Sunday-schools, debating societies, penny missionary affairs, anti - tobacco organizations, anti - profanity associations, and all such things; as a man, he was a quiet but steady and reliable helper in the church, the temperance societies, and in all movements looking to the aiding and uplifting of men. This excited no remark, attracted no attention — for it was his "natural bent."

Finally, the old people died. The will testified their loving pride in Edward, and left their little property to George—because he "needed it"; whereas, "owing to a bountiful Providence," such was not the case with Edward. The property was left to George conditionally: he must buy out Edward's partner with it; else it must go to a benevolent organization called the Prisoner's Friend Society. The old people left a letter, in which they begged their dear son Edward to take their place and watch over George, and help and shield him as they had done.

Edward dutifully acquiesced, and George became his partner in the business. He was not a valuable partner: he had been meddling with drink before; he soon developed into a constant tippler now, and his flesh and eyes showed the fact unpleasantly. Edward had been courting a sweet and kindly spirited girl for some time. They loved each other dearly, and— But about this period George began to haunt her tearfully and imploringly, and at last she went crying to Edward, and said her high and holy duty was plain before her—she must not let her own selfish desires interfere with it: she must marry "poor George" and "reform him." It would break her heart, she knew it would, and so on; but duty was duty. So she married George, and Edward's heart came very near breaking, as well as her own. How-

ever, Edward recovered, and married another girl—
a very excellent one she was, too.

Children came to both families. Mary did her
honest best to reform her husband, but the contract
was too large. George went on drinking, and by-
and-by he fell to misusing her and the little ones
sadly. A great many good people strove with
George—they were always at it, in fact—but he
calmly took such efforts as his due and their duty,
and did not mend his ways. He added a vice, presently—that of secret gambling. He got deeply in
debt; he borrowed money on the firm's credit, as
quietly as he could, and carried this system so far
and so successfully that one morning the sheriff took
possession of the establishment, and the two cousins
found themselves penniless.

Times were hard, now, and they grew worse. Edward moved his family into a garret, and walked the
streets day and night, seeking work. He begged for
it, but it was really not to be had. He was astonished to see how soon his face became unwelcome;
he was astonished and hurt to see how quickly the
ancient interest which people had had in him faded
out and disappeared. Still, he *must* get work; so he
swallowed his chagrin, and toiled on in search of it.
At last he got a job of carrying bricks up a ladder in
a hod, and was a grateful man in consequence; but
after that *nobody* knew him or cared anything about
him. He was not able to keep up his dues in the
various moral organizations to which he belonged,

and had to endure the sharp pain of seeing himself brought under the disgrace of suspension.

But the faster Edward died out of public knowledge and interest, the faster George rose in them. He was found lying, ragged and drunk, in the gutter one morning. A member of the Ladies' Temperance Refuge fished him out, took him in hand, got up a subscription for him, kept him sober a whole week, then got a situation for him. An account of it was published.

General attention was thus drawn to the poor fellow, and a great many people came forward, and helped him towards reform with their countenance and encouragement. He did not drink a drop for two months, and meantime was the pet of the good. Then he fell—in the gutter; and there was general sorrow and lamentation. But the noble sisterhood rescued him again. They cleaned him up, they fed him, they listened to the mournful music of his repentances, they got him his situation again. An account of this, also, was published, and the town was drowned in happy tears over the re-restoration of the poor beset and struggling victim of the fatal bowl. A grand temperance revival was got up, and after some rousing speeches had been made the chairman said, impressively: "We are now about to call for signers; and I think there is a spectacle in store for you which not many in this house will be able to view with dry eyes." There was an eloquent pause, and then George Benton, escorted by a red-sashed detachment of the Ladies of the Refuge, stepped forward upon the platform and signed the pledge. The air was rent with applause, and everybody cried for joy. Everybody wrung the hand of the new convert when the meeting was over; his salary was enlarged next day; he was the talk of the town, and its hero. An account of it was published.

George Benton fell, regularly, every three months, but was faithfully rescued and wrought with, every time, and good situations were found for him. Finally, he was taken around the country lecturing, as a reformed drunkard, and he had great houses an did an immense amount of good.

He was so popular at home, and so trusted—during his sober intervals—that he was enabled to use the name of a principal citizen, and get a large sum of money at the bank. A mighty pressure was brought to bear to save him from the consequences of his forgery, and it was partially successful—he was "sent up" for only two years. When, at the end of a year, the tireless efforts of the benevolent were crowned with success, and he emerged from the penitentiary with a pardon in his pocket, the Prisoner's Friend Society met him at the door with a situation and a comfortable salary, and all the other benevolent people came forward and gave him advice, encouragement, and help. Edward Mills had once applied to the Prisoner's Friend Society for a situation, when in dire need, but the question, "Have you been a prisoner?" made brief work of his case.

While all these things were going on, Edward Mills had been quietly making head against adversity. He was still poor, but was in receipt of a steady and sufficient salary, as the respected and trusted cashier of a bank. George Benton never came near him, and was never heard to inquire about him. George got to indulging in long absences from the town; there were ill reports about him, but nothing definite.

One winter's night some masked burglars forced their way into the bank, and found Edward Mills there alone. They commanded him to reveal the "combination," so that they could get into the safe. He refused. They threatened his life. He said his employers trusted him, and he could not be traitor to that trust. He could die, if he must, but while he lived he would be faithful; he would not yield up the "combination." The burglars killed him.

The detectives hunted down the criminals; the chief one proved to be George Benton. A wide sympathy was felt for the widow and orphans of the dead man, and all the newspapers in the land begged that all the banks in the land would testify their appreciation of the fidelity and heroism of the murdered cashier by coming forward with a generous contribution of money in aid of his family, now bereft of support. The result was a mass of solid cash amounting to upward of five hundred dollars—an average of nearly three-eighths of a cent for each bank in the Union. The cashier's own bank testified its gratitude by endeavoring to show (but humiliatingly failed in it) that the peerless servant's accounts were not square, and that he himself had knocked his brains out with a bludgeon to escape detection and punishment.

George Benton was arraigned for trial. Then everybody seemed to forget the widow and orphans in their solicitude for poor George. Everything that money and influence could do was done to save him, but it all failed; he was sentenced to death. Straightway the Governor was besieged with petitions for commutation or pardon; they were brought by tearful young girls; by sorrowful old maids; by deputations of pathetic widows; by shoals of impressive orphans. But no, the Governor—for once—would not yield.

Now George Benton experienced religion. The glad news flew all around. From that time forth his cell was always full of girls and women and fresh flowers; all the day long there was prayer, and hymnsinging, and thanksgivings, and homilies, and tears, with never an interruption, except an occasional five-minute intermission for refreshments.

This sort of thing continued up to the very gallows, and George Benton went proudly home, in the black cap, before a wailing audience of the sweetest and best that the region could produce. His grave had fresh flowers on it every day, for a while, and the head-stone bore these words, under a hand pointing aloft: "He has fought the good fight."

The brave cashier's head-stone has this inscrip-

10

tion: "Be pure, honest, sober, industrious, considerate, and you will never—"

Nobody knows who gave the order to leave it that way, but it was so given.

The cashier's family are in stringent circumstances, now, it is said; but no matter; a lot of appreciative people, who were not willing that an act so brave and true as his should go unrewarded, have collected forty-two thousand dollars—and built a Memorial Church with it.

SAINT JOAN OF ARC

I

THE evidence furnished at the Trials and Rehabilitation sets forth Joan of Arc's strange
and beautiful history in clear and minute detail.
Among all the multitude of biographies that freight
the shelves of the world's libraries, *this is the only
one whose validity is confirmed to us by oath*. It gives
us a vivid picture of a career and a personality of so
extraordinary a character that we are helped to accept them as actualities by the very fact that both

NOTE.—The Official Record of the Trials and Rehabilitation of Joan of Arc is the most remarkable history that exists in any language; yet there are few people in the world
who can say they have read it: in England and America it
has hardly been heard of.

Three hundred years ago Shakespeare did not know the
true story of Joan of Arc; in his day it was unknown even
in France. For four hundred years it existed rather as a
vaguely defined romance than as definite and authentic
history. The true story remained buried in the official
archives of France from the Rehabilitation of 1456 until
Quicherat dug it out and gave it to the world two generations ago, in lucid and understandable modern French. It
is a deeply fascinating story. But only in the Official Trials
and Rehabilitation can it be found in its entirety.—M. T.

are beyond the inventive reach of fiction. The public part of the career occupied only a mere breath of time—it covered but two years; but what a career it was! The personality which made it possible is one to be reverently studied, loved, and marvelled at, but not to be wholly understood and accounted for by even the most searching analysis.

In Joan of Arc at the age of sixteen there was no promise of a romance. She lived in a dull little village on the frontiers of civilization; she had been nowhere and had seen nothing; she knew none but simple shepherd folk; she had never seen a person of note; she hardly knew what a soldier looked like; she had never ridden a horse, nor had a warlike weapon in her hand; she could neither read nor write: she could spin and sew; she knew her catechism and her prayers and the fabulous histories of the saints, and this was all her learning. That was Joan at sixteen. What did she know of law? of evidence? of courts? of the attorney's trade? of legal procedure? Nothing. Less than nothing. Thus exhaustively equipped with ignorance, she went before the court at Toul to contest a false charge of breach of promise of marriage; she conducted her cause herself, without any one's help or advice or any one's friendly sympathy, and won it. She called no witnesses of her own, but vanquished the prosecution by using with deadly effectiveness its own testimony. The astonished judge threw the case out of court, and spoke of her as "this marvellous child."

She went to the veteran Commandant of Vaucouleurs and demanded an escort of soldiers, saying she
must march to the help of the King of France, since
she was commissioned of God to win back his lost
kingdom for him and set the crown upon his head.
The Commandant said, "What, you? you are only
a child." And he advised that she be taken back to
her village and have her ears boxed. But she said
she must obey God, and would come again, and
again, and yet again, and finally she would get the
soldiers. She said truly. In time he yielded, after
months of delay and refusal, and gave her the
soldiers; and took off his sword and gave her that,
and said, "Go—and let come what may." She made
her long and perilous journey through the enemy's
country, and spoke with the King, and convinced
him. Then she was summoned before the University of Poitiers to prove that she *was* commissioned of God and not of Satan, and daily during
three weeks she sat before that learned congress unafraid, and capably answered their deep questions
out of her ignorant but able head and her simple and
honest heart; and again she won her case, and with
it the wondering admiration of all that august company.

And now, aged seventeen, she was made Com-
mander-in-Chief, with a prince of the royal house
and the veteran generals of France for subordinates;
and at the head of the first army she had ever seen,
she marched to Orleans, carried the commanding

fortresses of the enemy by storm in three desperate assaults, and in ten days raised a siege which had defied the might of France for seven months.

After a tedious and insane delay caused by the King's instability of character and the treacherous counsels of his ministers, she got permission to take the field again. She took Jargeau by storm; then Meung; she forced Beaugency to surrender; then—in the open field—she won the memorable victory of Patay against Talbot, "the English lion," and broke the back of the Hundred Years' War. It was a campaign which cost but seven weeks of time; yet the political results would have been cheap if the time expended had been fifty years. Patay, that unsung and now long-forgotten battle, was the Moscow of the English power in France; from the blow struck that day it was destined never to recover. It was the beginning of the end of an alien dominion which had ridden France intermittently for three hundred years.

Then followed the great campaign of the Loire, the capture of Troyes by assault, and the triumphal march past surrendering towns and fortresses to Rheims, where Joan put the crown upon her King's head in the Cathedral, amid wild public rejoicings, and with her old peasant father there to see these things and believe his eyes if he could. She had restored the crown and the lost sovereignty; the King was grateful for once in his shabby poor life, and asked her to name her reward and have it. She asked for nothing for herself, but begged that the taxes of her native village might be remitted forever. The prayer was granted, and the promise kept for three hundred and sixty years. Then it was broken, and remains broken to-day. France was very poor then, she is very rich now; but she has been collecting those taxes for more than a hundred years.

Joan asked one other favor: that now that her mission was fulfilled she might be allowed to go back to her village and take up her humble life again with her mother and the friends of her childhood; for she had no pleasure in the cruelties of war, and the sight of blood and suffering wrung her heart. Sometimes in battle she did not draw her sword, lest in the splendid madness of the onset she might forget herself and take an enemy's life with it. In the Rouen Trials, one of her quaintest speeches—coming from the gentle and girlish source it did—was her naïve remark that she had "never killed any one." Her prayer for leave to go back to the rest and peace of her village home was not granted.

Then she wanted to march at once upon Paris, take it, and drive the English out of France. She was hampered in all the ways that treachery and the King's vacillation could devise, but she forced her way to Paris at last, and fell badly wounded in a successful assault upon one of the gates. Of course her men lost heart at once—she was the only heart they had. They fell back. She begged to be allowed to remain at the front, saying victory was sure. "I will take Paris now or die!" she said. But she was removed from the field by force; the King ordered a retreat, and actually disbanded his army. In accordance with a beautiful old military custom Joan devoted her silver armor and hung it up in the Cathedral of St. Denis. Its great days were over.

Then, by command, she followed the King and his frivolous court and endured a gilded captivity for a time, as well as her free spirit could; and whenever inaction became unbearable she gathered some men together and rode away and assaulted a stronghold and captured it.

At last in a sortie against the enemy, from Compiègne, on the 24th of May (when she was turned eighteen), she was herself captured, after a gallant fight. It was her last battle. She was to follow the drums no more.

Thus ended the briefest epoch-making military career known to history. It lasted only a year and a month, but it found France an English province, and furnishes the reason that France is France to-day and not an English province still. Thirteen months! It was, indeed, a short career; but in the centuries that have since elapsed five hundred millions of Frenchmen have lived and died blest by the benefactions it conferred; and so long as France shall endure, the mighty debt must grow. And France is grateful; we often hear her say it. Also thrifty: she collects the Domrémy taxes.

II

JOAN was fated to spend the rest of her life behind
bolts and bars. She was a prisoner of war, not a
criminal, therefore hers was recognized as an honorable captivity. By the rules of war she must be
held to ransom, and a fair price could not be refused
if offered. John of Luxembourg paid her the just
compliment of requiring a prince's ransom for her.
In that day that phrase represented a definite sum
—61,125 francs. It was, of course, supposable that
either the King or grateful France, or both, would
fly with the money and set their fair young benefactor free. But this did not happen. In five and
a half months neither King nor country stirred a
hand nor offered a penny. Twice Joan tried to escape. Once by a trick she succeeded for a moment,
and locked her jailer in behind her, but she was discovered and caught; in the other case she let herself
down from a tower sixty feet high, but her rope was
too short, and she got a fall that disabled her and
she could not get away.

Finally, Cauchon, Bishop of Beauvais, paid the
money and bought Joan—ostensibly for the Church,
to be tried for wearing male attire and for other im-
pieties, but really for the English, the enemy into

whose hands the poor girl was so piteously anxious not to fall. She was now shut up in the dungeons of the Castle of Rouen and kept in an iron cage, with her hands and feet and neck chained to a pillar; and from that time forth during all the months of her imprisonment, till the end, several rough English soldiers stood guard over her night and day— and not outside her room, but in it. It was a dreary and hideous captivity, but it did not conquer her: nothing could break that invincible spirit. From first to last she was a prisoner a year; and she spent the last three months of it on trial for her life before a formidable array of ecclesiastical judges, and disputing the ground with them foot by foot and inch by inch with brilliant generalship and dauntless pluck. The spectacle of that solitary girl, forlorn and friendless, without advocate or adviser, and without the help and guidance of any copy of the charges brought against her or rescript of the complex and voluminous daily proceedings of the court to modify the crushing strain upon her astonishing memory, fighting that long battle serene and undismayed against these colossal odds, stands alone in its pathos and its sublimity; it has nowhere its mate, either in the annals of fact or in the inventions of fiction.

And how fine and great were the things she daily said, how fresh and crisp—and she so worn in body, so starved, and tired, and harried! They run through the whole gamut of feeling and expression—

from scorn and defiance, uttered with soldierly fire
and frankness, all down the scale to wounded dignity
clothed in words of noble pathos; as, when her patience was exhausted by the pestering delvings and
gropings and searchings of her persecutors to find
out what kind of devil's witchcraft she had employed
to rouse the war spirit in her timid soldiers, she
burst out with, "What I said was, '*Ride these English down*'—and I did it myself!" and as, when in-
sultingly asked why it was that *her* standard had
place at the crowning of the King in the Cathedral
of Rheims rather than the standards of the other
captains, she uttered that touching speech, "*It had
borne the burden, it had earned the honor*"—a phrase
which fell from her lips without premeditation, yet
whose moving beauty and simple grace it would
bankrupt the arts of language to surpass.

Although she was on trial for her life, she was the
only witness called on either side; the only witness
summoned to testify before a packed jury commissioned with a definite task: to find her guilty, whether
she was guilty or not.   She must be convicted out of
her own mouth, there being no other way to accomplish it.   Every advantage that learning has over
ignorance, age over youth, experience over inexperience, chicane over artlessness, every trick and
trap and gin devisable by malice and the cunning of
sharp intellects practised in setting snares for the
unwary—all these were employed against her without shame; and when these arts were one by one de-

feated by the marvellous intuitions of her alert and
penetrating mind, Bishop Cauchon stooped to a final
baseness which it degrades human speech to describe: a priest who pretended to come from the
region of her own home and to be a pitying friend
and anxious to help her in her sore need was smuggled
into her cell, and he misused his sacred office to steal
her confidence; she confided to him the things sealed
from revealment by her Voices, and which her pros-
ecutors had tried so long in vain to trick her into be-
traying. A concealed confederate set it all down
and delivered it to Cauchon, who used Joan's secrets,
thus obtained, for her ruin.

Throughout the Trials, whatever the foredoomed
witness said was twisted from its true meaning when
possible, and made to tell against her; and whenever
an answer of hers was beyond the reach of twisting
it was not allowed to go upon the record. It was
upon one of these latter occasions that she uttered
that pathetic reproach—to Cauchon: "Ah, you set
down everything that is against me, but you will not
set down what is for me."

That this untrained young creature's genius for
war was wonderful, and her generalship worthy to
rank with the ripe products of a tried and trained
military experience, we have the sworn testimony of
two of her veteran subordinates — one, the Duc
d'Alençon, the other the greatest of the French generals of the time, Dunois, Bastard of Orleans; that
her genius was as great—possibly even greater—in

the subtle warfare of the forum we have for witness the records of the Rouen Trials, that protracted exhibition of intellectual fence maintained with credit against the master-minds of France; that her moral greatness was peer to her intellect we call the Rouen Trials again to witness, with their testimony to a fortitude which patiently and steadfastly endured during twelve weeks the wasting forces of captivity, chains, loneliness, sickness, darkness, hunger, thirst, cold, shame, insult, abuse, broken sleep, treachery, ingratitude, exhausting sieges of cross-examination, the threat of torture, with the rack before her and the executioner standing ready: yet never surrendering, never asking quarter, the frail wreck of her as unconquerable the last day as was her invincible spirit the first.

Great as she was in so many ways, she was perhaps even greatest of all in the lofty things just named— her patient endurance, her steadfastness, her granite fortitude. We may not hope to easily find her mate and twin in these majestic qualities; where we lift our eyes highest we find only a strange and curious contrast — there in the captive eagle beating his broken wings on the Rock of St. Helena.

THE Trials ended with her condemnation. But
as she had conceded nothing, confessed nothing, this
was victory for her, defeat for Cauchon. But his
evil resources were not yet exhausted. She was persuaded to agree to sign a paper of slight import, then
by treachery a paper was substituted which contained a recantation and a detailed confession of
everything which had been charged against her during the Trials and denied and repudiated by her persistently during the three months; and this false
paper she ignorantly signed. This was a victory for
Cauchon. He followed it eagerly and pitilessly up
by at once setting a trap for her which she could not
escape. When she realized this she gave up the long
struggle, denounced the treason which had been
practised against her, repudiated the false confession, reasserted the truth of the testimony which she
had given in the Trials, and went to her martyrdom
with the peace of God in her tired heart, and on her
lips endearing words and loving prayers for the cur
she had crowned and the nation of ingrates she had
saved.

When the fires rose about her and she begged for a
cross for her dying lips to kiss, it was not a friend

but an enemy, not a Frenchman but an alien, not a
comrade in arms but an English soldier, that answered that pathetic prayer. He broke a stick
across his knee, bound the pieces together in the
form of the symbol she so loved, and gave it her;
and his gentle deed is not forgotten, nor will be.

IV

TWENTY-FIVE years afterwards the Process of Rehabilitation was instituted, there being a growing
doubt as to the validity of a sovereignty that had
been rescued and set upon its feet by a person who
had been proven by the Church to be a witch and a
familiar of evil spirits. Joan's old generals, her
secretary, several aged relations and other villagers
of Domrémy, surviving judges and secretaries of the
Rouen and Poitiers Processes—a cloud of witnesses,
some of whom had been her enemies and persecutors,
—came and made oath and testified; and what they
said was written down. In that sworn testimony
the moving and beautiful history of Joan of Arc is
laid bare, from her childhood to her martyrdom.
From the verdict she rises stainlessly pure, in mind
and heart, in speech and deed and spirit, and will so
endure to the end of time.

She is the Wonder of the Ages. And when we
consider her origin, her early circumstances, her sex,
and that she did all the things upon which her renown rests while she was still a young girl, we recognize that while our race continues she will be also
the *Riddle* of the Ages. When we set about ac-
counting for a Napoleon or a Shakespeare or a

Raphael or a Wagner or an Edison or other extraordinary person, we understand that the measure of his talent will not explain the whole result, nor even the largest part of it; no, it is the atmosphere in which the talent was cradled that explains; it is the training which it received while it grew, the nurture it got from reading, study, example, the encouragement it gathered from self-recognition and recognition from the outside at each stage of its development: when we know all these details, then we know why the man was ready when his opportunity came. We should expect Edison's surroundings and atmosphere to have the largest share in discovering him to himself and to the world; and we should expect him to live and die undiscovered in a land where an inventor could find no comradeship, no sympathy, no ambition-rousing atmosphere of recognition and applause — Dahomey, for instance. Dahomey could not find an Edison out; in Dahomey an Edison could not find himself out. Broadly speaking, genius is not born with sight, but blind; and it is not itself that opens its eyes, but the subtle influences of a myriad of stimulating exterior circumstances.

We all know this to be not a guess, but a mere commonplace fact, a truism. Lorraine was Joan of Arc's Dahomey. And there the Riddle confronts us. We can understand how she could be born with military genius, with leonine courage, with incomparable fortitude, with a mind which was in several par-
11

ticulars a prodigy—a mind which included among its specialties the lawyer's gift of detecting traps laid by the adversary in cunning and treacherous arrangements of seemingly innocent words, the orator's gift of eloquence, the advocate's gift of presenting a case in clear and compact form, the judge's gift of sorting and weighing evidence, and finally, something recognizable as more than a mere trace of the statesman's gift of understanding a political situation and how to make profitable use of such opportunities as it offers; we can comprehend how she could be born with these great qualities, but we cannot comprehend how they became immediately usable and effective without the developing forces of a sympathetic atmosphere and the training which comes of teaching, study, practice—years of practice,—and the crowning and perfecting help of a thousand mistakes. We can understand how the possibilities of the future perfect peach are all lying hid in the humble bitter-almond, but we cannot conceive of the peach springing directly from the almond without the intervening long seasons of patient cultivation and development. Out of a cattle-pasturing peasant village lost in the remotenesses of an unvisited wilderness and atrophied with ages of stupefaction and ignorance we cannot see a Joan of Arc issue equipped to the last detail for her amazing career and hope to be able to explain the riddle of it, labor at it as we may.

It is beyond us. All the rules fail in this girl's

case. In the world's history she stands alone—quite alone. Others have been great in their first public exhibitions of generalship, valor, legal talent, diplomacy, fortitude; but always their previous years and associations had been in a larger or smaller degree a preparation for these things. There have been no exceptions to the rule. But Joan was competent in a law case at sixteen without ever having seen a law-book or a court-house before; she had no training in soldiership and no associations with it, yet she was a competent general in her first campaign; she was brave in her first battle, yet her courage had had no education—not even the education which a boy's courage gets from never-ceasing reminders that it is not permissible in a boy to be a coward, but only in a girl; friendless, alone, ignorant, in the blossom of her youth, she sat week after week, a prisoner in chains, before her assemblage of judges, enemies hunting her to her death, the ablest minds in France, and answered them out of an untaught wisdom which overmatched their learning, baffled their tricks and treacheries with a native sagacity which compelled their wonder, and scored every day a victory against these incredible odds and camped unchallenged on the field. In the history of the human intellect, untrained, inexperienced, and using only its birthright equipment of untried capacities, there is nothing which approaches this. Joan of Arc stands alone, and must continue to stand alone, by reason of the unfellowed fact that in the things wherein she was great she was so without shade or suggestion of help from preparatory teaching, practice, environment, or experience.   There is no one to compare her with, none to measure her by; for all others among the illustrious *grew* towards their high place in an atmosphere and surroundings which discovered their gift to them and nourished it and promoted it, intentionally or unconsciously.   There have been other young generals, but they were not girls; young generals, but they had been soldiers before they were generals: she *began* as a general; she commanded the first army she ever saw; she led it from victory to victory, and never lost a battle with it; there have been young commanders-in-chief, but none so young as she: she is the only soldier in history who has held the supreme command of a nation's armies at the age of seventeen.

Her history has still another feature which sets her apart and leaves her without fellow or competitor: there have been many uninspired prophets, but she was the only one who ever ventured the daring detail of naming, along with a foretold event, the event's precise nature, the special time-limit within which it would occur, and the place—*and scored fulfilment*.   At Vaucouleurs she said she must go to the King and be made his general, and break the English power, and crown her sovereign—"at Rheims." It all happened.   It was all to happen "next year" —and it did.   She foretold her first wound and its character and date a month in advance, and the prophecy was recorded in a public record-book three weeks in advance. She repeated it the morning of the date named, and it was fulfilled before night. At Tours she foretold the limit of her military career —saying it would end in one year from the time of its utterance—and she was right. She foretold her martyrdom—using *that word*, and naming a time three months away—and again she was right. At a time when France seemed hopelessly and permanently in the hands of the English she twice asserted in her prison before her judges that within seven years the English would meet with a mightier disaster than had been the fall of Orleans: it happened within five—the fall of Paris. Other prophecies of hers came true, both as to the event named and the time-limit prescribed.

She was deeply religious, and believed that she had daily speech with angels; that she saw them face to face, and that they counselled her, comforted and heartened her, and brought commands to her direct from God. She had a childlike faith in the heavenly origin of her apparitions and her Voices, and not any threat of any form of death was able to frighten it out of her loyal heart. She was a beautiful and simple and lovable character. In the records of the Trials this comes out in clear and shining detail. She was gentle and winning and affectionate; she loved her home and friends and her village life; she was miserable in the presence of pain and suffering; she was full of compassion: on the field of her most splendid victory she forgot her triumphs to hold in her lap the head of a dying enemy and comfort his passing spirit with pitying words; in an age when it was common to slaughter prisoners she stood dauntless between hers and harm, and saved them alive; she was forgiving, generous, unselfish, magnanimous; she was pure from all spot or stain of baseness. And always she was a *girl;* and dear and worshipful, as is meet for that estate: when she fell wounded, the first time, she was frightened, and cried when she saw her blood gushing from her breast; but she was Joan of Arc! and when presently she found that her generals were sounding the retreat, she staggered to her feet and led the assault again and took that place by storm.

There is no blemish in that rounded and beautiful character.

How strange it is!—that almost invariably the artist remembers only one detail—one minor and meaningless detail of the personality of Joan of Arc: to wit, that she was a peasant girl—and forgets all the rest; and so he paints her as a strapping middle-aged fishwoman, with costume to match, and in her face the spirituality of a ham. He is slave to his one idea, and forgets to observe that the supremely great souls are never lodged in gross bodies. No brawn, no muscle, could endure the work that their bodies must do; they do their miracles by the spirit, which has fifty times the strength and staying power of brawn and muscle. The Napoleons are little, not big; and they work twenty hours in the twenty-four, and come up fresh, while the big soldiers with the little hearts faint around them with fatigue. We know what Joan of Arc was like, without asking—merely by what she did. The artist should paint her *spirit*—then he could not fail to paint her body aright. She would rise before us, then, a vision to win us, not repel: a lithe young slender figure, instinct with "the unbought grace of youth," dear and bonny and lovable, the face beautiful, and transfigured with the light of that lustrous intellect and the fires of that unquenchable spirit.

Taking into account, as I have suggested before, all the circumstances—her origin, youth, sex, illiteracy, early environment, and the obstructing conditions under which she exploited her high gifts and made her conquests in the field and before the courts that tried her for her life,—she is easily and by far the most extraordinary person the human race has ever produced.

THE FIVE BOONS OF LIFE

I

IN the morning of life came the good fairy with her basket and said:

"Here are gifts. Take one, leave the others. And be wary, choose wisely; oh, choose wisely! for only one of them is valuable."

The gifts were five: Fame, Love, Riches, Pleasure, Death. The youth said, eagerly:

"There is no need to consider"; and he chose Pleasure.

He went out into the world and sought out the pleasures that youth delights in. But each in its turn was short-lived and disappointing, vain and empty; and each, departing, mocked him. In the end he said: "These years I have wasted. If I could but choose again, I would choose wisely."

II

THE fairy appeared, and said:

"Four of the gifts remain. Choose once more; and oh, remember—time is flying, and only one of them is precious."

The man considered long, then chose Love; and did not mark the tears that rose in the fairy's eyes.

After many, many years the man sat by a coffin, in an empty home. And he communed with himself, saying: "One by one they have gone away and left me; and now she lies here, the dearest and the last. Desolation after desolation has swept over me; for each hour of happiness the treacherous trader, Love, has sold me I have paid a thousand hours of grief. Out of my heart of hearts I curse him."

III

"Choose again." It was the fairy speaking. "The years have taught you wisdom—surely it must be so. Three gifts remain. Only one of them has any worth—remember it, and choose warily."

The man reflected long, then chose Fame; and the fairy, sighing, went her way.

Years went by and she came again, and stood behind the man where he sat solitary in the fading day, thinking. And she knew his thought:

"My name filled the world, and its praises were on every tongue, and it seemed well with me for a little while. How little a while it was! Then came envy; then detraction; then calumny; then hate; then persecution. Then derision, which is the beginning of the end. And last of all came pity, which is the funeral of fame. Oh, the bitterness and misery of renown! target for mud in its prime, for contempt and compassion in its decay."

IV

"CHOOSE yet again." It was the fairy's voice. "Two gifts remain. And do not despair. In the beginning there was but one that was precious, and it is still here."

"Wealth—which is power! How blind I was!" said the man. "Now, at last, life will be worth the living. I will spend, squander, dazzle. These mockers and despisers will crawl in the dirt before me, and I will feed my hungry heart with their envy. I will have all luxuries, all joys, all enchantments of the spirit, all contentments of the body that man holds dear. I will buy, buy, buy! deference, respect, esteem, worship — every pinchbeck grace of life the market of a trivial world can furnish forth. I have lost much time, and chosen badly heretofore, but let that pass; I was ignorant then, and could but take for best what seemed so."

Three short years went by, and a day came when the man sat shivering in a mean garret; and he was gaunt and wan and hollow-eyed, and clothed in rags; and he was gnawing a dry crust and mumbling:

"Curse all the world's gifts, for mockeries and gilded lies! And miscalled, every one. They are not gifts, but merely lendings. Pleasure, Love,

Fame, Riches: they are but temporary disguises for lasting realities—Pain, Grief, Shame, Poverty. The fairy said true; in all her store there was but one gift which was precious, only one that was not valueless. How poor and cheap and mean I know those others now to be, compared with that inestimable one, that dear and sweet and kindly one, that steeps in dreamless and enduring sleep the pains that persecute the body, and the shames and griefs that eat the mind and heart. Bring it! I am weary, I would rest."

V

THE fairy came, bringing again four of the gifts, but Death was wanting. She said:

"I gave it to a mother's pet, a little child. It was ignorant, but trusted me, asking me to choose for it. You did not ask me to choose."

"Oh, miserable me! What is there left for me?"

"What not even you have deserved: the wanton insult of Old Age."

THE FIRST WRITING-MACHINES

FROM MY UNPUBLISHED AUTOBIOGRAPHY

SOME days ago a correspondent sent in an old type-written sheet, faded by age, containing the following letter over the signature of Mark Twain:

"HARTFORD, *March 19, 1875.*

"Please do not use my name in any way. Please do not even divulge the fact that I own a machine. I have entirely stopped using the type-writer, for the reason that I never could write a letter with it to anybody without receiving a request by return mail that I would not only describe the machine, but state what progress I had made in the use of it, etc., etc. I don't like to write letters, and so I don't want people to know I own this curiosity-breeding little joker."

A note was sent to Mr. Clemens asking him if the letter was genuine and whether he really had a type-writer as long ago as that. Mr. Clemens replied that his best answer is in the following chapter from his unpublished autobiography:

1904. Villa Quarto, Florence, January.

Dictating autobiography to a type-writer is a new experience for me, but it goes very well, and is going to save time and "language"—the kind of language that soothes vexation.

I have dictated to a type-writer before—but not autobiography. Between that experience and the present one there lies a mighty gap—more than thirty years! It is a sort of lifetime. In that wide interval much has happened—to the type-machine as well as to the rest of us. At the beginning of that interval a type-machine was a curiosity. The person who owned one was a curiosity, too. But now it is the other way about: the person who *doesn't* own one is a curiosity. I saw a type-machine for the first time in—what year? I suppose it was 1873—because Nasby was with me at the time, and it was in Boston. We must have been lecturing, or we could not have been in Boston, I take it. I quitted the platform that season.

But never mind about that, it is no matter. Nasby and I saw the machine through a window, and went in to look at it. The salesman explained it to us, showed us samples of its work, and said it could do fifty-seven words a minute—a statement which we frankly confessed that we did not believe. So he put his type-girl to work, and we timed her by the watch. She actually did the fifty-seven in sixty seconds. We were partly convinced, but said it probably couldn't happen again. But it did. We timed the girl over and over again—with the same result always: she won out. She did her work on narrow slips of paper, and we pocketed them as fast as she turned them out, to show as curiosities. The price of the machine was $125. I bought one, and we went away very much excited.

At the hotel we got out our slips and were a little disappointed to find that they all contained the same words. The girl had economized time and labor by using a formula which she knew by heart. However, we argued—safely enough—that the *first* type-girl must naturally take rank with the first billiard-player: neither of them could be expected to get out of the game any more than a third or a half of what was in it. If the machine survived—*if* it survived—experts would come to the front, by-and-by, who would double this girl's output without a doubt. They would do one hundred words a minute — my talking speed on the platform. That score has long ago been beaten.

At home I played with the toy, repeating and repeating and repeating "The Boy stood on the Burning Deck," until I could turn that boy's adventure out at the rate of twelve words a minute; then I resumed the pen, for business, and only worked the machine to astonish inquiring visitors. They carried off many reams of the boy and his burning deck.

By-and-by I hired a young woman, and did my first dictating (letters, merely), and my last until now. The machine did not do both capitals and

lower case (as now), but only capitals. Gothic capitals they were, and sufficiently ugly. I remember
the first letter I dictated. It was to Edward Bok,
who was a boy then. I was not acquainted with
him at that time. His present enterprising spirit
is not new — he had it in that early day. He was
accumulating autographs, and was not content with
mere signatures, he wanted a whole autograph *letter*.
I furnished it—in type-machine capitals, *signature
and all*. It was long; it was a sermon; it contained
advice; also reproaches. I said writing was my
trade, my bread-and-butter; I said it was not fair to
ask a man to give away samples of his trade; would
he ask the blacksmith for a horseshoe? would he ask
the doctor for a corpse?

Now I come to an important matter—as I regard
it. In the year '74 the young woman copied a considerable part of a book of mine *on the machine*. In
a previous chapter of this Autobiography I have
claimed that I was the first person in the world that
ever had a telephone in his house for practical purposes; I will now claim—until dispossessed—that I
was the first person in the world to *apply the type-
machine to literature*. That book must have been
The Adventures of Tom Sawyer. I wrote the first
half of it in '72, the rest of it in '74. My machinist
type-copied a book for me in '74, so I concluded it
was that one.

That early machine was full of caprices, full of defects—devilish ones. It had as many immoralities

12

as the machines of to-day has virtues. After a year or two I found that it was degrading my character, so I thought I would give it to Howells. He was reluctant, for he was suspicious of novelties and unfriendly towards them, and he remains so to this day. But I persuaded him. He had great confidence in me, and I got him to believe things about the machine that I did not believe myself. He took it home to Boston, and my morals began to improve, but his have never recovered.

He kept it six months, and then returned it to me. I gave it away twice after that, but it wouldn't stay; it came back. Then I gave it to our coachman, Patrick McAleer, who was very grateful, because he did not know the animal, and thought I was trying to make him wiser and better. As soon as he got wiser and better he traded it to a heretic for a side-saddle which he could not use, and there my knowledge of its history ends.

ITALIAN WITHOUT A MASTER

IT is almost a fortnight now that I am domiciled in a mediæval villa in the country, a mile or two from Florence. I cannot speak the language; I am too old now to learn how, also too busy when I am busy, and too indolent when I am not; wherefore some will imagine that I am having a dull time of it. But it is not so. The "help" are all natives; they talk Italian to me, I answer in English; I do not understand them, they do not understand me, consequently no harm is done, and everybody is satisfied. In order to be just and fair, I throw in an Italian word when I have one, and this has a good influence. I get the word out of the morning paper. I have to use it while it is fresh, for I find

that Italian words do not keep in this climate. They fade towards night, and next morning they are gone. But it is no matter; I get a new one out of the paper before breakfast, and thrill the domestics with it while it lasts. I have no dictionary, and I do not

want one; I can select my words by the sound, or by orthographic aspect. Many of them have a French or German or English look, and these are the ones I enslave for the day's service. That is, as a rule. Not always. If I find a learnable phrase that has an imposing look and warbles musically along I do not care to know the meaning of it; I pay it out to the first applicant, knowing that if I pronounce it carefully *he* will understand it, and that's enough.

"SONO DISPIACENTISSIMO"

Yesterday's word was *avanti*. It sounds Shakespearian, and probably means Avaunt and quit my sight. To-day I have a whole phrase: *sono dispiacentissimo*. I do not know what it means, but it seems to fit in everywhere and give satisfaction. Although as a rule my words and phrases are good for one day and train only, I have several that stay by me all the time, for some unknown reason, and these come very handy when I get into a long conversation and need things to fire up with in monotonous stretches. One of the best ones is *Dov' è il gatto*. It nearly always produces a pleasant surprise, therefore I save it up for places where I want to express applause or admiration. The fourth word has a French sound, and I think the phrase means "that takes the cake."

During my first week in the deep and dreamy stillness of this woodsy and flowery place I was without news of the outside world, and was well content without it. It had been four weeks since I had seen a newspaper, and this lack seemed to give life a new charm and grace, and to saturate it with a feeling verging upon actual delight. Then came a change that was to be expected: the appetite for news began to rise again, after this invigorating rest. I had to feed it, but I was not willing to let it make me its helpless slave again; I determined to put it on a diet, and a strict and limited one. So I examined an Italian paper, with the idea of feeding it on that, and on that exclusively. On that exclusively, and without help of a dictionary. In this way I should surely be well protected against overloading and indigestion.

A glance at the telegraphic page filled me with encouragement. There were no scare-heads. That was good—supremely good. But there were headings—one-liners and two-liners—and that was good too; for without these, one must do as one does with a German paper—pay out precious time in finding out what an article is about, only to discover, in many cases, that there is nothing in it of interest to you. The head-line is a valuable thing.

Necessarily we are all fond of murders, scandals, swindles, robberies, explosions, collisions, and all such things, when we know the people, and when they are neighbors and friends, but when they are strangers we do not get any great pleasure out of them, as a rule. Now the trouble with an American paper is that it has no discrimination; it rakes the whole earth for blood and garbage, and the result is that you are daily overfed and suffer a surfeit. By habit you stow this muck every day, but you come by-and-by to take no vital interest in it—indeed, you almost get tired of it. As a rule, forty-nine-fiftieths of it concerns strangers only—people away off yonder, a thousand miles, two thousand miles, ten thousand miles from where you are. Why, when you come to think of it, who cares what becomes of those people? I would not give the assassination of one personal friend for a whole massacre of those others. And, to my mind, one relative or neighbor mixed up in a scandal is more interesting than a whole Sodom and Gomorrah of outlanders gone rotten. Give me the home product every time.

Very well. I saw at a glance that the Florentine paper would suit me: five out of six of its scandals and tragedies were local; they were adventures of

one's very neighbors, one might almost say one's
friends.   In the matter of world news there was not
too much, but just about enough.   I subscribed.   I
have had no occasion to regret it.   Every morning I
get all the news I need for the day; sometimes from
the head-lines, sometimes from the text.   I have
never had to call for a dictionary yet.   I read the
paper with ease.   Often I do not quite understand,
often some of the details escape me, but no matter, I
get the idea.   I will cut out a passage or two, then
you will see how limpid the language is:

The first line means that the Italian sovereigns are
coming back—they have been to England.   The
second line seems to mean that they enlarged the
King at the Italian hospital.   With a banquet, I suppose.   An English banquet has that effect.   Further:

Il ritorno dei Sovrani
a Roma
ROMA, 24, ore 22,50. - I Sovrani e le
Principessine Reali si attendono a Roma do-
mani alle ore 15,51.

Return of the sovereigns to Rome, you see.   Date
of the telegram, Rome, November 24, ten minutes

" THEY ENLARGED THE KING "

before twenty-three o'clock.   The telegram seems to say, "The Sovereigns and the Royal Children expect themselves at Rome to-morrow at fifty-one minutes after fifteen o'clock."

I do not know about Italian time, but I judge it begins at midnight and runs through the twenty-four hours without breaking bulk.   In the following ad. the theatres open at half-past twenty.   If these are not matinées, 20.30 must mean 8.30 P.M., by my reckoning.

Spettacoli del dì 25

TEATRO DELLA PERGOLA — (Ore 20,30)
— Opera : *Bohème.*
TEATRO ALFIERI. — Compagnia drammatica Drago — (Ore 20,30) — *La Legge.*
ALHAMBRA — (Ore 20,30) — Spettacolo variato.
SALA EDISON — Grandioso spettacolo Cinematografico: *Quo-Vadis?* — Inaugurazione della Chiesa Russa — In coda al Direttissimo — Vedute di Firenze con gran movimento — America: Trasporto tronchi giganteschi — I ladri in casa del Diavolo — Scene comiche.
CINEMATOGRAFO — Via Brunelleschi n. 4.
— Programma straordinario, *Don Chisciotte* — Prezzi popolari.

The whole of that is intelligible to me—and sane and rational, too—except the remark about the Inauguration of a Russian Cheese.   That one oversizes my hand.   Gimme five cards.

This is a four-page paper; and as it is set in long primer leaded and has a page of advertisements, there is no room for the crimes, disasters, and general sweepings of the outside world—thanks be! To-day I find only a single importation of the off-color sort:

> **Una principessa**
> che fugge con un cocchiere
> PARIGI, 24. - Il *Matin* ha da Berlino che la principessa Schovenbere-Waldenbure scomparve il 9 novembre. Sarebbe partita col suo cocchiere.
> La Principessa ha 27 anni.

Twenty-seven years old, and scomparve—scampered—on the 9th November. You see by the added detail that she departed with her coachman. I hope Sarebbe has not made a mistake, but I am afraid the chances are that she has. *Sono dispiacentissimo.*

There are several fires: also a couple of accidents. This is one of them:

> **Grave disgrazia sul Ponte Vecchio**
> Stamattina, circa le 7,80, mentre Giuseppe Sciatti, di anni 55, di Casellina e Torri, passava dal Ponte Vecchio, stando seduto sopra un barroccio carico di verdura, perse l'equilibrio e cadde al suolo, rimanendo con la gamba destra sotto una ruota del veicolo.
> Lo Sciatti fu subito raccolto da alcuni cittadini, che, per mezzo della pubblica vettura n. 365, lo trasportarono a San Giovanni di Dio.
> Ivi il medico di guardia gli riscontrò la frattura della gamba destra e alcune lievi escoriazioni giudicandolo guaribile in 50 giorni salvo complicazioni.

"I HOPE SAREBBE HAS NOT MADE A MISTAKE"

What it seems to say is this: "Serious Disgrace on the Old Old Bridge. This morning about 7.30, Mr. Joseph Sciatti, aged 55, of Casellina and Torri, while standing up in a sitting posture on top of a carico barrow of verdure (foliage? hay? vegetables?), lost his equilibrium and fell on himself, arriving with his left leg under one of the wheels of the vehicle.

"Said Sciatti was suddenly harvested (gathered in?) by several citizens, who by means of public cab No. 365 transported him to St. John of God."

Paragraph No. 3 is a little obscure, but I think it says that the medico set the broken left leg—right enough, since there was nothing the matter with the other one—and that several are encouraged to hope that fifty days will fetch him around in quite giudicandolo-guaribile way, if no complications intervene.

I am sure I hope so myself.

There is a great and peculiar charm about reading news-scraps in a language which you are not acquainted with—the charm that always goes with the mysterious and the uncertain. You can never be absolutely sure of the meaning of anything you read in such circumstances; you are chasing an alert and gamy riddle all the time, and the baffling turns and dodges of the prey make the life of the hunt. A dictionary would spoil it. Sometimes a single word of doubtful purport will cast a veil of dreamy and golden uncertainty over a whole paragraph of cold and practical certainties, and leave steeped in a haunting and adorable mystery an incident which

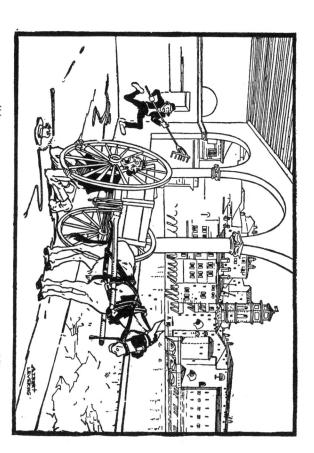

"'SERIOUS DISGRACE ON THE OLD OLD BRIDGE'"

had been vulgar and commonplace but for that bene-
faction. Would you be wise to draw a dictionary on
that gracious word? would you be properly grateful?

After a couple of days' rest I now come back to my
subject and seek a case in point. I find it without
trouble, in the morning paper; a cablegram from
Chicago and Indiana by way of Paris. All the words
save one are guessable by a person ignorant of
Italian:

Revolverate in teatro

PARIGI, 27. - La *Patrie* ha da Chicago:
Il guardiano del teatro dell'opera di Wallace (Indiana), avendo voluto espellere uno
spettatore che continuava a fumare malgrado
il divieto, questo spalleggiato dai suoi amici
tirò diversi colpi di rivoltella. Il guardiano
rispose. Nacque una scarica generale. Grande
panico tra gli spettatori. Nessun ferito.

Translation. — "REVOLVERATION IN THEATRE.
Paris, 27th. La Patrie has from Chicago: The cop
of the theatre of the opera of Wallace, Indiana, had
willed to expel a spectator which continued to smoke
in spite of the prohibition, who, spalleggiato by his
friends, tirò (Fr. *tiré*, Anglice *pulled*) manifold re-
volver-shots. The cop responded. Result, a general scare; great panic among the spectators. Nobody hurt."

It is bettable that that harmless cataclysm in the
theatre of the opera of Wallace, Indiana, excited not
a person in Europe but me, and so came near to not

"'THE REVOLVERATION IN THEATRE'"

being worth cabling to Florence by way of France.
But it does excite me. It excites me because I cannot make out, for sure, what it was that moved that
spectator to resist the officer. I was gliding along
smoothly and without obstruction or accident, until
I came to that word spalleggiato, then the bottom
fell out. You notice what a rich gloom, what a
sombre and pervading mystery, that word sheds all
over the whole Wallachian tragedy. That is the
charm of the thing, that is the delight of it. This is
where you begin, this is where you revel. You can
guess and guess, and have all the fun you like; you
need not be afraid there will be an end to it; none is
possible, for no amount of guessing will ever furnish
you a meaning for that word that you can be sure is
the right one. All the other words give you hints,
by their form, their sound, or their spelling—this one
doesn't, this one throws out no hints, this one keeps
its secret. If there is even the slightest slight
shadow of a hint anywhere, it lies in the very meagrely
suggestive fact that spalleggiato carries our word
"egg" in its stomach. Well, make the most out of
it, and then where are you at? You conjecture that
the spectator which was smoking in spite of the prohibition and become reprohibited by the guardians,
was "egged on" by his friends, and that it was owing
to that evil influence that he initiated the revolveration in theatre that has galloped under the sea and
come crashing through the European press without
exciting anybody but me. But are you sure, are

you dead sure, that that was the way of it? No. Then the uncertainty remains, the mystery abides, and with it the charm. Guess again.

If I had a phrase-book of a really satisfactory sort I would study it, and not give all my free time to un-dictionarial readings, but there is no such work on the market. The existing phrase-books are inade-quate. They are well enough as far as they go, but when you fall down and skin your leg they don't tell you what to say.

13

ITALIAN WITH GRAMMAR

I FOUND that a person of large intelligence could read this beautiful language with considerable facility without a dictionary, but I presently found that to such a person a grammar could be of use at times. It is because, if he does not know the *Were's* and the *Was's* and the *May-be's* and the *Has-been's* apart, confusions and uncertainties can arise. He can get the idea that a thing is going to happen next week when the truth is that it has already happened week before last. Even more previously, sometimes. Examination and inquiry showed me that the adjectives and such things were frank and fair-minded and straightforward, and did not shuffle; it was the Verb that mixed the hands, it was the Verb that lacked stability, it was the Verb that had no permanent opinion about anything, it was the Verb that was always dodging the issue and putting out the light and making all the trouble.

Further examination, further inquiry, further reflection, confirmed this judgment, and established beyond peradventure the fact that the Verb was the storm-centre. This discovery made plain the right and wise course to pursue in order to acquire certainty and exactness in understanding the statements which the newspaper was daily endeavoring to convey to me: I must catch a Verb and tame it. I must find out its ways, I must spot its eccentricities, I must penetrate its disguises, I must intelligently foresee and forecast at least the commoner of the dodges it was likely to try upon a stranger in given circumstances, I must get in on its main shifts and head them off, I must learn its game and play the limit.

I had noticed, in other foreign languages, that verbs are bred in families, and that the members of each family have certain features or resemblances that are common to that family and distinguish it from the other families—the other kin, the cousins and what not. I had noticed that this family-mark is not usually the nose or the hair, so to speak, but the tail— the Termination,—and that these tails are quite definitely differentiated; insomuch that an expert can tell a Pluperfect from a Subjunctive by its tail as easily and as certainly as a cowboy can tell a cow from a horse by the like process, the result of observation and culture. I should explain that I am speaking of legitimate verbs, those verbs which in the slang of the grammar are called Regular. There are others—I am not meaning to conceal this; others called Irregulars, born out of wedlock, of unknown and uninteresting parentage, and naturally destitute of family resemblances, as regards all features, tails included. But of these pathetic outcasts I have nothing to say. I do not approve of them, I do not encourage them; I am prudishly delicate and sensitive, and I do not allow them to be used in my presence.

But, as I have said, I decided to catch one of the others and break it to harness. One is enough. Once familiar with its assortment of tails, you are immune; after that, no regular verb can conceal its specialty from you and make you think it is working the past or the future or the conditional or the unconditional when it is engaged in some other line of business—its tail will give it away. I found out all these things by myself, without a teacher.

I selected the verb *Amare, to love*. Not for any personal reason, for I am indifferent about verbs; I care no more for one verb than for another, and have little or no respect for any of them; but in foreign languages you always begin with that one. Why, I do not know. It is merely habit, I suppose; the first teacher chose it, Adam was satisfied, and there hasn't been a successor since with originality enough to start a fresh one. For they *are* a pretty limited lot, you will admit that? Originality is not in their line; they can't think up anything new, anything to freshen up the old moss-grown dulness of the language lesson and put life and "go" into it, and charm and grace and picturesqueness.

I knew I must look after those details myself; therefore I thought them out and wrote them down, and sent for the *facchino* and explained them to him, and said he must arrange a proper plant, and get together a good stock company among the *contadini*,

and design the costumes, and distribute the parts;
and drill the troupe, and be ready in three days to
begin on this Verb in a shipshape and workman-like
manner. I told him to put each grand division of
it under a foreman, and each subdivision under a
subordinate of the rank of sergeant or corporal or
something like that, and to have a different uniform
for each squad, so that I could tell a Pluperfect from
a Compound Future without looking at the book;
the whole battery to be under his own special and
particular command, with the rank of Brigadier, and
I to pay the freight.

I then inquired into the character and possibilities
of the selected verb, and was much disturbed to find
that it was over my size, it being chambered for fifty-
seven rounds—fifty-seven ways of saying *I love* without reloading; and yet none of them likely to con-
vince a girl that was laying for a title, or a title that
was laying for rocks.

It seemed tò me that with my inexperience it
would be foolish to go into action with this mitrail-
leuse, so I ordered it to the rear and told the facchino
to provide something a little more primitive to start
with, something less elaborate, some gentle old-
fashioned flint-lock, smooth-bore, double-barrelled
thing, calculated to cripple at two hundred yards and
kill at forty—an arrangement suitable for a beginner
who could be satisfied with moderate results on the
offstart and did not wish to take the whole territory
in the first campaign.

But in vain. He was not able to mend the matter, all the verbs being of the same build, all Gatlings, all of the same calibre and delivery, fifty-seven to the volley, and fatal at a mile and a half. But he said the auxiliary verb AVERE, *to have*, was a tidy thing, and easy to handle in a seaway, and less likely to miss stays in going about than some of the others; so, upon his recommendation I chose that one, and told him to take it along and scrape its bottom and break out its spinnaker and get it ready for business.

I will explain that a facchino is a general-utility domestic. Mine was a horse-doctor in his better days, and a very good one.

At the end of three days the facchino-doctor-brigadier was ready. I was also ready, with a stenographer. We were in the room called the Rope-Walk. This is a formidably long room, as is indicated by its facetious name, and is a good place for reviews. At 9.30 the F.-D.-B. took his place near me and gave the word of command; the drums began to rumble and thunder, the head of the forces appeared at an upper door, and the "march-past" was on. Down they filed, a blaze of variegated color, each squad gaudy in a uniform of its own and bearing a banner inscribed with its verbal rank and quality: first the Present Tense in Mediterranean blue and old-gold, then the Past Definite in scarlet and black, then the Imperfect in green and yellow, then the Indicative Future in the stars and stripes, then the Old Red

Sandstone Subjunctive in purple and silver—and so on and so on, fifty-seven privates and twenty commissioned and non-commissioned officers; certainly one of the most fiery and dazzling and eloquent sights I have ever beheld. I could not keep back the tears. Presently—

"Halt!" commanded the Brigadier.

"Front—face!"

"Right dress!"

"Stand at ease!"

"One—two—three. In unison—*recite!*"

It was fine. In one noble volume of sound all the fifty-seven Haves in the Italian language burst forth in an exalting and splendid confusion. Then came the commands—

"About—face! Eyes—front! Helm alee—hard aport! Forward—march!" and the drums let go again.

When the last Termination had disappeared, the commander said the instruction drill would now begin, and asked for suggestions. I said:

"They say *I have, thou hast, he has,* and so on, but they don't say *what.* It will be better, and more definite, if they have something to have; just an object, you know, a something—anything will do; anything that will give the listener a sort of personal as well as grammatical interest in their joys and complaints, you see."

He said:

"It is a good point. Would a dog do?"

I said I did not know, but we could try a dog and
see. So he sent out an aide-de-camp to give the
order to add the dog.

The six privates of the Present Tense now filed in,
in charge of Sergeant AVERE (*to have*), and displaying
their banner. They formed in line of battle, and re-
cited, one at a time, thus:

"*Io ho un cane*, I have a dog."

"*Tu hai un cane*, thou hast a dog."

"*Egli ha un cane*, he has a dog."

"*Noi abbiamo un cane*, we have a dog."

"*Voi avete un cane*, you have a dog."

"*Eglino hanno un cane*, they have a dog."

No comment followed. They returned to camp,
and I reflected a while. The commander said:

"I fear you are disappointed."

"Yes," I said; "they are too monotonous, too
singsong, too dead-and-alive; they have no expression, no elocution. It isn't natural; it could never
happen in real life. A person who has just acquired
a dog is either blame' glad or blame' sorry. He is
not on the fence. I never saw a case. What the
nation do you suppose is the matter with these
people?"

He thought maybe the trouble was with the dog.
He said:

"These are *contadini*, you know, and they have a
prejudice against dogs—that is, against marimane.
Marimana dogs stand guard over people's vines and

olives, you know, and are very savage, and thereby a grief and an inconvenience to persons who want other people's things at night.   In my judgment they have taken this dog for a marimana, and have soured on him."

I saw that the dog was a mistake, and not function-able: we must try something else; something, if pos-sible, that could evoke sentiment, interest, feeling.

"What is cat, in Italian?" I asked.

"Gatto."

"Is it a gentleman cat, or a lady?"

"Gentleman cat."

"How are these people as regards that animal?"

"We-ll, they—they—"

"You hesitate: that is enough.   How are they about chickens?"

He tilted his eyes towards heaven in mute ecstasy. I understood.

"What is chicken in Italian?" I asked.

"Pollo, *podere*."   (Podere is Italian for master.   It is a title of courtesy, and conveys reverence and admiration.)   "Pollo is one chicken by itself; when there are enough present to constitute a plural, it is *polli*."

"Very well, polli will do.   Which squad is detailed for duty next?"

"The Past Definite."

"Send out and order it to the front—with chickens. And let them understand that we don't want any more of this cold indifference."

He gave the order to an aide, adding, with a haunting tenderness in his tone and a watering mouth in his aspect:

"Convey to them the conception that these are unprotected chickens." He turned to me, saluting with his hand to his temple, and explained, "It will inflame their interest in the poultry, sire."

A few minutes elapsed. Then the squad marched in and formed up, their faces glowing with enthusiasm, and the file-leader shouted:

"*Ebbi polli*, I had chickens!"

"Good!" I said. "Go on, the next."

"*Avesti polli*, thou hadst chickens!"

"Fine! Next!"

"*Ebbe polli*, he had chickens!"

"Moltimoltissimo! Go on, the next!"

"*Avemmo polli*, we had chickens!"

"Basta - basta aspettatto avanti — last man — *charge!*"

"*Ebbero polli*, they had chickens!"

Then they formed in echelon, by column of fours, refusing the left, and retired in great style on the double-quick. I was enchanted, and said:

"Now, doctor, that is something *like!* Chickens are the ticket, there is no doubt about it. What is the next squad?"

"The Imperfect."

"How does it go?"

"*Io aveva*, I had, *tu avevi*, thou hadst, *egli aveva*, he had, *noi av—*"

"Wait—we've just *had* the hads. What are you giving me?"

"But this is another breed."

"What do we want of another breed? Isn't one breed enough? *Had* is HAD, and your tricking it out in a fresh way of spelling isn't going to make it any hadder than it was before; now you know that yourself."

"But there is a distinction—they are not just the same Hads."

"How do you make it out?"

"Well, you use that first Had when you are referring to something that happened at a named and sharp and perfectly definite moment; you use, the other when the thing happened at a vaguely defined time and in a more prolonged and indefinitely continuous way."

"Why, doctor, it is pure nonsense; you know it yourself. Look here: If I have had a had, or have wanted to have had a had, or was in a position right then and there to have had a had that hadn't had any chance to go out hadding on account of this foolish discrimination which lets one Had go hadding in any kind of indefinite grammatical weather but restricts the other one to definite and datable meteoric convulsions, and keeps it pining around and watching the barometer all the time, and liable to get sick through confinement and lack of exercise, and all that sort of thing, why—why, the inhumanity of it is enough, let alone the wanton superfluity and useless-

ness of any such a loafing consumptive hospital-bird
of a Had taking up room and cumbering the place for
nothing. These finical refinements revolt me; it is
not right, it is not honorable; it is constructive
nepotism to keep in office a Had that is so delicate
it can't come out when the wind's in the nor'west—I
won't have this dude on the pay-roll. Cancel his
exequatur; and look here—"

"But you miss the point. It is like this. You
see—"

"Never mind explaining, I don't care anything
about it. Six Hads is enough for me; anybody that
needs twelve, let him subscribe; I don't want any
stock in a Had Trust. Knock out the Prolonged and
Indefinitely Continuous; four-fifths of it is water,
anyway."

"But I beg you, podere! It is often quite indispensable in cases where—"

"Pipe the next squad to the assault!"

But it was not to be; for at that moment the dull
boom of the noon gun floated up out of far-off Florence,
followed by the usual softened jangle of church-bells,
Florentine and suburban, that bursts out in murmur-
ous response; by labor-union law the *colazione*[1] must
stop; stop promptly, stop instantly, stop definitely,
like the chosen and best of the breed of Hads.

---

[1] Colazione is Italian for a collection, a meeting, a séance,
a sitting.—M. T.

A BURLESQUE BIOGRAPHY

TWO or three persons having at different times intimated that if I would write an autobiography they would read it when they got leisure, I yield at last to this frenzied public demand and herewith tender my history.

Ours is a noble old house, and stretches a long way back into antiquity. The earliest ancestor the Twains have any record of was a friend of the family by the name of Higgins. This was in the eleventh century, when our people were living in Aberdeen, county of Cork, England. Why it is that our long line has ever since borne the maternal name (except when one of them now and then took a playful refuge in an alias to avert foolishness), instead of Higgins, is a mystery which none of us has ever felt much desire to stir. It is a kind of vague, pretty romance, and we leave it alone. All the old families do that way.

Arthour Twain was a man of considerable note—a solicitor on the highway in William Rufus's time. At about the age of thirty he went to one of those fine old English places of resort called Newgate, to see about something, and never returned again. While there he died suddenly.

Augustus Twain seems to have made something of a stir about the year 1160. He was as full of fun as he could be, and used to take his old sabre and sharpen it up, and get in a convenient place on a dark night, and stick it through people as they went by, to see them jump. He was a born humorist. But he got to going too far with it; and the first time he was found stripping one of these parties, the authorities removed one end of him, and put it up on a nice high place on Temple Bar, where it could contemplate the people and have a good time. He never liked any situation so much or stuck to it so long.

Then for the next two hundred years the family tree shows a succession of soldiers—noble, high-spirit-

OUR FAMILY TREE

ed fellows, who always went into battle singing, right behind the army, and always went out a-whooping, right ahead of it.

This is a scathing rebuke to old dead Froissart's poor witticism that our family tree never had but one limb to it, and that that one stuck out at right angles, and bore fruit winter and summer.

Early in the fifteenth century we have Beau Twain,
called "the Scholar." He wrote a beautiful, beautiful hand. And he could imitate anybody's hand so
closely that it was enough to make a person laugh his
head off to see it. He had infinite sport with his
talent. But by-and-by he took a contract to break
stone for a road, and the roughness of the work spoiled
his hand. Still, he enjoyed life all the time he was in
the stone business, which, with inconsiderable intervals, was some forty-two years. In fact, he died in
harness. During all those long years he gave such
satisfaction that he never was through with one contract a week till the government gave him another.
He was a perfect pet. And he was always a favorite
with his fellow-artists, and was a conspicuous member of their benevolent secret society, called the Chain
Gang. He always wore his hair short, had a preference for striped clothes, and died lamented by the
government. He was a sore loss to his country. For
he was so regular.

Some years later we have the illustrious John Morgan Twain. He came over to this country with
Columbus in 1492 as a passenger. He appears to
have been of a crusty, uncomfortable disposition.
He complained of the food all the way over, and was
always threatening to go ashore unless there was a
change. He wanted fresh shad. Hardly a day
passed over his head that he did not go idling about
the ship with his nose in the air, sneering about the
commander, and saying he did not believe Columbus

knew where he was going to or had ever been there
before. The memorable cry of "Land ho!" thrilled
every heart in the ship but his. He gazed a while
through a piece of smoked glass at the pencilled line
lying on the distant water, and then said: "Land be
hanged,—it's a raft!"

When this questionable passenger came on board
the ship, he brought nothing with him but an old
newspaper containing a handkerchief marked "B. G.,"
one cotton sock marked "L. W. C.," one woollen one
marked "D. F.," and a night-shirt marked "O. M. R."
And yet during the voyage he worried more about his
"trunk," and gave himself more airs about it, than
all the rest of the passengers put together. If the ship
was "down by the head," and would not steer, he
would go and move his "trunk" farther aft, and then
watch the effect. If the ship was "by the stern," he
would suggest to Columbus to detail some men to
"shift that baggage." In storms he had to be gagged,
because his wailings about his "trunk" made it impossible for the men to hear the orders. The man
does not appear to have been openly charged with
any gravely unbecoming thing, but it is noted in the
ship's log as a "curious circumstance" that albeit he
brought his baggage on board the ship in a newspaper,
he took it ashore in four trunks, a queensware crate,
and a couple of champagne baskets. But when he
came back insinuating, in an insolent, swaggering way,
that some of his things were missing, and was going
to search the other passengers' baggage, it was too

much, and they threw him overboard.   They watched long and wonderingly for him to come up, but not even a bubble rose on the quietly ebbing tide.   But while every one was most absorbed in gazing over the side, and the interest was momentarily increasing, it was observed with consternation that the vessel was adrift and the anchor-cable hanging limp from the bow.   Then in the ship's dimmed and ancient log we find this quaint note:

"In time it was discouvered yt ye troblesome passenger hadde gonne downe and got ye anchor, and toke ye same and solde it to ye dam sauvages from ye interior, saying yt he hadde founde it, ye sonne of a ghun!"

Yet this ancestor had good and noble instincts, and it is with pride that we call to mind the fact that he was the first white person who ever interested himself in the work of elevating and civilizing our Indians. He built a commodious jail and put up a gallows, and to his dying day he claimed with satisfaction that he had had a more restraining and elevating influence on the Indians than any other reformer that ever labored among them.   At this point the chronicle becomes less frank and chatty, and closes abruptly by saying that the old voyager went to see his gallows perform on the first white man ever hanged in America, and while there received injuries which terminated in his death.

The great-grandson of the "Reformer" flourished in sixteen hundred and something, and was known

14

in our annals as "the old Admiral," though in history he had other titles. He was long in command of fleets of swift vessels, well armed and manned, and did great service in hurrying up merchantmen. Vessels which he followed and kept his eagle eye on, always made good fair time across the ocean. But if a ship still loitered in spite of all he could do, his indignation would grow till he could contain himself no longer—and then he would take that ship home where he lived and keep it there carefully, expecting the owners to come for it, but they never did. And he would try to get the idleness and sloth out of the sailors of that ship by compelling them to take invigorating exercise and a bath. He called it "walking a plank." All the pupils liked it. At any rate they never found any fault with it after trying it. When the owners were late coming for their ships, the Admiral always burned them, so that the insurance money should not be lost. At last this fine old tar was cut down in the fulness of his years and honors. And to her dying day, his poor heart-broken widow believed that if he had been cut down fifteen minutes sooner he might have been resuscitated.

Charles Henry Twain lived during the latter part of the seventeenth century, and was a zealous and distinguished missionary. He converted sixteen thousand South Sea islanders, and taught them that a dog-tooth necklace and a pair of spectacles was not enough clothing to come to divine service in. His poor flock loved him very, very dearly; and when his funeral was over, they got up in a body (and came out of the restaurant) with tears in their eyes, and saying, one to another, that he was a good tender missionary, and they wished they had some more of him.

Pah-go-to-wah-wah-pukketekeewis (Mighty-Hunter-with-a-Hog-Eye-Twain) adorned the middle of the eighteenth century, and aided General Braddock with all his heart to resist the oppressor Washington. It was this ancestor who fired seventeen times at our Washington from behind a tree. So far the beautiful romantic narrative in the moral story-books is correct; but when that narrative goes on to say that at the seventeenth round the awe-stricken savage said solemnly that that man was being reserved by the Great Spirit for some mighty mission, and he dared not lift his sacrilegious rifle against him again, the narrative seriously impairs the integrity of history. What he did say was:

"It ain't no (hic) no use. 'At man's so drunk he can't stan' still long enough for a man to hit him. I (hic) I can't 'ford to fool away any more am'nition on him."

That was why he stopped at the seventeenth round, and it was a good, plain, matter-of-fact reason, too, and one that easily commends itself to us by the eloquent, persuasive flavor of probability there is about it.

I always enjoyed the story-book narrative, but I felt a marring misgiving that every Indian at Brad-

dock's Defeat who fired at a soldier a couple of times
(two easily grows to seventeen in a century), and
missed him, jumped to the conclusion that the Great
Spirit was reserving that soldier for some grand
mission; and so I somehow feared that the only
reason why Washington's case is remembered and
the others forgotten is, that in his the prophecy came
true, and in that of the others it didn't. There are
not books enough on earth to contain the record of
the prophecies Indians and other unauthorized parties
have made; but one may carry in his overcoat-pockets
the record of all the prophecies that have been fulfilled.

I will remark here, in passing, that certain ancestors
of mine are so thoroughly well-known in history by
their aliases, that I have not felt it to be worth while
to dwell upon them, or even mention them in the
order of their birth. Among these may be mentioned
Richard Brinsley Twain, alias Guy Fawkes; John
Wentworth Twain, alias Sixteen-String Jack; William Hogarth Twain, alias Jack Sheppard; Ananias
Twain, alias Baron Munchausen; John George Twain,
alias Captain Kydd; and then there are George Francis
Train, Tom Pepper, Nebuchadnezzar, and Baalam's
Ass—they all belong to our family, but to a branch
of it somewhat distinctly removed from the honorable
direct line—in fact, a collateral branch, whose members chiefly differ from the ancient stock in that, in
order to acquire the notoriety we have always yearned
and hungered for, they have got into a low way of
going to jail instead of getting hanged.

It is not well, when writing an autobiography, to follow your ancestry down too close to your own time —it is safest to speak only vaguely of your great-grandfather, and then skip from there to yourself, which I now do.

I was born without teeth—and there Richard III. had the advantage of me; but I was born without a humpback, likewise, and there I had the advantage of him. My parents were neither very poor nor conspicuously honest.

But now a thought occurs to me. My own history would really seem so tame contrasted with that of my ancestors, that it is simply wisdom to leave it unwritten until I am hanged. If some other biographies I have read had stopped with the ancestry until a like event occurred, it would have been a felicitous thing for the reading public. How does it strike you?

GENERAL WASHINGTON'S NEGRO
BODY-SERVANT

A BIOGRAPHICAL SKETCH

THE stirring part of this celebrated colored man's life properly began with his death — that is to say, the notable features of his biography begin with the first time he died. He had been little heard of up to that time, but since then we have never ceased to hear of him; we have never ceased to hear of him at stated, unfailing intervals. His was a most remarkable career, and I have thought that its history would make a valuable addition to our biographical literature. Therefore, I have carefully collated the materials for such a work, from authentic sources, and here present them to the public. I have rigidly excluded from these pages everything of a doubtful character, with the object in view of introducing my work into the schools for the instruction of the youth of my country.

The name of the famous body-servant of General Washington was George. After serving his illustrious master faithfully for half a century, and enjoying throughout this long term his high regard and confidence, it became his sorrowful duty at last to lay that beloved master to rest in his peaceful grave by the Potomac. Ten years afterwards—in 1809—full of years and honors, he died himself, mourned by all who knew him. The Boston *Gazette* of that date thus refers to the event:

"George, the favorite body-servant of the lamented Washington, died in Richmond, Va., last Tuesday, at the ripe age of 95 years. His intellect was unimpaired, and his memory tenacious, up to within a few minutes of his decease. He was present at the second installation of Washington as President, and also at his funeral, and distinctly remembered all the prominent incidents connected with those noted events."

From this period we hear no more of the favorite body-servant of General Washington until May, 1825, at which time he died again. A Philadelphia paper thus speaks of the sad occurrence:

"At Macon, Ga., last week, a colored man named George, who was the favorite body-servant of General Washington, died, at the advanced age of 95 years. Up to within a few hours of his dissolution he was in full possession of all his faculties, and could distinctly recollect the second installation of Washington, his death and burial, the surrender of Cornwallis, the battle of Trenton, the griefs and hardships of Valley Forge, etc. Deceased was followed to the grave by the entire population of Macon."

On the Fourth of July, 1830, and also of 1834 and 1836, the subject of this sketch was exhibited in great state upon the rostrum of the orator of the day, and

in November of 1840 he died again. The St. Louis
Republican of the 25th of that month spoke as
follows:

"ANOTHER RELIC OF THE REVOLUTION GONE

"George, once the favorite body-servant of General
Washington, died yesterday at the house of Mr. John
Leavenworth, in this city, at the venerable age of 95
years. He was in the full possession of his faculties up
to the hour of his death, and distinctly recollected the
first and second installations and death of President
Washington, the surrender of Cornwallis, the battles
of Trenton and Monmouth, the sufferings of the patriot
army at Valley Forge, the proclamation of the Declaration of Independence, the speech of Patrick Henry in
the Virginia House of Delegates, and many other old-
time reminiscences of stirring interest. Few white men
die lamented as was this aged negro. The funeral was
very largely attended."

During the next ten or eleven years the subject of
this sketch appeared at intervals at Fourth-of-July
celebrations in various parts of the country, and was
exhibited upon the rostrum with flattering success.
But in the fall of 1855 he died again. The California
papers thus speak of the event:

"ANOTHER OLD HERO GONE

"Died, at Dutch Flat, on the 7th of March, George
(once the confidential body-servant of General Washington), at the great age of 95 years. His memory, which
did not fail him till the last, was a wonderful storehouse

of interesting reminiscences. He could distinctly recollect the first and second installations and death of
President Washington, the surrender of Cornwallis, the
battles of Trenton and Monmouth, and Bunker Hill,
the proclamation of the Declaration of Independence,
and Braddock's Defeat. George was greatly respected
in Dutch Flat, and it is estimated that there were
10,000 people present at his funeral."

The last time the subject of this sketch died was
in June, 1864; and until we learn the contrary, it is
just to presume that he died permanently this time.
The Michigan papers thus refer to the sorrowful event:

"ANOTHER CHERISHED REMNANT OF THE REVOLUTION GONE

"George, a colored man, and once the favorite body-
servant of General Washington, died in Detroit last
week, at the patriarchal age of 95 years.   To the moment
of his death his intellect was unclouded, and he could
distinctly remember the first and second installations
and death of Washington, the surrender of Cornwallis,
the battles of Trenton and Monmouth, and Bunker Hill,
the proclamation of the Declaration of Independence,
Braddock's Defeat, the throwing over of the tea in Boston harbor, and the landing of the Pilgrims.   He died
greatly respected, and was followed to the grave by a
vast concourse of people."

The faithful old servant is gone! We shall never
see him more until he turns up again.   He has closed
his long and splendid career of dissolution, for the
present, and sleeps peacefully, as only they sleep who

have earned their rest. He was in all respects a remarkable man. He held his age better than any celebrity that has figured in history; and the longer he lived the stronger and longer his memory grew. If he lives to die again, he will distinctly recollect the discovery of America.

The above résumé of his biography I believe to be substantially correct, although it is possible that he may have died once or twice in obscure places where the event failed of newspaper notoriety.   One fault I find in all notices of his death which I have quoted, and this ought to be corrected.   In them he uniformly and impartially died at the age of 95.   This could not have been.   He might have done that once, or maybe twice, but he could not have continued it indefinitely. Allowing that when he first died, he died at the age of 95, he was 151 years old when he died last, in 1864. But his age did not keep pace with his recollections. When he died the last time, he distinctly remembered the landing of the Pilgrims, which took place in 1620. He must have been about twenty years old when he witnessed that event, wherefore it is safe to assert that the body-servant of General Washington was in the neighborhood of two hundred and sixty or seventy years old when he departed this life finally.

Having waited a proper length of time, to see if the subject of this sketch had gone from us reliably and irrevocably, I now publish his biography with confidence, and respectfully offer it to a mourning nation.

P. S.—I see by the papers that this infamous old fraud has just died again, in Arkansas. This makes six times that he is known to have died, and always in a new place. The death of Washington's body-servant has ceased to be a novelty; its charm is gone; the people are tired of it; let it cease. This well-meaning but misguided negro has now put six different communities to the expense of burying him in state, and has swindled tens of thousands of people into following him to the grave under the delusion that a select and peculiar distinction was being conferred upon them. Let him stay buried for good now; and let that newspaper suffer the severest censure that shall ever, in all future time, publish to the world that General Washington's favorite colored body-servant has died again.

WIT INSPIRATIONS OF THE "TWO-YEAR-OLDS"

ALL infants appear to have an impertinent and disagreeable fashion nowadays of saying "smart" things on most occasions that offer, and especially on occasions when they ought not to be saying anything at all. Judging by the average published specimens of smart sayings, the rising generation of children are little better than idiots. And the parents must surely be but little better than the children, for in most cases they are the publishers of the sunbursts of infantile imbecility which dazzle us from the pages of our periodicals. I may seem to speak with some heat, not to say a suspicion of personal spite; and I do admit that it nettles me to hear about so many gifted infants in these days, and remember that I seldom said anything smart when I was a child. I tried it once or twice, but it was not popular. The family were not expecting brilliant remarks from me, and so they snubbed me sometimes and spanked me the rest. But it makes my flesh creep and my blood run cold to think what might have happened to me if I had dared to utter some of the smart things of this generation's "four-year-olds" where my father could hear me. To have simply skinned me alive and considered his duty at an end would have seemed to him criminal leniency towards one so sinning. He was a stern unsmiling man, and hated all forms of precocity. If I had said some of the things I have referred to, and said them in his hearing, he would have destroyed me. He would, indeed. He would, provided the opportunity remained with him. But it would not, for I would have had judgment enough to take some strychnine first and say my smart thing afterwards. The fair record of my life has been tarnished by just one pun. My father overheard that, and he hunted me over four or five townships seeking to take my life. If I had been full-grown, of course he would have been right; but, child as I was, I could not know how wicked a thing I had done.

I made one of those remarks ordinarily called "smart things" before that, but it was not a pun. Still, it came near causing a serious rupture between my father and myself. My father and mother, my uncle Ephraim and his wife, and one or two others were present, and the conversation turned on a name for me. I was lying there trying some India-rubber rings of various patterns, and endeavoring to make a selection, for I was tired of trying to cut my teeth on people's fingers, and wanted to get hold of something that would enable me to hurry the thing through and get something else. Did you ever notice what a nuisance it was cutting your teeth on your nurse's finger, or how back-breaking and tiresome it was trying to cut them on your big toe? And did you never get out of patience and wish your teeth were in Jericho long before you got them half cut? To me it seems as if these things happened yesterday. And they did, to some children. But I digress. I was lying there trying the India-rubber rings. I remember looking at the clock and noticing that in an hour and twenty-five minutes I would be two weeks old, and thinking how little I had done to merit the blessings that were so unsparingly lavished upon me. My father said:

"Abraham is a good name. My grandfather was named Abraham."

My mother said:

"Abraham is a good name. Very well. Let us have Abraham for one of his names."

I said:

"Abraham suits the subscriber."

My father frowned, my mother looked pleased; my aunt said:

"What a little darling it is!"

My father said:

"Isaac is a good name, and Jacob is a good name."

My mother assented, and said:

"No names are better. Let us add Isaac and Jacob to his names."

I said:

"All right. Isaac and Jacob are good enough for

yours truly. Pass me that rattle, if you please. I can't chew India-rubber rings all day."

Not a soul made a memorandum of these sayings of mine, for publication. I saw that, and did it myself, else they would have been utterly lost. So far from meeting with a generous encouragement like other children when developing intellectually, I was now furiously scowled upon by my father; my mother looked grieved and anxious, and even my aunt had about her an expression of seeming to think that maybe I had gone too far. I took a vicious bite out of an India-rubber ring, and covertly broke the rattle over the kitten's head, but said nothing. Presently my father said:

"Samuel is a very excellent name."

I saw that trouble was coming. Nothing could prevent it. I laid down my rattle; over the side of the cradle I dropped my uncle's silver watch, the clothes-brush, the toy dog, my tin soldier, the nut-meg-grater, and other matters which I was accustomed to examine, and meditate upon and make pleasant noises with, and bang and batter and break when I needed wholesome entertainment. Then I put on my little frock and my little bonnet, and took my pygmy shoes in one hand and my licorice in the other, and climbed out on the floor. I said to myself, Now, if the worst comes to worst, I am ready. Then I said aloud, in a firm voice:

"Father, I cannot, cannot wear the name of Samuel."

"My son!"

"Father, I mean it. I cannot."

"Why?"

"Father, I have an invincible antipathy to that name."

"My son, this is unreasonable. Many great and good men have been named Samuel."

"Sir, I have yet to hear of the first instance."

"What! There was Samuel the prophet. Was not he great and good?"

"Not so very."

"My son! With His own voice the Lord called him."

"Yes, sir, and had to call him a couple of times before he would come!"

And then I sallied forth, and that stern old man sallied forth after me. He overtook me at noon the following day, and when the interview was over I had acquired the name of Samuel, and a thrashing, and other useful information; and by means of this compromise my father's wrath was appeased and a misunderstanding bridged over which might have become a permanent rupture if I had chosen to be unreasonable. But just judging by this episode, what would my father have done to me if I had ever uttered in his hearing one of the flat, sickly things these "two-year-olds" say in print nowadays? In my opinion there would have been a case of infanticide in our family.

AN ENTERTAINING ARTICLE

I TAKE the following paragraph from an article in the Boston *Advertiser*:

"AN ENGLISH CRITIC ON MARK TWAIN

"Perhaps the most successful flights of the humor of Mark Twain have been descriptions of the persons who did not appreciate his humor at all. We have become familiar with the Californians who were thrilled with terror by his burlesque of a newspaper reporter's way of telling a story, and we have heard of the Pennsylvania clergyman who sadly returned his *Innocents Abroad* to the book-agent with the remark that 'the man who could shed tears over the tomb of Adam must be an idiot.' But Mark Twain may now add a much more glorious instance to his string of trophies. The *Saturday Review*, in its number of October 8th, reviews his book of travels, which has been republished in England, and reviews it seriously. We can imagine the delight of the humorist in reading this tribute to his power; and indeed it is so amusing in itself that he can hardly do better than reproduce the article in full in his next monthly Memoranda."

(Publishing the above paragraph thus, gives me a sort of authority for reproducing the *Saturday Review's* article in full in these pages. I dearly wanted to do it, for I cannot write anything half so delicious myself. If I had a cast-iron dog that could read this English criticism and preserve his austerity, I would drive him off the door-step.)

(From the London " Saturday Review.")

"REVIEWS OF NEW BOOKS

"THE INNOCENTS ABROAD. A Book of Travels. By Mark Twain. London: Hotten, publisher. 1870.

"Lord Macaulay died too soon. We never felt this so deeply as when we finished the last chapter of the above-named extravagant work. Macaulay died too soon—for none but he could mete out complete and comprehensive justice to the insolence, the impertinence, the presumption, the mendacity, and, above all, the majestic ignorance of this author.

"To say that the *Innocents Abroad* is a curious book, would be to use the faintest language—would be to speak of the Matterhorn as a neat elevation or of Niagara as being 'nice' or 'pretty.' 'Curious' is too tame a word wherewith to describe the imposing insanity of this work. There is no word that is large enough or long enough. Let us, therefore, photograph a passing glimpse of book and author, and trust the rest to the reader. Let the cultivated English student of human nature picture to himself this Mark Twain as a person capable of doing the following-described things—and not only doing them, but with incredible innocence *printing them* calmly and tranquilly in a book. For instance:

"He states that he entered a hair-dresser's in Paris to get shaved, and the first '*rake*' the barber gave with his razor it *loosened his 'hide'* and *lifted him out of the chair*.

"This is unquestionably exaggerated. In Florence

he was so annoyed by beggars that he pretends to have seized and eaten one in a frantic spirit of revenge. There is, of course, no truth in this. He gives at full length a theatrical programme seventeen or eighteen hundred years old, which he professes to have found in the ruins of the Coliseum, among the dirt and mould and rubbish. It is a sufficient comment upon this statement to remark that even a cast-iron programme would not have lasted so long under such circumstances. In Greece he plainly betrays both fright and flight upon one occasion, but with frozen effrontery puts the latter in this falsely tame form: 'We *sidled* towards the Piræus.' 'Sidled,' indeed! He does not hesitate to intimate that at Ephesus, when his mule strayed from the proper course, he got down, took him under his arm, carried him to the road again, pointed him right, remounted, and went to sleep contentedly till it was time to restore the beast to the path once more. He states that a growing youth among his ship's passengers was in the constant habit of appeasing his hunger with soap and oakum between meals. In Palestine he tells of ants that came eleven miles to spend the summer in the desert and brought their provisions with them; yet he shows by his description of the country that the feat was an impossibility. He mentions, as if it were the most commonplace of matters, that he cut a Moslem in two in broad daylight in Jerusalem, with Godfrey de Bouillon's sword, and would have shed more blood *if he had had a graveyard of his own.* These statements are unworthy a moment's attention. Mr. Twain or any other foreigner who did such a thing in Jerusalem would be mobbed, and would infallibly lose his life. But why go on? Why repeat more of his audacious and exasperating falsehoods? Let us close fittingly with this one: he affirms that 'in the mosque of St. Sophia at Constantinople I got my feet so stuck up with a complication of gums, slime, and general impurity, that I wore out more than two thousand pair of bootjacks getting my boots off that night, and even then some Christian hide peeled off with them.' It is monstrous. Such statements are simply lies—there is no other name for them. Will the reader longer marvel at the brutal ignorance that pervades the American nation when we tell him that we are informed upon perfectly good authority that this extravagant compilation of falsehoods, this exhaustless mine of stupendous lies, this *Innocents Abroad*, has actually been adopted by the schools and colleges of several of the States as a text-book!

"But if his falsehoods are distressing, his innocence and his ignorance are enough to make one burn the book and despise the author. In one place he was so appalled at the sudden spectacle of a murdered man, unveiled by the moonlight, that he jumped out of the window, going through sash and all, and then remarks with the most childlike simplicity that he 'was not scared, but was considerably agitated.' It puts us out of patience to note that the simpleton is densely unconscious that Lucrezia Borgia ever existed off the stage. He is vulgarly ignorant of all foreign languages, but is frank enough to criticise the Italians' use of their own tongue. He says they spell the name of their great painter 'Vinci, but pronounce it Vinchy'—and then adds with a naïveté possible only to helpless ignorance, 'foreigners always spell better than they pronounce.' In another place he commits the bald absurdity of putting the phrase 'tare an ouns' into an Italian's mouth. In Rome he unhesitatingly believes the legend that St. Philip Neri's heart was so inflamed with divine love that it burst his ribs— believes it wholly because an author with a learned list of university degrees strung after his name endorses it— 'otherwise,' says this gentle idiot, 'I should have felt a curiosity to know what Philip had for dinner.' Our author makes a long, fatiguing journey to the Grotto del

Cane on purpose to test its poisoning powers on a dog—got elaborately ready for the experiment, and then discovered that he had no dog. A wiser person would have kept such a thing discreetly to himself, but with this harmless creature everything comes out. He hurts his foot in a rut two thousand years old in exhumed Pompeii, and presently, when staring at one of the cinder-like corpses unearthed in the next square, conceives the idea that may be it is the remains of the ancient Street Commissioner, and straightway his horror softens down to a sort of chirpy contentment with the condition of things. In Damascus he visits the well of Ananias, three thousand years old, and is as surprised and delighted as a child to find that the water is 'as pure and fresh as if the well had been dug yesterday.' In the Holy Land he gags desperately at the hard Arabic and Hebrew Biblical names, and finally concludes to call them Baldwinsville, Williamsburgh, and so on, 'for convenience of spelling.'

"We have thus spoken freely of this man's stupefying simplicity and innocence, but we cannot deal similarly with his colossal ignorance. We do not know where to begin. And if we knew where to begin, we certainly would not know where to leave off. We will give one specimen, and one only. He did not know, until he got to Rome, that Michael Angelo was dead! And then, instead of crawling away and hiding his shameful ignorance somewhere, he proceeds to express a pious, grateful sort of satisfaction that he is gone and out of his troubles!

"No, the reader may seek out the author's exhibition of his uncultivation for himself. The book is absolutely dangerous, considering the magnitude and variety of its misstatements, and the convincing confidence with which they are made. And yet it is a text-book in the schools of America.

The poor blunderer mouses among the sublime crea-
tions of the Old Masters, trying to acquire the elegant
proficiency in art-knowledge, which he has a groping
sort of comprehension is a proper thing for the travelled
man to be able to display.   But what is the manner of
his study?   And what is the progress he achieves?   To
what extent does he familiarize himself with the great
pictures of Italy, and what degree of appreciation does
he arrive at?   Read:

"'When we see a monk going about with a lion and
looking up into heaven, we know that that is St. Mark.
When we see a monk with a book and a pen, looking
tranquilly up to heaven, trying to think of a word, we
know that that is St. Matthew.   When we see a monk
sitting on a rock, looking tranquilly up to heaven, with
a human skull beside him, and without other baggage,
we know that that is St. Jerome.   Because we know
that he always went flying light in the matter of baggage.   When we see other monks looking tranquilly up
to heaven, but having no trade-mark, we always ask
who those parties are.   We do this because we humbly
wish to learn.'

"He then enumerates the thousands and thousands
of copies of these several pictures which he has seen, and
adds with accustomed simplicity that he feels encouraged
to believe that when he has seen 'Some More' of each,
and had a larger experience, he will eventually 'begin
to take an absorbing interest in them'—the vulgar boor.

"That we have shown this to be a remarkable book,
we think no one will deny.   That it is a pernicious book
to place in the hands of the confiding and uninformed, we
think we have also shown.   That the book is a deliberate
and wicked creation of a diseased mind, is apparent upon
every page.   Having placed our judgment thus upon
record, let us close with what charity we can, by remarking that even in this volume there is some good to

be found; for whenever the author talks of his own country and lets Europe alone, he never fails to make himself interesting, and not only interesting, but instructive. No one can read without benefit his occasional chapters and paragraphs, about life in the gold and silver mines of California and Nevada; about the Indians of the plains and deserts of the West, and their cannibalism; about the raising of vegetables in kegs of gunpowder by the aid of two or three teaspoonfuls of guano; about the moving of small farms from place to place at night in wheelbarrows to avoid taxes; and about a sort of cows and mules in the Humboldt mines, that climb down chimneys and disturb the people at night. These matters are not only new, but are well worth knowing. It is a pity the author did not put in more of the same kind. His book is well written and is exceedingly entertaining, and so it just barely escaped being quite valuable also."

(One month later)

Latterly I have received several letters, and see a number of newspaper paragraphs, all upon a certain subject, and all of about the same tenor. I here give honest specimens. One is from a New York paper, one is from a letter from an old friend, and one is from a letter from a New York publisher who is a stranger to me. I humbly endeavor to make these bits toothsome with the remark that the article they are praising (which appeared in the December *Galaxy*, and *pretended* to be a criticism from the London *Saturday Review* on my *Innocents Abroad*) *was written by myself, every line of it*:

"The *Herald* says the richest thing out is the 'serious critique' in the London *Saturday Review*, on Mark

Twain's *Innocents Abroad*. We thought before we read it that it must be 'serious,' as everybody said so, and were even ready to shed a few tears; but since perusing it, we are bound to confess that next to Mark Twain's 'Jumping Frog' it's the finest bit of humor and sarcasm that we've come across in many a day."

(I do not get a compliment like that every day.)

"I used to think that your writings were pretty good, but after reading the criticism in *The Galaxy* from the *London Review*, have discovered what an ass I must have been. If suggestions are in order, mine is, that you put that article in your next edition of the *Innocents*, as an extra chapter, if you are not afraid to put your own humor in competition with it.   It is as rich a thing as I ever read."

(Which is strong commendation from a book publisher.)

"The London Reviewer, my friend, is not the stupid, 'serious' creature he pretends to be, *I* think; but, on the contrary, has a keen appreciation and enjoyment of your book. As I read his article in *The Galaxy*, I could imagine him giving vent to many a hearty laugh. But he is writing for Catholics and Established Church people, and high-toned, antiquated, conservative gentility, whom it is a delight to him to help you shock, while he pretends to shake his head with owlish density. He is a magnificent humorist himself."

(Now that is graceful and handsome. I take off my hat to my life-long friend and comrade, and with my feet together and my fingers spread over my heart, I say, in the language of Alabama, "You do me proud.")

I stand guilty of the authorship of the article, but I did not mean any harm. I saw by an item in the Boston *Advertiser* that a solemn, serious critique on the English edition of my book had appeared in the London *Saturday Review*, and the idea of *such* a literary breakfast by a stolid, ponderous British ogre of the quill was too much for a naturally weak virtue, and I went home and burlesqued it—revelled in it, I may say. I never saw a copy of the real *Saturday Review* criticism until after my burlesque was written and mailed to the printer. But when I did get hold of a copy, I found it to be vulgar, awkwardly written, ill-natured, and entirely serious and in earnest. The gentleman who wrote the newspaper paragraph above quoted had not been misled as to its character.

If any man doubts my word now, I will kill him. No, I will not kill him; I will win his money. I will bet him twenty to one, and let any New York publisher hold the stakes, that the statements I have above made as to the authorship of the article in question are entirely true. Perhaps I may get wealthy at this, for I am willing to take all the bets that offer; and if a man wants larger odds, I will give him all he requires. But he ought to find out whether I am betting on what is termed "a sure thing" or not before he ventures his money, and he can do that by going to a public library and examin-

ing the London *Saturday Review* of October 8th, which
contains the real critique.

Bless me, some people thought that *I* was the "sold"
person!

P. S.—I cannot resist the temptation to toss in this
most savory thing of all—this easy, graceful, philosophical disquisition, with its happy, chirping confidence.   It is from the Cincinnati *Enquirer:*

"Nothing is more uncertain than the value of a fine
cigar.   Nine smokers out of ten would prefer an ordinary
domestic article, three for a quarter, to a fifty-cent
Partaga, if kept in ignorance of the cost of the latter.
The flavor of the Partaga is too delicate for palates that
have been accustomed to Connecticut seed leaf.   So it is
with humor.   The finer it is in quality, the more danger
of its not being recognized at all.   Even Mark Twain
has been taken in by an English review of his *Innocents
Abroad*.   Mark Twain is by no means a coarse humorist,
but the Englishman's humor is so much finer than his,
that he mistakes it for solid earnest, and 'larfs most
consumedly.' "

A man who cannot learn stands in his own light.
Hereafter, when I write an article which I know to
be good, but which I may have reason to fear will
not, in some quarters, be considered to amount to
much, coming from an American, I will aver that an
Englishman wrote it and that it is copied from a
London journal.   And then I will occupy a back seat
and enjoy the cordial applause.

(Still later)

"Mark Twain at last sees that the *Saturday Review's* criticism of his *Innocents Abroad* was not serious, and he is intensely mortified at the thought of having been so badly sold. He takes the only course left him, and in the last *Galaxy* claims that *he* wrote the criticism himself, and published it in *The Galaxy* to sell the public. This is ingenious, but unfortunately it is not true. If any of our readers will take the trouble to call at this office we will show them the original article in the *Saturday Review* of October 8th, which, on comparison, will be found to be identical with the one published in *The Galaxy*. The best thing for Mark to do will be to admit that he was sold, and say no more about it."

The above is from the Cincinnati *Enquirer*, and is a falsehood. Come to the proof. If the *Enquirer* people, through any agent, will produce at *The Galaxy* office a London *Saturday Review* of October 8th, containing an "article which, on comparison, will be found to be identical with the one published in *The Galaxy*, I will pay to that agent five hundred dollars cash. Moreover, if at any specified time I fail to produce at the same place a copy of the London *Saturday Review* of October 8th, containing a lengthy criticism upon the *Innocents Abroad*, entirely different, in every paragraph and sentence, from the one I published in *The Galaxy*, I will pay to the *Enquirer* agent another five hundred dollars cash. I offer Sheldon & Co., publishers, 500 Broadway, New York, as my "backers." Any one in New York, authorized by the *Enquirer*, will receive prompt attention. It is an easy and profitable way for the *Enquirer* people to prove that they have not uttered a pitiful, deliberate falsehood in the above paragraphs. Will they swallow that falsehood ignominiously, or will they send an agent to *The Galaxy* office? I think the Cincinnati *Enquirer* must be edited by children.

A LETTER TO THE SECRETARY OF THE TREASURY

Riverdale-on-the-Hudson,
October 13, 1902.

*The Hon. the Secretary of the Treasury, Washington,
D. C.:*

Sir, — Prices for the customary kinds of winter fuel having reached an altitude which puts them out of the reach of literary persons in straitened circumstances, I desire to place with you the following order:

Forty-five tons best old dry government bonds, suitable for furnace, gold 7 per cents., 1864, preferred.

Twelve tons early greenbacks, range size, suitable for cooking.

Eight barrels seasoned 25 and 50 cent postal currency, vintage of 1866, eligible for kindlings.

Please deliver with all convenient dispatch at my house in Riverdale at lowest rates for spot cash, and send bill to   Your obliged servant,

                              Mark Twain,

who will be very grateful, and will vote right.

AMENDED OBITUARIES

To the Editor:

Sir, — I am approaching seventy; it is in sight; it is only three years away. Necessarily, I must go soon. It is but matter-of-course wisdom, then, that I should begin to set my worldly house in order now, so that it may be done calmly and with thoroughness, in place of waiting until the last day, when, as we have often seen, the attempt to set both houses in order at the same time has been marred by the necessity for haste and by the confusion and waste of time arising from the inability of the notary and the ecclesiastic to work together harmoniously, taking turn about and giving each other friendly assistance —not perhaps in fielding, which could hardly be expected, but at least in the minor offices of keeping game and umpiring; by consequence of which conflict of interests and absence of harmonious action a draw has frequently resulted where this ill-fortune could not have happened if the houses had been set in order one at a time and hurry avoided by beginning in season, and giving to each the amount of time fairly and justly proper to it.

In setting my earthly house in order I find it of
moment that I should attend in person to one or two
matters which men in my position have long had the
habit of leaving wholly to others, with consequences
often most regrettable.   I wish to speak of only one
of these matters at this time: Obituaries.   Of necessity, an Obituary is a thing which cannot be so judi-

ciously edited by any hand as by that of the subject
of it.   In such a work it is not the Facts that are of
chief importance, but the light which the obituarist
shall throw upon them, the meanings which he shall
dress them in, the conclusions which he shall draw
from them, and the judgments which he shall deliver

upon them. The Verdicts, you understand: that is the danger-line.

In considering this matter, in view of my approaching change, it has seemed to me wise to take such measures as may be feasible, to acquire, by courtesy of the press, access to my standing obituaries, with the privilege—if this is not asking too much—of editing, not their Facts, but their Verdicts. This, not for present profit, further than as concerns my family, but as a favorable influence usable on the Other Side, where there are some who are not friendly to me.

With this explanation of my motives, I will now ask you of your courtesy to make an appeal for me to the public press. It is my desire that such journals and periodicals as have obituaries of me lying in their pigeon-holes, with a view to sudden use some day, will not wait longer, but will publish them now, and kindly send me a marked copy. My address is simply New York city—I have no other that is permanent and not transient.

I will correct them—not the Facts, but the Verdicts—striking out such clauses as could have a deleterious influence on the Other Side, and replacing them with clauses of a more judicious character. I should, of course, expect to pay double rates for both the omissions and the substitutions; and I should also expect to pay quadruple rates for all obituaries which proved to be rightly and wisely worded in the originals, thus requiring no emendations at all.

It is my desire to leave these Amended Obituaries

neatly bound behind me as a perennial consolation and entertainment to my family, and as an heirloom which shall have a mournful but definite commercial value for my remote posterity.

I beg, sir, that you will insert this Advertisement (1t-eow, agate, inside), and send the bill to

Yours very respectfully,
Mark Twain.

P. S.—For the best Obituary—one suitable for me to read in public, and calculated to inspire regret— I desire to offer a Prize, consisting of a Portrait of me done entirely by myself in pen and ink without previous instructions. The ink warranted to be the kind used by the very best artists.

16

A MONUMENT TO ADAM

SOME one has revealed to the *Tribune* that I once suggested to Rev. Thomas K. Beecher, of Elmira, New York, that we get up a monument to Adam, and that Mr. Beecher favored the project. There is more to it than that. The matter started as a joke, but it came somewhat near to materializing.

It is long ago—thirty years. Mr. Darwin's *Descent of Man* had been in print five or six years, and the storm of indignation raised by it was still raging in pulpits and periodicals. In tracing the genesis of the human race back to its sources, Mr. Darwin had left Adam out altogether. We had monkeys, and "missing links," and plenty of other kinds of ancestors, but no Adam. Jesting with Mr. Beecher and other friends in Elmira, I said there seemed to be a likelihood that the world would discard Adam and accept the monkey, and that in the course of time Adam's very name would be forgotten in the earth; therefore this calamity ought to be averted; a monument would accomplish this, and Elmira ought not to waste this honorable opportunity to do Adam a favor and herself a credit.

Then the unexpected happened. Two bankers
came forward and took hold of the matter—not for
fun, not for sentiment, but because they saw in the
monument certain commercial advantages for the
town. The project had seemed gently humorous
before—it was more than that now, with this stern
business gravity injected into it. The bankers discussed the monument with me. We met several
times. They proposed an indestructible memorial,
to cost twenty-five thousand dollars. The insane
oddity of a monument set up in a village to preserve
a name that would outlast the hills and the rocks
without any such help, would advertise Elmira to the
ends of the earth—and draw custom. It would be
the only monument on the planet to Adam, and in
the matter of interest and impressiveness could never
have a rival until somebody should set up a monument to the Milky Way.

People would come from every corner of the globe
and stop off to look at it, no tour of the world would
be complete that left out Adam's monument. Elmira
would be a Mecca; there would be pilgrim ships at
pilgrim rates, pilgrim specials on the continent's railways; libraries would be written about the monument, every tourist would kodak it, models of it
would be for sale everywhere in the earth, its form
would become as familiar as the figure of Napoleon.

One of the bankers subscribed five thousand dollars,
and I think the other one subscribed half as much,
but I do not remember with certainty now whether

that was the figure or not.　We got designs made—
some of them came from Paris.

In the beginning—as a detail of the project when
it was as yet a joke—I had framed a humble and beseeching and perfervid petition to Congress begging the
government to build the monument, as a testimony
of the Great Republic's gratitude to the Father of the
Human Race and as a token of her loyalty to him in
this dark day of his humiliation when his older children were doubting him and deserting him.　It seemed
to me that this petition ought to be presented, now—
it would be widely and feelingly abused and ridiculed
and cursed, and would advertise our scheme and
make our ground-floor stock go off briskly.　So I sent
it to General Joseph R. Hawley, who was then in the
House, and he said he would present it.　But he did
not do it.　I think he explained that when he came to
read it he was afraid of it: it was too serious, too gushy,
too sentimental—the House might take it for earnest.

We ought to have carried out our monument
scheme; we could have managed it without any great
difficulty, and Elmira would now be the most celebrated town in the universe.

Very recently I began to build a book in which one
of the minor characters touches incidentally upon a
project for a monument to Adam, and now the
Tribune has come upon a trace of the forgotten jest
of thirty years ago.　Apparently mental telegraphy
is still in business.　It is odd; but the freaks of
mental telegraphy are usually odd.

A HUMANE WORD FROM SATAN

[The following letter, signed by Satan and purporting to come from him, we have reason to believe was not written by him, but by Mark Twain.—EDITOR.]

To the Editor of Harper's Weekly:

DEAR SIR AND KINSMAN,—Let us have done with this frivolous talk. The American Board accepts contributions from me every year: then why shouldn't it from Mr. Rockefeller? In all the ages, three-fourths of the support of the great charities has been conscience-money, as my books will show: then what becomes of the sting when that term is applied to Mr. Rockefeller's gift? The American Board's trade is financed mainly from the graveyards. Bequests, you understand. Conscience-money. Confession of an old crime and deliberate perpetration of a new one; for deceased's contribution is a robbery of his heirs. Shall the Board decline bequests because they stand for one of these offences every time and generally for both?

Allow me to continue. The charge most persistently and resentfully and remorselessly dwelt upon is, that Mr. Rockefeller's contribution is incurably tainted by perjury—perjury proved against him in the courts. *It makes us smile*—down in my place! Because there isn't a rich man in your vast city who doesn't perjure himself every year before the tax board. They are all caked with perjury, many layers thick. Iron clad, so to speak. If there is one that isn't, I desire to acquire him for my museum, and will pay Dinosaur rates. Will you say it isn't infraction of law, but only annual evasion of it? Comfort yourselves with that nice distinction if you like—*for the present*. But by-and-by, when you arrive, I will show you something interesting: a whole hell-full of evaders! Sometimes a frank law-breaker turns up elsewhere, but I get those others every time.

To return to my muttons. I wish you to remember that my rich perjurers are contributing to the American Board with frequency: it is money filched from the sworn-off personal tax; therefore it is the wages of sin; therefore it is my money; therefore it is *I* that contribute it; and, finally, it is therefore as I have said: since the Board daily accepts contributions from me, why should it decline them from Mr. Rockefeller, who is as good as I am, let the courts say what they may?

..   ..   .. SATAN.

INTRODUCTION TO "THE NEW GUIDE OF THE CONVERSATION IN PORTUGUESE AND ENGLISH"

BY PEDRO CAROLINO

IN this world of uncertainties, there is, at any rate, one thing which may be pretty confidently set down as a certainty: and that is, that this celebrated little phrase-book will never die while the English language lasts. Its delicious unconscious ridiculousness, and its enchanting naïveté, are as supreme and unapproachable, in their way, as are Shakespeare's sublimities. Whatsoever is perfect in its kind, in literature, is imperishable: nobody can add to the absurdity of this book, nobody can imitate it successfully, nobody can hope to produce its fellow; it is perfect, it must and will stand alone: its immortality is secure.

It is one of the smallest books in the world, but few big books have received such wide attention, and been so much pondered by the grave and the learned, and so much discussed and written about by the thoughtful, the thoughtless, the wise, and the foolish. Long notices of it have appeared, from time to time, in the great English reviews, and in erudite and authoritative philological periodicals; and it has been laughed at, danced upon, and tossed in a blanket by nearly every newspaper and magazine in the English-speaking world. Every scribbler, almost, has had his little fling at it, at one time or another; I had mine fifteen years ago. The book gets out of print, every now and then, and one ceases to hear of it for a season; but presently the nations and near and far colonies of our tongue and lineage call for it once more, and once more it issues from some London or Continental or American press, and runs a new course around the globe, wafted on its way by the wind of a world's laughter.

Many persons have believed that this book's miraculous stupidities were studied and disingenuous; but no one can read the volume carefully through and keep that opinion. It was written in serious good faith and deep earnestness, by an honest and upright idiot who believed he knew something of the English language, and could impart his knowledge to others. The amplest proof of this crops out somewhere or other upon each and every page. There are sentences in the book which could have been manufactured by a man in his right mind, and with an intelligent and deliberate purpose to seem innocently ignorant; but there are other sentences, and paragraphs, which no mere pretended ignorance could ever achieve—nor yet even the most genuine and comprehensive ignorance, when unbacked by inspiration.

It is not a fraud who speaks in the following paragraph of the author's Preface, but a good man, an honest man, a man whose conscience is at rest, a man who believes he has done a high and worthy work for his nation and his generation, and is well pleased with his performance:

"We expect then, who the little book (for the care what we wrote him, and for her typographical correction) that may be worth the acceptation of the studious persons, and especialy of the Youth, at which we dedicate him particularly."

One cannot open this book anywhere and not find richness. To prove that this is true, I will open it at random and copy the page I happen to stumble upon. Here is the result:

"DIALOGUE 16

" FOR TO SEE THE TOWN

"Anthony, go to accompany they gentilsmen, do they see the town.

"We won't to see all that is it remarquable here.

"Come with me, if you please. I shall not folget nothing what can to merit your attention. Here we are near to cathedral; will you come in there?

"We will first to see him in oudside, after we shall go in there for to look the interior.

"Admire this master piece gothic architecture's.

"The chasing of all they figures is astonishing'indeed.

"The cupola and the nave are not less curious to see.

"What is this palace how I see youder?

"It is the town hall.

"And this tower here at this side?

"It is the Observatory.

"The bridge is very fine, it have ten archs, and is constructed of free stone.

"The streets are very layed out by line and too paved.

"What is the circuit of this town?

"Two leagues.

"There is it also hospitals here?

"It not fail them.

"What are then the edifices the worthest to have seen?

"It is the arsnehal, the spectacle's hall, the Cusiom-house, and the Purse.

"We are going too see the others monuments such that the public pawnbroker's office, the plants garden's, the money office's, the library.

"That it shall be for another day; we are tired."

"DIALOGUE 17

"TO INFORM ONE'SELF OF A PERSON

"How is that gentilman who you did speak by and by?

"Is a German.

"I did think him Englishman.

"He is of the Saxony side.

"He speak the french very well.

"Tough he is German, he speak so much well italyan, french, spanish and english, that among the Italyans, they believe him Italyan, he speak the frenche as the Frenches himselves. The Spanishesmen believe him

Spanishing, and the Englishes, Englisman.   It is difficult
to enjoy well so much several langages."

The last remark contains a general truth; but it
ceases to be a truth when one contracts it and applies
it to an individual—provided that that individual is
the author of this book, Senhor Pedro Carolino.   I
am sure I should not find it difficult "to enjoy well
so much several langages"—or even a thousand of
them—if he did the translating for me from the
originals into his ostensible English.

ADVICE TO LITTLE GIRLS

GOOD little girls ought not to make mouths at their teachers for every trifling offence. This retaliation should only be resorted to under peculiarly aggravated circumstances.

If you have nothing but a rag-doll stuffed with sawdust, while one of your more fortunate little play-mates has a costly China one, you should treat her with a show of kindness nevertheless. And you ought not to attempt to make a forcible swap with her unless your conscience would justify you in it, and you know you are able to do it.

You ought never to take your little brother's "chewing-gum" away from him by main force; it is better to rope him in with the promise of the first two dollars and a half you find floating down the river on a grindstone. In the artless simplicity natural to his time of life, he will regard it as a perfectly fair transaction. In all ages of the world this eminently plausible fiction has lured the obtuse infant to financial ruin and disaster.

If at any time you find it necessary to correct your brother, do not correct him with mud—never, on any account, throw mud at him, because it will spoil his clothes. It is better to scold him a little, for then you obtain desirable results. You secure his immediate attention to the lessons you are inculcating, and at the same time your hot water will have a tendency to move impurities from his person, and possibly the skin, in spots.

If your mother tells you to do a thing, it is wrong to reply that you won't. It is better and more becoming to intimate that you will do as she bids you, and then afterwards act quietly in the matter according to the dictates of your best judgment.

You should ever bear in mind that it is to your kind parents that you are indebted for your food, and your nice bed, and for your beautiful clothes, and for the privilege of staying home from school when you let on that you are sick. Therefore you ought to respect their little prejudices, and humor their little whims, and put up with their little foibles until they get to crowding you too much.

Good little girls always show marked deference for the aged. You ought never to "sass" old people unless they "sass" you first.

POST-MORTEM POETRY [1]

IN Philadelphia they have a custom which it would be pleasant to see adopted throughout the land. It is that of appending to published death-notices a little verse or two of comforting poetry. Any one who is in the habit of reading the daily Philadelphia *Ledger*, must frequently be touched by these plaintive tributes to extinguished worth. In Philadelphia, the departure of a child is a circumstance which is not more surely followed by a burial than by the accustomed solacing poesy in the *Public Ledger*. In that city death loses half its terror because the knowledge of its presence comes thus disguised in the sweet drapery of verse. For instance, in a late *Ledger* I find the following (I change the surname):

"DIED

"HAWKS.—On the 17th inst., Clara, the daughter of Ephraim and Laura Hawks, aged 21 months and 2 days.

"That merry shout no more I hear,
No laughing child I see,
No little arms are round my neck,
No feet upon my knee;

[1] Written in 1870.

No kisses drop upon my cheek,
  These lips are sealed to me.
Dear Lord, how could I give Clara up
  To any but to Thee?"

A child thus mourned could not die wholly discontented. From the *Ledger* of the same date I make the following extract, merely changing the surname, as before:

"BECKET.—On Sunday morning, 19th inst., John P., infant son of George and Julia Becket, aged 1 year, 6 months, and 15 days.

  "That merry shout no more I hear,
    No laughing child I see,
  No little arms are round my neck,
    No feet upon my knee;
  No kisses drop upon my cheek,
    These lips are sealed to me.
  Dear Lord, how could I give Johnnie up
    To any but to Thee?"

The similarity of the emotions as produced in the mourners in these two instances is remarkably evidenced by the singular similarity of thought which they experienced, and the surprising coincidence of language used by them to give it expression.

In the same journal, of the same date, I find the following (surname suppressed, as before):

"WAGNER.—On the 10th inst., Ferguson G., the son of William L. and Martha Theresa Wagner, aged 4 weeks and 1 day.

"That merry shout no more I hear,
    No laughing child I see,
No little arms are round my neck,
    No feet upon my knee;
No kisses drop upon my cheek,
    These lips are sealed to me.
Dear Lord, how could I give Ferguson up
    To any but to Thee?"

It is strange what power the reiteration of an essentially poetical thought has upon one's feelings. When we take up the *Ledger* and read the poetry about little Clara, we feel an unaccountable depression of the spirits. When we drift further down the column and read the poetry about little Johnnie, the depression of spirits acquires an added emphasis, and we experience tangible suffering. When we saunter along down the column further still and read the poetry about little Ferguson, the word torture but vaguely suggests the anguish that rends us.

In the *Ledger* (same copy referred to above) I find the following (I alter surname, as usual):

"WELCH.—On the 5th inst., Mary C. Welch, wife of William B. Welch, and daughter of Catharine and George W. Markland, in the 29th year of her age.

"A mother dear, a mother kind,
    Has gone and left us all behind.
Cease to weep, for tears are vain,
    Mother dear is out of pain.

"Farewell, husband, children dear,
    Serve thy God with filial fear,
    And meet me in the land above,
    Where all is peace, and joy, and love."

What could be sweeter than that? No collection
of salient facts (without reduction to tabular form)
could be more succinctly stated than is done in the
first stanza by the surviving relatives, and no more
concise and comprehensive programme of farewells,
post-mortuary general orders, etc., could be framed
in any form than is done in verse by deceased in the
last stanza. These things insensibly make us wiser
and tenderer, and better. Another extract:

"BALL.—On the morning of the 15th inst, Mary E.,
daughter of John and Sarah F. Ball.

"'Tis sweet to rest in lively hope
    That when my change shall come
    Angels will hover round my bed,
    To waft my spirit home."

The following is apparently the customary form for
heads of families:

"BURNS.—On the 20th inst., Michael Burns, aged 40
years.

"Dearest father, thou hast left us,
    Here thy loss we deeply feel;
    But 'tis God that has bereft us,
    He can all our sorrows heal.

"Funeral at 2 o'clock sharp."

17

There is something very simple and pleasant about the following, which, in Philadelphia, seems to be the usual form for consumptives of long standing. (It deplores four distinct cases in the single copy of the *Ledger* which lies on the Memoranda editorial table):

"BROMLEY.—On the 29th inst., of consumption, Philip Bromley, in the 50th year of his age.

"Affliction sore long time he bore,
    Physicians were in vain—
Till God at last did hear him mourn,
    And eased him of his pain.

"The friend whom death from us has torn,
    We did not think so soon to part;
An anxious care now sinks the thorn
    Still deeper in our bleeding heart."

This beautiful creation loses nothing by repetition. On the contrary, the oftener one sees it in the *Ledger*, the more grand and awe-inspiring it seems.

With one more extract I will close:

"DOBLE.—On the 4th inst., Samuel Peveril Worthington Doble, aged 4 days.

"Our little Sammy's gone,
    His tiny spirit's fled;
Our little boy we loved so dear
    Lies sleeping with the dead.

"A tear within a father's eye,
    A mother's aching heart,
Can only tell the agony
    How hard it is to part."

Could anything be more plaintive than that, without requiring further concessions of grammar? Could
anything be likely to do more towards reconciling
deceased to circumstances, and making him willing
to go? Perhaps not. The power of song can hardly
be estimated. There is an element about some poetry
which is able to make even physical suffering and
death cheerful things to contemplate and consumma-
tions to be desired. This element is present in the
mortuary poetry of Philadelphia degree of development.

The custom I have been treating of is one that
should be adopted in all the cities of the land.

It is said that once a man of small consequence
died, and the Rev. T. K. Beecher was asked to preach
the funeral sermon—a man who abhors the lauding
of people, either dead or alive, except in dignified and
simple language, and then only for merits which they
actually possessed or possess, not merits which they
merely ought to have possessed. The friends of the
deceased got up a stately funeral. They must have
had misgivings that the corpse might not be praised
strongly enough, for they prepared some manuscript
headings and notes in which nothing was left unsaid
on that subject that a fervid imagination and an un-
abridged dictionary could compile, and these they

handed to the minister as he entered the pulpit. They were merely intended as suggestions, and so the friends were filled with consternation when the minister stood up in the pulpit and proceeded to read off the curious odds and ends in ghastly detail and in a loud voice! And their consternation solidified to petrification when he paused at the end, contemplated the multitude reflectively, and then said, impressively:

"The man would be a fool who tried to add anything to that. Let us pray!"

And with the same strict adhesion to truth it can be said that the man would be a fool who tried to add anything to the following transcendent obituary poem. There is something so innocent, so guileless, so complacent, so unearthly serene and self-satisfied about this peerless "hogwash," that the man must be made of stone who can read it without a dulcet ecstasy creeping along his backbone and quivering in his marrow. There is no need to say that this poem is genuine and in earnest, for its proofs are written all over its face. An ingenious scribbler might imitate it after a fashion, but Shakespeare himself could not counterfeit it. It is noticeable that the country editor who published it did not know that it was a treasure and the most perfect thing of its kind that the storehouses and museums of literature could show. He did not dare to say no to the dread poet—for such a poet must have been something of an apparition— but he just shovelled it into his paper anywhere that came handy, and felt ashamed, and put that disgusted

"Published by Request" over it, and hoped that his subscribers would overlook it or not feel an impulse to read it:

"(*Published by request*)

"LINES

'Composed on the death of Samuel and Catharine Belknap's children

" BY M. A. GLAZE

"Friends and neighbors all draw near,
    And listen to what I have to say;
And never leave your children dear
    When they are small, and go away.

"But always think of that sad fate,
    That happened in year of '63;
Four children with a house did burn,
    Think of their awful agony.

"Their mother she had gone away,
    And left them there alone to stay;
The house took fire and down did burn,
    Before their mother did return.

"Their piteous cry the neighbors heard,
    And then the cry of fire was given;
But, ah! before they could them reach,
    Their little spirits had flown to heaven.

"Their father he to war had gone,
    And on the battle-field was slain;
But little did he think when he went away,
    But what on earth they would meet again.

"The neighbors often told his wife
    Not to leave his children there,
Unless she got someone to stay,
    And of the little ones take care.

"The oldest he was years not six,
    And the youngest only eleven months old,
But often she had left them there alone,
    As, by the neighbors, I have been told.

"How can she bear to see the place.
    Where she so oft has left them there,
Without a single one to look to them,
    Or of the little ones to take good care.

"Oh, can she look upon the spot,
    Whereunder their little burnt bones lay,
But what she thinks she hears them say,
    ' 'Twas God had pity, and took us on high.'

"And there may she kneel down and pray,
    And ask God her to forgive;
And she may lead a different life
    While she on earth remains to live.

"Her husband and her children too,
    God has took from pain and woe.
May she reform and mend her ways,
    That she may also to them go.

"And when it is God's holy will,
    O, may she be prepared
To meet her God and friends in peace,
    And leave this world of care."

A DECEPTION

YOU may remember that I lectured lately for the young gentlemen of the Clayonian Society? During the afternoon of that day I was talking with one of the young gentlemen referred to, and he said he had an uncle who, from some cause or other, seemed to have grown permanently bereft of all emotion. And with tears in his eyes this young man said:

"Oh, if I could only see him laugh once more! Oh, if I could only see him weep!"

I was touched. I could never withstand distress. I said:

"Bring him to my lecture. I'll start him for you."

"Oh, if you could but do it! If you could but do it, all our family would bless you for evermore; for he is very dear to us. Oh, my benefactor, can you make him laugh? Can you bring soothing tears to those parched orbs?"

I was profoundly moved. I said:

"My son, bring the old party round. I have got some jokes in my lecture that will make him laugh, if there is any laugh in him; and, if they miss fire, I have got some others that'll make him cry or kill him, one or the other."

Then the young man wept on my neck, and presently spread both hands on my head and looked up towards heaven, mumbling something reverently; and then he went after his uncle. He placed him in full view, in the second row of benches, that night, and I began on him. I tried him with mild jokes—then with severe ones; I dosed him with bad jokes, and riddled him with good ones; I fired old, stale jokes on him, and peppered him fore and aft with red-hot new ones. I warmed up to my work, and assaulted him on the right and left, in front and behind; I fumed, and charged, and ranted, till I was hoarse and sick, and frantic and furious; but I never moved him once — I never started a smile or a tear! Never a ghost of a smile, and never a suspicion of moisture! I was astounded. I closed the lecture at last with one despairing shriek—with one wild burst of humor —and hurled a joke of supernatural atrocity full at him. It never phased him! Then I sat down bewildered and exhausted.

The president of the society came up and bathed my head with cold water, and said:

"What made you carry on so towards the last?"

I said, "I was trying to make that confounded old idiot laugh in the second row."

And he said, "Well, you were wasting your time; because he is deaf and dumb, and as blind as a badger."

Now was that any way for that old man's nephew to impose on a stranger and an orphan like me?

THE DANGER OF LYING IN BED

THE man in the ticket-office said:

"Have an accident insurance ticket, also?"

"No," I said, after studying the matter over a little. "No, I believe not; I am going to be travelling by rail all day to-day. However, to-morrow I don't travel. Give me one for to-morrow."

The man looked puzzled. He said:

"But it is for accident insurance, and if you are going to travel by rail—"

"If I am going to travel by rail I sha'n't need it. Lying at home in bed is the thing *I* am afraid of."

I had been looking into this matter. Last year I travelled twenty thousand miles, almost entirely by rail; the year before, I travelled over twenty-five thousand miles, half by sea and half by rail; and the year before that I travelled in the neighborhood of ten thousand miles, exclusively by rail. I suppose if I put in all the little odd journeys here and there, I may say I have travelled sixty thousand miles during the three years I have mentioned. *And never an accident.*

For a good while I said to myself every morning:

"Now I have escaped thus far, and so the chances are just that much increased that I shall catch it this time. I will be shrewd, and buy an accident ticket." And to a dead moral certainty I drew a blank, and went to bed that night without a joint started or a bone splintered. I got tired of that sort of daily bother, and fell to buying accident tickets that were good for a month. I said to myself, "A man *can't* buy thirty blanks in one bundle."

But I was mistaken. There was never a prize in the lot. I could read of railway accidents every day —the newspaper atmosphere was foggy with them; but somehow they never came my way. I found I had spent a good deal of money in the accident business, and had nothing to show for it. My suspicions were aroused, and I began to hunt around for somebody that had won in this lottery. I found plenty of people who had invested, but not an individual that had ever had an accident or made a cent. I stopped buying accident tickets and went to ciphering. The result was astounding. THE PERIL LAY NOT IN TRAVELLING, BUT IN STAYING AT HOME.

I hunted up statistics, and was amazed to find that after all the glaring newspaper headings concerning railroad disasters, less than *three hundred* people had really lost their lives by those disasters in the preceding twelve months. The Erie road was set down as the most murderous in the list. It had killed forty-six—or twenty-six, I do not exactly remember which, but I know the number was double that of any other road. But the fact straightway suggested itself that the Erie was an immensely long road, and did more business than any other line in the country; so the double number of killed ceased to be matter for surprise.

By further figuring, it appeared that between New York and Rochester the Erie ran eight passenger trains each way every day—sixteen altogether; and carried a daily average of 6000 persons. That is about a million in six months—the population of New York City. Well, the Erie kills from thirteen to twenty-three persons out of *its* million in six months; and in the same time 13,000 of New York's million die in their beds! My flesh crept, my hair stood on end. "This is appalling!" I said. "The danger isn't in travelling by rail, but in trusting to those deadly beds. I will never sleep in a bed again."

I had figured on considerably less than one-half the length of the Erie road. It was plain that the entire road must transport at least eleven or twelve thousand people every day. There are many short roads running out of Boston that do fully half as much; a great many such roads. There are many roads scattered about the Union that do a prodigious passenger business. Therefore it was fair to presume that an average of 2500 passengers a day for each road in the country would be about correct. There are 846 railway lines in our country, and 846 times 2500 are 2,115,000. So the railways of America move more than two millions of people every day; six hundred and fifty millions of people a year, without counting the Sundays. They do that, too—there is no question about it; though where they get the raw material is clear beyond the jurisdiction of my arithmetic; for I have hunted the census through and through, and I find that there are not that many people in the United States, by a matter of six hundred and ten millions at the very least. They must use some of the same people over again, likely.

San Francisco is one-eighth as populous as New York; there are 60 deaths a week in the former and 500 a week in the latter—if they have luck. That is 3120 deaths a year in San Francisco, and eight times as many in New York—say about 25,000 or 26,000. The health of the two places is the same. So we will let it stand as a fair presumption that this will hold good all over the country, and that consequently 25,000 out of every million of people we have must die every year. That amounts to one-fortieth of our total population. One million of us, then, die annually. Out of this million ten or twelve thousand are stabbed, shot, drowned, hanged, poisoned, or meet a similarly violent death in some other popular way, such as perishing by kerosene lamp and hoop-skirt conflagrations, getting buried in coal-mines, falling off house-tops, breaking through church or lecture-room floors, taking patent medicines, or committing suicide in other forms. The Erie railroad kills from 23 to 46; the other 845 railroads kill an average of one-third of a man each; and the rest of that million, amounting in the aggregate to the appalling figure of nine hundred and eighty-seven thousand six hundred and thirty-one corpses, die naturally in their beds!

You will excuse me from taking any more chances on those beds. The railroads are good enough for me.

And my advice to all people is, Don't stay at home any more than you can help; but when you have *got* to stay at home a while, buy a package of those insurance tickets and sit up nights. You cannot be too cautious.

[One can see now why I answered that ticket-agent in the manner recorded at the top of this sketch.]

The moral of this composition is, that thoughtless people grumble more than is fair about railroad management in the United States. When we consider that every day and night of the year full fourteen thousand railway trains of various kinds, freighted with life and armed with death, go thundering over the land, the marvel is, *not* that they kill three hundred human beings in a twelvemonth, but that they do not kill three hundred times three hundred!

PORTRAIT OF KING WILLIAM III

I NEVER can look at those periodical portraits in
The Galaxy magazine without feeling a wild, tem-
pestuous ambition to be an artist. I have seen thousands and thousands of pictures in my time—acres of
them here and leagues of them in the galleries of Europe—but never any that moved me as these portraits do.

There is the portrait of Monsignore Capel in the
November number, now *could* anything be sweeter
than that? And there was Bismarck's, in the October
number; who can look at that without being purer
and stronger and nobler for it? And Thurlow Weed's
picture in the September number; I would not have
died without seeing that, no, not for anything this
world can give. But look back still further and recall
my own likeness as printed in the August number; if
I had been in my grave a thousand years when that
appeared, I would have got up and visited the artist.

I sleep with all these portraits under my pillow
every night, so that I can go on studying them as soon
as the day dawns in the morning. I know them all
as thoroughly as if I had made them myself; I know

every line and mark about them. Sometimes when
company are present I shuffle the portraits all up together, and then pick them out one by one and call
their names, without referring to the printing at the
bottom. I seldom make a mistake—never, when I
am calm.

I have had the portraits framed for a long time,
waiting till my aunt gets everything ready for hanging them up in the parlor. But first one thing and
then another interferes, and so the thing is delayed.
Once she said they would have more of the peculiar
kind of light they needed in the attic. The old simpleton! it is as dark as a tomb up there. But she does
not know anything about art, and so she has no
reverence for it. When I showed her my "Map of
the Fortifications of Paris," she said it was rubbish.

Well, from nursing those portraits so long, I have
come at last to have a perfect infatuation for art. I
have a teacher now, and my enthusiasm continually
and tumultuously grows, as I learn to use with more
and more facility the pencil, brush, and graver. I
am studying under De Mellville, the house and portrait
painter. [His name was Smith when he lived West.]
He does any kind of artist work a body wants, having
a genius that is universal, like Michael Angelo. Resembles that great artist, in fact. The back of his
head is like his, and he wears his hat-brim tilted down
on his nose to expose it.

I have been studying under De Mellville several

months now. The first month I painted fences, and
gave general satisfaction. The next month I whitewashed a barn. The third, I was doing tin roofs;
the fourth, common signs; the fifth, statuary to stand
before cigar shops. This present month is only the
sixth, and I am already in portraits!

The humble offering which accompanies these remarks — the portrait of his Majesty William III.,
King of Prussia—is my fifth attempt in portraits, and
my greatest success. It has received unbounded
praise from all classes of the community, but that
which gratifies me most is the frequent and cordial
verdict that it resembles the *Galaxy* portraits. Those
were my first love, my earliest admiration, the original
source and incentive of my art-ambition. Whatever
I am in Art to-day, I owe to these portraits. I ask
no credit for myself—I deserve none. And I never
take any, either. Many a stranger has come to my
exhibition (for I have had my portrait of King William
on exhibition at one dollar a ticket), and would have
gone away blessing *me*, if I had let him, but I never
did. I always stated where I got the idea.

King William wears large bushy side-whiskers, and
some critics have thought that this portrait would be
more complete if they were added. But it was not
possible. There was not room for side-whiskers and
epaulettes both, and so I let the whiskers go, and put
in the epaulettes, for the sake of style. That thing
on his hat is an eagle. The Prussian eagle—it is a
national emblem. When I say hat I mean helmet;

WILLIAM III.,
King of Prussia.

but it seems impossible to make a picture oi a helmet that a body can have confidence in.

I wish kind friends everywhere would aid me in my endeavor to attract a little attention to the *Galaxy* portraits. I feel persuaded it can be accomplished, if the course to be pursued be chosen with judgment. I write for that magazine all the time, and so do many abler men, and if I can get these portraits into universal favor, it is all I ask; the reading matter will take care of itself.

COMMENDATIONS OF THE PORTRAIT

There is nothing like it in the Vatican.　Pius IX.

It has none of that vagueness, that dreamy spirituality about it, which many of the first critics of Arkansas have objected to in the Murillo school of Art.

Ruskin.

The expression is very interesting.　J. W. Titian.

(Keeps a macaroni store in Venice, at the old family stand.)

It is the neatest thing in still life I have seen for years.　Rosa Bonheur.

The smile may be almost called unique.　Bismarck.

I never saw such character portrayed in a pictured face before.　De Mellville.

There is a benignant simplicity about the execution of this work which warms the heart towards it as much, full as much, as it fascinates the eye.　Landseer.

One cannot see it without longing to contemplate the artist.   FREDERICK WILLIAM.

Send me the entire edition—together with the plate and the original portrait—and name your own price. And—would you like to come over and stay a while with Napoleon at Wilhelmshöhe? It shall not cost you a cent.   WILLIAM III.

DOES THE RACE OF MAN LOVE A LORD?

Often a quite assified remark becomes sanctified by use and petrified by custom; it is then a permanency, its term of activity a geologic period.

THE day after the arrival of Prince Henry I met an English friend, and he rubbed his hands and broke out with a remark that was charged to the brim with joy—joy that was evidently a pleasant salve to an old sore place:

"Many a time I've had to listen without retort to an old saying that is irritatingly true, and until now seemed to offer no chance for a return jibe: 'An Englishman does dearly love a lord'; but after this I shall talk back, and say 'How about the Americans?'"

It is a curious thing, the currency that an idiotic saying can get. The man that first says it thinks he has made a discovery. The man he says it to, thinks the same. It departs on its travels, is received everywhere with admiring acceptance, and not only as a piece of rare and acute observation, but as being exhaustively true and profoundly wise; and so it

presently takes its place in the world's list of recognized and established wisdoms, and after that no
one thinks of examining it to see whether it is really
entitled to its high honors or not. I call to mind
instances of this in two well - established proverbs,
whose dulness is not surpassed by the one about the
Englishman and his love for a lord: one of them
records the American's Adoration of the Almighty
Dollar, the other the American millionaire-girl's ambition to trade cash for a title, with a husband
thrown in.

It isn't merely the American that adores the Almighty Dollar, it is the human race. The human
race has always adored the hatful of shells, or the
bale of calico, or the half - bushel of brass rings, or
the handful of steel fish-hooks, or the houseful of
black wives, or the zareba full of cattle, or the two
score camels and asses, or the factory, or the farm,
or the block of buildings, or the railroad bonds, or
the bank stock, or the hoarded cash, or—anything
that stands for wealth and consideration and independence, and can secure to the possessor that most
precious of all things, another man's envy. It was
a dull person that invented the idea that the American's devotion to the dollar is more strenuous than
another's.

Rich American girls do buy titles, but they did not
invent that idea; it had been worn threadbare several
hundred centuries before America was discovered.
European girls still exploit it as briskly as ever; and,

when a title is not to be had for the money in hand,
they buy the husband without it. They must put up
the "dot," or there is no trade. The commercializa-
tion of brides is substantially universal, except in
America. It exists with us, to some little extent, but
in no degree approaching a custom.

"The Englishman dearly loves a lord."

What is the soul and source of his love? I think
the thing could be more correctly worded:

"The human race dearly envies a lord."

That is to say, it envies the lord's place. Why?
On two accounts, I think: its Power and its Conspicuousness.

Where Conspicuousness carries with it a Power
which, by the light of our own observation and experience, we are able to measure and comprehend, I
think our envy of the possessor is as deep and as
passionate as is that of any other nation. No one
can care less for a lord than the backwoodsman, who
has had no personal contact with lords and has seldom heard them spoken of; but I will not allow that
any Englishman has a profounder envy of a lord
than has the average American who has lived long
years in a European capital and fully learned how
immense is the position the lord occupies.

Of any ten thousand Americans who eagerly gather,
at vast inconvenience, to get a glimpse of Prince
Henry, all but a couple of hundred will be there out
of an immense curiosity; they are burning up with
desire to see a personage who is so much talked about.

They envy him; but it is Conspicuousness they envy
mainly, not the Power that is lodged in his royal
quality and position, for they have but a vague and
spectral knowledge and appreciation of that; through
their environment and associations they have been
accustomed to regard such things lightly, and as not
being very real; consequently, they are not able to
value them enough to consumingly envy them.

But, whenever an American (or other human being)
is in the presence, for the first time, of a combination of great Power and Conspicuousness which he
thoroughly understands and appreciates, his eager
curiosity and pleasure will be well-sodden with that
other passion—envy—whether he suspect it or not.
At any time, on any day, in any part of America,
you can confer a happiness upon any passing stranger
by calling his attention to any other passing stranger
and saying:

"Do you see that gentleman going along there?
It is Mr. Rockefeller."

Watch his eye. It is a combination of power and
conspicuousness which the man understands.

When we understand rank, we always like to rub
against it. When a man is conspicuous, we always
want to see him. Also, if he will pay us an attention
we will manage to remember it. Also, we will mention it now and then, casually; sometimes to a friend,
or if a friend is not handy, we will make out with a
stranger.

Well, then, what is rank, and what is conspicuousness? At once we think of kings and aristocracies, and of world-wide celebrities in soldiership, the arts, letters, etc., and we stop there. But that is a mistake. Rank holds its court and receives its homage on every round of the ladder, from the emperor down to the rat-catcher; and distinction, also, exists on every round of the ladder, and commands its due of deference and envy.

To worship rank and distinction is the dear and valued privilege of all the human race, and it is freely and joyfully exercised in democracies as well as in monarchies—and even, to some extent, among those creatures whom we impertinently call the Lower Animals. For even they have some poor little vanities and foibles, though in this matter they are paupers as compared to us.

A Chinese Emperor has the worship of his four hundred millions of subjects, but the rest of the world is indifferent to him. A Christian Emperor has the worship of his subjects and of a large part of the Christian world outside of his dominions; but he is a matter of indifference to all China. A king, class A, has an extensive worship; a king, class B, has a less extensive worship; class C, class D, class E get a steadily diminishing share of worship; class L (Sultan of Zanzibar), class P (Sultan of Sulu), and class W (half-king of Samoa), get no worship at all outside their own little patch of sovereignty.

Take the distinguished people along down. Each has his group of homage-payers. In the navy, there

are many groups; they start with the Secretary and
the Admiral, and go down to the quartermaster—
and below; for there will be groups among the sailors,
and each of these groups will have a tar who is distinguished for his battles, or his strength, or his
daring, or his profanity, and is admired and envied
by his group. The same with the army; the same
with the literary and journalistic craft; the publishing craft; the cod-fishery craft; Standard Oil; U. S.
Steel; the class A hotel—and the rest of the alphabet
in that line; the class A prize-fighter—and the rest of
the alphabet in his line—clear down to the lowest
and obscurest six-boy gang of little gamins, with its
one boy that can thrash the rest, and to whom he is
king of Samoa, bottom of the royal race, but looked
up to with a most ardent admiration and envy.

There is something pathetic, and funny, and pretty,
about this human race's fondness for contact with
power and distinction, and for the reflected glory it
gets out of it. The king, class A, is happy in the
state banquet and the military show which the
emperor provides for him, and he goes home and
gathers the queen and the princelings around him in
the privacy of the spare room, and tells them all
about it, and says:

"His Imperial Majesty put his hand on my shoulder
in the most friendly way—just as friendly and familiar, oh, you can't imagine it!—and everybody *seeing*
him do it; charming, perfectly charming!"

The king, class G, is happy in the cold collation

and the police-parade provided for him by the king, class B, and goes home and tells the family all about it, and says:

"And His Majesty took me into his own private cabinet for a smoke and a chat, and there we sat just as sociable, and talking away and laughing and chatting, just the same as if we had been born in the same bunk; and all the servants in the anteroom could see us doing it! Oh, it was too lovely for anything!"

The king, class Q, is happy in the modest entertainment furnished him by the king, class M, and goes home and tells the household about it, and is as grateful and joyful over it as were his predecessors in the gaudier attentions that had fallen to their larger lot.

Emperors, kings, artisans, peasants, big people, little people—at bottom we are all alike and all the same; all just alike on the inside, and when our clothes are off, nobody can tell which of us is which. We are unanimous in the pride we take in good and genuine compliments paid us, in distinctions conferred upon us, in attentions shown us. There is not one of us, from the emperor down, but is made like that. Do I mean attentions shown us by the great? No, I mean simply flattering attentions, let them come whence they may. We despise no source that can pay us a pleasing attention—there is no source that is humble enough for that. You have heard a dear little girl say of a frowzy and disreputable dog: "He

came right to me and let me pat him on the head, and
he wouldn't let the others touch him!" and you have
seen her eyes dance with pride in that high distinction. You have often seen that. If the child were
a princess, would that random dog be able to confer
the like glory upon her with his pretty compliment?
Yes; and even in her mature life and seated upon a
throne, she would still remember it, still recall it, still
speak of it with frank satisfaction. That charming
and lovable German princess and poet, Carmen Sylva,
Queen of Roumania, remembers yet that the flowers
of the woods and fields "talked to her" when she was
a girl, and she sets it down in her latest book; and
that the squirrels conferred upon her and her father
the valued compliment of not being afraid of them;
and "once one of them, holding a nut between its
sharp little teeth, ran right up against my father"—
it has the very note of "He came right to me and let
me pat him on the head"—"and when it saw itself
reflected in his boot it was very much surprised, and
stopped for a long time to contemplate itself in the
polished leather"—then it went its way. And the
birds! she still remembers with pride that "they
came boldly into my room," when she had neglected
her "duty" and put no food on the window-sill for
them; she knew all the wild birds, and forgets the
royal crown on her head to remember with pride that
they knew her; also that the wasp and the bee were
personal friends of hers, and never forgot that gracious
relationship to her injury: "never have I been stung

by a wasp or a bee." And here is that proud note again that sings in that little child's elation in being singled out, among all the company of children, for the random dog's honor-conferring attentions. "Even in the very worst summer for wasps, when, in lunching out-of-doors, our table was covered with them and every one else was stung, they never hurt me."

When a queen whose qualities of mind and heart and character are able to add distinction to so distinguished a place as a throne, remembers with grateful exultation, after thirty years, honors and distinctions conferred upon her by the humble, wild creatures of the forest, we are helped to realize that complimentary attentions, homage, distinctions, are of no caste, but are above all caste — that they are a nobility-conferring power apart.

We all like these things. When the gate-guard at the railway station passes me through unchallenged and examines other people's tickets, I feel as the king, class A, felt when the emperor put the imperial hand on his shoulder, "everybody seeing him do it"; and as the child felt when the random dog allowed her to pat his head and ostracized the others; and as the princess felt when the wasps spared her and stung the rest; and I felt just so, four years ago in Vienna (and remember it yet), when the helmeted police shut me off, with fifty others, from a street which the Emperor was to pass through, and the captain of the squad turned and saw the situation and said indignantly to that guard:

"Can't you see it is the Herr Mark Twain? Let him through!"

It was four years ago; but it will be four hundred before I forget the wind of self-complacency that rose in me, and strained my buttons when I marked the deference for me evoked in the faces of my fellow-rabble, and noted, mingled with it, a puzzled and resentful expression which said, as plainly as speech could have worded it: "And who in the nation is the Herr Mark Twain *um Gotteswillen?*"

How many times in your life have you heard this boastful remark:

"I stood as close to him as I am to you; I could have put out my hand and touched him."

We have all heard it many and many a time. It was a proud distinction to be able to say those words. It brought envy to the speaker, a kind of glory; and he basked in it and was happy through all his veins. And who was it he stood so close to? The answer would cover all the grades. Sometimes it was a king; sometimes it was a renowned highwayman; sometimes it was an unknown man killed in an extraordinary way and made suddenly famous by it; always it was a person who was for the moment the subject of public interest—the public interest of a nation, maybe only the public interest of a village.

"I was there, and I saw it myself." That is a common and envy-compelling remark. It can refer to a battle; to a hanging; to a coronation, to the killing of Jumbo by the railway train; to the arrival

of Jenny Lind at the Battery; to the meeting of the
President and Prince Henry; to the chase of a murderous maniac; to the disaster in the tunnel; to the
explosion in the subway; to a remarkable dog-fight;
to a village church struck by lightning. It will be
said, more or less casually, by everybody in America
who has seen Prince Henry do anything, or try to.
The man who was absent and didn't see him do anything, will scoff. It is his privilege; and he can make
capital out of it, too; he will seem, even to himself,
to be different from other Americans, and better.
As his opinion of his superior Americanism grows, and
swells, and concentrates and coagulates, he will go
further and try to belittle the distinction of those
that saw the Prince do things, and will spoil their
pleasure in it if he can. My life has been embittered
by that kind of persons. If you are able to tell of a
special distinction that has fallen to your lot, it
gravels them; they cannot bear it; and they try to
make believe that the thing you took for a special
distinction was nothing of the kind and was meant
in quite another way. Once I was received in private
audience by an emperor. Last week I was telling a
jealous person about it, and I could see him wince
under it, see it bite, see him suffer. I revealed the
whole episode to him with considerable elaboration
and nice attention to detail. When I was through,
he asked me what had impressed me most. I said:

"His Majesty's delicacy. They told me to be sure
and back out from the presence, and find the door-

knob as best I could; it was not allowable to face
around.   Now the Emperor knew it would be a difficult ordeal for me, because of lack of practice; and
so, when it was time to part, he turned, with exceed-
ing delicacy, and pretended to fumble with things on
his desk, so that I could get out in my own way,
without his seeing me."

It went home! It was vitriol! I saw the envy
and disgruntlement rise in the man's face; he couldn't
keep it down. I saw him trying to fix up something
in his mind to take the bloom off that distinction. I
enjoyed that, for I judged that he had his work cut
out for him. He struggled along inwardly for quite
a while; then he said, with the manner of a person
who has to say something and hasn't anything rele-
vant to say:

"You said he had a handful of special-brand cigars
lying on the table?"

"Yes; I never saw anything to match them."

I had him again. He had to fumble around in his
mind as much as another minute before he could play;
then he said in as mean a way as I ever heard a person
say anything:

"He could have been counting the cigars, you
know."

I cannot endure a man like that. It is nothing to
him how unkind he is, so long as he takes the bloom
off. It is all he cares for.

"An Englishman (or other human being) does
dearly love a lord," (or other conspicuous person).

It includes us all. We love to be noticed by the conspicuous person; we love to be associated with such, or with a conspicuous event, even in a seventh-rate fashion, even in a forty-seventh, if we cannot do better. This accounts for some of our curious tastes in mementos. It accounts for the large private trade in the Prince of Wales's hair, which chambermaids were able to drive in that article of commerce when the Prince made the tour of the world in the long ago —hair which probably did not always come from his brush, since enough of it was marketed to refurnish a bald comet; it accounts for the fact that the rope which lynches a negro in the presence of ten thousand Christian spectators is saleable five minutes later at two dollars an inch; it accounts for the mournful fact that a royal personage does not venture to wear buttons on his coat in public.

We do love a lord—and by that term I mean any person whose situation is higher than our own. The lord of a group, for instance: a group of peers, a group of millionaires, a group of hoodlums, a group of sailors, a group of newsboys, a group of saloon politicians, a group of college girls. No royal person has ever been the object of a more delirious loyalty and slavish adoration than is paid by the vast Tammany herd to its squalid idol of Wantage. There is not a bifurcated animal in that menagerie that would not be proud to appear in a newspaper-picture in his company. At the same time, there are some in that organization who would scoff at the people who have been daily pictured in company with Prince Henry, and would say vigorously that *they* would not consent to be photographed with him — a statement which would not be true in any instance. There are hundreds of people in America who would frankly say to you that they would not be proud to be photographed in a group with the Prince, if invited; and some of these unthinking people would believe it when they said it; yet in no instance would it be true. We have a large population, but we have not a large enough one, by several millions, to furnish that man. He has not yet been begotten, and in fact he is not begettable.

You may take any of the printed groups, and there isn't a person in it who isn't visibly glad to be there; there isn't a person in the dim background who isn't visibly trying to be vivid; if it is a crowd of ten thousand — ten thousand proud, untamed democrats, horny-handed sons of toil and of politics, and fliers of the eagle—there isn't one who isn't conscious of the camera, there isn't one who is trying to keep out of range, there isn't one who isn't plainly meditating a purchase of the paper in the morning, with the intention of hunting himself out in the picture and of framing and keeping it if he shall find so much of his person in it as his starboard ear.

We all love to get some of the drippings of Conspicuousness, and we will put up with a single, humble drip, if we can't get any more. We may pretend otherwise, in conversation; but we can't pretend it

19

to ourselves privately—and we don't. We do confess
in public that we are the noblest work of God, being
moved to it by long habit, and teaching, and supersti-
tion; but deep down in the secret places of our souls
we recognize that, if we *are* the noblest work, the less
said about it the better.

We of the North poke fun at the South for its fondness for titles—a fondness for titles pure and simple,
regardless of whether they are genuine or pinchbeck.
We forget that whatever a Southerner likes the rest
of the human race likes, and that there is no law of
predilection lodged in one people that is absent from
another people. There is no variety in the human
race. We are all children, all children of the one
Adam, and we love toys. We can soon acquire that
Southern disease if some one will give it a start. It
already has a start, in fact. I have been personally
acquainted with over eighty-four thousand persons
who, at one time or another in their lives, have served
for a year or two on the staffs of our multitudinous
governors, and through that fatality have been generals temporarily, and colonels temporarily, and judge-
advocates temporarily; but I have known only nine
among them who could be hired to let the title go
when it ceased to be legitimate. I know thousands
and thousands of governors who ceased to be governors
away back in the last century; but I am acquainted
with only three who would answer your letter if you
failed to call them "Governor" in it. I know acres
and acres of men who have done time in a legislature

in prehistoric days, but among them is not half an acre whose resentment you would not raise if you addressed them as "Mr." instead of "Hon." The first thing a legislature does is to convene in an impressive legislative attitude, and get itself photographed. Each member frames his copy and takes it to the woods and hangs it up in the most aggressively conspicuous place in his house; and if you visit the house and fail to inquire what that accumulation is, the conversation will be brought around to it by that aforetime legislator, and he will show you a figure in it which in the course of years he has almost obliterated with the smut of his finger-marks, and say with a solemn joy, "It's me!"

Have you ever seen a country Congressman enter the hotel breakfast-room in Washington with his letters?—and sit at his table and let on to read them? —and wrinkle his brows and frown statesman-like?— keeping a furtive watch-out over his glasses all the while to see if he is being observed and admired?— those same old letters which he fetches in every morning? Have you seen it? Have you seen him show off? It is *the* sight of the national capital. Except one; a pathetic one. That is the ex-Congressman: the poor fellow whose life has been ruined by a two-year taste of glory and of fictitious consequence; who has been superseded, and ought to take his heartbreak home and hide it, but cannot tear himself away from the scene of his lost little grandeur; and so he lingers, and still lingers, year after year, unconsidered, sometimes snubbed, ashamed of his fallen estate, and valiantly trying to look otherwise; dreary and depressed, but counterfeiting breeziness and gayety, hailing with chummy familiarity, which is not always welcomed, the more-fortunates who are still in place and were once his mates. Have you seen him? He clings piteously to the one little shred that is left of his departed distinction—the "privilege of the floor"; and works it hard and gets what he can out of it. That is the saddest figure I know of.

Yes, we do so love our little distinctions! And then we loftily scoff at a Prince for enjoying his larger ones; forgetting that if we only had his chance—ah! "Senator" is not a legitimate title. A Senator has no more right to be addressed by it than have you or I; but, in the several State capitals and in Washington, there are five thousand Senators who take very kindly to that fiction, and who purr gratefully when you call them by it—which you may do quite unrebuked. Then those same Senators smile at the self-constructed majors and generals and judges of the South!

Indeed, we do love our distinctions, get them how we may. And we work them for all they are worth. In prayer we call ourselves "worms of the dust," but it is only on a sort of tacit understanding that the remark shall not be taken at par. *We*—worms of the dust! Oh, no, we are not that. Except in fact; and we do not deal much in fact when we are contemplating ourselves.

As a race, we do certainly love a lord—let him be

Croker, or a duke, or a prize-fighter, or whatever other personage shall chance to be the head of our group. Many years ago, I saw a greasy youth in overalls standing by the *Herald* office, with an expectant look in his face. Soon a large man passed out, and gave him a pat on the shoulder. That was what the boy was waiting for—the large man's notice. The pat made him proud and happy, and the exultation inside of him shone out through his eyes; and his mates were there to see the pat and envy it and wish they could have that glory. The boy belonged down cellar in the press-room, the large man was king of the upper floors, foreman of the composing-room. The light in the boy's face was worship, the foreman was his lord, head of his group. The pat was an accolade. It was as precious to the boy as it would have been if he had been an aristocrat's son and the accolade had been delivered by his sovereign with a sword. The quintessence of the honor was all there; there was no difference in values; in truth there was no difference present except an artificial one—clothes.

All the human race loves a lord—that is, it loves to look upon or be noticed by the possessor of Power or Conspicuousness; and sometimes animals, born to better things and higher ideals, descend to man's level in this matter. In the Jardin des Plantes I have seen a cat that was so vain of being the personal friend of an elephant that I was ashamed of her.

EVE'S DIARY

TRANSLATED FROM THE ORIGINAL

SATURDAY. — I am almost a whole day old, now. I arrived yesterday. That is as it seems to me. And it must be so, for if there was a day-before-yesterday I was not there when it happened, or I should remember it. It could be, of course, that it did happen, and that I was not noticing. Very well; I will be very watchful, now, and if any day-before-yesterdays happen I will make a note of it. It will be best to start right and not let the record get confused, for some instinct tells me that these details are going to be important to the historian some day. For I feel like an experiment, I feel exactly like an experiment; it would be impossible for a person to feel more like an experiment than I do, and so I am coming to feel convinced that that is what I *am*—an experiment; just an experiment, and nothing more.

Then if I am an experiment, am I the whole of it? No, I think not; I think the rest of it is part of it. I am the main part of it, but I think the rest of it has its share in the matter. Is my position assured, or do I have to watch it and take care of it? The latter, perhaps. Some instinct tells me that eternal vigilance is the price of supremacy. [That is a good phrase, I think, for one so young.]

Everything looks better to-day than it did yesterday. In the rush of finishing up yesterday, the mountains were left in a ragged condition, and some of the plains were so cluttered with rubbish and remnants that the aspects were quite distressing. Noble and beautiful works of art should not be subjected to haste; and this majestic new world is indeed a most noble and beautiful work. And certainly marvellously near to being perfect, notwithstanding the shortness of the time. There are too many stars in some places and not enough in others, but that can be remedied presently, no doubt. The moon got loose last night, and slid down and fell out of the scheme—a very great loss; it breaks my heart to think of it. There isn't another thing among the ornaments and decorations that is comparable to it for beauty and finish. It should have been fastened better. If we can only get it back again—

But of course there is no telling where it went to. And besides, whoever gets it will hide it; I know it because I would do it myself. I believe I can be honest in all other matters, but I already begin to realize that the core and centre of my nature is love of the beautiful, a passion for the beautiful, and that it would not be safe to trust me with a moon that

belonged to another person and that person didn't
know I had it. I could give up a moon that I found
in the daytime, because I should be afraid some one
was looking; but if I found it in the dark, I am sure
I should find some kind of an excuse for not saying
anything about it. For I do love moons, they are
so pretty and so romantic. I wish we had five or
six; I would never go to bed; I should never get
tired lying on the moss-bank and looking up at them.

Stars are good, too. I wish I could get some to
put in my hair. But I suppose I never can. You
would be surprised to find how far off they are, for
they do not look it. When they first showed, last
night, I tried to knock some down with a pole, but it
didn't reach, which astonished me; then I tried clods
till I was all tired out, but I never got one. It was
because I am left-handed and cannot throw good.
Even when I aimed at the one I wasn't after I
couldn't hit the other one, though I did make some
close shots, for I saw the black blot of the clod sail
right into the midst of the golden clusters forty or fifty
times, just barely missing them, and if I could have
held out a little longer maybe I could have got one.

So I cried a little, which was natural, I suppose,
for one of my age, and after I was rested I got a
basket and started for a place on the extreme rim of
the circle, where the stars were close to the ground
and I could get them with my hands, which would
be better, anyway, because I could gather them ten-
derly then, and not break them. But it was farther

than I thought, and at last I had to give it up; I was so tired I couldn't drag my feet another step; and besides, they were sore and hurt me very much.

I couldn't get back home; it was too far and turning cold; but I found some tigers and nestled in among them and was most adorably comfortable, and their breath was sweet and pleasant, because they live on strawberries. I had never seen a tiger before, but I knew them in a minute by the stripes. If I could have one of those skins, it would make a lovely gown.

To-day I am getting better ideas about distances. I was so eager to get hold of every pretty thing that I giddily grabbed for it, sometimes when it was too far off, and sometimes when it was but six inches away but seemed a foot—alas, with thorns between! I learned a lesson; also I made an axiom, all out of my own head—my very first one: *The scratched Experiment shuns the thorn.* I think it is a very good one for one so young.

I followed the other Experiment around, yesterday afternoon, at a distance, to see what it might be for, if I could. But I was not able to make out. I think it is a man. I had never seen a man, but it looked like one, and I feel sure that that is what it is. I realize that I feel more curiosity about it than about any of the other reptiles. If it is a reptile, and I suppose it is; for it has frowsy hair and blue eyes, and looks like a reptile. It has no hips; it tapers like a carrot; when it stands, it spreads itself apart like a derrick; so I think it is a reptile, though it may be architecture.

I was afraid of it at first, and started to run every time it turned around, for I thought it was going to chase me; but by-and-by I found it was only trying to get away, so after that I was not timid any more, but tracked it along, several hours, about twenty yards behind, which made it nervous and unhappy. At last it was a good deal worried, and climbed a tree. I waited a good while, then gave it up and went home.

To-day the same thing over. I've got it up the tree again.

Sunday.—It is up there yet. Resting, apparently. But that is a subterfuge: Sunday isn't the day of rest; Saturday is appointed for that. It looks to me like a creature that is more interested in resting than in anything else. It would tire me to rest so much. It tires me just to sit around and watch the tree. I do wonder what it is for; I never see it do anything.

They returned the moon last night, and I was *so* happy! I think it is very honest of them. It slid down and fell off again, but I was not distressed; there is no need to worry when one has that kind of neighbors; they will fetch it back. I wish I could do something to show my appreciation. I would like to send them some stars, for we have more than we can use. I mean I, not we, for I can see that the reptile cares nothing for such things.

It has low tastes, and is not kind.   When I went there yesterday evening in the gloaming it had crept down and was trying to catch the little speckled fishes that play in the pool, and I had to clod it to make it go up the tree again and let them alone.   I wonder if *that* is what it is for?   Hasn't it any heart? Hasn't it any compassion for those little creatures? Can it be that it was designed and manufactured for such ungentle work?   It has the look of it.   One of the clods took it back of the ear, and it used language.   It gave me a thrill, for it was the first time I had ever heard speech, except my own.   I did not understand the words, but they seemed expressive.

When I found it could talk I felt a new interest in it, for I love to talk; I talk, all day, and in my sleep, too, and I am very interesting, but if I had another to talk to I could be twice as interesting, and would never stop, if desired.

If this reptile is a man, it isn't an *it*, is it?   That wouldn't be grammatical, would it?   I think it would be *he*.   I think so.   In that case one would parse it thus: nominative, *he;* dative, *him;* possessive, *his'n*.   Well, I will consider it a man and call it he until it turns out to be something else.   This will be handier than having so many uncertainties.

Next week Sunday.—All the week I tagged around atter him and tried to get acquainted.   I had to do the talking, because he was shy, but I didn't mind it.   He seemed pleased to have me around, and I

used the sociable "we" a good deal, because it
seemed to flatter him to be included.

Wednesday.—We are getting along very well indeed, now, and getting better and better acquainted.
He does not try to avoid me any more, which is a
good sign, and shows that he likes to have me with
him.   That pleases me, and I study to be useful to
him in every way I can, so as to increase his regard.
During the last day or two I have taken all the work
of naming things off his hands, and this has been a
great relief to him, for he has no gift in that line, and
is evidently very grateful.   He can't think of a rational name to save him, but I do not let him see
that I am aware of his defect.   Whenever a new
creature comes along I name it before he has time
to expose himself by an awkward silence.   In this
way I have saved him many embarrassments.   I
have no defect like his.   The minute I set eyes on
an animal I know what it is.   I don't have to reflect
a moment; the right name comes out instantly, just
as if it were an inspiration, as no doubt it is, for I
am sure it wasn't in me half a minute before.   I
seem to know just by the shape of the creature and
the way it acts what animal it is.

When the dodo came along he thought it was a
wild-cat — I saw it in his eye.   But I saved him.
And I was careful not to do it in a way that could·
hurt his pride.   I just spoke up in a quite natural
way of pleased surprise, and not as if I was **dreaming**

of conveying information, and said, "Well, I do de-
clare, if there isn't the dodo!" I explained—without seeming to be explaining—how I knew it for a
dodo, and although I thought maybe he was a little
piqued that I knew the creature when he didn't,
it was quite evident that he admired me. That
was very agreeable, and I thought of it more than
once with gratification before I slept. How little a
thing can make us happy when we feel that we have
earned it.

Thursday.—My first sorrow. Yesterday he avoided me and seemed to wish I would not talk to him.
I could not believe it, and thought there was some
mistake, for I loved to be with him, and loved to
hear him talk, and so how could it be that he could
feel unkind towards me when I had not done anything? But at last it seemed true, so I went away
and sat lonely in the place where I first saw him the
morning that we were made and I did not know
what he was and was indifferent about him; but now
it was a mournful place, and every little thing spoke
of him, and my heart was very sore. I did not
know why very clearly, for it was a new feeling; I
had not experienced it before, and it was all a mystery, and I could not make it out.

But when night came I could not bear the lone-
someness, and went to the new shelter which he has
built, to ask him what I had done that was wrong
and how I could mend it and get back his kindness

again; but he put me out in the rain, and it was my first sorrow.

Sunday.—It is pleasant again, now, and I am happy; but those were heavy days; I do not think of them when I can help it.

I tried to get him some of those apples, but I cannot learn to throw straight. I failed, but I think the good intention pleased him. They are forbidden, and he says I shall come to harm; but so I come to harm through pleasing him, why shall I care for that harm?

Monday.—This morning I told him my name, hoping it would interest him. But he did not care for it. It is strange. If he should tell me his name, I would care. I think it would be pleasanter in my ears than any other sound.

He talks very little. Perhaps it is because he is not bright, and is sensitive about it and wishes to conceal it. It is such a pity that he should feel so, for brightness is nothing; it is in the heart that the values lie. I wish I could make him understand that a loving good heart is riches, and riches enough, and that without it intellect is poverty.

Although he talks so little he has quite a considerable vocabulary. This morning he used a surprisingly good word. He evidently recognized, himself, that it was a good one, for he worked it in twice afterwards, casually. It was not good casual art, still it showed that he possesses a certain quality of perception. Without a doubt that seed can be made to grow, if cultivated.

Where did he get that word? I do not think I have ever used it.

No, he took no interest in my name. I tried to hide my disappointment, but I suppose I did not succeed. I went away and sat on the moss-bank with my feet in the water. It is where I go when I hunger for companionship, some one to look at, some one to talk to. It is not enough—that lovely white body painted there in the pool—but it is something, and something is better than utter loneliness. It talks when I talk; it is sad when I am sad; it comforts me with its sympathy; it says, "Do not be downhearted, you poor friendless girl; I will be your friend." It *is* a good friend to me, and my only one; it is my sister.

That first time that she forsook me! ah, I shall never forget that—never, never. My heart was lead in my body! I said, "She was all I had, and now she is gone!" In my despair I said, "Break, my heart; I cannot bear my life any more!" and hid my face in my hands, and there was no solace for me. And when I took them away, after a little, there she was again, white and shining and beautiful, and I sprang into her arms!

That was perfect happiness; I had known happiness before, but it was not like this, which was ecstasy. I never doubted her afterwards. Sometimes she stayed away—maybe an hour, maybe al-

most the whole day, but I waited and did not doubt;
I said, "She is busy, or she is gone a journey, but
she will come." And it was so: she always did. At
night she would not come if it was dark, for she was
a timid little thing; but if there was a moon she
would come. I am not afraid of the dark, but she is
younger than I am; she was born after I was. Many
and many are the visits I have paid her; she is my
comfort and my refuge when my life is hard—and it
is mainly that.

Tuesday.—All the morning I was at work improving the estate; and I purposely kept away from him
in the hope that he would get lonely and come. But
he did not.

At noon I stopped for the day and took my recrea-
tion by flitting all about with the bees and the but-
terflies and revelling in the flowers, those beautiful
creatures that catch the smile of God out of the sky
and preserve it! I gathered them, and made them
into wreaths and garlands and clothed myself in
them while I ate my luncheon — apples, of course;
then I sat in the shade and wished and waited. But
he did not come.

But no matter. Nothing would have come of it,
for he does not care for flowers. He calls them rubbish, and cannot tell one from another, and thinks
it is superior to feel like that. He does not care for
me, he does not care for flowers, he does not care
for the painted sky at eventide—is there anything

20

he does care for, except building shacks to coop himself up in from the good clean rain, and thumping the melons, and sampling the grapes, and fingering the fruit on the trees, to see how those properties are coming along?

I laid a dry stick on the ground and tried to bore a hole in it with another one, in order to carry out a scheme that I had, and soon I got an awful fright. A thin, transparent bluish film rose out of the hole, and I dropped everything and ran! I thought it was a spirit, and I *was* so frightened! But I looked back, and it was not coming; so I leaned against a rock and rested and panted, and let my limbs go on trembling until they got steady again; then I crept warily back, alert, watching, and ready to fly if there was occasion; and when I was come near, I parted the branches of a rose-bush and peeped through—wishing the man was about, I was looking so cunning and pretty—but the sprite was gone. I went there, and there was a pinch of delicate pink dust in the hole. I put my finger in, to feel it, and said *ouch!* and took it out again. It was a cruel pain. I put my finger in my mouth; and by standing first on one foot and then the other, and grunting, I presently eased my misery; then I was full of interest, and began to examine.

I was curious to know what the pink dust was. Suddenly the name of it occurred to me, though I had never heard of it before. It was *fire!* I was as certain of it as a person could be of anything in the world. So without hesitation I named it that—fire.

I had created something that didn't exist before; I had added a new thing to the world's uncountable properties; I realized this, and was proud of my achievement, and was going to run and find him and tell him about it, thinking to raise myself in his esteem—but I reflected, and did not do it. No—he would not care for it. He would ask what it was good for, and what could I answer? for if it was not *good* for something, but only beautiful, merely beautiful—

So I sighed, and did not go. For it wasn't good for anything; it could not build a shack, it could not improve melons, it could not hurry a fruit crop; it was useless, it was a foolishness and a vanity; he would despise it and say cutting words. But to me it was not despicable; I said, "Oh, you fire, I love you, you dainty pink creature, for you are *beautiful* —and that is enough!" and was going to gather it to my breast. But refrained. Then I made another maxim out of my own head, though it was so nearly like the first one that I was afraid it was only a plagiarism: "*The burnt Experiment shuns the fire.*"

I wrought again; and when I had made a good deal of fire-dust I emptied it into a handful of dry brown grass, intending to carry it home and keep it always and play with it; but the wind struck it and it sprayed up and spat out at me fiercely, and I dropped it and ran. When I looked back the blue spirit was towering up and stretching and rolling away like a cloud, and instantly I thought of the name of it—*smoke!*—though, upon my word, I had never heard of smoke before.

Soon, brilliant yellow-and-red flares shot up through the smoke, and I named them in an instant —*flames!*—and I was right, too, though these were the very first flames that had ever been in the world. They climbed the trees, they flashed splendidly in and out of the vast and increasing volume of tumbling smoke, and I had to clap my hands and laugh and dance in my rapture, it was so new and strange and so wonderful and so beautiful!

He came running, and stopped and gazed, and said not a word for many minutes. Then he asked what it was. Ah, it was too bad that he should ask such a direct question. I had to answer it, of course, and I did. I said it was fire. If it annoyed him that I should know and he must ask, that was not my fault; I had no desire to annoy him. After a pause he asked:

"How did it come?"

Another direct question, and it also had to have a direct answer.

"I made it."

The fire was travelling farther and farther off. He went to the edge of the burned place and stood looking down, and said:

"What are these?"

"Fire-coals."

He picked up one to examine it, but changed his mind and put it down again. Then he went away. *Nothing* interests him.

But I was interested. There were ashes, gray and soft and delicate and pretty — I knew what they were at once. And the embers; I knew the embers, too. I found my apples, and raked them out, and was glad; for I am very young and my appetite is active. But I was disappointed; they were all burst open and spoiled. Spoiled apparently; but it was not so; they were better than raw ones. Fire is beautiful; some day it will be useful, I think.

Friday.—I saw him again, for a moment, last Monday at nightfall, but only for a moment. I was hoping he would praise me for trying to improve the estate, for I had meant well and had worked hard. But he was not pleased, and turned away and left me. He was also displeased on another account: I tried once more to persuade him to stop going over the Falls. That was because the fire had revealed to me a new passion—quite new, and distinctly different from love, grief, and those others which I had already discovered — *fear*. And it is horrible! — I wish I had never discovered it; it gives me dark moments, it spoils my happiness, it makes me shiver and tremble and shudder. But I could not persuade him, for he has not discovered fear yet, and so he could not understand me.

Extract from Adam's Diary

Perhaps I ought to remember that she is very young, a mere girl, and make allowances. She is all interest, eagerness, vivacity, the world is to her a charm, a wonder, a mystery, a joy; she can't speak for delight when she finds a new flower, she must pet it and caress it and smell it and talk to it, and pour out endearing names upon it. And she is color-mad: brown rocks, yellow sand, gray moss, green foliage, blue sky; the pearl of the dawn, the purple shadows on the mountains, the golden islands floating in crimson seas at sunset, the pallid moon sailing through the shredded cloud-rack, the star-jewels glittering in the wastes of space—none of them is of any practical value, so far as I can see, but because they have color and majesty, that is enough for her, and she loses her mind over them. If she could quiet down and keep still a couple of minutes at a time, it would be a reposeful spectacle. In that case I think I could enjoy looking at her; indeed I am sure I could, for I am coming to realize that she is a quite remarkably comely creature — lithe, slender, trim, rounded, shapely, nimble, graceful; and once when she was standing marble-white and sun-drenched on a bowlder, with her young head tilted back and her hand shading her eyes, watching the flight of a bird in the sky, I recognized that she was beautiful.

Monday noon.—If there is anything on the planet that she is not interested in it is not in my list. There are animals that I am indifferent to, but it is not so with her. She has no discrimination, she takes to all of them, she thinks they are all treasures, every new one is welcome.

When the mighty brontosaurus came striding into camp, she regarded it as an acquisition, I considered it a calamity; that is a good sample of the lack of harmony that prevails in our views of things. She wanted to domesticate it, I wanted to make it a present of the homestead and move out. She believed it could be tamed by kind treatment and would be a good pet; I said a pet twenty-one feet high and eighty-four feet long would be no proper thing to have about the place, because, even with the best intentions and without meaning any harm, it could sit down on the house and mash it, for any one could see by the look of its eye that it was absent-minded.

Still, her heart was set upon having that monster, and she couldn't give it up. She thought we could start a dairy with it, and wanted me to help her milk it; but I wouldn't; it was too risky. The sex wasn't right, and we hadn't any ladder anyway. Then she wanted to ride it, and look at the scenery. Thirty or forty feet of its tail was lying on the ground, like a fallen tree, and she thought she could climb it, but she was mistaken; when she got to the steep place it was too slick and down she came, and would have hurt herself but for me.

Was she satisfied now? No. Nothing ever satisfies her but demonstration; untested theories are not in her line, and she won't have them. It is the right spirit, I concede it; it attracts me; I feel the influence of it; if I were with her more I think I should take it up myself. Well, she had one theory remaining about this colossus: she thought that if we could tame him and make him friendly we could stand him in the river and use him for a bridge. It turned out that he was already plenty tame enough—at least as far as she was concerned—so she tried her theory, but it failed: every time she got him properly placed in the river and went ashore to cross over on him, he came out and followed her around like a pet mountain. Like the other animals. They all do that.

Friday.—Tuesday — Wednesday — Thursday — and to-day: all without seeing him. It is a long time to be alone; still, it is better to be alone than unwelcome.

I *had* to have company—I was made for it, I think—so I made friends with the animals. They are just charming, and they have the kindest disposition and the politest ways; they never look sour, they never let you feel that you are intruding, they smile at you and wag their tail, if they've got one, and they are always ready for a romp or an excursion or anything you want to propose. I think they are perfect gentlemen. All these days we have had such good times, and it hasn't been lonesome for me, ever. Lonesome! No, I should say not. Why, there's always a swarm of them around—sometimes as much as four or five acres—you can|t count them; and when you stand on a rock in the midst and look out over the furry expanse it is so mottled and splashed and gay with color and frisking sheen and sun-flash, and so rippled with stripes, that you might think it was a lake, only you know it isn't; and there's storms of sociable birds, and hurricanes of whirring wings; and when the sun strikes all that feathery commotion, you have a blazing up of all the colors you can think of, enough to put your eyes out.

We have made long excursions, and I have seen a

great deal of the world; almost all of it, I think; and so I am the first traveller, and the only one. When we are on the march, it is an imposing sight—there's nothing like it anywhere. For comfort I ride a tiger or a leopard, because it is soft and has a round back that fits me, and because they are such pretty animals; but for long distance or for scenery I ride the elephant. He hoists me up with his trunk, but I can get off myself; when we are ready to camp, he sits and I slide down the back way.

The birds and animals are all friendly to each other, and there are no disputes about anything. They all talk, and they all talk to me, but it must be a foreign language, for I cannot make out a word they say; yet they often understand me when I talk back, particularly the dog and the elephant. It makes me ashamed. It shows that they are brighter than I am, and are therefore my superiors. It annoys me, for I want to be the principal Experiment myself—and I intend to be, too.

I have learned a number of things, and am educated, now, but I wasn't at first. I was ignorant at first. At first it used to vex me because, with all my watching, I was never smart enough to be around when the water was running up-hill; but now I do not mind it. I have experimented and experimented until now I know it never does run up-hill, except in the dark. I know it does in the dark, because the pool never goes dry; which it would, of course, if the water didn't come back in the night.

It is best to prove things by actual experiment; then you *know;* whereas if you depend on guessing and supposing and conjecturing, you will never get educated.

Some things you *can't* find out; but you will never know you can't by guessing and supposing: no, you have to be patient and go on experimenting until you find out that you can't find out. And it is delightful to have it that way, it makes the world so interesting. If there wasn't anything to find out, it would be dull. Even trying to find out and not finding out is just as interesting as trying to find out and finding out, and I don't know but more so. The secret of the water was a treasure until I *got* it; then the excitement all went away, and I recognized a sense of loss.

By experiment I know that wood swims, and dry leaves, and feathers, and plenty of other things; therefore by all that cumulative evidence you know that a rock will swim; but you have to put up with simply knowing it, for there isn't any way to prove it—up to now. But I shall find a way—then *that* excitement will go. Such things make me sad; because by-and-by when I have found out everything there won't be any more excitements, and I do love excitements so! The other night I couldn't sleep for thinking about it.

At first I couldn't make out what I was made for, but now I think it was to search out the secrets of this wonderful world and be happy and thank the Giver of it all for devising it. I think there are

many things to learn yet—I hope so; and by econo-
mizing and not hurrying too fast I think they will
last weeks and weeks. I hope so. When you cast
up a feather it sails away on the air and goes out of
sight; then you throw up a clod and it doesn't. It
comes down, every time. I have tried it and tried
it, and it is always so. I wonder why it is? Of
course it *doesn't* come down, but why should it *seem*
to? I suppose it is an optical illusion. I mean, one
of them is. I don't know which one. It may be
the feather, it may be the clod; I can't prove which
it is, I can only demonstrate that one or the other is
a fake, and let a person take his choice.

By watching, I know that the stars are not going
to last. I have seen some of the best ones melt and
run down the sky. Since one can melt, they can all
melt; since they can all melt, they can all melt the
same night. That sorrow will come—I know it. I
mean to sit up every night and look at them as long as
I can keep awake; and I will impress those sparkling
fields on my memory, so that by-and-by when they
are taken away I can by my fancy restore those lovely
myriads to the black sky and make them sparkle
again, and double them by the blur of my tears.

AFTER THE FALL

When I look back, the Garden is a dream to me.
It was beautiful, surpassingly beautiful, enchant-
ingly beautiful; and now it is lost, and I shall not see
it any more.

The Garden is lost, but I have found *him*, and am content.   He loves me as well as he can; I love him with all the strength of my passionate nature, and this, I think, is proper to my youth and sex.   If I ask myself why I love him, I find I do not know, and do not really much care to know; so I suppose that this kind of love is not a product of reasoning and statistics, like one's love for other reptiles and animals.   I think that this must be so.   I love certain birds because of their song; but I do not love Adam on account of his singing—no, it is not that; the more he sings the more I do not get reconciled to it.   Yet I ask him to sing, because I wish to learn to like everything he is interested in.   I am sure I can learn, because at first I could not stand it, but now I can.   It sours the milk, but it doesn't matter; I can get used to that kind of milk.

It is not on account of his brightness that I love him—no, it is not that.   He is not to blame for his brightness, such as it is, for he did not make it himself; he is as God made him, and that is sufficient.   There was a wise purpose in it, *that* I know.   In time it will develop, though I think it will not be sudden; and besides, there is no hurry; he is well enough just as he is.

It is not on account of his gracious and considerate ways and his delicacy that I love him.   No, he has lacks in these regards, but he is well enough just so, and is improving.

It is not on account of his industry that I love

him—no, it is not that. I think he has it in him, and I do not know why he conceals it from me. It is my only pain. Otherwise he is frank and open with me, now. I am sure he keeps nothing from me but this. It grieves me that he should have a secret from me, and sometimes it spoils my sleep, thinking of it, but I will put it out of my mind; it shall not trouble my happiness, which is otherwise full to overflowing.

It is not on account of his education that I love him—no, it is not that. He is self-educated, and does really know a multitude of things, but they are not so.

It is not on account of his chivalry that I love him—no, it is not that. He told on me, but I do not blame him; it is a peculiarity of sex, I think, and he did not make his sex. Of course I would not have told on him, I would have perished first; but that is a peculiarity of sex, too, and I do not take credit for it, for I did not make my sex.

Then why is it that I love him? *Merely because he is masculine*, I think.

At bottom he is good, and I love him for that, but I could love him without it. If he should beat me and abuse me, I should go on loving him. I know it. It is a matter of sex, I think.

He is strong and handsome, and I love him for that, and I admire him and am proud of him, but I could love him without those qualities. If he were plain, I should love him; if he were a wreck, I should love him; and I would work for him, and slave over him, and pray for him, and watch by his bedside until I died.

Yes, I think I love him merely because he is *mine* and is *masculine*. There is no other reason, I suppose. And so I think it is as I first said: that this kind of love is not a product of reasonings and statistics. It just *comes* — none knows whence — and cannot explain itself. And doesn't need to.

It is what I think. But I am only a girl, and the first that has examined this matter, and it may turn out that in my ignorance and inexperience I have not got it right.

FORTY YEARS LATER

It is my prayer, it is my longing, that we may pass from this life together—a longing which shall never perish from the earth, but shall have place in the heart of every wife that loves, until the end of time; and it shall be called by my name.

But if one of us must go first, it is my prayer that it shall be I; for he is strong, I am weak, I am not so necessary to him as he is to me—life without him would not be life; how could I endure it? This prayer is also immortal, and will not cease from being offered up while my race continues. I am the first wife; and in the last wife I shall be repeated.

AT EVE'S GRAVE

ADAM: Wheresoever she was, *there* was Eden.

THE INVALID'S STORY

I SEEM sixty and married, but these effects are due to my condition and sufferings, for I am a bachelor, and only forty-one. It will be hard for you to believe that I, who am now but a shadow, was a hale, hearty man two short years ago,— a man of iron, a very athlete! — yet such is the simple truth. But stranger still than this fact is the way in which I lost my health. I lost it through helping to take care of a box of guns on a two-hundred-mile railway journey one winter's night. It is the actual truth, and I will tell you about it.

I belong in Cleveland, Ohio. One winter's night, two years ago, I reached home just after dark, in a driving snow-storm, and the first thing I heard when I entered the house was that my dearest boyhood friend and schoolmate, John B. Hackett, had died the day before, and that his last utterance had been a desire that I would take his remains home to his poor old father and mother in Wisconsin. I was greatly shocked and grieved, but there was no time to waste in emotions; I must start at once. I took the card, marked "Deacon Levi Hackett, Bethlehem, Wisconsin," and hurried off through the whistling storm to the railway station. Arrived there I found the long white-pine box which had been described to me; I fastened the card to it with some tacks, saw it put safely aboard the express car, and then ran into the eating-room to provide myself with a sandwich and some cigars. When I returned, presently, there was my coffin-box *back again*, apparently, and a young fellow examining around it, with a card in his hands, and some tacks and a hammer! I was astonished and puzzled. He began to nail on his card, and I rushed out to the express car, in a good deal of a state of mind, to ask for an explanation. But no — there was my box, all right, in the express car; it hadn't been disturbed. [The fact is that without my suspecting it a prodigious mistake had been made. I was carrying off a box of *guns* which that young fellow had come to the station to ship to a rifle company in Peoria, Illinois, and *he* had got my corpse!] Just then the conductor sung out "All aboard," and I jumped into the express car and got a comfortable seat on a bale of buckets. The expressman was there, hard at work,— a plain man of fifty, with a simple, honest, good-natured face, and a breezy, practical heartiness in his general style. As the train moved off a stranger skipped into the car and set a package of peculiarly mature and capable Limburger cheese on one end of my coffin-box — I mean my box of guns. That is

21

to say, I know *now* that it was Limburger cheese, but at that time I never had heard of the article in my life, and of course was wholly ignorant of its character. Well, we sped through the wild night, the bitter storm raged on, a cheerless misery stole over me, my heart went down, down, down! The old expressman made a brisk remark or two about the tempest and the arctic weather, slammed his sliding doors to, and bolted them, closed his window down tight, and then went bustling around, here and there and yonder, setting things to rights, and all the time contentedly humming " Sweet By and By,'' in a low tone, and flatting a good deal. Presently I began to detect a most evil and searching odor stealing about on the frozen air. This depressed my spirits still more, because of course I attributed it to my poor departed friend. There was something infinitely saddening about his calling himself to my remembrance in this dumb pathetic way, so it was hard to keep the tears back. Moreover, it distressed me on account of the old expressman, who, I was afraid, might notice it. However, he went humming tranquilly on, and gave no sign; and for this I was grateful. Grateful, yes, but still uneasy; and soon I began to feel more and more uneasy every minute, for every minute that went by that odor thickened up the more, and got to be more and more gamey and hard to stand. Presently, having got things arranged to his satisfaction, the expressman got some wood and made up a tremendous fire in his stove.

This distressed me more than I can tell, for I could not but feel that it was a mistake. I was sure that the effect would be deleterious upon my poor departed friend. Thompson — the expressman's name was Thompson, as I found out in the course of the night — now went poking around his car, stopping up whatever stray cracks he could find, remarking that it didn't make any difference what kind of a night it was outside, he calculated to make *us* comfortable, anyway. I said nothing, but I believed he was not choosing the right way. Meantime he was humming to himself just as before; and meantime, too, the stove was getting hotter and hotter, and the place closer and closer. I felt myself growing pale and qualmish, but grieved in silence and said nothing. Soon I noticed that the " Sweet By and By " was gradually fading out; next it ceased altogether, and there was an ominous stillness. After a few moments Thompson said,—

" Pfew ! I reckon it ain't no cinnamon 't I've loaded up thish-yer stove with !"

He gasped once or twice, then moved toward the cof—gun-box, stood over that Limburger cheese part of a moment, then came back and sat down near me, looking a good deal impressed. After a contemplative pause, he said, indicating the box with a gesture,—

" Friend of yourn ?"

" Yes," I said with a sigh.

" He's pretty ripe, *ain't* he !"

Nothing further was said for perhaps a couple of minutes, each being busy with his own thoughts; then Thompson said, in a low, awed voice,—

" Sometimes it's uncertain whether they're really gone or not,— *seem* gone, you know — body warm, joints limber — and so, although you *think* they're gone, you don't really know. I've had cases in my car. It's perfectly awful, becuz *you* don't know what minute they'll rise up and look at you!" Then, after a pause, and slightly lifting his elbow toward the box,—" But *he* ain't in no trance! No, sir, I go bail for *him!*"

We sat some time, in meditative silence, listening to the wind and the roar of the train; then Thompson said, with a good deal of feeling,—

" Well-a-well, we've all got to go, they ain't no getting around it. Man that is born of woman is of few days and far between, as Scriptur' says. Yes, you look at it any way you want to, it's awful solemn and cur'us: they ain't *nobody* can get around it; *all's* got to go — just *everybody*, as you may say. One day you're hearty and strong" — here he scrambled to his feet and broke a pane and stretched his nose out at it a moment or two, then sat down again while I struggled up and thrust my nose out at the same place, and this we kept on doing every now and then —" and next day he's cut down like the grass, and the places which knowed him then knows him no more forever, as Scriptur' says. Yes'ndeedy, it's awful solemn and cur'us; but we've all got to go, one time or another; they ain't no getting around it."

There was another long pause; then,—

" What did he die of?"

I said I didn't know.

" How long has he ben dead?"

It seemed judicious to enlarge the facts to fit the probabilities; so I said,—

" Two or three days."

But it did no good; for Thompson received it with an injured look which plainly said, " Two or three *years*, you mean." Then he went right along, placidly ignoring my statement, and gave his views at considerable length upon the unwisdom of putting off burials too long. Then he lounged off toward the box, stood a moment, then came back on a sharp trot and visited the broken pane, observing,—

" 'Twould 'a' ben a dum sight better, all around, if they'd started him along last summer."

Thompson sat down and buried his face in his red silk handkerchief, and began to slowly sway and rock his body like one who is doing his best to endure the almost unendurable. By this time the fragrance — if you may call it fragrance — was just about suffocating, as near as you can come at it. Thompson's face was turning gray; I knew mine hadn't any color left in it. By and by Thompson rested his forehead in his left hand, with his elbow on his knee, and sort of waved his red handkerchief towards the box with his other hand, and said,—

" I've carried a many a one of 'em,— some of 'em considerable overdue, too,— but, lordy, he just lays over 'em all ! — and does it *easy*.   Cap., they was heliotrope to *him!* "

This recognition of my poor friend gratified me, in spite of the sad circumstances, because it had so much the sound of a compliment.

Pretty soon it was plain that something had got to be done.   I suggested cigars.   Thompson thought it was a good idea.   He said,—

" Likely it'll modify him some."

We puffed gingerly along for a while, and tried hard to imagine that things were improved.   But it wasn't any use.   Before very long, and without any consultation, both cigars were quietly dropped from our nerveless fingers at the same moment. Thompson said, with a sigh,—

" No, Cap., it don't modify him worth a cent. Fact is, it makes him worse, becuz it appears to stir up his ambition.   What do you reckon we better do, now ?"

I was not able to suggest anything; indeed, I had to be swallowing and swallowing, all the time, and did not like to trust myself to speak.   Thompson fell to maundering, in a desultory and low-spirited way, about the miserable experiences of this night; and he got to referring to my poor friend by various titles,— sometimes   military   ones,   sometimes   civil ones; and I noticed that as fast as my poor friend's effectiveness   grew,   Thompson   promoted   him   ac-

cordingly,— gave him a bigger title. Finally he
said,—

" I've got an idea.   Suppos'n we buckle down to
it and give the Colonel a bit of a shove towards
t'other end of the car? — about ten foot, say.   He
wouldn't have so much influence, then, don't you
reckon?"

I said it was a good scheme.   So we took in
a good fresh breath at the broken pane, calculating to hold it till we got through; then we went
there and bent over that deadly cheese and took a
grip on the box.   Thompson nodded " All ready,"
and then we threw ourselves forward with all our
might; but Thompson slipped, and slumped down
with his nose on the cheese, and his breath got
loose.   He gagged and gasped, and floundered up
and made a break for the door, pawing the air
and saying hoarsely, " Don't hender me! — gimme
the road! I'm a-dying; gimme the road!"   Out
on the cold platform I sat down and held his head
a while, and he revived.   Presently he said,—

" Do you reckon we started the Gen'rul any?"
I said no; we hadn't budged him.

" Well, then, *that* idea's up the flume.   We got
to think up something else.   He's suited wher' he
is, I reckon; and if that's the way he feels about it,
and has made up his mind that he don't wish to be
disturbed, you bet he's a-going to have his own way
in the business.   Yes, better leave him right wher'
he is, long as he wants it so; becuz he holds all the

trumps, don't you know, and so it stands to reason that the man that lays out to alter his plans for him is going to get left."

But we couldn't stay out there in that mad storm; we should have frozen to death. So we went in again and shut the door, and began to suffer once more and take turns at the break in the window. By and by, as we were starting away from a station where we had stopped a moment Thompson pranced in cheerily, and exclaimed,—

"We're all right, now! I reckon we've got the Commodore this time. I judge I've got the stuff here that'll take the tuck out of him."

It was carbolic acid. He had a carboy of it. He sprinkled it all around everywhere; in fact he drenched everything with it, rifle-box, cheese and all. Then we sat down, feeling pretty hopeful. But it wasn't for long. You see the two perfumes began to mix, and then — well, pretty soon we made a break for the door; and out there Thompson swabbed his face with his bandanna and said in a kind of disheartened way,—

"It ain't no use. We can't buck agin *him*. He just utilizes everything we put up to modify him with, and gives it his own flavor and plays it back on us. Why, Cap., don't you know, it's as much as a hundred times worse in there now than it was when he first got a-going. I never *did* see one of 'em warm up to his work so, and take such a dumnation interest in it. No, sir, I never did, as long as I've

"AND BREAKING FOR THE PLATFORM, THOMPSON GOT
SUFFOCATED AND FELL"

ben on the road; and I've carried a many a one of 'em, as I was telling you."

We went in again after we were frozen pretty stiff; but my, we couldn't *stay* in, now.   So we just waltzed back and forth, freezing, and thawing, and stifling, by turns.   In about an hour we stopped at another station; and as we left it Thompson came in with a bag, and said,—

" Cap., I'm a-going to chance him once more,— just this once; and if we don't fetch him this time, the thing for us to do, is to just throw up the sponge and withdraw from the canvass.   That's the way *I* put it up."

He had brought a lot of chicken feathers, and dried apples, and leaf tobacco, and rags, and old shoes, and sulphur, and asafœtida, and one thing or another; and he piled them on a breadth of sheet iron in the middle of the floor, and set fire to them.

When they got well started, I couldn't see, myself, how even the corpse could stand it.   All that went before was just simply poetry to that smell,—but mind you, the original smell stood up out of it just as sublime as ever,—fact is, these other smells just seemed to give it a better hold; and my, how rich it was!   I didn't make these reflections there — there wasn't time — made them on the platform.   And breaking for the platform, Thompson got suffocated and fell; and before I got him dragged out, which I did by the collar, I was mighty near gone myself. When we revived, Thompson said dejectedly,—

"We got to stay out here, Cap. We got to do it. They ain't no other way. The Governor wants to travel alone, and he's fixed so he can outvote us."

And presently he added,—

"And don't you know, we're *pisoned*. It's *our* last trip, you can make up your mind to it. Typhoid fever is what's going to come of this. I feel it a-coming right now. Yes, sir, we're elected, just as sure as you're born."

We were taken from the platform an hour later, frozen and insensible, at the next station, and I went straight off into a virulent fever, and never knew anything again for three weeks. I found out, then, that I had spent that awful night with a harmless box of rifles and a lot of innocent cheese; but the news was too late to save *me;* imagination had done its work, and my health was permanently shattered; neither Bermuda nor any other land can ever bring it back to me. This is my last trip; I am on my way home to die.

THE CAPTAIN'S STORY

THERE was a good deal of pleasant gossip about old Captain " Hurricane " Jones, of the Pacific Ocean,— peace to his ashes! Two or three of us present had known him; I, particularly well, for I had made four sea-voyages with him. He was a very remarkable man. He was born on a ship; he picked up what little education he had among his shipmates; he began life in the forecastle, and climbed grade by grade to the captaincy. More than fifty years of his sixty-five were spent at sea. He had sailed all oceans, seen all lands, and borrowed a tint from all climates. When a man has been fifty years at sea, he necessarily knows nothing of men, nothing of the world but its surface, nothing of the world's thought, nothing of the world's learning but its A B C, and that blurred and distorted by the unfocused lenses of an untrained mind. Such a man is only a gray and bearded child. That is what old Hurricane Jones was,— simply an innocent, lovable old infant. When his spirit was in repose he was as sweet and gentle as a girl; when his wrath was up he was a hurricane that made his nickname seem tamely descriptive. He was formidable in a fight, for he was of powerful build and dauntless courage. He was frescoed from head to heel with pictures and mottoes tattooed in red and blue India ink. I was with him one voyage when he got his last vacant space tattooed; this vacant space was around his left ankle. During three days he stumped about the ship with his ankle bare and swollen, and this legend gleaming red and angry out from a clouding of India ink: " Virtue is its own R'd." (There was a lack of room.) He was deeply and sincerely pious, and swore like a fish-woman. He considered swearing blameless, because sailors would not understand an order unillumined by it. He was a profound Biblical scholar, — that is, he thought he was. He believed everything in the Bible, but he had his own methods of arriving at his beliefs. He was of the " advanced " school of thinkers, and applied natural laws to the interpretation of all miracles, somewhat on the plan of the people who make the six days of creation six geological epochs, and so forth. Without being aware of it, he was a rather severe satire on modern scientific religionists. Such a man as I have been describing is rabidly fond of disquisition and argument; one knows that without being told it.

One trip the captain had a clergyman on board, but did not know he was a clergyman, since the passenger list did not betray the fact. He took a great liking to this Rev. Mr. Peters, and talked with him a great deal: told him yarns, gave him toothsome scraps of personal history, and wove a glittering streak of profanity through his garrulous fabric that was refreshing to a spirit weary of the dull neutralities of undecorated speech. One day the captain said, "Peters, do you ever read the Bible?"

" Well — yes."

" I judge it ain't often, by the way you say it. Now, you tackle it in dead earnest once, and you'll find it'll pay. Don't you get discouraged, but hang right on. First, you won't understand it; but by and by things will begin to clear up, and then you wouldn't lay it down to eat."

" Yes, I have heard that said."

" And it's so, too. There ain't a book that begins with it. It lays over 'em all, Peters. There's some pretty tough things in it,— there ain't any getting around that,— but you stick to them and think them out, and when once you get on the inside everything's plain as day."

" The miracles, too, captain?"

" Yes, sir! the miracles, too. Every one of them. Now, there's that business with the prophets of Baal; like enough that stumped you?"

" Well, I don't know but —"

" Own up, now; it stumped you. Well, I don't wonder. You hadn't had any experience in raveling such things out, and naturally it was too many for you. Would you like to have me explain that thing to you, and show you how to get at the meat of these matters?''

'' Indeed, I would, captain, if you don't mind.''

Then the captain proceeded as follows: '' I'll do it with pleasure. First, you see, I read and read, and thought and thought, till I got to understand what sort of people they were in the old Bible times, and then after that it was clear and easy. Now, this was the way I put it up, concerning Isaac* and the prophets of Baal. There was some mighty sharp men amongst the public characters of that old ancient day, and Isaac was one of them. Isaac had his failings,— plenty of them, too; it ain't for me to apologize for Isaac; he played on the prophets of Baal, and like enough he was justifiable, considering the odds that was against him. No, all I say is, 't wa'n't any miracle, and that I'll show you so's't you can see it yourself.

'' Well, times had been getting rougher and rougher for prophets,— that is, prophets of Isaac's denomination. There were four hundred and fifty prophets of Baal in the community, and only one Presbyterian; that is, if Isaac *was* a Presbyterian, which I reckon he was, but it don't say. Naturally, the prophets of Baal took all the trade. Isaac was pretty low-spirited, I reckon, but he was a good deal of a man, and no doubt he went a-prophesying around, letting on to be doing a land-office busi-

---

* This is the captain's own mistake.

ness, but 't wa'n't any use; he couldn't run any opposition to amount to anything. By and by things got desperate with him; he sets his head to work and thinks it all out, and then what does he do? Why, he begins to throw out hints that the other parties are this and that and t'other,— nothing very definite, may be, but just kind of undermining their reputation in a quiet way. This made talk, of course, and finally got to the king. The king asked Isaac what he meant by his talk. Says Isaac, 'Oh, nothing particular; only, can they pray down fire from heaven on an altar? It ain't much, maybe, your majesty, only can they *do* it? That's the idea.' So the king was a good deal disturbed, and he went to the prophets of Baal, and they said, pretty airy, that if he had an altar ready, *they* were ready; and they intimated he better get it insured, too.

" So next morning all the children of Israel and their parents and the other people gathered themselves together. Well, here was that great crowd of prophets of Baal packed together on one side, and Isaac walking up and down all alone on the other, putting up his job. When time was called, Isaac let on to be comfortable and indifferent; told the other team to take the first innings. So they went at it, the whole four hundred and fifty, praying around the altar, very hopeful, and doing their level best. They prayed an hour,— two hours,— three hours,— and so on, plumb till noon. It wa'n't any use; they

hadn't took a trick. Of course they felt kind
of ashamed before all those people, and well they
might. Now, what would a magnanimous man
do? Keep still, wouldn't he? Of course. What
did Isaac do? He graveled the prophets of Baal
every way he could think of. Says he, ' You
don't speak up loud enough; your god's asleep,
like enough, or maybe he's taking a walk; you
want to holler, you know,' — or words to that effect; I don't recollect the exact language. Mind,
I don't apologize for Isaac; he had his faults.

" Well, the prophets of Baal prayed along the best
they knew how all the afternoon, and never raised a
spark. At last, about sundown, they were all
tuckered out, and they owned up and quit.

" What does Isaac do, now? He steps up and
says to some friends of his, there, ' Pour four barrels
of water on the altar ! ' Everybody was astonished;
for the other side had prayed at it dry, you know,
and got whitewashed. They poured it on. Says he,
' Heave on four more barrels.' Then he says,
' Heave on four more.' Twelve barrels, you see,
altogether. The water ran all over the altar, and all
down the sides, and filled up a trench around it that
would hold a couple of hogsheads,—' measures,' it
says; I reckon it means about a hogshead. Some
of the people were going to put on their things and
go, for they allowed he was crazy. They didn't
know Isaac. Isaac knelt down and began to pray:
he strung along, and strung along, about the heathen

in distant lands, and about the sister churches, and about the state and the country at large, and about those that's in authority in the government, and all the usual programme, you know, till everybody had got tired and gone to thinking about something else, and then, all of a sudden, when nobody was noticing, he outs with a match and rakes it on the under side of his leg, and pff! up the whole thing blazes like a house afire! Twelve barrels of *water ? Petroleum*, sir, PETROLEUM! that's what it was!''

"Petroleum, captain?"

"Yes, sir; the country was full of it. Isaac knew all about that. You read the Bible. Don't you worry about the tough places. They ain't tough when you come to think them out and throw light on them. There ain't a thing in the Bible but what is true; all you want is to go prayerfully to work and cipher out how 't was done.''

22

MARK TWAIN

A BIOGRAPHICAL SKETCH

By SAMUEL E. MOFFETT

IN 1835 the creation of the Western empire of America had just begun. In the whole region west of the Mississippi, which now contains 21,-000,000 people — nearly twice the entire population of the United States at that time — there were less than half a million white inhabitants. There were only two states beyond the great river, Louisiana and Missouri. There were only two considerable groups of population, one about New Orleans, the other about St. Louis. If we omit New Orleans, which is east of the river, there was only one place in all that vast domain with any pretension to be called a city. That was St. Louis, and that metropolis, the wonder and pride of all the Western country, had no more than 10,000 inhabitants.

It was in this frontier region, on the extreme fringe of settlement " that just divides the desert from the sown," that Samuel Langhorne Clemens was born, November 30, 1835, in the hamlet of Florida, Missouri. His parents had come there to be in the thick of the Western boom, and by a fate for which no lack of foresight on their part was to blame, they found themselves in a place which succeeded in accumulating 125 inhabitants in the next sixty years. When we read of the westward sweep of population and wealth in the United States, it seems as if those who were in the van of that movement must have been inevitably carried on to fortune. But that was a tide full of eddies and back currents, and Mark Twain's parents possessed a faculty for finding them that appears nothing less than miraculous. The whole Western empire was before them where to choose. They could have bought the entire site of Chicago for a pair of boots. They could have taken up a farm within the present city limits of St. Louis. What they actually did was to live for a time in Columbia, Kentucky, with a small property in land, and six inherited slaves, then to move to Jamestown, on the Cumberland plateau of Tennessee, a place that was then no farther removed from the currents of the world's life than Uganda, but which no resident of that or any other part of Central Africa would now regard as a serious competitor, and next to migrate to Missouri, passing St. Louis and settling first in Florida, and afterward in Hannibal. But when the whole map was blank the promise of fortune glowed as rosily in these regions as anywhere else. Florida had great expectations when Jackson was President. When John Marshall Clemens took up 80,000 acres of land in Tennessee, he thought he had established his children as territorial magnates. That phantom vision of wealth furnished later one of the motives of " The Gilded Age." It conferred no other benefit.

If Samuel Clemens missed a fortune he inherited good blood. On both sides his family had been settled in the South since early colonial times. His father, John Marshall Clemens, of Virginia, was a descendant of Gregory Clemens, who became one of the judges that condemned Charles I. to death, was excepted from the amnesty after the Restoration in consequence, and lost his head. A cousin of John M. Clemens, Jeremiah Clemens, represented Alabama in the United States Senate from 1849 to 1853.

Through his mother, Jane Lampton (Lambton), the boy was descended from the Lambtons of Durham, whose modern English representatives still possess the lands held by their ancestors of the same name since the twelfth century. Some of her forbears on the maternal side, the Montgomerys, went with Daniel Boone to Kentucky, and were in the thick of the romantic and tragic events that accompanied the settlement of the " Dark and Bloody Ground," and she herself was born there twenty-nine years after the first log cabin was built within the limits of the present commonwealth. She was one of the earliest, prettiest, and brightest of the many belles that have given Kentucky such an enviable reputation as a nursery of fair women, and her vivacity and wit left no doubt in the minds of her friends concerning the source of her son's genius.

John Marshall Clemens, who had been trained for the bar in Virginia, served for some years as a magistrate at Hannibal, holding for a time the position of county judge. With his death, in March, 1847, Mark Twain's formal education came to an end, and his education in real life began. He had always been a delicate boy, and his father, in consequence, had been lenient in the matter of enforcing attendance at school, although he had been profoundly anxious that his children should be well educated. His wish was fulfilled, although not in the way he had expected. It is a fortunate thing for literature that Mark Twain was never ground into smooth uniformity under the scholastic emery wheel. He has made the world his university, and in men, and books, and strange places, and all the phases of an infinitely varied life, has built an education broad and deep, on the foundations of an undisturbed individuality.

His high school was a village printing-office, where his elder brother Orion was conducting a newspaper. The thirteen-year-old boy served in all capacities, and in the occasional absences of his chief he reveled in personal journalism, with original illustrations hacked on wooden blocks with a jackknife, to an extent that riveted the town's attention, " but not its admiration," as his brother plaintively confessed. The editor spoke with feeling, for he had to take the consequences of these exploits on his return.

From his earliest childhood young Clemens had
been of an adventurous disposition. Before he was
thirteen, he had been extracted three times from the
Mississippi, and six times from Bear Creek, in a substantially drowned condition, but his mother, with
the high confidence in his future that never deserted
her, merely remarked: " People who are born to be
hanged are safe in the water."   By 1853 the Hannibal tether had become too short for him.   He
disappeared from home and wandered from one
Eastern printing-office to another.   He saw the
World's Fair at New York, and other marvels,
and supported himself by setting type. At the
end of this *Wanderjahr* financial stress drove him
back to his family.   He lived at St. Louis, Mus-
catine, and Keokuk until 1857, when he induced
the great Horace Bixby to teach him the mystery
of steamboat piloting.   The charm of all this
warm, indolent existence in the sleepy river towns
has colored his whole subsequent life.   In "Tom
Sawyer," "Huckleberry Finn," "Life on the
Mississippi," and "Pudd'nhead Wilson," every
phase of that vanished estate is lovingly dwelt upon.

Native character will always make itself felt, but
one may wonder whether Mark Twain's humor would
have developed in quite so sympathetic and buoyant
a vein if he had been brought up in Ecclefechan
instead of in Hannibal, and whether Carlyle might
not have been a little more human if he had spent his
boyhood in Hannibal instead of in Ecclefechan.

A Mississippi pilot in the later fifties was a personage of imposing grandeur. He was a miracle of attainments; he was the absolute master of his boat while it was under way, and just before his fall he commanded a salary precisely equal to that earned at that time by the Vice-President of the United States or a Justice of the Supreme Court. The best proof of the superlative majesty and desirability of his position is the fact that Samuel Clemens deliberately subjected himself to the incredible labor necessary to attain it — a labor compared with which the efforts needed to acquire the degree of Doctor of Philosophy at a University are as light as a summer course of modern novels. To appreciate the full meaning of a pilot's marvelous education, one must read the whole of "Life on the Mississippi," but this extract may give a partial idea of a single feature of that training — the cultivation of the memory:

" First of all, there is one faculty which a pilot must incessantly cultivate until he has brought it to absolute perfection. Nothing short of perfection will do. That faculty is memory. He cannot stop with merely thinking a thing is so and so; he must *know* it; for this is eminently one of the exact sciences. With what scorn a pilot was looked upon, in the old times, if he ever ventured to deal in that feeble phrase ' I think,' instead of the vigorous one ' I know!' One cannot easily realize what a tremendous thing it is to know every trivial detail of twelve hundred miles of river, and know it with absolute exactness. If you will take the longest street in New York, and travel up and down it, conning its features patiently until you know every house, and window, and door, and lamp-post, and big and little sign by heart, and know them so accurately that you can instantly name the one you are abreast of when you are set down at random in that street in the middle of an inky black night, you will then have a tolerable notion of the amount and the exactness of a pilot's knowledge who carries the Mississippi River in his head. And then, if you will go on until you know every street crossing, the character, size, and position of the crossing-stones, and the varying depth of mud in each of those numberless places, you will have some idea of what the pilot must know in order to keep a Mississippi steamer out of trouble. Next, if you will take half of the signs in that long street and *change their places* once a month, and still manage to know their new positions accurately on dark nights, and keep up with these repeated changes without making any mistakes, you will understand what is required of a pilot's peerless memory by the fickle Mississippi.

"I think a pilot's memory is about the most wonderful thing in the world. To know the Old and New Testaments by heart, and be able to recite them glibly, forward or backward, or begin at random anywhere in the book and recite both ways, and never trip or make a mistake, is no extravagant mass of knowledge, and no marvelous facility, compared to a pilot's massed knowledge of the Mississippi, and his marvelous facility in handling it.

" And how easily and comfortably the pilot's memory does its work; how placidly effortless is its way; how *unconsciously* it lays up its vast stores, hour by hour, day by day, and never loses or mislays a single valuable package of them all! Take an instance. Let a leadsman say: ' Half twain! half twain! half twain! half twain! half twain!' until it becomes as monotonous as the ticking of a clock; let conversation be going on all the time, and the pilot be doing his share of the talking, and no longer consciously listening to the leadsman; and in the midst of this endless string of half twains let a single ' quarter twain!' be interjected, without emphasis, and then the half twain cry go on again, just as before: two or three weeks later that pilot can describe with precision the boat's position in the river when that quarter twain was uttered, and give you such a lot of head marks, stern marks, and side marks to guide you that you ought to be able to take the boat there and put her in that same spot again yourself! The cry of ' Quarter twain ' did not really take his mind from his talk, but his trained faculties instantly photographed the bearings, noted the change of depth, and laid up the important details for future reference without requiring any assistance from him in the matter.''

Young Clemens went through all that appalling training, stored away in his head the bewildering mass of knowledge a pilot's duties required, received the license that was the diploma of the river university, entered into regular employment, and regarded himself as established for life, when the outbreak of the Civil War wiped out his occupation at a stroke, and made his weary apprenticeship a useless labor. The commercial navigation of the lower Mississippi was stopped by a line of fire, and black, squat gunboats, their sloping sides plated with railroad iron, took the place of the gorgeous white side-wheelers, whose pilots had been the envied aristocrats of the river towns. Clemens was in New Orleans when Louisiana seceded, and started North the next day. The boat ran a blockade every day of her trip, and on the last night of the voyage the batteries at the Jefferson barracks, just below St. Louis, fired two shots through her chimneys.

Brought up in a slaveholding atmosphere, Mark Twain naturally sympathized at first with the South. In June he joined the Confederates in Ralls County, Missouri, as a Second Lieutenant under General Tom Harris. His military career lasted for two weeks. Narrowly missing the distinction of being captured by Colonel Ulysses S. Grant, he resigned, explaining that he had become "incapacitated by fatigue" through persistent retreating. In his subsequent writings he has always treated his brief experience of warfare as a burlesque episode, although the official reports and correspondence of the Confederate commanders speak very respectfully of the work of the raw countrymen of the Harris Brigade. The elder Clemens brother, Orion, was *persona grata* to the Administration of President Lincoln, and received in consequence an appointment as the first Secretary of the new Territory of Nevada. He offered his speedily reconstructed junior the position of private secretary to himself, " with nothing to do and no salary." The two crossed the plains in the overland coach in eighteen days — almost precisely the time it will take to go from New York to Vladivostok when the Trans-Siberian Railway is finished.

A year of variegated fortune hunting among the silver mines of the Humboldt and Esmeralda regions followed. Occasional letters written during this time to the leading newspaper of the Territory, the Virginia City *Territorial Enterprise*, attracted the attention of the proprietor, Mr. J. T. Goodman, a man of keen and unerring literary instinct, and he offered the writer the position of local editor on his staff. With the duties of this place were combined those of legislative correspondent at Carson City, the capital. The work of young Clemens created a sensation among the lawmakers. He wrote a weekly letter, spined with barbed personalities. It appeared every Sunday, and on Mondays the legislative business was obstructed with the complaints of members who rose to questions of privilege, and expressed their opinion of the correspondent with acerbity. This encouraged him to give his letters more individuality by signing them. For this purpose he adopted the old Mississippi leadsman's call for two fathoms (twelve feet)—"Mark Twain."

At that particular period dueling was a passing fashion on the Comstock. The refinements of Parisian civilization had not penetrated there, and a Washoe duel seldom left more than one survivor. The weapons were always Colt's navy revolvers — distance, fifteen paces; fire and advance; six shots allowed. Mark Twain became involved in a quarrel with Mr. Laird, the editor of the Virginia *Union*, and the situation seemed to call for a duel. Neither combatant was an expert with the pistol, but Mark Twain was fortunate enough to have a second who was. The men were practicing in adjacent gorges, Mr. Laird doing fairly well, and his opponent hitting everything but the mark. A small bird lit on a sage bush thirty yards away, and Mark Twain's second fired and knocked off its head. At that moment the enemy came over the ridge, saw the dead bird, observed the distance, and learned from Gillis, the humorist's second, that the feat had been performed by Mark Twain, for whom such an exploit was nothing remarkable. They withdrew for consultation, and then offered a formal apology, after which peace was restored, leaving Mark Twain with the honors of war.

However, this incident was the means of effecting another change in his life. There was a new law which prescribed two years' imprisonment for any one who should send, carry, or accept a challenge. The fame of the proposed duel had reached the capital, eighteen miles away, and the governor wrathfully gave orders for the arrest of all concerned, announcing his intention of making an example that would be remembered. A friend of the duelists heard of their danger, outrode the officers of the law; and hurried the parties over the border into California.

Mark Twain found a berth as city editor of the San Francisco *Morning Call*, but he was not adapted to routine newspaper work, and in a couple of years he made another bid for fortune in the mines. He tried the " pocket mines " of California, this time, at Jackass Gulch, in Calaveras County, but was fortunate enough to find no pockets. Thus he escaped the hypnotic fascination that has kept some intermittently successful pocket miners willing prisoners in Sierra cabins for life, and in three months he was back in San Francisco, penniless, but in the line of literary promotion. He wrote letters for the Virginia *Enterprise* for a time, but tiring of that, welcomed an assignment to visit Hawaii for the Sacramento *Union*, and write about the sugar interests. It was in Honolulu that he accomplished one of his greatest feats of "straight newspaper work." The clipper *Hornet* had been burned on " the line," and when the skeleton survivors arrived, after a passage of forty-three days in an open boat on ten days' provisions, Mark Twain gathered their stories, worked all day and all night, and threw a complete account of the horror aboard a schooner that had already cast off. It was the only full account that reached California, and it was not only a clean " scoop " of unusual magnitude, but an admirable piece of literary art. The *Union* testified its appreciation by paying the correspondent ten times the current rates for it.

After six months in the Islands, Mark Twain returned to California, and made his first venture upon the lecture platform. He was warmly received, and delivered several lectures with profit. In 1867 he went East by way of the Isthmus, and joined the Quaker City excursion to Europe and the Holy Land, as correspondent of the *Alta California*, of San Francisco. During this tour of five or six months the party visited the principal ports of the Mediterranean and the Black Sea. From this trip grew " The Innocents Abroad," the creator of Mark Twain's reputation as a literary force of the first order. " The Celebrated Jumping Frog of Calaveras County " had preceded it, but " The Innocents " gave the author his first introduction to international literature. A hundred thousand copies were sold the first year, and as many more later.

Four years of lecturing followed — distasteful, but profitable. Mark Twain always shrank from the public exhibition of himself on the platform, but he was a popular favorite there from the first. He was one of a little group, including Henry Ward Beecher and two or three others, for whom every lyceum committee in the country was bidding, and whose capture at any price insured the success of a lecture course.

The Quaker City excursion had a more important result than the production of " The Innocents Abroad." Through her brother, who was one of the party, Mr. Clemens became acquainted with Miss Olivia L. Langdon, the daughter of Jervis Langdon, of Elmira, New York, and this acquaintance led, in February, 1870, to one of the most ideal marriages in literary history.

Four children came of this union. The eldest, Langdon, a son, was born in November, 1870, and died in 1872. The second, Susan Olivia, a daughter, was born in the latter year, and lived only twenty-four years, but long enough to develop extraordinary mental gifts and every grace of character. Two other daughters, Clara Langdon and Jean, were born in 1874 and 1880, respectively, and still live (1899).

Mark Twain's first home as a man of family was in Buffalo, in a house given to the bride by her father as a wedding present. He bought a third interest in a daily newspaper, the Buffalo *Express*, and joined its staff. But his time for jogging in harness was past. It was his last attempt at regular newspaper work, and a year of it was enough. He had become assured of a market for anything he might produce, and he could choose his own place and time for writing.

There was a tempting literary colony at Hartford;

the place was steeped in an atmosphere of antique peace and beauty, and the Clemens family were captivated by its charm. They moved there in October, 1871, and soon built a house which was one of the earliest fruits of the artistic revolt against the mid-century Philistinism of domestic architecture in America. For years it was an object of wonder to the simple-minded tourist. The facts that its rooms were arranged for the convenience of those who were to occupy them, and that its windows, gables, and porches were distributed with an eye to the beauty, comfort, and picturesqueness of that particular house, instead of following the traditional lines laid down by the carpenters and contractors who designed most of the dwellings of the period, distracted the critics, and gave rise to grave discussions in the newspapers throughout the country of " Mark Twain's practical joke."

The years that followed brought a steady literary development. " Roughing It," which was written in 1872, and scored a success hardly second to that of " The Innocents," was, like that, simply a humorous narrative of personal experiences, variegated by brilliant splashes of description; but with " The Gilded Age," which was produced in the same year, in collaboration with Mr. Charles Dudley Warner, the humorist began to evolve into the philosopher. " Tom Sawyer," appearing in 1876, was a veritable manual of boy nature, and its sequel, " Huckleberry Finn," which was published nine years later, was not only an advanced treatise in the same science, but a most moving study of the workings of the untutored human soul, in boy and man. "The Prince and the Pauper," 1882, "A Connecticut Yankee at King Arthur's Court" (1890), and "Pudd'nhead Wilson" (first published serially in 1893-94), were all alive with a comprehensive and passionate sympathy to which their humor was quite subordinate, although Mark Twain never wrote, and probably never will write, a book that could be read without laughter. His humor is as irrepressible as Lincoln's, and like that, it bubbles out on the most solemn occasions; but still, again like Lincoln's, it has a way of seeming, in spite of the surface incongruity, to belong there. But it was in the "Personal Recollections of Joan of Arc," whose anonymous serial publication in 1894-95 betrayed some critics of reputation into the absurdity of attributing it to other authors, notwithstanding the characteristic evidences of its paternity that obtruded themselves on every page, that Mark Twain became most distinctly a prophet of humanity. Here, at last, was a book with nothing ephemeral about it — one that will reach the elemental human heart as well among the flying machines of the next century, as it does among the automobiles of to-day, or as it would have done among the stage coaches of a hundred years ago.

And side by side with this spiritual growth had come a growth in knowledge and in culture. The

Mark Twain of " The Innocents," keen-eyed, quick of understanding, and full of fresh, eager interest in all Europe had to show, but frankly avowing that he " did not know what in the mischief the Renaissance was," had developed into an accomplished scholar and a man of the world for whom the globe had few surprises left.   The Mark Twain of 1895 might conceivably have written " The Innocents Abroad," although it would have required an effort to put himself in the necessary frame of mind, but the Mark Twain of 1869 could no more have written " Joan of Arc " than he could have deciphered the Maya hieroglyphics.

In 1873 the family spent some months in England and Scotland, and Mr. Clemens lectured for a few weeks in London.   Another European journey followed in 1878.

" A Tramp Abroad " was the result of this tour, which lasted eighteen months.   " The Prince and the Pauper," " Life on the Mississippi," and " Huckleberry Finn " appeared in quick succession in 1882, 1883, and 1885.   Considerably more amusing than anything the humorist ever wrote was the fact that the trustees of some village libraries in New England solemnly voted that " Huckleberry Finn," whose power of moral uplift has hardly been surpassed by any book of our time, was too demoralizing to be allowed on their shelves.

All this time fortune had been steadily favorable, and Mark Twain had been spoken of by the press, sometimes with admiration, as an example of the financial success possible in literature, and sometimes with uncharitable envy, as a haughty millionaire, forgetful of his humble friends. But now began the series of unfortunate investments that swept away the accumulations of half a lifetime of hard work, and left him loaded with debts incurred by other men. In 1885 he financed the publishing house of Charles L. Webster & Company in New York. The firm began business with the prestige of a brilliant *coup*. It secured the publication of the Memoirs of General Grant, which achieved a sale of more than 600,000 volumes. The first check received by the Grant heirs was for $200,000, and this was followed a few months later by one for $150,000. These are the largest checks ever paid for an author's work on either side of the Atlantic. Meanwhile, Mr. Clemens was spending great sums on a type-setting machine of such seductive ingenuity as to captivate the imagination of everybody who saw it. It worked to perfection, but it was too complicated and expensive for commercial use, and after sinking a fortune in it between 1886 and 1889, Mark Twain had to write off the whole investment as a dead loss.

On top of this the publishing house, which had been supposed to be doing a profitable business, turned out to have been incapably conducted, and all the money that came into its hands was lost. Mark Twain contributed $65,000 in efforts to save its life, but to no purpose, and when it finally failed, he found that it had not only absorbed everything he had put in, but had incurred liabilities of $96,000, of which less than one-third was covered by assets.

He could easily have avoided any legal liability for the debts, but as the credit of the company had been based largely upon his name, he felt bound in honor to pay them. In 1895-96 he took his wife and second daughter on a lecturing tour around the world, wrote " Following the Equator," and cleared off the obligations of the house in full.

The years 1897, 1898, and 1899 were spent in England, Switzerland, and Austria. Vienna took the family to its heart, and Mark Twain achieved such a popularity among all classes there as is rarely won by a foreigner anywhere. He saw the manufacture of a good deal of history in that time. It was his fortune, for instance, to be present in the Austrian Reichsrath on the memorable occasion when it was invaded by sixty policemen, and sixteen refractory members were dragged roughly out of the hall. That momentous event in the progress of parliamentary government profoundly impressed him.

Mark Twain, although so characteristically American in every fiber, does not appeal to Americans alone, nor even to the English-speaking race. His work has stood the test of translation into French, German, Russian, Italian, Swedish, Norwegian, and Magyar. That is pretty good evidence that it possesses the universal quality that marks the master.

Another evidence of its fidelity to human nature is the readiness with which it lends itself to dramatization. " The Gilded Age," " Tom Sawyer," " The Prince and the Pauper," and "Pudd'nhead Wilson " have all been successful on the stage.

In the thirty-eight years of his literary activity Mark Twain has seen generation after generation of " American humorists " rise, expand into sudden popularity, and disappear, leaving hardly a memory behind. If he has not written himself out like them, if his place in literature has become every year more assured, it is because his " humor " has been something radically different from theirs. It has been irresistibly laughter-provoking, but its sole end has never been to make people laugh. Its more important purpose has been to make them think and feel. And with the progress of the years Mark Twain's own thoughts have become finer, his own feelings deeper and more responsive. Sympathy with the suffering, hatred of injustice and oppression, and enthusiasm for all that tends to make the world a more tolerable place for mankind to live in, have grown with his accumulating knowledge of life as it is. That is why Mark Twain has become a classic, not only at home, but in all lands whose people read and think about the common joys and sorrows of humanity.

IN MEMORIAM

OLIVIA SUSAN CLEMENS

Died August 18, 1896; Aged 24

IN a fair valley — oh, how long ago, how long ago!
   Where all the broad expanse was clothed in vines
And fruitful fields and meadows starred with flowers,
And clear streams wandered at their idle will,
And still lakes slept, their burnished surfaces
A dream of painted clouds, and soft airs
Went whispering with odorous breath,
And all was peace — in that fair vale,
Shut from the troubled world, a nameless hamlet
   drowsed.

   Hard by, apart, a temple stood;
And strangers from the outer world
Passing, noted it with tired eyes,
And seeing, saw it not:
A glimpse of its fair form — an answering momen-
   tary thrill —
And they passed on, careless and unaware.

They could not know the cunning of its make;
They could not know the secret shut up in its heart;
Only the dwellers of the hamlet knew:

They knew that what seemed brass was gold;
What marble seemed, was ivory;
The glories that enriched the milky surfaces —
The trailing vines, and interwoven flowers,
And tropic birds awing, clothed all in tinted fire —
They knew for what they were, not what they
    seemed:
Encrustings all of gems, not perishable splendors of
    the brush.
They knew the secret spot where one must stand —
They knew the surest hour, the proper slant of
    sun —
To gather in, unmarred, undimmed,
The vision of the fane in all its fairy grace,
A fainting dream against the opal sky.
    And more than this.   They knew
That in the temple's inmost place a spirit dwelt,
Made all of light!
    For glimpses of it they had caught
Beyond the curtains when the priests
That served the altar came and went.

    All loved that light and held it dear
That had this partial grace;
But the adoring priests alone who lived
By day and night submerged in its immortal glow
Knew all its power and depth, and could appraise
    the loss
If it should fade and fail and come no more.

    All this was long ago — so long ago!

The light burned on; and they that worship'd it,
And they that caught its flash at intervals and held
    it dear,
Contented lived in its secure possession.   Ah,
How long ago it was!
                  And then when they
Were nothing fearing, and God's peace was in the
    air,
And none was prophesying harm —
The vast disaster fell:
Where stood the temple when the sun went down,
Was vacant desert when it rose again!

    Ah, yes! 'Tis ages since it chanced!
                      So long ago it was,
That from the memory of the hamlet-folk the Light
    has passed —
They scarce believing, now, that once it was,
Or, if believing, yet not missing it,
And reconciled to have it gone.

    Not so the priests!   Oh, not so
The stricken ones that served it day and night,
Adoring it, abiding in the healing of its peace:
They stand, yet, where erst they stood
Speechless in that dim morning long ago;
And still they gaze, as then they gazed,
And murmur, " It will come again;
It knows our pain — it knows — it knows —
Ah, surely it will come again."
                                S. L. C.

LAKE LUCERNE, August 18, 1897.

THE BELATED RUSSIAN PASSPORT

" One fly makes a summer."—Pudd'nhead Wilson's Calendar.

I

A GREAT beer - saloon in the Friedrichstrasse, Berlin, towards mid - afternoon. At a hundred round tables gentlemen sat smoking and drinking; flitting here and there and everywhere were white-aproned waiters bearing foaming mugs to the thirsty. At a table near the main entrance were grouped half a dozen lively young fellows—American students— drinking good-bye to a visiting Yale youth on his travels, who had been spending a few days in the German capital.

"But why do you cut your tour short in the middle, Parrish?" asked one of the students. "I wish I had your chance. What do you want to go home for?"

"Yes," said another, "what is the idea? You want to explain, you know, because it looks like insanity. Homcsick?"

A girlish blush rose in Parrish's fresh young face,

and after a little hesitation he confessed that that was his trouble.

"I was never away from home before," he said, "and every day I get more and more lonesome. I have not seen a friend for weeks, and it's been horrible. I meant to stick the trip through, for pride's sake, but seeing you boys has finished me. It's been heaven to me, and I can't take up that companionless dreariness again. If I had company— but I haven't, you know, so it's no use. They used to call me Miss Nancy when I was a small chap, and I reckon I'm that yet—girlish and timorous, and all that. I ought to have *been* a girl! I can't stand it; I'm going home."

The boys rallied him good-naturedly, and said he was making the mistake of his life; and one of them added that he ought at least to see St. Petersburg before turning back.

"Don't!" said Parrish, appealingly. "It was my dearest dream, and I'm throwing it away. Don't say a word more on that head, for I'm made of water, and can't stand out against anybody's persuasion. I *can't* go alone; I think I should die." He slapped his breast-pocket, and added: "Here is my protection against a change of mind; I've bought ticket and sleeper for Paris, and I leave to-night. Drink, now—this is on me—bumpers—this is for home!"

The good-byes were said, and Alfred Parrish was left to his thoughts and his loneliness. But for a

moment only. A sturdy, middle-aged man with a
brisk and business-like bearing, and an air of decision
and confidence suggestive of military training, came
bustling from the next table, and seated himself at
Parrish's side, and began to speak, with concentrated interest and earnestness. His eyes, his face,
his person, his whole system, seemed to exude energy. He was full of steam—racing pressure—one
could almost hear his gauge-cocks sing. He extended a frank hand, shook Parrish cordially, and
said, with a most convincing air of strenuous conviction:

"Ah, but you *mustn't;* really you mustn't; it
would be the greatest mistake; you would always
regret it. Be persuaded, I beg you; don't do it—
don't!"

There was such a friendly note in it, and such a
seeming of genuineness, that it brought a sort of uplift to the youth's despondent spirits, and a telltale
moisture betrayed itself in his eyes, an unintentional
confession that he was touched and grateful. The
alert stranger noted that sign, was quite content
with that response, and followed up his advantage
without waiting for a spoken one:

"No, don't do it; it would be a mistake. I have
heard everything that was said—you will pardon
that—I was so close by that I couldn't help it.
And it troubled me to think that you would cut
your travels short when you really *want* to see St.
Petersburg, and are right here almost in sight of it!

Reconsider it—ah, you *must* reconsider it. It is such a short distance—it is very soon done and very soon over—and think what a memory it will be!"

Then he went on and made a picture of the Russian capital and its wonders, which made Alfred Parrish's mouth water and his roused spirits cry out with longing. Then—

"Of course you must see St. Petersburg—you *must!* Why, it will be a joy to you—a joy! I know, because I know the place as familiarly as I know my own birthplace in America. Ten years—I've known it ten years. Ask anybody there; they'll tell you; they all know me—Major Jackson The very dogs know me. Do go; oh, you must go; you must, indeed."

Alfred Parrish was quivering with eagerness now. He would go. His face said it as plainly as his tongue could have done it. Then—the old shadow fell, and he said, sorrowfully:

"Oh no—no, it's no use; I can't. I should die of the loneliness."

The Major said, with astonishment: "The—loneliness! Why, I'm going *with* you!"

It was startlingly unexpected. And not quite pleasant. Things were moving too rapidly. Was this a trap? Was this stranger a sharper? Whence all this gratuitous interest in a wandering and unknown lad? Then he glanced at the Major's frank and winning and beaming face, and was ashamed; and wished he knew how to get out of this scrape without hurting the feelings of its contriver. But he

was not handy in matters of diplomacy, **and went at**
the difficulty with conscious awkwardness and small
confidence.   He said, with a quite overdone show of
unselfishness:

"Oh no, no, you are too kind; I couldn't — I
couldn't allow you to put yourself to such an inconvenience on my—"

"Inconvenience?   None in the world, my boy; I
was going to-night, anyway; I leave in the express
at nine.   Come! we'll go together.   You sha'n't
be lonely a single minute.   Come along — say the
word!"

So that excuse had failed.   What to do now?
Parrish was disheartened; it seemed to him that no
subterfuge which his poor invention could contrive
would ever rescue him from these toils.   Still, he
must make another effort, and he did; and before he
had finished his new excuse he thought he recognized that it was unanswerable:

"Ah, but most unfortunately luck is against me,
and it is impossible.   Look at these"—and he took
out his tickets and laid them on the table.   "I am
booked through to Paris, and I couldn't get these
tickets and baggage coupons changed for St. Petersburg, of course, and would have to lose the money;
and if I could afford to lose the money I should be
rather short after I bought the new tickets—for
there is all the cash I've got about me"—and he laid
a five-hundred-mark bank-note on the table.

In a moment the Major had the tickets and cou-

pons and was on his feet, and saying, with enthusiasm:

"Good! It's all right, and everything safe.
They'll change the tickets and baggage pasters for
me; they all know me—everybody knows me. Sit
right where you are; I'll be back right away." Then
he reached for the bank-note, and added, "I'll take
this along, for there will be a little extra pay on the
new tickets, maybe"—and the next moment he was
flying out at the door.

II

ALFRED PARRISH was paralyzed. It was all so sudden. So sudden, so daring, so incredible, so impossible. His mouth was open, but his tongue wouldn't work; he tried to shout "Stop him," but his lungs were empty; he wanted to pursue, but his legs refused to do anything but tremble; then they gave way under him and let him down into his chair. His throat was dry, he was gasping and swallowing with dismay, his head was in a whirl. What must he do? He did not know. One thing seemed plain, however—he must pull himself together, and try to overtake that man. Of course the man could not get back the ticket money, but would he throw the tickets away on that account? No; he would certainly go to the station and sell them to some one at half-price; and to-day, too, for they would be worthless to-morrow, by German custom. These reflections gave him hope and strength, and he rose and started. But he took only a couple of steps, then he felt a sudden sickness, and tottered back to his chair again, weak with a dread that his movement had been noticed—for the last round of beer was at his expense; it had not been paid for, and he hadn't a pfennig. He was a prisoner—Heaven only could know what might happen if he tried to leave the place. He was timid, scared, crushed; and he had not German enough to state his case and beg for help and indulgence.

Then his thoughts began to persecute him. How could he have been such a fool? What possessed him to listen to such a manifest adventurer? *And here comes the waiter!* He buried himself in the newspaper — trembling. The waiter passed by. It filled him with thankfulness. The hands of the clock seemed to stand still, yet he could not keep his eyes from them.

Ten minutes dragged by. The waiter again! Again he hid behind the paper. The waiter paused —apparently a week—then passed on.

Another ten minutes of misery—once more the waiter; this time he wiped off the table, and seemed to be a month at it; then paused two months, and went away.

Parrish felt that he could not endure another visit; he must take the chances: he must run the gantlet; he must escape. But the waiter stayed around about the neighborhood for five minutes — months and months seemingly, Parrish watching him with a despairing eye, and feeling the infirmities of age creeping upon him and his hair gradually turning gray.

At last the waiter wandered away—stopped at a table, collected a bill, wandered farther, collected another bill, wandered farther — Parrish's praying eye riveted on him all the time, his heart thumping, his breath coming and going in quick little gasps of anxiety mixed with hope.

The waiter stopped again to collect, and Parrish said to himself, it is now or never! and started for the door. One step — two steps — three — four — he was nearing the door—five—his legs shaking under him—was that a swift step behind him?—the thought shrivelled his heart — six steps — seven, and he was out! — eight — nine — ten — eleven — twelve — there *is* a pursuing step!—he turned the corner, and picked up his heels to fly — a heavy hand fell on his shoulder, and the strength went out of his body!

It was the Major. He asked not a question, he showed no surprise. He said, in his breezy and exhilarating fashion:

"Confound those people, they delayed me; that's why I was gone so long. New man in the ticket-office, and he didn't know me, and wouldn't make the exchange because it was irregular; so I had to hunt up my old friend, the great mogul—the station-master, you know—hi, there, cab! cab!—jump in, Parrish!—Russian consulate, cabby, and let them fly!—so, as I say, that all cost time. But it's all right now, and everything straight; your luggage re-weighed, rechecked, fare-ticket and sleeper changed, and I've got the documents for it in my pocket; also the change — I'll keep it for you. Whoop along, cabby, whoop along; don't let them go to sleep!"

Poor Parrish was trying his best to get in a word
24

edgeways, as the cab flew farther and farther from the bilked beer-hall, and now at last he succeeded, and wanted to return at once and pay his little bill.

"Oh, never mind about that," said the Major, placidly; "that's all right, they know me, everybody knows me—I'll square it next time I'm in Berlin—push along, cabby, push along—no great lot of time to spare, now."

They arrived at the Russian consulate, a moment after hours, and hurried in. No one there but a clerk. The Major laid his card on the desk, and said, in the Russian tongue, "Now, then, if you'll visé this young man's passport for Petersburg as quickly as—"

"But, dear sir, I'm not authorized, and the consul has just gone."

"Gone where?"

"Out in the country, where he lives."

"And he'll be back—"

"Not till morning."

"Thunder! Oh, well, look here, I'm Major Jackson—he knows me, everybody knows me. You visé it yourself; tell him Major Jackson asked you; it 'll be all right."

But it would be desperately and fatally irregular; the clerk could not be persuaded; he almost fainted at the idea.

"Well, then, I'll tell you what to do," said the Major. "Here's stamps and the fee—visé it in the morning, and start it along by mail."

The clerk said, dubiously, "He—well, he may perhaps do it, and so—"

"May? He *will!* He knows me — everybody knows me."

"Very well," said the clerk, "I will tell him what you say." He looked bewildered, and in a measure subjugated; and added, timidly: "But—but—you know you will beat it to the frontier twenty-four hours. There are no accommodations there for so long a wait."

"Who's going to *wait?* Not I, if the court knows herself."

The clerk was temporarily paralyzed, and said, "Surely, sir, you don't wish it sent to Petersburg!"

"And why not?"

"And the owner of it tarrying at the frontier, twenty-five miles away? It couldn't do him any good, in those circumstances."

"Tarry—the mischief! Who said he was going to do any tarrying?"

"Why, you know, of course, they'll stop him at the frontier if he has no passport."

"Indeed they won't! The Chief Inspector knows me—everybody does. I'll be responsible for the young man. You send it straight through to Petersburg—Hôtel de l'Europe, care Major Jackson: tell the consul not to worry, I'm taking all the risks myself."

The clerk hesitated, then chanced one more appeal:

"You must bear in mind, sir, that the risks are

peculiarly serious, just now. The new edict is in force."

"What is it?"

"Ten years in Siberia for being in Russia without a passport."

"Mm—damnation!" He said it in English, for the Russian tongue is but a poor stand-by in spiritual emergencies. He mused a moment, then brisked up and resumed in Russian: "Oh, it's all right— label her St. Petersburg and let her sail! I'll fix it. They all know me there—all the authorities—everybody."

III

THE Major turned out to be an adorable travelling companion, and young Parrish was charmed with him. His talk was sunshine and rainbows, and lit up the whole region around, and kept it gay and happy and cheerful; and he was full of accommodating ways, and knew all about how to do things, and when to do them, and the best way. So the long journey was a fairy dream for that young lad who had been so lonely and forlorn and friendless so many homesick weeks. At last, when the two travellers were approaching the frontier, Parrish said something about passports; then started, as if recollecting something, and added:

"Why, come to think, I don't remember your bringing my passport away from the consulate. But you did, didn't you?"

"No; it's coming by mail," said the Major, comfortably.

"K—coming—by—mail!" gasped the lad; and all the dreadful things he had heard about the terrors and disasters of passportless visitors to Russia rose in his frightened mind and turned him white to the lips. "Oh, Major—oh, my goodness, what will become of me! How *could* you do such a thing?"

The Major laid a soothing hand upon the youth's shoulder and said:

"Now don't you worry, my boy, don't you worry a bit. I'm taking care of you, and I'm not going to let any harm come to you. The Chief Inspector knows me, and I'll explain to him, and it 'll be all right—you'll see. Now don't you give yourself the least discomfort—I'll fix it all up, easy as nothing."

Alfred trembled, and felt a great sinking inside, but he did what he could to conceal his misery, and to respond with some show of heart to the Major's kindly pettings and reassurings.

At the frontier he got out and stood on the edge of the great crowd, and waited in deep anxiety while the Major ploughed his way through the mass to "explain to the Chief Inspector." It seemed a cruelly long wait, but at last the Major reappeared. He said, cheerfully, ' Damnation, it's a new inspector, and I don't know him!"

Alfred fell up against a pile of trunks, with a despairing, "Oh, dear, dear, I might have known it!" and was slumping limp and helpless to the ground, but the Major gathered him up and seated him on a box, and sat down by him, with a supporting arm around him, and whispered in his ear:

"Don't worry, laddie, don't—it's going to be all right; you just trust to me. The sub-inspector's as near-sighted as a shad. I watched him, and I know it's so. Now I'll tell you how to do. I'll go and get my passport chalked, then I'll stop right yonder inside the grille where you see those peasants with their packs. You be there, and I'll back up against the grille, and slip my passport to you through the bars, then you tag along after the crowd and hand it in, and trust to Providence and that shad. Mainly the shad. You'll pull through all right—now don't you be afraid."

"But, oh dear, dear, *your* description and *mine* don't tally any more than—"

"Oh, that's all right—difference between fifty-one and nineteen—just entirely imperceptible to that shad—don't you fret, it's going to come out as right as nails."

Ten minutes later Alfred was tottering towards the train, pale, and in a collapse, but he had played the shad successfully, and was as grateful as an untaxed dog that has evaded the police.

"I told you so," said the Major, in splendid spirits. "I knew it would come out all right if you trusted in Providence like a little, trusting child and didn't try to improve on His ideas—it always does."

Between the frontier and Petersburg the Major laid himself out to restore his young comrade's life, and work up his circulation, and pull him out of his despondency, and make him feel again that life was a joy and worth living. And so, as a consequence, the young fellow entered the city in high feather and marched into the hotel in fine form, and registered his name. But instead of naming a room, the clerk glanced at him inquiringly, and waited. The

Major came promptly to the rescue, and said, cordially:

"It's all right—you know me—set him down, I'm responsible." The clerk looked grave, and shook his head. The Major added: "It's all right, it 'll be here in twenty-four hours — it's coming by mail. Here's mine, and his is coming right along."

The clerk was full of politeness, full of deference, but he was firm. He said, in English:

"Indeed, I wish I could accommodate you, Major, and certainly I would if I could; but I have no choice, I must ask him to go; I cannot allow him to remain in the house a moment."

Parrish began to totter, and emitted a moan; the Major caught him and stayed him with an arm, and said to the clerk, appealingly:

"Come, you know me—everybody does—just let him stay here the one night, and I give you my word—"

The clerk shook his head, and said:

"But, Major, you are endangering me, you are endangering the house. I—I hate to do such a thing, but I—I *must* call the police."

"Hold on, don't do that. Come along, my boy, and don't you fret—it's going to come out all right. Hi, there, cabby! Jump in, Parrish. Palace of the General of the Secret Police — turn them loose, cabby! Let them go! Make them whiz! Now we're off, and don't you give yourself any uneasiness. Prince Bossloffsky knows me, knows me like a book; he'll soon fix things all right for us."

They tore through the gay streets and arrived at the palace, which was brilliantly lighted. But it was half-past eight; the Prince was about going in to dinner, the sentinel said, and couldn't receive any one.

"But he'll receive *me*," said the Major, robustly, and handed his card. "I'm Major Jackson. Send it in; it 'll be all right."

The card was sent in, under protest, and the Major and his waif waited in a reception-room for some time. At length they were sent for, and conducted to a sumptuous private office and confronted with the Prince, who stood there gorgeously arrayed and frowning like a thunder-cloud. The Major stated his case, and begged for a twenty-four-hour stay of proceedings until the passport should be forthcoming.

"Oh, impossible!" said the Prince, in faultless English. "I marvel that you should have done so insane a thing as to bring the lad into the country without a passport, Major, I marvel at it; why, it's ten years in Siberia, and no help for it—catch him! support him!" for poor Parrish was making another trip to the floor. "Here—quick, give him this. There—take another draught; brandy's the thing, don't you find it so, lad? Now you feel better, poor fellow. Lie down on the sofa. How stupid it was of you, Major, to get him into such a horrible scrape."

The Major eased the boy down with his strong arms, put a cushion under his head, and whispered in his ear:

"Look as damned sick as you can! Play it for all it's worth; he's touched, you see; got a tender heart under there somewhere; fetch a groan, and say, 'Oh, mamma, mamma'; it 'll knock him out, sure as guns."

Parrish was going to do these things anyway, from native impulse, so they came from him promptly, with great and moving sincerity, and the Major whispered: "Splendid! Do it again; Bernhardt couldn't beat it."

What with the Major's eloquence and the boy's misery, the point was gained at last; the Prince struck his colors, and said:

"Have it your way; though you deserve a sharp lesson and you ought to get it. I give you exactly twenty-four hours. If the passport is not here then, don't come near me; it's Siberia without hope of pardon."

While the Major and the lad poured out their thanks, the Prince rang in a couple of soldiers, and in their own language he ordered them to go with these two people, and not lose sight of the younger one a moment for the next twenty-four hours; and if, at the end of that term, the boy could not show a passport, impound him in the dungeons of St. Peter and St. Paul, and report.

The unfortunates arrived at the hotel with their guards, dined under their eyes, remained in Parrish's room until the Major went off to bed, after cheering up the said Parrish, then one of the soldiers locked himself and Parrish in, and the other one stretched himself across the door outside and soon went off to sleep.

So also did not Alfred Parrish. The moment he was alone with the solemn soldier and the voiceless silence his machine-made cheerfulness began to waste away, his medicated courage began to give off its supporting gases and shrink towards normal, and his poor little heart to shrivel like a raisin. Within thirty minutes he struck bottom; grief, misery, fright, despair, could go no lower. Bed? Bed was not for such as he; bed was not for the doomed, the lost! Sleep? He was not the Hebrew children, he could not sleep in the fire! He could only walk the floor. And not only could, but must. And did, by the hour. And mourned, and wept, and shuddered, and prayed.

Then all-sorrowfully he made his last dispositions, and prepared himself, as well as in him lay, to meet his fate. As a final act, he wrote a letter:

"MY DARLING MOTHER,—When these sad lines shall have reached you your poor Alfred will be no more. No; worse than that, far worse! Through my own fault and foolishness I have fallen into the hands of a sharper or a lunatic; I do not know which, but in either case I feel that I am lost. Sometimes I think he is a sharper, but most of the time I think he is only mad, for he has a kind, good heart, I know, and he certainly seems to try the hardest that ever a person tried to get me out of the fatal difficulties he has gotten me into.

"In a few hours I shall be one of a nameless horde plodding the snowy solitudes of Russia, under the lash, and bound for that land of mystery and misery and termless oblivion, Siberia! I shall not live to see it; my heart is broken and I shall die. Give my picture to *her*, and ask her to keep it in memory of me, and to so live that in the appointed time she may join me in that better world where there is no marriage nor giving in marriage, and where there are no more separations, and troubles never come. Give my yellow dog to Archy Hale, and the other one to Henry Taylor; my blazer I give to brother Will, and my fishing things and Bible.

"There is no hope for me. I cannot escape; the soldier stands there with his gun and never takes his eyes off me, just blinks; there is no other movement, any more than if he was dead. I cannot bribe him, the maniac has my money. My letter of credit is in my trunk, and may never come—*will* never come, I know. Oh, what is to become of me! Pray for me, darling mother, pray for your poor Alfred. But it will do no good."

IV

In the morning Alfred came out looking scraggy and worn when the Major summoned him to an early breakfast. They fed their guards, they lit cigars, the Major loosened his tongue and set it going, and under its magic influence Alfred gradually and gratefully became hopeful, measurably cheerful, and almost happy once more.

But he would not leave the house. Siberia hung over him black and threatening, his appetite for sights was all gone, he could not have borne the shame of inspecting streets and galleries and churches with a soldier at each elbow and all the world stopping and staring and commenting—no, he would stay within and wait for the Berlin mail and his fate. So, all day long the Major stood gallantly by him in his room, with one soldier standing stiff and motionless against the door with his musket at his shoulder, and the other one drowsing in a chair outside; and all day long the faithful veteran spun campaign yarns, described battles, reeled off explosive anecdotes, with unconquerable energy and sparkle and resolution, and kept the scared student alive and his pulses functioning. The long day wore to a close, and the pair, followed by their guards, went down to the great dining-room and took their seats.

"The suspense will be over before long, now," sighed poor Alfred.

Just then a pair of Englishmen passed by, and one of them said, "So we'll get no letters from Berlin to-night."

Parrish's breath began to fail him. The Englishmen seated themselves at a near-by table, and the other one said:

"No, it isn't as bad as that." Parrish's breathing improved. "There is later telegraphic news. The accident did detain the train formidably, but that is all. It will arrive here three hours late to-night."

Parrish did not get to the floor this time, for the Major jumped for him in time. He had been listening, and foresaw what would happen. He patted Parrish on the back, hoisted him out of his chair, and said, cheerfully:

"Come along, my boy, cheer up, there's absolutely nothing to worry about. I know a way out. Bother the passport; let it lag a week if it wants to, we can do without it."

Parrish was too sick to hear him; hope was gone, Siberia present; he moved off on legs of lead, upheld by the Major, who walked him to the American legation, heartening him on the way with assurances that on his recommendation the minister wouldn't hesitate a moment to grant him a new passport.

"I had that card up my sleeve all the time," he

said. "The minister knows me—knows me familiarly—chummed together hours and hours under a pile of other wounded at Cold Harbor; been chummies ever since, in spirit, though we haven't met much in the body. Cheer up, laddie, everything's looking splendid! By gracious! I feel as cocky as a buck angel. Here we are, and our troubles are at an end! If we ever really had any."

There, alongside the door, was the trade-mark of the richest and freest and mightiest republic of all the ages: the pine disk, with the planked eagle spread upon it, his head and shoulders among the stars, and his claws full of out-of-date war material; and at that sight the tears came into Alfred's eyes, the pride of country rose in his heart, "Hail Columbia" boomed up in his breast, and all his fears and sorrows vanished away; for here he was safe, safe! not all the powers of the earth would venture to cross that threshold to lay a hand upon him!

For economy's sake the mightiest republic's legations in Europe consist of a room and a half on the ninth floor, when the tenth is occupied, and the legation furniture consists of a minister or an ambassador with a brakeman's salary, a secretary of legation who sells matches and mends crockery for a living, a hired girl for interpreter and general utility, pictures of the American liners, a chromo of the reigning President, a desk, three chairs, kerosene-lamp, a cat, a clock, and a cuspidor with motto, "In God We Trust."

The party climbed up there, followed by the escort. A man sat at the desk writing official things on wrapping-paper with a nail. He rose and faced about; the cat climbed down and got under the desk; the hired girl squeezed herself up into the corner by the vodka-jug to make room; the soldiers squeezed themselves up against the wall alongside of her, with muskets at shoulder arms. Alfred was radiant with happiness and the sense of rescue. The Major cordially shook hands with the official, rattled off his case in easy and fluent style, and asked for the desired passport.

The official seated his guests, then said: "Well, I am only the secretary of legation, you know, and I wouldn't like to grant a passport while the minister is on Russian soil. There is far too much responsibility."

"All right, send for him."

The secretary smiled, and said: "That's easier said than done. He's away up in the wilds, somewhere, on his vacation."

"Ger-reat Scott!" ejaculated the Major.

Alfred groaned; the color went out of his face, and he began to slowly collapse in his clothes. The secretary said, wonderingly:

"Why, what are you Great-Scotting about, Major? The Prince gave you twenty-four hours. Look at the clock; you're all right; you've half an hour left; the train is just due; the passport will arrive in time."

"Man, there's news! The train is three hours behind time! This boy's life and liberty are wasting
away by minutes, and only thirty of them left! In
half an hour he's the same as dead and damned to
all eternity! By God, we *must* have the passport!"

"Oh, I am dying, I know it!" wailed the lad, and
buried his face in his arms on the desk. A quick
change came over the secretary, his placidity vanished away, excitement flamed up in his face and
eyes, and he exclaimed:

"I see the whole ghastliness of the situation, but,
Lord help us, what can I do? What can you suggest?"

"Why, hang it, give him the passport!"

"Impossible! totally impossible! You know nothing about him; three days ago you had never heard
of him; there's no way in the world to identify him.
He is lost, lost — there's no possibility of saving
him!"

The boy groaned again, and sobbed out, "Lord,
Lord, it's the last of earth for Alfred Parrish!"

Another change came over the secretary.

In the midst of a passionate outburst of pity, vexation, and hopelessness, he stopped short, his manner calmed down, and he asked, in the indifferent
voice which one uses in introducing the subject of
the weather when there is nothing to talk about, "Is
that your name?"

The youth sobbed out a yes.

"Where are you from?"
25

"Bridgeport."

The secretary shook his head—shook it again—
and muttered to himself. After a moment:

"Born there?"

"No; New Haven."

"Ah-h." The secretary glanced at the Major,
who was listening intently, with blank and unen-
lightened face, and indicated rather than said,
"There is vodka there, in case the soldiers are
thirsty. The Major sprang up, poured for them,
and received their gratitude. The questioning went
on.

"How long did you live in New Haven?"

"Till I was fourteen. Came back two years ago
to enter Yale."

"When you lived there, what street did you live
on?"

"Parker Street."

With a vague half-light of comprehension dawning
in his eye, the Major glanced an inquiry at the secretary. The secretary nodded, the Major poured
vodka again.

"What number?"

"It hadn't any."

The boy sat up and gave the secretary a pathetic
look which said, "Why do you want to torture me
with these foolish things, when I am miserable
enough without it?"

The secretary went on, unheeding: "What kind of
a house was it?"

"Brick—two-story."

"Flush with the sidewalk?"

"No, small yard in front."

"Iron fence?"

"No, palings."

The Major poured vodka again—without instructions—poured brimmers this time; and his face had cleared and was alive now.

"What do you see when you enter the door?"

"A narrow hall; door at the end of it, and a door at your right."

"Anything else?"

"Hat-rack."

"Room at the right?"

"Parlor."

"Carpet?"

"Yes."

"Kind of carpet?"

"Old-fashioned Wilton."

"Figures?"

"Yes—hawking-party, horseback."

The Major cast an eye at the clock — only six minutes left! He faced about with the jug, and as he poured he glanced at the secretary, then at the clock—inquiringly. The secretary nodded; the Major covered the clock from view with his body a moment, and set the hands back half an hour; then he refreshed the men—double rations.

"Room beyond the hall and hat-rack?"

"Dining-room."

"Stove?"

"Grate."

"Did your people own the house?"

"Yes."

"Do they own it yet?"

"No; sold it when we moved to Bridgeport."

The secretary paused a little, then said, "Did you have a nickname among your playmates?"

The color slowly rose in the youth's pale cheeks, and he dropped his eyes. He seemed to struggle with himself a moment or two, then he said, plaintively, "They called me Miss Nancy."

The secretary mused awhile, then he dug up another question:

"Any ornaments in the dining-room?"

"Well, y—no."

"*None?* None at *all?*"

"No."

"The mischief! Isn't that a little odd? Think!"

The youth thought and thought; the secretary waited, slightly panting. At last the imperilled waif looked up sadly and shook his head.

"Think—*think!*" cried the Major, in anxious solicitude; and poured again.

"Come!" said the secretary, "not even a *picture?*"

"Oh, certainly! but you said ornament."

"Ah! What did your father think of it?"

The color rose again. The boy was silent.

"Speak," said the secretary.

"Speak," cried the Major, and his trembling hand poured more vodka outside the glasses than inside.

"I—I can't tell you what he said," murmured the boy.

"Quick! quick!" said the secretary; "out with it; there's no time to lose—home and liberty or Siberia and death depend upon the answer."

"Oh, have pity! he is a clergyman, and—"

"No matter; out with it, or—"

"He said it was the hellfiredest nightmare he ever struck!"

"Saved!" shouted the secretary, and seized his nail and a blank passport. "*I* identify you; I've lived in the house, and I painted the picture myself!"

"Oh, come to my arms, my poor rescued boy!" cried the Major. "We will always be grateful to God that He made this artist!—if He did."

TWO LITTLE TALES

FIRST STORY: THE MAN WITH A MESSAGE FOR THE
DIRECTOR-GENERAL

SOME days ago, in this second month of 1900,
a friend made an afternoon call upon me here
in London. We are of that age when men who are
smoking away their time in chat do not talk quite so
much about the pleasantnesses of life as about its
exasperations. By and by this friend began to
abuse the War Office. It appeared that he had a
friend who had been inventing something which
could be made very useful to the soldiers in South
Africa. It was a light and very cheap and durable
boot, which would remain dry in wet weather, and
keep its shape and firmness. The inventor wanted
to get the government's attention called to it, but he
was an unknown man and knew the great officials
would pay no heed to a message from him.

"This shows that he was an ass — like the rest of
us," I said, interrupting. "Go on."

"But why have you said that? The man spoke
the truth."

"The man spoke a lie. Go on."

"I will *prove* that he —"

"You can't prove anything of the kind. I am very old and very wise. You must not argue with me: it is irreverent and offensive. Go on."

"Very well. But you will presently see. I am not unknown, yet even *I* was not able to get the man's message to the Director-General of the Shoe-Leather Department."

"This is another lie. Pray go on."

"But I assure you on my honor that I failed."

"Oh, certainly. I knew *that*. You didn't need to tell me."

"Then where is the lie?"

"It is in your intimation that you were *not able* to get the Director-General's immediate attention to the man's message. It is a lie, because you *could* have gotten his immediate attention to it."

"I tell you I couldn't. In three months I haven't accomplished it."

"Certainly. Of course. I could know that without your telling me. You *could* have gotten his immediate attention if you had gone at it in a sane way; and so could the other man."

"I *did* go at it in a sane way."

"You didn't."

"How do *you* know? What do you know about the circumstances?"

"Nothing at all. But you didn't go at it in a sane way. That much I know to a certainty."

"How can you know it, when you don't know what method I used?"

"I know by the result. The result is perfect proof. You went at it in an insane way. I am very old and very w—"

"Oh, yes, I know. But will you let me tell you *how* I proceeded? I think that will settle whether it was insanity or not."

"No; that has already been settled. But go on, since you so desire to expose yourself. I am very o—"

"Certainly, certainly. I sat down and wrote a courteous letter to the Director-General of the Shoe-Leather Department, explai—"

"Do you know him personally?"

"No."

"You have scored one for my side. You began insanely. Go on."

"In the letter I made the great value and inexpensiveness of the invention clear, and offered to —"

"Call and see him? Of course you did. Score two against yourself. I am v—"

"He didn't answer for three days."

"Necessarily. Proceed."

"Sent me three gruff lines thanking me for my trouble, and proposing —"

"Nothing."

"That's it — proposing nothing. Then I wrote him more elaborately and —"

"Score three —"

"— and got no answer. At the end of a week I wrote and asked, with some touch of asperity, for an answer to that letter."

"Four. Go on."

"An answer came back saying the letter had not been received, and asking for a copy. I traced the letter through the post-office, and found that it *had* been received; but I sent a copy and said nothing. Two weeks passed without further notice of me. In the mean time I gradually got myself cooled down to a polite-letter temperature. Then I wrote and proposed an interview for next day, and said that if I did not hear from him in the mean time I should take his silence for assent."

"Score five."

"I arrived at twelve sharp, and was given a chair in the anteroom and told to wait. I waited until half-past one; then I left, ashamed and angry. I waited another week, to cool down; then I wrote and made another appointment with him for next day noon."

"Score six."

"He answered, assenting. I arrived promptly, and kept a chair warm until half-past two. I left then, and shook the dust of that place from my shoes for good and all. For rudeness, inefficiency, incapacity, indifference to the army's interests, the Director-General of the Shoe-Leather Department of the War Office is, in my o—"

"Peace! I am very old and very wise, and have seen many seemingly intelligent people who hadn't common sense enough to go at a simple and easy thing like this in a common-sense way. You are not a curiosity to me; I have personally known millions and billions like you. You have lost three months quite unnecessarily; the inventor has lost three months; the soldiers have lost three — nine months altogether. I will now read you a little tale which I wrote last night. Then you will call on the Director-General at noon to-morrow and transact your business."

"Splendid! Do you know him?"

"No; but listen to the tale."

SECOND STORY: HOW THE CHIMNEY-SWEEP GOT THE EAR OF THE EMPEROR

I

Summer was come, and all the strong were bowed by the burden of the awful heat, and many of the weak were prostrate and dying. For weeks the army had been wasting away with a plague of dysentery, that scourge of the soldier, and there was but little help. The doctors were in despair; such efficacy as their drugs and their science had once had — and it was not much at its best — was a thing of the past, and promised to remain so.

The Emperor commanded the physicians of greatest renown to appear before him for a consultation, for he was profoundly disturbed. He was very severe with them, and called them to account for letting his soldiers die: and asked them if they knew their trade, or didn't; and were they properly healers, or merely assassins? Then the principal assassin, who was also the oldest doctor in the land and the most venerable in appearance, answered and said:

"We have done what we could, your Majesty, and for a good reason it has been little. No medicine and no physician can cure that disease; only nature and a good constitution can do it. I am old, and I know. No doctor and no medicine can cure it — I repeat it and I emphasize it. Sometimes they seem to help nature a little, — a very little, — but as a rule, they merely do damage."

The Emperor was a profane and passionate man, and he deluged the doctors with rugged and unfamiliar names, and drove them from his presence.

Within a day he was attacked by that fell disease himself. The news flew from mouth to mouth, and carried consternation with it over all the land.

All the talk was about this awful disaster, and there was general depression, for few had hope. The Emperor himself was very melancholy, and sighed and said:

"The will of God be done. Send for the assassins again, and let us get over with it."

They came, and felt his pulse and looked at his tongue, and fetched the drug store and emptied it into him, and sat down patiently to wait — for they were not paid by the job, but by the year.

II

Tommy was sixteen and a bright lad, but he was not in society. His rank was too humble for that,

and his employment too base. In fact, it was the
lowest of all employments, for he was second in
command to his father, who emptied cesspools and
drove a night-cart.   Tommy's closest friend was
Jimmy the chimney-sweep, a slim little fellow of
fourteen, who was honest and industrious, and had a
good heart, and supported a bedridden mother by
his dangerous and unpleasant trade.

About a month after the Emperor fell ill, these
two lads met one evening about nine. Tommy was
on his way to his night-work, and of course was not
in his Sundays, but in his dreadful work-clothes, and
not smelling very well.   Jimmy was on his way
home from his day's labor, and was blacker than
any other object imaginable, and he had his brushes
on his shoulder and his soot-bag at his waist, and no
feature of his sable face was distinguishable except
his lively eyes.

They sat down on the curbstone to talk; and of
course it was upon the one subject — the nation's
calamity, the Emperor's disorder.   Jimmy was full of
a great project, and burning to unfold it.   He said:

"Tommy, I can cure his Majesty.   I know how
to do it."

Tommy was surprised.

"What!   You?"

"Yes, I."

"Why, you little fool, the best doctors can't."

"I don't care: I can do it.   I can cure him in
fifteen minutes."

"Oh, come off! What are you giving me?"

"The facts — that's all."

Jimmy's manner was so serious that it sobered Tommy, who said:

"I believe you are in earnest, Jimmy. Are you in earnest?"

"I give you my word."

"What is the plan? How'll you cure him?"

"Tell him to eat a slice of ripe watermelon."

It caught Tommy rather suddenly, and he was shouting with laughter at the absurdity of the idea before he could put on a stopper. But he sobered down when he saw that Jimmy was wounded. He patted Jimmy's knee affectionately, not minding the soot, and said:

"I take the laugh all back. I didn't mean any harm, Jimmy, and I won't do it again. You see, it seemed so funny, because wherever there's a soldier-camp and dysentery, the doctors always put up a sign saying anybody caught bringing watermelons there will be flogged with the cat till he can't stand."

"I know it — the idiots!" said Jimmy, with both tears and anger in his voice. "There's plenty of watermelons, and not one of all those soldiers ought to have died."

"But, Jimmy, what put the notion into your head?"

"It isn't a notion; it's a fact. Do you know that old gray-headed Zulu? Well, this long time back he has been curing a lot of our friends, and my mother has seen him do it, and so have I. It takes only one or two slices of melon, and it don't make any difference whether the disease is new or old; it cures it."

"It's very odd. But, Jimmy, if it is so, the Emperor ought to be told of it."

"Of course; and my mother has told people, hoping they could get the word to him; but they are poor working-folks and ignorant, and don't know how to manage it."

"Of course they don't, the blunderheads," said Tommy, scornfully. "*I'll* get it to him!"

"You? You night-cart polecat!" And it was Jimmy's turn to laugh. But Tommy retorted sturdily:

"Oh, laugh if you like; but I'll *do* it!"

It had such an assured and confident sound that it made an impression, and Jimmy asked gravely:

"Do you know the Emperor?"

"Do *I* know him? Why, how you talk! Of course I don't."

"Then how'll you do it?"

"It's very simple and very easy. Guess. How would *you* do it, Jimmy?"

"Send him a letter. I never thought of it till this minute. But I'll bet that's your way."

"I'll bet it ain't. Tell me, how would you send it?"

"Why, through the mail, of course."

Tommy overwhelmed him with scoffings, and said:

"Now, don't you suppose every crank in the

empire is doing the same thing? Do you mean to say you haven't thought of that?"

"Well — no," said Jimmy, abashed.

"You *might* have thought of it, if you weren't so young and inexperienced. Why, Jimmy, when even a common *general*, or a poet, or an actor, or anybody that's a little famous gets sick, all the cranks in the kingdom load up the mails with certain-sure quack cures for him. And so, what's bound to happen when it's the Emperor?"

"I suppose it's worse," said Jimmy, sheepishly.

"Well, I should think so! Look here, Jimmy: every single night we cart off as many as six loads of that kind of letters from the back yard of the palace, where they're thrown. Eighty thousand letters in one night! Do you reckon anybody reads them? Sho! not a single one. It's what would happen to your letter if you wrote it — which you won't, I reckon?"

"No," sighed Jimmy, crushed.

"But it's all right, Jimmy. Don't you fret: there's more than one way to skin a cat. *I'll* get the word to him."

"Oh, if you only *could*, Tommy, I should love you forever!"

"I'll do it, I tell you. Don't you worry; you depend on me."

"Indeed I will, Tommy, for you do know so much. You're not like other boys: they never know anything. How'll you manage, Tommy?"

Tommy was greatly pleased. He settled himself for reposeful talk, and said:

"Do you know that ragged poor thing that thinks he's a butcher because he goes around with a basket and sells cat's meat and rotten livers? Well, to begin with, I'll tell *him*."

Jimmy was deeply disappointed and chagrined, and said:

"Now, Tommy, it's a shame to talk so. You know my heart's in it, and it's not right."

Tommy gave him a love-pat, and said:

"Don't you be troubled, Jimmy. *I* know what I'm about. Pretty soon you'll see. That half-breed butcher will tell the old woman that sells chestnuts at the corner of the lane — she's his closest friend, and I'll ask him to; then, by request, she'll tell her rich aunt that keeps the little fruit-shop on the corner two blocks above; and that one will tell her particular friend, the man that keeps the game-shop; and he will tell his friend the sergeant of police; and the sergeant will tell his captain, and the captain will tell the magistrate, and the magistrate will tell his brother-in-law the county judge, and the county judge will tell the sheriff, and the sheriff will tell the Lord Mayor, and the Lord Mayor will tell the President of the Council, and the President of the Council will tell the —"

"By George, but it's a wonderful scheme, Tommy! How ever *did* you —"

"—Rear-Admiral, and the Rear will tell the Vice,

and the Vice will tell the Admiral of the Blue, and
the Blue will tell the Red, and the Red will tell the
White, and the White will tell the First Lord of the
Admiralty, and the First Lord will tell the Speaker
of the House, and the Speaker—''

"Go it, Tommy; you're 'most there!"

"—will tell the Master of the Hounds, and the
Master will tell the Head Groom of the Stables, and
the Head Groom will tell the Chief Equerry, and
the Chief Equerry will tell the First Lord in Waiting,
and the First Lord will tell the Lord High Chamberlain, and the Lord High Chamberlain will tell the
Master of the Household, and the Master of the
Household will tell the little pet page that fans the
flies off the Emperor, and the page will get down on
his knees and whisper it to his Majesty—and the
game's made!"

"I've *got* to get up and hurrah a couple of times,
Tommy. It's the grandest idea that ever was.
What ever put it into your head?"

"Sit down and listen, and I'll give you some
wisdom—and don't you ever forget it as long as
you live. Now, then, who is the closest friend
you've got, and the one you couldn't and wouldn't
ever refuse anything in the world to?"

"Why, it's you, Tommy. You know that."

"Suppose you wanted to ask a pretty large favor
of the cat's-meat man. Well, you don't know him,
and he would tell you to go to thunder, for he is that
kind of a person; but he is my next best friend after
26

you, and would run his legs off to do me a kindness
— *any* kindness, he don't care what it is. Now, I'll
ask you: which is the most common-sensible — for
you to go and ask him to tell the chestnut-woman
about your watermelon cure, or for you to get me
to do it for you?"

"To get you to do it for me, of course. I
wouldn't ever have thought of that, Tommy; it's
splendid!"

"It's a *philosophy*, you see. Mighty good word —
and large. It goes on this idea: everybody in the
world, little and big, has one *special* friend, a friend
that he's *glad* to do favors to — not sour about it,
but *glad* — glad clear to the marrow. And so, I
don't care where you start, you can get at anybody's
ear that you want to — I don't care how low you are,
nor how high he is. And it's so simple: you've
only to find the *first* friend, that is all; that ends
your part of the work. He finds the next friend
himself, and that one finds the third, and so on,
friend after friend, link after link, like a chain; and
you can go up it or down it, as high as you like or
as low as you like."

"It's just beautiful, Tommy."

"It's as simple and easy as a-b-c; but did you
ever hear of anybody trying it? No; everybody is
a fool. He goes to a stranger without any introduction, or writes him a letter, and of course he
strikes a cold wave — and serves him gorgeously
right. Now, the Emperor don't know me, but

that's no matter — he'll eat his watermelon to-mor-row. You'll see. Hi-hi — stop! It's the cat's-meat man. Good-by, Jimmy; I'll overtake him."

He did overtake him, and said:

" Say, will you do me a favor? "

" *Will* I? Well, I should *say* ! I'm your man. Name it, and see me fly ! "

" Go tell the chestnut-woman to put down every-thing and carry this message to her first-best friend, and tell the friend to pass it along." He worded the message, and said, " Now, then, rush ! "

The next moment the chimney-sweep's word to the Emperor was on its way.

III

The next evening, toward midnight, the doctors sat whispering together in the imperial sick-room, and they were in deep trouble, for the Emperor was in very bad case. They could not hide it from them-selves that every time they emptied a fresh drug-store into him he got worse. It saddened them, for they were expecting that result. The poor emaci-ated Emperor lay motionless, with his eyes closed, and the page that was his darling was fanning the flies away and crying softly. Presently the boy heard the silken rustle of a portière, and turned and saw the Lord High Great Master of the Household peering in at the door and excitedly motioning to him to come. Lightly and swiftly the page tiptoed his way to his dear and worshiped friend the Master, who said:

" Only you can persuade him, my child, and oh, don't fail to do it!   Take this, make him eat it, and he is saved.''

" On my head be it.   He shall eat it! ''

It was a couple of great slices of ruddy, fresh watermelon.

The next morning the news flew everywhere that the Emperor was sound and well again, and had hanged the doctors.   A wave of joy swept the land, and frantic preparations were made to illuminate.

After breakfast his Majesty sat meditating.   His gratitude was unspeakable, and he was trying to devise a reward rich enough to properly testify it to his benefactor.   He got it arranged in his mind, and called the page, and asked him if he had invented that cure.   The boy said no — he got it from the Master of the Household.

He was sent away, and the Emperor went to devising again.   The Master was an earl; he would make him a duke, and give him a vast estate which belonged to a member of the Opposition.   He had him called, and asked him if he was the inventor of the remedy.   But the Master was an honest man, and said he got it of the Grand Chamberlain.   He was sent away, and the Emperor thought some more.   The Chamberlain was a viscount; he would make him an earl, and give him a large income. But the Chamberlain referred him to the First Lord in Waiting, and there was some more thinking; his Majesty thought out a smaller reward.   But the

"JIMMY SAVES THE EMPEROR"

First Lord in Waiting referred him back further, and he had to sit down and think out a further and becomingly and suitably smaller reward.

Then, to break the tediousness of the inquiry and hurry the business, he sent for the Grand High Chief Detective, and commanded him to trace the cure to the bottom, so that he could properly reward his benefactor.

At nine in the evening the High Chief Detective brought the word. He had traced the cure down to a lad named Jimmy, a chimney-sweep. The Emperor said, with deep feeling:

"Brave boy, he saved my life, and shall not regret it!"

And sent him a pair of his own boots; and the next best ones he had, too. They were too large for Jimmy, but they fitted the Zulu, so it was all right, and everything as it should be.

CONCLUSION TO THE FIRST STORY

"There — do you get the idea?"

"I am obliged to admit that I do. And it will be as you have said. I will transact the business to-morrow. I intimately know the Director-General's nearest friend. He will give me a note of introduction, with a word to say my matter is of real importance to the government. I will take it along, without an appointment, and send it in, with my card, and I shan't have to wait so much as half a minute."

That turned out true to the letter, and the government adopted the boots.

DIPLOMATIC PAY AND CLOTHES

VIENNA, *January 5.*— I find in this morning's
papers the statement that the Government of
the United States has paid to the two members of
the Peace Commission entitled to receive money for
their services $100,000 each for their six weeks'
work in Paris.

I hope that this is true. I will allow myself the
satisfaction of considering that it *is* true, and of
treating it as a thing finished and settled.

It is a precedent; and ought to be a welcome one
to our country. A precedent always has a chance
to be valuable (as well as the other way); and its
best chance to be valuable (or the other way) is
when it takes such a striking form as to fix a whole
nation's attention upon it. If it come justified out
of the discussion which will follow, it will find a
career ready and waiting for it.

We realize that the edifice of public justice is built
of precedents, from the ground upward; but we do
not always realize that all the other details of our
civilization are likewise built of precedents. The
changes also which they undergo are due to the in-

trusion of new precedents, which hold their ground against opposition, and keep their place. A precedent may die at birth, or it may live — it is mainly a matter of luck. If it be imitated once, it has a chance; if twice a better chance; if three times it is reaching a point where account must be taken of it; if four, five, or six times, it has probably come to stay — for a whole century, possibly. If a town start a new bow, or a new dance, or a new temperance project, or a new kind of hat, and can get the precedent adopted in the next town, the career of that precedent is begun; and it will be unsafe to bet as to where the end of its journey is going to be. It may not get this start at all, and may have no career; but if a crown prince introduce the precedent, it will attract vast attention, and its chances for a career are so great as to amount almost to a certainty.

For a long time we have been reaping damage from a couple of disastrous precedents. One is the precedent of shabby pay to public servants standing for the power and dignity of the Republic in foreign lands; the other is a precedent condemning them to exhibit themselves officially in clothes which are not only without grace or dignity, but are a pretty loud and pious rebuke to the vain and frivolous costumes worn by the other officials. To our day an American ambassador's official costume remains under the reproach of these defects. At a public function in a European court all foreign representatives except ours wear clothes which in some way distinguish them from the unofficial throng, and mark them as standing for their *countries*. But our representative appears in a plain black swallow-tail, which stands for neither country nor people. It has no nationality. It is found in all countries; it is as international as a night-shirt. It has no particular meaning: but our Government tries to give it one; it tries to make it stand for Republican Simplicity, modesty and unpretentiousness. Tries, and without doubt fails, for it is not conceivable that this loud ostentation of simplicity deceives any one. The statue that advertises its modesty with a fig-leaf really brings its modesty under suspicion. Worn officially, our nonconforming swallow-tail is a declaration of ungracious independence in the matter of manners, and is uncourteous. It says to all around: " In Rome we do not choose to do as Rome does; we refuse to respect your tastes and your traditions; we make no sacrifices to any one's customs and prejudices; we yield no jot to the courtesies of life; we prefer our manners, and intrude them here."

That is not the true American spirit, and those clothes misrepresent us. When a foreigner comes among us and trespasses against our customs and our code of manners, we are offended, and justly so: but our Government commands our ambassadors to wear abroad an official dress which is an offense against foreign manners and customs; and the discredit of it falls upon the nation.

We did not dress our public functionaries in un-
distinguished raiment before Franklin's time; and
the change would not have come if he had been an
obscurity. But he was such a colossal figure in the
world that whatever he did of an unusual nature
attracted the world's attention, and became a precedent. In the case of clothes, the next representative after him, and the next, had to imitate it. After
that, the thing was custom: and custom is a petri-
faction; nothing but dynamite can dislodge it for a
century. We imagine that our queer official cos-
tumery was deliberately devised to symbolize our Republican Simplicity — a quality which we have never
possessed, and are too old to acquire now, if we had
any use for it or any leaning toward it. But it is
not so; there was nothing deliberate about it: it
grew naturally and heedlessly out of the precedent
set by Franklin.

If it had been an intentional thing, and based
upon a principle, it would not have stopped where
it did: we should have applied it further. Instead
of clothing our admirals and generals, for courts-
martial and other public functions, in superb dress
uniforms blazing with color and gold, the Government would put them in swallow-tails and white
cravats, and make them look like ambassadors and
lackeys. If I am wrong in making Franklin the
father of our curious official clothes, it is no matter
— he will be able to stand it.

It is my opinion — and I make no charge for the

suggestion — that, whenever we appoint an ambassador or a minister, we ought to confer upon him the
temporary rank of admiral or general, and allow
him to wear the corresponding uniform at public
functions in foreign countries. I would recommend
this for the reason that it is not consonant with the
dignity of the United States of America that her
representative should appear upon occasions of state
in a dress which makes him glaringly conspicuous;
and that is what his present undertaker-outfit does
when it appears, with its dismal smudge, in the
midst of the butterfly splendors of a Continental
court. It is a most trying position for a shy man, a
modest man, a man accustomed to being like other
people. He is the most striking figure present;
there is no hiding from the multitudinous eyes. It
would be funny, if it were not such a cruel spectacle,
to see the hunted creature in his solemn sables
scuffling around in that sea of vivid color, like a
mislaid Presbyterian in perdition. We are all aware
that our representative's dress should not compel too
much attention; for anybody but an Indian chief
knows that that is a vulgarity. I am saying these
things in the interest of our national pride and
dignity. Our representative is the flag. He is the
Republic. He is the United States of America.
And when these embodiments pass by, we do not
want them scoffed at; we desire that people shall
be obliged to concede that they are worthily clothed,
and politely.

Our Government is oddly inconsistent in this matter of official dress. When its representative is a civilian who has not been a soldier, it restricts him to the black swallow-tail and white tie; but if he is a civilian who has been a soldier, it allows him to wear the uniform of his former rank as an official dress. When General Sickles was minister to Spain, he always wore, when on official duty, the dress uniform of a major-general. When General Grant visited foreign courts, he went handsomely and properly ablaze in the uniform of a full general, and was introduced by diplomatic survivals of his own Presidential Administration. The latter, by official necessity, went in the meek and lowly swallow-tail — a deliciously sarcastic contrast: the one dress representing the honest and honorable dignity of the nation; the other, the cheap hypocrisy of the Republican Simplicity tradition. In Paris our present representative can perform his official functions reputably clothed; for he was an officer in the Civil War. In London our late ambassador was similarly situated; for he also was an officer in the Civil War. But Mr. Choate must represent the Great Republic — even at official breakfast at seven in the morning — in that same old funny swallow-tail.

Our Government's notions about proprieties of costume are indeed very, very odd — as suggested by that last fact. The swallow-tail is recognized the world over as not wearable in the daytime; it is a night-dress, and a night-dress only — a night-shirt is

not more so. Yet, when our representative makes
an official visit in the morning, he is obliged by his
Government to go in that night-dress. It makes the
very cab-horses laugh.

The truth is, that for a while during the present
century, and up to something short of forty years
ago, we had a lucid interval, and dropped the
Republican Simplicity sham, and dressed our foreign
representatives in a handsome and becoming official
costume. This was discarded by and by, and the
swallow-tail substituted. I believe it is not now
known which statesman brought about this change;
but we all know that, stupid as he was as to diplomatic proprieties in dress, he would not have sent his
daughter to a state ball in a corn-shucking costume,
nor to a corn-shucking in a state ball costume, to be
harshly criticised as an ill-mannered offender against
the proprieties of custom in both places. And we
know another thing, viz.: that he himself would not
have wounded the tastes and feelings of a family of
mourners by attending a funeral in their house in a
costume which was an offense against the dignities
and decorum prescribed by tradition and sanctified
by custom. Yet that man was so heedless as not to
reflect that *all* the social customs of civilized peoples
are entitled to respectful observance, and that no
man with a right spirit of courtesy in him ever has
any disposition to transgress these customs.

There is still another argument for a rational
diplomatic dress — a business argument. We are a

trading nation; and our representative is our business agent. If he is respected, esteemed, and liked where he is stationed, he can exercise an influence which can extend our trade and forward our prosperity. A considerable number of his business activities have their field in his social relations; and clothes which do not offend against local manners and customs and prejudices are a valuable part of his equipment in this matter — would be, if Franklin had died earlier.

I have not done with gratis suggestions yet. We made a great and valuable advance when we instituted the office of ambassador. That lofty rank endows its possessor with several times as much influence, consideration, and effectiveness as the rank of minister bestows. For the sake of the country's dignity and for the sake of her advantage commercially, we should have ambassadors, not ministers, at the great courts of the world.

But not at present salaries! No; if we are to maintain present salaries, let us make no more ambassadors; and let us unmake those we have already made. The great position, without the means of respectably maintaining it — there could be no wisdom in that. A foreign representative, to be valuable to his country, must be on good terms with the officials of the capital and with the rest of the influential folk. He must mingle with this society; he cannot sit at home — it is not business, it butters no commercial parsnips. He must attend the dinners, banquets,

suppers, balls, receptions, and must *return* these
hospitalities. He should return as good as he gets,
too, for the sake of the dignity of his country, and
for the sake of Business. Have we ever had a minister or an ambassador who could do this on his
salary? No — not once, from Franklin's time to
ours. Other countries understand the commercial
value of properly lining the pockets of their representatives; but apparently our Government has not
learned it. England is the most successful trader of
the several trading nations; and she takes good care
of the watchmen who keep guard in her commercial
towers. It has been a long time, now, since we
needed to blush for our representatives abroad. It
has become custom to send our fittest. We send
men of distinction, cultivation, character — our
ablest, our choicest, our best. Then we cripple
their efficiency through the meagreness of their pay.
Here is a list of salaries for English and American
ministers and ambassadors:

CITY.						SALARIES.	
						AMERICAN.	ENGLISH.
Paris	.	.	.	.	.	$17,500	$45,000
Berlin	.	.	.	.	.	17,500	40,000
Vienna	.	.	.	.	.	12,000	40,000
Constantinople	.	.	.	.	.	10,000	40,000
St. Petersburg	.	.	.	.	.	17,500	39,000
Rome	.	.	.	.	.	12,000	35,000
Washington	.	.	.	.	.	—	32,500

Sir Julian Pauncefote, the English ambassador at Washington, has a very fine house besides — at no damage to his salary.

English ambassadors pay no house-rent; they live in palaces owned by England. Our representatives pay house-rent out of their salaries. You can judge by the above figures what kind of houses the United States of America has been used to living in abroad, and what sort of return-entertaining she has done. There is not a salary in our list which would properly house the representative receiving it, and, in addition, pay $3,000 toward his family's bacon and doughnuts — the strange but economical and customary fare of the American ambassador's household, except on Sundays, when petrified Boston crackers are added.

The ambassadors and ministers of foreign nations not only have generous salaries, but their Governments provide them with money wherewith to pay a considerable part of their hospitality bills. I believe our Government pays no hospitality bills except those incurred by the navy. Through this concession to the navy, that arm is able to do us credit in foreign parts; and certainly that is well and politic. But why the Government does not think it well and politic that our diplomats should be able to do us like credit abroad is one of those mysterious inconsistencies which have been puzzling me ever since I stopped trying to understand baseball and took up statesmanship as a pastime.

To return to the matter of house-rent. Good
houses, properly furnished, in European capitals, are
not to be had at small figures. Consequently, our
foreign representatives have been accustomed to live
in garrets — sometimes on the roof. Being poor
men, it has been the best they could do on the salary
which the Government has paid them. How could
they adequately return the hospitalities shown them?
It was impossible. It would have exhausted the
salary in three months. Still, it was their official
duty to entertain the influentials after some sort of
fashion; and they did the best they could with their
limited purse. In return for champagne they furnished lemonade; in return for game they furnished
ham; in return for whale they furnished sardines; in
return for liquors they furnished condensed milk;
in return for the battalion of liveried and powdered
flunkeys they furnished the hired girl; in return for
the fairy wilderness of sumptuous decorations they
draped the stove with the American flag; in return
for the orchestra they furnished zither and ballads
by the family; in return for the ball — but they
didn't return the ball, except in cases where the
United States lived on the roof and had room.

Is this an exaggeration? It can hardly be called
that. I saw nearly the equivalent of it once, a good
many years ago. A minister was trying to create
influential friends for a project which might be worth
ten millions a year to the agriculturists of the Republic; and our Government had furnished him ham

and lemonade to persuade the opposition with. The minister did not succeed. He might not have succeeded if his salary had been what it ought to have been — $50,000 or $60,000 a year — but his chances would have been very greatly improved. And in any case, he and his dinners and his country would not have been joked about by the hard-hearted and pitied by the compassionate.

Any experienced ''drummer'' will testify that, when you want to do business, there is no economy in ham and lemonade. The drummer takes his country customer to the theatre, the opera, the circus; dines him, wines him, entertains him all the day and all the night in luxurious style; and plays upon his human nature in all seductive ways. For he knows, by old experience, that this is the best way to get a profitable order out of him. He has his reward. All Governments except our own play the same policy, with the same end in view; and they also have their reward. But ours refuses to do business by business ways, and sticks to ham and lemonade. This is the most expensive diet known to the diplomatic service of the world.

Ours is the only country of first importance that pays its foreign representatives trifling salaries. If we were poor, we could not find great fault with these economies, perhaps — at least one could find a sort of plausible excuse for them. But we are not poor; and the excuse fails. As shown above, some of our important diplomatic representatives receive

27

$12,000; others $17,500. These salaries are all ham
and lemonade, and unworthy of the flag. When we
have a rich ambassador in London or Paris, he lives
as the ambassador of a country like ours ought to
live, and it costs him $100,000 a year to do it. But
why should we allow him to pay that out of his
private pocket? There is nothing fair about it; and
the Republic is no proper subject for any one's
charity. In several cases our salaries of $12,000
should be $50,000; and all of the salaries of $17,-
500 ought to be $75,000 or $100,000, since we pay
no representative's house-rent. Our State Department realizes the mistake which we are making, and
would like to rectify it, but it has not the power.

When a young girl reaches eighteen she is recognized as being a woman. She adds six inches to her
skirt, she unplaits her dangling braids and balls her
hair on top of her head, she stops sleeping with her
little sister and has a room to herself, and becomes
in many ways a thundering expense. But she is in
society now; and papa has to stand it. There is no
avoiding it. Very well. The Great Republic length-
ened her skirts last year, balled up her hair, and
entered the world's society. This means that, if
she would prosper and stand fair with society, she
must put aside some of her dearest and darlingest
young ways and superstitions, and do as society
does. Of course, she can decline if she wants to;
but this would be unwise. She ought to realize,
now that she has "come out," that this is a right

and proper time to change a part of her style. She is in Rome; and it has long been granted that when one is in Rome it is good policy to do as Rome does. To advantage Rome? No — to advantage herself.

If our Government has really paid representatives of ours on the Paris Commission $100,000 apiece for six weeks' work, I feel sure that it is the best cash investment the nation has made in many years. For it seems quite impossible that, with that precedent on the books, the Government will be able to find excuses for continuing its diplomatic salaries at the present mean figure.

P. S.— VIENNA, *January 10.*— I see, by this morning's telegraphic news, that I am not to be the new ambassador here, after all. This — well, I hardly know what to say. I — well, of course, I do not care anything about it; but it is at least a surprise. I have for many months been using my influence at Washington to get this diplomatic see expanded into an ambassadorship, with the idea, of course, th— But never mind. Let it go. It is of no consequence. I say it calmly; for I am calm. But at the same time — However, the subject has no interest for me, and never had. I never really intended to take the place, anyway — I made up my mind to it months and months ago, nearly a year. But now, while I am calm, I would like to say this — that so long as I shall continue to possess an American's proper pride in the honor and dignity of his

country, I will not take any ambassadorship in the
gift of the flag at a salary short of $75,000 a year.
If I shall be charged with wanting to live beyond my
country's means, I cannot help it.   A country which
cannot afford ambassador's wages should be ashamed
to have ambassadors.

Think of a Seventeen-thousand-five-hundred-dollar
ambassador !   Particularly for *America*.   Why, it is
the most ludicrous spectacle, the most inconsistent and
incongruous spectacle, contrivable by even the most
diseased imagination.   It is a billionaire in a paper
collar, a king in a breechclout, an archangel in a tin
halo.   And, for pure sham and hypocrisy, the salary
is just the match of the ambassador's official clothes
— that boastful advertisement of a Republican Simplicity which manifests itself at home in Fifty-thou-
sand-dollar salaries to insurance presidents and railway lawyers, and in domestic palaces whose fittings
and furnishings often transcend in costly display and
splendor and richness the fittings and furnishings of
the palaces of the sceptred masters of Europe; and
which has invented and exported to the Old World
the palace-car, the sleeping-car, the tram-car, the
electric trolley, the best bicycles, the best motor-
cars, the steam-heater, the best and smartest systems
of electric calls and telephonic aids to laziness and
comfort, the elevator, the private bath-room (hot
and cold water on tap), the palace-hotel, with its
multifarious conveniences, comforts, shows, and
luxuries, the — oh, the list is interminable !   In a

word, Republican Simplicity found Europe with one shirt on her back, so to speak, as far as *real* luxuries, conveniences, and the comforts of life go, and has clothed her to the chin with the latter. We are the lavishest and showiest and most luxury-loving people on the earth; and at our masthead we fly one true and honest symbol, the gaudiest flag the world has ever seen. Oh, Republican Simplicity, there are many, many humbugs in the world, but none to which you need take off *your* hat!

EXTRACTS FROM ADAM'S DIARY

MONDAY.— This new creature with the long hair is a good deal in the way. It is always hanging around and following me about. I don't like this; I am not used to company. I wish it would stay with the other animals. . . . Cloudy to-day, wind in the east; think we shall have rain. . . . *We?* Where did I get that word?—I remember now —- the new creature uses it.

TUESDAY.— Been examining the great waterfall. It is the finest thing on the estate, I think. The new creature calls it Niagara Falls — why, I am sure I do not know. Says it *looks* like Niagara Falls. That is not a reason, it is mere waywardness and imbecility. I get no chance to name anything myself. The new creature names everything that comes along, before I can get in a protest. And always that same pretext is offered — it *looks* like the thing. There is the dodo, for instance. Says the moment one looks at it one sees at a glance that it " looks like a dodo." It will have to keep that name, no doubt. It wearies me to fret about it, and it does no good, anyway. Dodo! It looks no more like a dodo than I do.

WEDNESDAY.— Built me a shelter against the rain,

but could not have it to myself in peace.   The new
creature intruded.   When I tried to put it out it shed
water out of the holes it looks with, and wiped it
away with the back of its paws, and made a noise
such as some of the other animals make when they
are in distress.   I wish it would not talk; it is
always talking.   That sounds like a cheap fling at
the poor creature, a slur; but I do not mean it so.
I have never heard the human voice before, and any
new and strange sound intruding itself here upon the
solemn hush of these dreaming solitudes offends my
ear and seems a false note.   And this new sound is so
close to me; it is right at my shoulder, right at my ear,
first on one side and then on the other, and I am used
only to sounds that are more or less distant from me.

FRIDAY.— The naming goes recklessly on, in
spite of anything I can do.   I had a very good
name for the estate, and it was musical and pretty
— GARDEN OF EDEN.   Privately, I continue to call
it that, but not any longer publicly.   The new
creature says it is all woods and rocks and scenery,
and therefore has no resemblance to a garden.
Says it *looks* like a park, and does not look like
anything *but* a park.   Consequently, without con-
sulting me, it has been new-named — NIAGARA
FALLS PARK.   This is sufficiently high-handed, it
seems to me.   And already there is a sign up:

KEEP OFF
THE GRASS

My life is not as happy as it was.

SATURDAY.— The new creature eats too much fruit. We are going to run short, most likely. "We" again — that is *its* word; mine, too, now, from hearing it so much. Good deal of fog this morning. I do not go out in the fog myself. The new creature does. It goes out in all weathers, and stumps right in with its muddy feet. And talks. It used to be so pleasant and quiet here.

SUNDAY.— Pulled through. This day is getting to be more and more trying. It was selected and set apart last November as a day of rest. I had already six of them per week before. This morning found the new creature trying to clod apples out of that forbidden tree.

MONDAY.— The new creature says its name is Eve. That is all right, I have no objections. Says it is to call it by, when I want it to come. I said it was superfluous, then. The word evidently raised me in its respect; and indeed it is a large, good word and will bear repetition. It says it is not an It, it is a She. This is probably doubtful; yet it is all one to me; what she is were nothing to me if she would but go by herself and not talk.

TUESDAY. — She has littered the whole estate with execrable names and offensive signs:

THIS WAY TO THE WHIRLPOOL.
THIS WAY TO GOAT ISLAND.
CAVE OF THE WINDS THIS WAY.

She says this park would make a tidy summer resort if there was any custom for it. Summer

"WRITING HIS DIARY"

resort — another invention of hers — just words, without any meaning. What is a summer resort? But it is best not to ask her, she has such a rage for explaining.

FRIDAY. — She has taken to beseeching me to stop going over the Falls. What harm does it do? Says it makes her shudder. I wonder why; I have always done it — always liked the plunge, and the excitement and the coolness. I supposed it was what the Falls were for. They have no other use that I can see, and they must have been made for something. She says they were only made for scenery — like the rhinoceros and the mastodon.

I went over the Falls in a barrel — not satisfactory to her. Went over in a tub — still not satisfactory. Swam the Whirlpool and the Rapids in a fig-leaf suit. It got much damaged. Hence, tedious complaints about my extravagance. I am too much hampered here. What I need is change of scene.

SATURDAY. — I escaped last Tuesday night, and traveled two days, and built me another shelter in a secluded place, and obliterated my tracks as well as I could, but she hunted me out by means of a beast which she has tamed and calls a wolf, and came making that pitiful noise again, and shedding that water out of the places she looks with. I was obliged to return with her, but will presently emigrate again when occasion offers. She engages herself in many foolish things; among others, to study out why the animals called lions and tigers live on grass and flowers, when, as she says, the sort of teeth they wear would indicate that they were intended to eat each other. This is foolish, because to do that would be to kill each other, and that would introduce what, as I understand it, is called " death "; and death, as I have been told, has not yet entered the Park. Which is a pity, on some accounts.

SUNDAY.— Pulled through.

MONDAY.— I believe I see what the week is for: it is to give time to rest up from the weariness of Sunday. It seems a good idea. . . . She has been climbing that tree again. Clodded her out of it. She said nobody was looking. Seems to consider that a sufficient justification for chancing any dangerous thing. Told her that. The word justification moved her admiration — and envy, too, I thought. It is a good word.

TUESDAY.— She told me she was made out of a rib taken from my body. This is at least doubtful, if not more than that. I have not missed any rib. . . . She is in much trouble about the buzzard; says grass does not agree with it; is afraid she can't raise it; thinks it was intended to live on decayed flesh. The buzzard must get along the best it can with what it is provided. We cannot overturn the whole scheme to accommodate the buzzard.

SATURDAY.— She fell in the pond yesterday when she was looking at herself in it, which she is always doing. She nearly strangled, and said it was most uncomfortable. This made her sorry for the crea-

tures which live in there, which she calls fish, for
she continues to fasten names on to things that don't
need them and don't come when they are called by
them, which is a matter of no consequence to her,
she is such a numskull, anyway; so she got a lot of
them out and brought them in last night and put
them in my bed to keep warm, but I have noticed
them now and then all day and I don't see that they
are any happier there than they were before, only
quieter. When night comes I shall throw them
outdoors. I will not sleep with them again, for I
find them clammy and unpleasant to lie among when
a person hasn't anything on.

SUNDAY.— Pulled through.

TUESDAY.— She has taken up with a snake now.
The other animals are glad, for she was always experimenting with them and bothering them; and I
am glad because the snake talks, and this enables me
to get a rest.

FRIDAY.— She says the snake advises her to try
the fruit of that tree, and says the result will be a
great and fine and noble education. I told her there
would be another result, too — it would introduce
death into the world. That was a mistake — it had
been better to keep the remark to myself; it only
gave her an idea — she could save the sick buzzard,
and furnish fresh meat to the despondent lions and
tigers. I advised her to keep away from the tree.
She said she wouldn't. I foresee trouble. Will
emigrate.

WEDNESDAY.— I have had a variegated time. I escaped last night, and rode a horse all night as fast as he could go, hoping to get clear out of the Park and hide in some other country before the trouble should begin; but it was not to be. About an hour after sun-up, as I was riding through a flowery plain where thousands of animals were grazing, slumbering, or playing with each other, according to their wont, all of a sudden they broke into a tempest of frightful noises, and in one moment the plain was a frantic commotion and every beast was destroying its neighbor. I knew what it meant — Eve had eaten that fruit, and death was come into the world. . . . The tigers ate my horse, paying no attention when I ordered them to desist, and they would have eaten me if I had stayed — which I didn't, but went away in much haste. . . . I found this place, outside the Park, and was fairly comfortable for a few days, but she has found me out. Found me out, and has named the place Tonawanda — says it *looks* like that. In fact I was not sorry she came, for there are but meagre pickings here, and she brought some of those apples. I was obliged to eat them, I was so hungry. It was against my principles, but I find that principles have no real force except when one is well fed. . . . She came curtained in boughs and bunches of leaves, and when I asked her what she meant by such nonsense, and snatched them away and threw them down, she tittered and blushed. I had never seen a person titter and blush before, and to me it seemed unbecoming and idiotic. She said I would soon know how it was myself. This was correct. Hungry as I was, I laid down the apple half-eaten — certainly the best one I ever saw, considering the lateness of the season —and arrayed myself in the discarded boughs and branches, and then spoke to her with some severity and ordered her to go and get some more and not make such a spectacle of herself. She did it, and after this we crept down to where the wild-beast battle had been, and collected some skins, and I made her patch together a couple of suits proper for public occasions. They are uncomfortable, it is true, but stylish, and that is the main point about clothes. . . . I find she is a good deal of a companion. I see I should be lonesome and depressed without her, now that I have lost my property. Another thing, she says it is ordered that we work for our living hereafter. She will be useful. I will superintend.

TEN DAYS LATER.— She accuses *me* of being the cause of our disaster! She says, with apparent sincerity and truth, that the Serpent assured her that the forbidden fruit was not apples, it was chestnuts. I said I was innocent, then, for I had not eaten any chestnuts. She said the Serpent informed her that "chestnut" was a figurative term meaning an aged and mouldy joke. I turned pale at that, for I have made many jokes to pass the weary time, and some of them could have been of that sort, though I had

honestly supposed that they were new when I made
them.   She asked me if I had made one just at the
time of the catastrophe.   I was obliged to admit that
I had made one to myself, though not aloud.   It
was this.   I was thinking about the Falls, and I said
to myself, ".How wonderful it is to see that vast
body of water tumble down there!"   Then in an
instant a bright thought flashed into my head, and I
let it fly, saying, " It would be a deal more wonderful
to see it tumble *up* there!" — and I was just about
to kill myself with laughing at it when all nature
broke loose in war and death and I had to flee for
my life.   "There," she said, with triumph, "that
is just it; the Serpent mentioned that very jest, and
called it the First Chestnut, and said it was coeval
with the creation."   Alas, I am indeed to blame.
Would that I were not witty; oh, that I had never
had that radiant thought!

NEXT YEAR.— We have named it Cain.   She
caught it while I was up country trapping on the
North Shore of the Erie; caught it in the timber a
couple of miles from our dug-out — or it might have
been four, she isn't certain which.   It resembles us
in some ways, and may be a relation.   That is what
she thinks, but this is an error, in my judgment.
The difference in size warrants the conclusion that
it is a different and new kind of animal — a fish, perhaps, though when I put it in the water to see, it
sank, and she plunged in and snatched it out before
there was opportunity for the experiment to deter-

mine the matter.   I still think it is a fish, but she is
indifferent about what it is, and will not let me have
it to try.   I do not understand this.   The coming
of the creature seems to have changed her whole
nature and made her unreasonable about experiments.   She thinks more of it than she does of any
of the other animals, but is not able to explain why.
Her mind is disordered — everything shows it.
Sometimes she carries the fish in her arms half the
night when it complains and wants to get to the
water.   At such times the water comes out of the
places in her face that she looks out of, and she pats
the fish on the back and makes soft sounds with her
mouth to soothe it, and betrays sorrow and solicitude
in a hundred ways.   I have never seen her do like
this with any other fish, and it troubles me greatly.
She used to carry the young tigers around so, and
play with them, before we lost our property, but it
was only play; she never took on about them like
this when their dinner disagreed with them.

SUNDAY.— She doesn't work, Sundays, but lies
around all tired out, and likes to have the fish wallow
over her; and she makes fool noises to amuse it,
and pretends to chew its paws, and that makes it
laugh.   I have not seen a fish before that could
laugh.   This makes me doubt. . . . I have come
to like Sunday myself.   Superintending all the week
tires a body so.   There ought to be more Sundays.
In the old days they were tough, but now they
come handy.

WEDNESDAY.— It isn't a fish. I cannot quite make out what it is. It makes curious devilish noises when not satisfied, and says " goo-goo " when it is. It is not one of us, for it doesn't walk; it is not a bird, for it doesn't fly; it is not a frog, for it doesn't hop; it is not a snake, for it doesn't crawl; I feel sure it is not a fish, though I cannot get a chance to find out whether it can swim or not. It merely lies around, and mostly on its back, with its feet up. I have not seen any other animal do that before. I said I believed it was an enigma; but she only admired the word without understanding it. In my judgment it is either an enigma or some kind of a bug. If it dies, I will take it apart and see what its arrangements are. I never had a thing perplex me so.

THREE MONTHS LATER.— The perplexity augments instead of diminishing. I sleep but little. It has ceased from lying around, and goes about on its four legs now. Yet it differs from the other four-legged animals, in that its front legs are unusually short, consequently this causes the main part of its person to stick up uncomfortably high in the air, and this is not attractive. It is built much as we are, but its method of traveling shows that it is not of our breed. The short front legs and long hind ones indicate that it is of the kangaroo family, but it is a marked variation of the species, since the true kangaroo hops, whereas this one never does. Still it is a curious and interesting variety, and has not been

catalogued before.   As I discovered it, I have felt
justified in securing the credit of the discovery by
attaching my name to it, and hence have called it
Kangaroorum Adamiensis. . . . It must have been
a young one when it came, for it has grown exceedingly since.   It must be five times as big, now, as it
was then, and when discontented it is able to make
from twenty-two to thirty-eight times the noise it
made at first.   Coercion does not modify this, but
has the contrary effect.   For this reason I discon-
tinued the system.   She reconciles it by persuasion,
and by giving it things which she had previously told
it she wouldn't give it.   As already observed, I was
not at home when it first came, and she told me she
found it in the woods.   It seems odd that it should
be the only one, yet it must be so, for I have worn
myself out these many weeks trying to find another
one to add to my collection, and for this one to play
with; for surely then it would be quieter and we
could tame it more easily.   But I find none, nor any
vestige of any; and strangest of all, no tracks.   It
has to live on the ground, it cannot help itself;
therefore, how does it get about without leaving a
track?   I have set a dozen traps, but they do no
good.   I catch all small animals except that one;
animals that merely go into the trap out of curiosity,
I think, to see what the milk is there for.   They
never drink it.

THREE MONTHS LATER.— The Kangaroo still
continues to grow, which is very strange and per-

28

plexing. I never knew one to be so long getting its growth. It has fur on its head now; not like kangaroo fur, but exactly like our hair except that it is much finer and softer, and instead of being black is red. I am like to lose my mind over the capricious and harassing developments of this unclassifiable zoölogical freak. If I could catch another one — but that is hopeless; it is a new variety, and the only sample; this is plain. But I caught a true kangaroo and brought it in, thinking that this one, being lonesome, would rather have that for company than have no kin at all, or any animal it could feel a nearness to or get sympathy from in its forlorn condition here among strangers who do not know its ways or habits, or what to do to make it feel that it is among friends; but it was a mistake — it went into such fits at the sight of the kangaroo that I was convinced it had never seen one before. I pity the poor noisy little animal, but there is nothing I can do to make it happy. If I could tame it — but that is out of the question; the more I try the worse I seem to make it. It grieves me to the heart to see it in its little storms of sorrow and passion. I wanted to let it go, but she wouldn't hear of it. That seemed cruel and not like her; and yet she may be right. It might be lonelier than ever; for since I cannot find another one, how could *it?*

FIVE MONTHS LATER.—It is not a kangaroo. No, for it supports itself by holding to her finger, and thus goes a few steps on its hind legs, and then falls down. It is probably some kind of a bear; and yet it has no tail — as yet — and no fur, except on its head. It still keeps on growing — that is a curious circumstance, for bears get their growth earlier than this. Bears are dangerous — since our catastrophe — and I shall not be satisfied to have this one prowling about the place much longer without a muzzle on. I have offered to get her a kangaroo if she would let this one go, but it did no good — she is determined to run us into all sorts of foolish risks, I think. She was not like this before she lost her mind.

A FORTNIGHT LATER.— I examined its mouth. There is no danger yet: it has only one tooth. It has no tail yet. It makes more noise now than it ever did before — and mainly at night. I have moved out. But I shall go over, mornings, to breakfast, and see if it has more teeth. If it gets a mouthful of teeth it will be time for it to go, tail or no tail, for a bear does not need a tail in order to be dangerous.

FOUR MONTHS LATER.— I have been off hunting and fishing a month, up in the region that she calls Buffalo; I don't know why, unless it is because there are not any buffaloes there. Meantime the bear has learned to paddle around all by itself on its hind legs, and says " poppa " and " momma." It is certainly a new species. This resemblance to words may be purely accidental, of course, and may have no purpose or meaning; but even in that case it is still extraordinary, and is a thing which no other bear can do. This imitation of speech, taken together with general absence of fur and entire absence of tail, sufficiently indicates that this is a new kind of bear. The further study of it will be exceedingly interesting. Meantime I will go off on a far expedition among the forests of the north and make an exhaustive search. There must certainly be another one somewhere, and this one will be less dangerous when it has company of its own species. I will go straightway; but I will muzzle this one first.

THREE MONTHS LATER.— It has been a weary, weary hunt, yet I have had no success. In the meantime, without stirring from the home estate, she has caught another one! I never saw such luck. I might have hunted these woods a hundred years, I never would have run across that thing.

NEXT DAY.— I have been comparing the new one with the old one, and it is perfectly plain that they are the same breed. I was going to stuff one of them for my collection, but she is prejudiced against it for some reason or other; so I have relinquished the idea, though I think it is a mistake. It would be an irreparable loss to science if they should get away. The old one is tamer than it was and can laugh and talk like the parrot, having learned this, no doubt, from being with the parrot so much, and having the imitative faculty in a highly developed degree. I shall be astonished if it turns out to be a new kind of parrot; and yet I ought not to be astonished, for it has already been everything else it could think of since those first days when it was a fish. The new one is as ugly now as the old one was at first; has the same sulphur-and-raw-meat complexion and the same singular head without any fur on it. She calls it Abel.

TEN YEARS LATER.—They are *boys;* we found it out long ago. It was their coming in that small, immature shape that puzzled us; we were not used to it. There are some girls now. Abel is a good boy, but if Cain had stayed a bear it would have improved him. After all these years, I see that I was mistaken about Eve in the beginning; it is better to live outside the Garden with her than inside it without her. At first I thought she talked too much; but now I should be sorry to have that voice fall silent and pass out of my life. Blessed be the chestnut that brought us near together and taught me to know the goodness of her heart and the sweetness of her spirit!

THE DEATH DISK *

I

THIS was in Oliver Cromwell's time. Colonel
Mayfair was the youngest officer of his rank
in the armies of the Commonwealth, he being but
thirty years old. But young as he was, he was a
veteran soldier, and tanned and warworn, for he
had begun his military life at seventeen; he had
fought in many battles, and had won his high place
in the service and in the admiration of men, step
by step, by valor in the field. But he was in deep
trouble now; a shadow had fallen upon his fortunes.

The winter evening was come, and outside were
storm and darkness; within, a melancholy silence;
for the Colonel and his young wife had talked their
sorrow out, had read the evening chapter and prayed
the evening prayer, and there was nothing more to
do but sit hand in hand and gaze into the fire, and
think — and wait. They would not have to wait
long; they knew that, and the wife shuddered at
the thought.

---

* The text for this story is a touching incident mentioned in Carlyle's
Letters and Speeches of Oliver Cromwell.— M. T.

They had one child — Abby, seven years old, their idol. She would be coming presently for the good-night kiss, and the Colonel spoke now, and said:

" Dry away the tears and let us seem happy, for her sake. We must forget, for the time, that which is to happen."

" I will. I will shut them up in my heart, which is breaking."

" And we will accept what is appointed for us, and bear it in patience, as knowing that whatsoever He doeth is done in righteousness and meant in kindness — "

" Saying, His will be done. Yes, I can say it with all my mind and soul — I would I could say it with my heart. Oh, if I could! if this dear hand which I press and kiss for the last time — "

" 'Sh! sweetheart, she is coming!"

A curly-headed little figure in nightclothes glided in at the door and ran to the father, and was gathered to his breast and fervently kissed once, twice, three times.

"Why, papa, you mustn't kiss me like that: you rumple my hair."

" Oh, I am so sorry — so sorry: do you forgive me, dear?"

" Why, of course, papa. But *are* you sorry? — not pretending, but real, right down sorry?"

" Well, you can judge for yourself, Abby," and he covered his face with his hands and made believe to sob. The child was filled with remorse to see this

tragic thing which she had caused, and she began to
cry herself, and to tug at the hands, and say:

"Oh, don't, papa, please don't cry; Abby didn't
mean it; Abby wouldn't ever do it again. Please,
papa!" Tugging and straining to separate the
fingers, she got a fleeting glimpse of an eye behind
them, and cried out: "Why, you naughty papa,
you are not crying at all! You are only fooling!
And Abby is going to mamma, now: you don't
treat Abby right."

She was for climbing down, but her father wound
his arms about her and said: "No, stay with me,
dear: papa *was* naughty, and confesses it, and is
sorry — there, let him kiss the tears away — and he
begs Abby's forgiveness, and will do anything Abby
says he must do, for a punishment; they're all
kissed away now, and not a curl rumpled — and
whatever Abby commands — "

And so it was made up; and all in a moment the
sunshine was back again and burning brightly in the
child's face, and she was patting her father's cheeks
and naming the penalty — "A story! a story!"

Hark!

The elders stopped breathing, and listened. Footsteps! faintly caught between the gusts of wind.
They came nearer, nearer — louder, louder — then
passed by and faded away. The elders drew deep
breaths of relief, and the papa said: "A story, is
it? A gay one?"

"No, papa: a dreadful one."

"HARK! THE ELDERS STOPPED BREATHING AND LISTENED"

Papa wanted to shift to the gay kind, but the child stood by her rights — as per agreement, she was to have anything she commanded. He was a good Puritan soldier and had passed his word — he saw that he must make it good. She said:

"Papa, we mustn't always have gay ones. Nurse says people don't always have gay times. Is that true, papa? She *says* so."

The mamma sighed, and her thoughts drifted to her troubles again. The papa said, gently: "It is true, dear. Troubles have to come; it is a pity, but it is true."

"Oh, then tell a story about them, papa — a dreadful one, so that we'll shiver, and feel just as if it was *us*. Mamma, you snuggle up close, and hold one of Abby's hands, so that if it's too dreadful it'll be easier for us to bear it if we are all snuggled up together, you know. Now you can begin, papa."

"Well, once there were three Colonels —"

"Oh, goody! *I* know Colonels, just as easy! It's because you are one, and I know the clothes. Go on, papa."

"And in a battle they had committed a breach of discipline."

The large words struck the child's ear pleasantly, and she looked up, full of wonder and interest, and said:

"Is it something good to eat, papa?"

The parents almost smiled, and the father answered:

"No, quite another matter, dear.   They exceeded their orders."

"Is *that* someth—"

"No; it's as uneatable as the other.   They were ordered to feign an attack on a strong position in a losing fight, in order to draw the enemy about and give the Commonwealth's forces a chance to retreat; but in their enthusiasm they overstepped their orders, for they turned the feint into a fact, and carried the position by storm, and won the day and the battle.   The Lord General was very angry at their disobedience, and praised them highly, and ordered them to London to be tried for their lives."

"Is it the great General Cromwell, papa?"

"Yes."

"Oh, I've seen *him*, papa! and when he goes by our house so grand on his big horse, with the soldiers, he looks so — so — well, I don't know just how, only he looks as if he isn't satisfied, and you can see the people are afraid of him; but *I'm* not afraid of him, because he didn't look like that at me."

"Oh, you dear prattler!   Well, the Colonels came prisoners to London, and were put upon their honor, and allowed to go and see their families for the last—"

Hark!

They listened.   Footsteps again; but again they passed by.   The mamma leaned her head upon her husband's shoulder to hide her paleness.

"They arrived this morning."

The child's eyes opened wide.

"Why, papa! is it a *true* story?"

"Yes, dear."

"Oh, how good! Oh, it's ever so much better! Go on, papa. Why, mamma! — *dear* mamma, are you crying?"

"Never mind me, dear — I was thinking of the — of the — the poor families."

"But *don't* cry, mamma: it'll all come out right — you'll see; stories always do. Go on, papa, to where they lived happy ever after; then she won't cry any more. You'll see, mamma. Go on, papa."

"First, they took them to the Tower before they let them go home."

"Oh, *I* know the Tower! We can see it from here. Go on, papa."

"I am going on as well as I can, in the circumstances. In the Tower the military court tried them for an hour, and found them guilty, and condemned them to be shot."

"*Killed*, papa?"

"Yes."

"Oh, how naughty! *Dear* mamma, you are crying again. Don't, mamma; it'll soon come to the good place — you'll see. Hurry, papa, for mamma's sake; you don't go fast enough."

"I know I don't, but I suppose it is because I stop so much to reflect."

"But you mustn't *do* it, papa; you must go right on."

"Very well, then. The three Colonels— "

"Do you know them, papa?"

"Yes, dear."

"Oh, I wish I did! I love Colonels. Would they let me kiss them, do you think?" The Colonel's voice was a little unsteady when he answered —

"*One* of them would, my darling! There — kiss me for him."

"There, papa — and these two are for the others. I think they would let me kiss them, papa; for I would say, 'My papa is a Colonel, too, and brave, and he would do what you did; so it *can't* be wrong, no matter what those people say, and you needn't be the least bit ashamed;' then they would let me,— wouldn't they, papa?"

"God knows they would, child!"

"Mamma! — oh, mamma, you mustn't. He's soon coming to the happy place; go on, papa."

"Then, some were sorry — they all were; that military court, I mean; and they went to the Lord General, and said they had done their duty — for it *was* their duty, you know — and now they begged that two of the Colonels might be spared, and only the other one shot. One would be sufficient for an example for the army, they thought. But the Lord General was very stern, and rebuked them forasmuch as, having done *their* duty and cleared their consciences, they would beguile him to do less, and so smirch his soldierly honor. But they answered that they were asking nothing of him that they would not do themselves if they stood in his great place and held in their hands the noble prerogative of mercy. That struck him, and he paused and stood thinking, some of the sternness passing out of his face. Presently he bid them wait, and he retired to his closet to seek counsel of God in prayer; and when he came again, he said: 'They shall cast lots. That shall decide it, and two of them shall live.' "

" And did they, papa, did they? And which one is to die? — ah, that poor man ! "

" No. They refused."

" They wouldn't do it, papa? "

" No."

" Why? "

" They said that the one that got the fatal bean would be sentencing himself to death by his own voluntary act, and it would be but suicide, call it by what name one might. They said they were Christians, and the Bible forbade men to take their own lives. They sent back that word, and said they were ready—let the court's sentence be carried into effect."

" What does that mean, papa? "

" They — they will all be shot."

Hark!

The wind? No. Tramp — tramp — tramp — r-r-r-umble-dumdum, r-r-rumble-dumdum —

" Open — in the Lord General's name ! "

" Oh, goody, papa, it's the soldiers ! — I love the soldiers ! Let *me* let them in, papa, let *me!* "

She jumped down, and scampered to the door and pulled it open, crying joyously: "Come in! come in! Here they are, papa! Grenadiers! *I* know the Grenadiers!"

The file marched in and straightened up in line at shoulder arms; its officer saluted, the doomed Colonel standing erect and returning the courtesy, the soldier wife standing at his side, white, and with features drawn with inward pain, but giving no other sign of her misery, the child gazing on the show with dancing eyes. . . .

One long embrace, of father, mother, and child; then the order, "To the Tower — forward!" Then the Colonel marched forth from the house with military step and bearing, the file following; then the door closed.

"Oh, mamma, didn't it come out beautiful! I *told* you it would; and they're going to the Tower, and he'll *see* them! He—"

"Oh, come to my arms, you poor innocent thing!" . . . .

II

The next morning the stricken mother was not able to leave her bed; doctors and nurses were watching by her, and whispering together now and then; Abby could not be allowed in the room; she was told to run and play — mamma was very ill. The child, muffled in winter wraps, went out and played in the street awhile; then it struck her as strange, and also wrong, that her papa should be allowed to stay at the Tower in ignorance at such a time as this. This must be remedied; she would attend to it in person.

An hour later the military court were ushered into the presence of the Lord General. He stood grim and erect, with his knuckles resting upon the table, and indicated that he was ready to listen. The spokesman said: "We have urged them to reconsider; we have implored them: but they persist. They will not cast lots. They are willing to die, but not to defile their religion."

The Protector's face darkened, but he said nothing. He remained a time in thought, then he said: "They shall not all die; the lots shall be cast *for* them." Gratitude shone in the faces of the court. "Send for them. Place them in that room there. Stand them side by side with their faces to the wall and their wrists crossed behind them. Let me have notice when they are there."

When he was alone he sat down, and presently gave this order to an attendant: "Go, bring me the first little child that passes by."

The man was hardly out at the door before he was back again — leading Abby by the hand, her garments lightly powdered with snow. She went straight to the Head of the State, that formidable personage at the mention of whose name the principalities and powers of the earth trembled, and climbed up in his lap, and said:

"I know *you*, sir: you are the Lord General; I have seen you; I have seen you when you went by my house. Everybody was afraid; but *I* wasn't afraid, because you didn't look cross at *me;* you remember, don't you? I had on my red frock — the one with the blue things on it down the front. Don't you remember that?"

A smile softened the austere lines of the Protector's face, and he began to struggle diplomatically with his answer:

"Why, let me see — I — "

"I was standing right by the house — *my* house, you know."

"Well, you dear little thing, I ought to be ashamed, but you know — "

The child interrupted, reproachfully:

"Now you *don't* remember it. Why, I didn't forget *you*."

"Now I *am* ashamed: but I will never forget you again, dear; you have my word for it. You will forgive me now, won't you, and be good friends with me, always and forever?"

"Yes, indeed I will, though I don't know how you came to forget it; you must be very forgetful: but I am too, sometimes. I can forgive you without any trouble, for I think you *mean* to be good and do right, and I think you are just as kind — but you must snuggle me better, the way papa does — it's cold."

"You shall be snuggled to your heart's content,

little new friend of mine, always to be *old* friend of
mine hereafter, isn't it? You mind me of my little
girl — not little any more, now — but she was dear,
and sweet, and daintily made, like you. And she
had your charm, little witch —your all-conquering
sweet confidence in friend and stranger alike, that
wins to willing slavery any upon whom its precious
compliment falls. She used to lie in my arms, just
as you are doing now; and charm the weariness and
care out of my heart and give it peace, just as
you are doing now; and we were comrades, and
equals, and playfellows together. Ages ago it
was, since that pleasant heaven faded away and
vanished, and you have brought it back again; —
take a burdened man's blessing for it, you tiny
creature, who are carrying the weight of England
while I rest!"

"Did you love her very, very, *very* much?"

"Ah, you shall judge by this: she commanded
and I obeyed!"

"I think you are lovely! Will you kiss me?"

"Thankfully— and hold it a privilege, too.
There — this one is for you; and there — this one
is for her. You made it a request; and you could
have made it a command, for you are representing
her, and what you command I must obey."

The child clapped her hands with delight at the
idea of this grand promotion — then her ear caught
an approaching sound: the measured tramp of
marching men.

29

"Soldiers! — soldiers, Lord General! Abby
wants to see them!"

"You shall, dear; but wait a moment, I have a
commission for you."

An officer entered and bowed low, saying, "They
are come, your Highness," bowed again, and retired.

The Head of the Nation gave Abby three little
disks of sealing-wax: two white, and one a ruddy
red — for this one's mission was to deliver death to
the Colonel who should get it.

"Oh, what a lovely red one! Are they for me?"

"No, dear; they are for others. Lift the corner
of that curtain, there, which hides an open door;
pass through, and you will see three men standing
in a row, with their backs toward you and their
hands behind their backs — so — each with one hand
open, like a cup. Into each of the open hands drop
one of those things, then come back to me."

Abby disappeared behind the curtain, and the
Protector was alone. He said, reverently: "Of a
surety that good thought came to me in my perplexity from Him who is an ever present help to
them that are in doubt and seek His aid. He
knoweth where the choice should fall, and has sent
His sinless messenger to do His will. Another
would err, but He cannot err. Wonderful are His
ways, and wise — blessed be His holy Name!"

The small fairy dropped the curtain behind her
and stood for a moment conning with alert curiosity
the appointments of the chamber of doom, and the

rigid figures of the soldiery and the prisoners; then her face lighted merrily, and she said to herself: "Why, one of them is papa! I know his back. He shall have the prettiest one!" She tripped gayly forward and dropped the disks into the open hands, then peeped around under her father's arm and lifted her laughing face and cried out:

"Papa! papa! look what you've got. *I* gave it to you!"

He glanced at the fatal gift, then sunk to his knees and gathered his innocent little executioner to his breast in an agony of love and pity. Soldiers, officers, released prisoners, all stood paralyzed, for a moment, at the vastness of this tragedy, then the pitiful scene smote their hearts, their eyes filled, and they wept unashamed. There was deep and reverent silence during some minutes, then the officer of the guard moved reluctantly forward and touched his prisoner on the shoulder, saying, gently:

"It grieves me, sir, but my duty commands."

"Commands what?" said the child.

"I must take him away. I am so sorry."

"Take him away? Where?"

"To — to — God help me! — to another part of the fortress."

"Indeed you can't. My mamma is sick, and I am going to take him home." She released herself and climbed upon her father's back and put her arms around his neck. "Now Abby's ready, papa — come along."

"My poor child, I can't.   I must go with them."

The child jumped to the ground and looked about her, wondering.   Then she ran and stood before the officer and stamped her small foot indignantly and cried out:

"I told you my mamma is sick, and you might have listened.   Let him go — you *must!*"

"Oh, poor child, would God I could, but indeed I must take him away.   Attention, guard! . . . . fall in! . . . . shoulder arms!" . . . .

Abby was gone — like a flash of light.   In a moment she was back, dragging the Lord Protector by the hand.   At this formidable apparition all present straightened up, the officers saluting and the soldiers presenting arms.

"Stop them, sir!   My mamma is sick and wants my papa, and I *told* them so, but they never even listened to me, and are taking him away."

The Lord General stood as one dazed.

"*Your* papa, child?   Is he your papa?"

"Why, of course — he was *always* it.   Would I give the pretty red one to any other, when I love him so?   No!"

A shocked expression rose in the Protector's face, and he said:

"Ah, God help me! through Satan's wiles I have done the cruelest thing that ever man did — and there is no help, no help!   What can I do?"

Abby cried out, distressed and impatient: "Why, you can make them let him go," and she began to sob. "Tell them to do it! You told me to command, and now the very first time I tell you to do a thing you don't do it!"

A tender light dawned in the rugged old face, and the Lord General laid his hand upon the small tyrant's head and said: "God be thanked for the saving accident of that unthinking promise; and you, inspired by Him, for reminding me of my forgotten pledge, O incomparable child! Officer, obey her command — she speaks by my mouth. The prisoner is pardoned; set him free!"

WE OUGHT NEVER TO DO WRONG WHEN
PEOPLE ARE LOOKING

A DOUBLE-BARRELED DETECTIVE STORY

CHAPTER I.

THE first scene is in the country, in Virginia; the time, 1880. There has been a wedding, between a handsome young man of slender means and a rich young girl — a case of love at first sight and a precipitate marriage; a marriage bitterly opposed by the girl's widowed father.

Jacob Fuller, the bridegroom, is twenty-six years old, is of an old but unconsidered family which had by compulsion emigrated from Sedgemoor, and for King James's purse's profit, so everybody said — some maliciously, the rest merely because they believed it. The bride is nineteen and beautiful. She is intense, high-strung, romantic, immeasurably proud of her Cavalier blood, and passionate in her love for her young husband. For its sake she braved her father's displeasure, endured his reproaches, listened with loyalty unshaken to his warning predictions, and went from his house without his blessing, proud and happy in the proofs she was thus giving of the quality of the affection which had made its home in her heart.

The morning after the marriage there was a sad surprise for her. Her husband put aside her proffered caresses, and said:

"Sit down. I have something to say to you. I loved you. That was before I asked your father to give you to me. His refusal is not my grievance — I could have endured that. But the things he said of me to you — that is a different matter. There — you needn't speak; I know quite well what they were; I got them from authentic sources. Among other things he said that my character was written in my face; that I was treacherous, a dissembler, a coward, and a brute without sense of pity or compassion: the 'Sedgemoor trade-mark,' he called it — and 'white-sleeve badge.' Any other man in my place would have gone to his house and shot him down like a dog. I wanted to do it, and was minded to do it, but a better thought came to me: to put him to shame; to break his heart; to kill him by inches. How to do it? Through my treatment of you, his idol! I would marry you; and then — Have patience. You will see."

From that moment onward, for three months, the young wife suffered all the humiliations, all the insults, all the miseries that the diligent and inventive mind of the husband could contrive, save physical injuries only. Her strong pride stood by her, and

"HE   . PROCEEDED TO LASH HER TO A TREE"

she kept the secret of her troubles. Now and then the husband said, "Why don't you go to your father and tell him?" Then he invented new tortures, applied them, and asked again. She always answered, "He shall never know by my mouth," and taunted him with his origin; said she was the lawful slave of a scion of slaves, and must obey, and would — up to that point, but no further; he could kill her if he liked, but he could not break her; it was not in the Sedgemoor breed to do it. At the end of the three months he said, with a dark significance in his manner, "I have tried all things but one" — and waited for her reply. "Try that," she said, and curled her lip in mockery.

That night he rose at midnight and put on his clothes, then said to her,

"Get up and dress!"

She obeyed — as always, without a word. He led her half a mile from the house, and proceeded to lash her to a tree by the side of the public road; and succeeded, she screaming and struggling. He gagged her then, struck her across the face with his cowhide, and set his bloodhounds on her. They tore the clothes off her, and she was naked. He called the dogs off, and said:

"You will be found — by the passing public. They will be dropping along about three hours from now, and will spread the news — do you hear? Good-by. You have seen the last of me."

He went away then. She moaned to herself:

"I shall bear a child — to *him!* God grant it may be a boy!"

The farmers released her by and by — and spread the news, which was natural. They raised the country with lynching intentions, but the bird had flown. The young wife shut herself up in her father's house; he shut himself up with her, and thenceforth would see no one. His pride was broken, and his heart; so he wasted away, day by day, and even his daughter rejoiced when death relieved him.

Then she sold the estate and disappeared.

CHAPTER II.

IN 1886 a young woman was living in a modest house near a secluded New England village, with no company but a little boy about five years old. She did her own work, she discouraged acquaintanceships, and had none. The butcher, the baker, and the others that served her could tell the villagers nothing about her further than that her name was Stillman, and that she called the child Archy. Whence she came they had not been able to find out, but they said she talked like a Southerner. The child had no playmates and no comrade, and no teacher but the mother. She taught him diligently and intelligently, and was satisfied with the results — even a little proud of them. One day Archy said,

"Mamma, am I different from other children?"

"Well, I suppose not. Why?"

"There was a child going along out there and asked me if the postman had been by and I said yes, and she said how long since I saw him and I said I hadn't seen him at all, and she said how did I know he'd been by, then, and I said because I smelt his track on the sidewalk, and she said I was a dum

fool and made a mouth at me. What did she do
that for?''

The young woman turned white, and said to herself, ''It's a birthmark! The gift of the bloodhound is in him.'' She snatched the boy to her
breast and hugged him passionately, saying, '' God
has appointed the way!'' Her eyes were burning
with a fierce light and her breath came short and
quick with excitement. She said to herself: '' The
puzzle is solved now; many a time it has been a
mystery to me, the impossible things the child has
done in the dark, but it is all clear to me now.''

She set him in his small chair, and said,

''Wait a little till I come, dear; then we will talk
about the matter.''

She went up to her room and took from her
dressing-table several small articles and put them
out of sight: a nail-file on the floor under the bed;
a pair of nail-scissors under the bureau; a small
ivory paper-knife under the wardrobe. Then she
returned, and said:

''There! I have left some things which I ought
to have brought down.'' She named them, and
said, '' Run up and bring them, dear.''

The child hurried away on his errand and was soon
back again with the things.

'' Did you have any difficulty, dear?''

'' No, mamma; I only went where you went.''

During his absence she had stepped to the bookcase, taken several books from the bottom shelf,

opened each, passed her hand over a page, noting its number in her memory, then restored them to their places.   Now she said:

"I have been doing something while you have been gone, Archy.   Do you think you can find out what it was?"

The boy went to the bookcase and got out the books that had been touched, and opened them at the pages which had been stroked.

The mother took him in her lap, and said:

"I will answer your question now, dear.   I have found out that in one way you are quite different from other people.   You can see in the dark, you can smell what other people cannot, you have the talents of a bloodhound.   They are good and valuable things to have, but you must keep the matter a secret.   If people found it out, they would speak of you as an odd child, a strange child, and children would be disagreeable to you, and give you nicknames.   In this world one must be like everybody else if he doesn't want to provoke scorn or envy or jealousy.   It is a great and fine distinction which has been born to you, and I am glad; but you will keep it a secret, for mamma's sake, won't you?"

The child promised, without understanding.

All the rest of the day the mother's brain was busy with excited thinkings; with plans, projects, schemes, each and all of them uncanny, grim, and dark.   Yet they lit up her face; lit it with a fell light of their own; lit it with vague fires of hell.

She was in a fever of unrest; she could not sit,
stand, read, sew; there was no relief for her but in
movement. She tested her boy's gift in twenty
ways, and kept saying to herself all the time, with
her mind in the past: "He broke my father's
heart, and night and day all these years I have tried,
and all in vain, to think out a way to break his. I
have found it now — I have found it now."

When night fell, the demon of unrest still possessed
her. She went on with her tests; with a candle she
traversed the house from garret to cellar, hiding
pins, needles, thimbles, spools, under pillows, under
carpets, in cracks in the walls, under the coal in the
bin; then sent the little fellow in the dark to find
them; which he did, and was happy and proud when
she praised him and smothered him with caresses.

From this time forward life took on a new complexion for her. She said, "The future is secure—
I can wait, and enjoy the waiting." The most of
her lost interests revived. She took up music again,
and languages, drawing, painting, and the other long-
discarded delights of her maidenhood. She was
happy once more, and felt again the zest of life.
As the years drifted by she watched the development of her boy, and was contented with it. Not
altogether, but nearly that. The soft side of his
heart was larger than the other side of it. It was
his only defect, in her eyes. But she considered
that his love for her and worship of her made up for
it. He was a good hater — that was well; but it

was a question if the materials of his hatreds were of as tough and enduring a quality as those of his friendships — and that was not so well.

The years drifted on. Archy was become a handsome, shapely, athletic youth, courteous, dignified, companionable, pleasant in his ways, and looking perhaps a trifle older than he was, which was sixteen. One evening his mother said she had something of grave importance to say to him, adding that he was old enough to hear it now, and old enough and possessed of character enough and stability enough to carry out a stern plan which she had been for years contriving and maturing. Then she told him her bitter story, in all its naked atrociousness. For a while the boy was paralyzed; then he said:

"I understand. We are Southerners; and by our custom and nature there is but one atonement. I will search him out and kill him."

"Kill him? No! Death is release, emancipation; death is a favor. Do I owe him favors? You must not hurt a hair of his head."

The boy was lost in thought awhile; then he said:

"You are all the world to me, and your desire is my law and my pleasure. Tell me what to do and I will do it."

The mother's eyes beamed with satisfaction, and she said:

"You will go and find him. I have known his hiding-place for eleven years; it cost me five years and more of inquiry, and much money, to locate it.
30

He is a quartz-miner in Colorado, and well-to-do. He lives in Denver. His name is Jacob Fuller. There — it is the first time I have spoken it since that unforgettable night. Think! That name could have been yours if I had not saved you that shame and furnished you a cleaner one. You will drive him from that place; you will hunt him down and drive him again; and yet again, and again, and again, persistently, relentlessly, poisoning his life, filling it with mysterious terrors, loading it with weariness and misery, making him wish for death, and that he had a suicide's courage; you will make of him another wandering Jew; he shall know no rest any more, no peace of mind, no placid sleep; you shall shadow him, cling to him, persecute him, till you break his heart, as he broke my father's and mine.''

'' I will obey, mother.''

'' I believe it, my child. The preparations are all made; everything is ready. Here is a letter of credit; spend freely, there is no lack of money. At times you may need disguises. I have provided them; also some other conveniences.'' She took from the drawer of the typewriter table several squares of paper. They all bore these typewritten words:

$10,000 REWARD.

It is believed that a certain man who is wanted in an Eastern State is sojourning here. In 1880, in the night, he tied his young wife to a tree by the public road, cut her across the face with a cowhide, and made his dogs tear her clothes from her, leaving her naked. He left her there, and fled the country. A blood-relative of hers has searched for him for seventeen years. Address ...., ..., Post-office. The above reward will be paid in cash to the person who will furnish the seeker, in a personal interview, the criminal's address.

" When you have found him and acquainted your-self with his scent, you will go in the night and placard one of these upon the building he occupies, and another one upon the post-office or in some other prominent place. It will be the talk of the region. At first you must give him several days in which to force a sale of his belongings at something approaching their value. We will ruin him by and by, but gradually; we must not impoverish him at once, for that could bring him to despair and injure his health, possibly kill him."

She took three or four more typewritten forms from the drawer — duplicates — and read one:

.........., ..., 18......

To Jacob Fuller:

You have .... days in which to settle your affairs. You will not be disturbed during that limit, which will expire at ...... M., on the ...... of ...... You must then MOVE ON. If you are still in the place after the named hour, I will placard you on all the dead walls, detailing your crime once more, and adding the date, also the scene of it, with all names concerned, including your own. Have no fear of bodily injury — it will in no circumstances ever be inflicted upon you. You brought misery upon an old man, and ruined his life and broke his heart. What he suffered, you are to suffer.

"You will add no signature. He must receive this before he learns of the reward placard — before he rises in the morning — lest he lose his head and fly the place penniless."

" I shall not forget."

" You will need to use these forms only in the beginning — once may be enough.   Afterward, when
you are ready for him to vanish out of a place, see
that he gets a copy of *this* form, which merely says:

MOVE ON.   You have ...... days.

" He will obey.   That is sure."

CHAPTER III.

EXTRACTS from letters to the mother:

DENVER, April 3, 1897.

I have now been living several days in the same hotel with Jacob Fuller. I have his scent; I could track him through ten divisions of infantry and find him. I have often been near him and heard him talk. He owns a good mine, and has a fair income from it; but he is not rich. He learned mining in a good way — by working at it for wages. He is a cheerful creature, and his forty-three years sit lightly upon him; he could pass for a younger man — say thirty-six or thirty-seven. He has never married again — passes himself off for a widower. He stands well, is liked, is popular, and has many friends. Even I feel a drawing toward him — the paternal blood in me making its claim. How blind and unreasoning and arbitrary are some of the laws of nature —the most of them, in fact! My task is become hard now—you realize it? you comprehend, and make allowances? — and the fire of it has cooled, more than I like to confess to myself. But I will carry it out. Even with the pleasure paled, the duty remains, and I will not spare him.

And for my help, a sharp resentment rises in me when I reflect that he who committed that odious crime is the only one who has not suffered by it. The lesson of it has manifestly reformed his character, and in the change he is happy. He, the guilty party, is absolved from all suffering; you, the innocent, are borne down with it. But be comforted—he shall harvest his share.

SILVER GULCH, May 19.

I placarded Form No. 1 at midnight of April 3; an hour later I slipped Form No. 2 under his chamber door, notifying him to leave Denver at or before 11.50 the night of the 14th.

Some late bird of a reporter stole one of my placards, then hunted the town over and found the other one, and stole that. In this manner he accomplished what the profession call a "scoop"—that is, he got a valuable item, and saw to it that no other paper got it. And so his paper—the principal one in the town—had it in glaring type on the editorial page in the morning, followed by a Vesuvian opinion of our wretch a column long, which wound up by adding a thousand dollars to our reward on the *paper's* account! The journals out here know how to do the noble thing—when there's business in it.

At breakfast I occupied my usual seat—selected because it afforded a view of papa Fuller's face, and was near enough for me to hear the talk that went on at his table. Seventy-five or a hundred people were in the room, and all discussing that item, and saying they hoped the seeker would find that rascal and remove the pollution of his presence from the town—with a rail, or a bullet, or something.

When Fuller came in he had the Notice to Leave—folded up—in one hand, and the newspaper in the other; and it gave me more than half a pang to see him. His cheerfulness was all gone, and he looked old and pinched and ashy. And then—only think of the things he had to listen to! Mamma, he heard his own unsuspecting friends describe him with epithets and characterizations drawn from the very dictionaries and phrase-books of Satan's own authorized editions down below. And more than that, he had to *agree* with the verdicts and applaud them. His applause tasted bitter in his mouth, though; he could not disguise that from me; and it was observable that his appetite was gone; he only nibbled; he couldn't eat. Finally a man said:

"It is quite likely that that relative is in the room and hearing what this town thinks of that unspeakable scoundrel. I hope so."

Ah, dear, it was pitiful the way Fuller winced, and glanced around scared! He couldn't endure any more, and got up and left.

During several days he gave out that he had bought a mine in Mexico, and wanted to sell out and go down there as soon as he could, and give the property his personal attention. He played his cards well; said he would take $40,000—a quarter in cash, the rest in safe notes; but that as he greatly needed money on account of his new purchase, he would diminish his terms for cash in full. He sold out for $30,000. And then, what do you think he did? He asked for *greenbacks*, and took them, saying the man in Mexico was a New-Englander, with a head full of crotchets, and preferred greenbacks to gold or drafts. People thought it queer, since a draft on New York could produce greenbacks quite conveniently. There was talk of this odd thing, but only for a day; that is as long as any topic lasts in Denver.

I was watching, all the time. As soon as the sale was completed and the money paid — which was on the 11th — I began to stick to Fuller's track without dropping it for a moment. That night — no, 12th, for it was a little past midnight — I tracked him to his room, which was four doors from mine in the same hall; then I went back and put on my muddy day-laborer disguise, darkened my complexion, and sat down in my room in the gloom, with a gripsack handy, with a change in it, and my door ajar. For I suspected that the bird would take wing now. In half an hour an old woman passed by, carrying a grip: I caught the familiar whiff, and followed with my grip, for it was Fuller. He left the hotel by a side entrance, and at the corner he turned up an unfrequented street and walked three blocks in a light rain and a heavy darkness, and got into a two-horse hack, which of course was waiting for him by appointment. I took a seat (uninvited) on the trunk platform behind, and we drove briskly off. We drove ten miles, and the hack stopped at a way-station and was discharged. Fuller got out and took a seat on a barrow under the awning, as far as he could get from the light; I went inside, and watched the ticket-office. Fuller bought no ticket; I bought none. Presently the train came along, and he boarded a car; I entered the same car at the other end, and came down the aisle and took the seat behind him. When he paid the conductor and named his objective point, I dropped back several seats, while the conductor was changing a bill, and when he came to me I paid to the same place — about a hundred miles westward.

From that time for a week on end he led me a dance. He traveled here and there and yonder — always on a general westward trend — but he was not a woman after the first day. He was a laborer, like myself, and wore bushy false whiskers. His outfit was perfect, and he could do the character without thinking about it, for he had served the trade for wages. His nearest friend could not have recognized him. At last he located himself here, the obscurest little mountain camp in Montana; he has a shanty, and goes out prospecting daily; is gone all day, and avoids society. I am living at a miner's boarding-house, and it is an awful place: the bunks, the food, the dirt — everything.

We have been here four weeks, and in that time I have seen him but once; but every night I go over his track and post myself. As soon as

he engaged a shanty here I went to a town fifty miles away and tele-
graphed that Denver hotel to keep my baggage till I should send for it.
I need nothing here but a change of army shirts, and I brought that
with me.

SILVER GULCH, June 12.

The Denver episode has never found its way here, I think.   I know
the most of the men in camp, and they have never referred to it, at least
in my hearing.   Fuller doubtless feels quite safe in these conditions.
He has located a claim, two miles away, in an out-of-the-way place in
the mountains; it promises very well, and he is working it diligently.
Ah, but the change in him!   He never smiles, and he keeps quite
to himself, consorting with no one — he who was so fond of company
and so cheery only two months ago.   I have seen him passing along
several times recently — drooping, forlorn, the spring gone from his
step, a pathetic figure.   He calls himself David Wilson.

I can trust him to remain here until we disturb him.   Since you
insist, I will banish him again, but I do not see how he can be unhappier than he already is.   I will go back to Denver and treat myself to a
little season of comfort, and edible food, and endurable beds, and bodily
decency; then I will fetch my things, and notify poor papa Wilson
to move on.

DENVER, June 19.

They miss him here.   They all hope he is prospering in Mexico, and
they do not say it just with their mouths, but out of their hearts.   You
know you can always tell.   I am loitering here overlong, I confess it.
But if you were in my place you would have charity for me.   Yes,
I know what you will say, and you are right: if I were in *your* place,
and carried your scalding memories in my heart —

I will take the night train back to-morrow.

DENVER, June 20.

God forgive us, mother, we are hunting the *wrong man!*   I have
not slept any all night.   I am now waiting, at dawn, for the *morning*
train — and how the minutes drag, how they drag!

This Jacob Fuller is a *cousin* of the guilty one.   How stupid we
have been not to reflect that the guilty one would never again wear his
own name after that fiendish deed!   The Denver Fuller is four years
younger than the other one; he came here a young widower in '79,
aged twenty-one — a year before you were married; and the documents

to prove it are innumerable. Last night I talked with familiar friends
of his who have known him from the day of his arrival. I said nothing,
but a few days from now I will land him in this town again, with the
loss upon his mine made good; and there will be a banquet, and a
torch-light procession, and there will not be any expense on anybody
but me. Do you call this "gush"? I am only a boy, as you well
know; it is my privilege. By and by I shall not be a boy any more.

SILVER GULCH, July 3.

Mother, he is gone! Gone, and left no trace. The scent was cold
when I came. To-day I am out of bed for the first time since. I wish
I were not a boy; then I could stand shocks better. They all think he
went west. I start to-night, in a wagon — two or three hours of that,
then I get a train. I don't know where I'm going, but I must go; to
try to keep still would be torture.

Of course he has effaced himself with a new name and a disguise.
This means that *I may have to search the whole globe to find him*. In-
deed it is what I expect. Do you see, mother? It is *I* that am the
Wandering Jew. The irony of it! We arranged that for another.

Think of the difficulties! And there would be none if I only could
advertise for him. But if there is any way to do it that would not
frighten him, I have not been able to think it out, and I have tried till
my brains are addled. "If the gentleman who lately bought a mine in
Mexico and sold one in Denver will send his address to" (to whom,
mother!), "it will be explained to him that it was all a mistake; his
forgiveness will be asked, and full reparation made for a loss which he
sustained in a certain matter." Do you see? He would think it a
trap. Well, any one would. If I should say, "It is now known that
he was not the man wanted, but another man — a man who once bore
the same name, but discarded it for good reasons" — would that
answer? But the Denver people would wake up then and say "Oho!"
and they would remember about the suspicious greenbacks, and say,
"Why did he run away if he wasn't the right man? — it is too thin."
If I failed to find him he would be ruined there — there where there is
no taint upon him now. You have a better head than mine. Help me.

I have one clew, and only one. I know his handwriting. If he puts
his new false name upon a hotel register and does not disguise it too
much, it will be valuable to me if I ever run across it.

SAN FRANCISCO, June 28, 1898.

You already know how well I have searched the States from Colorado to the Pacinc, and how nearly I came to getting him once. Well, I have had another close miss. It was here, yesterday. I struck his trail, *hot*, on the street, and followed it on a run to a cheap hotel. That was a costly mistake; a dog would have gone the other way. But I am only part dog, and can get very humanly stupid when excited. He had been stopping in that house ten days; I almost know, now, that he stops long nowhere, the past six or eight months, but is restless and has to keep moving. I understand that feeling! and I know what it is to feel it. He still uses the name he had registered when I came so near catching him nine months ago — "James Walker"; doubtless the same he adopted when he fled from Silver Gulch. An unpretending man, and has small taste for fancy names. I recognized the hand easily, through its slight disguise. A square man, and not good at shams and pretenses.

They said he was just gone, on a journey; left no address; didn't say where he was going; looked frightened when asked to leave his address; had no baggage but a cheap valise; carried it off on foot — a "stingy old person, and not much loss to the house." " *Old!* " I suppose he is, now. I hardly heard; I was there but a moment. I rushed along his trail, and it led me to a wharf. Mother, the smoke of the steamer he had taken was just fading out on the horizon! I should have saved half an hour if I had gone in the right direction at first. I could have taken a fast tug, and should have stood a chance of catching that vessel. She is bound for Melbourne.

HOPE CANYON, CALIFORNIA, October 3, 1900.

You have a right to complain. " A letter a year " *is* a paucity; I freely acknowledge it; but how can one write when there is nothing to write about but failures? No one can keep it up; it breaks the heart.

I told you — it seems ages ago, now — how I missed him at Melbourne, and then chased him all over Australasia for months on end.

Well, then, after that I followed him to India; almost *saw* him in Bombay; traced him all around — to Baroda, Rawal-Pindi, Lucknow, Lahore, Cawnpore, Allahabad, Calcutta, Madras — oh, everywhere; week after week, month after month, through the dust and swelter — always approximately on his track, sometimes close upon him, yet never catching him. And down to Ceylon, and then to — Never mind; by and by I will write it all out.

I chased him home to California, and down to Mexico, and back again to California. Since then I have been hunting him about the State from the first of last January down to a month ago. I feel almost sure he is not far from Hope Canyon; I traced him to a point thirty miles from here, but there I lost the trail; some one gave him a lift in a wagon, I suppose.

I am taking a rest, now — modified by searchings for the lost trail. I was tired to death, mother, and low-spirited, and sometimes coming uncomfortably near to losing hope; but the miners in this little camp are good fellows, and I am used to their sort this long time back; and their breezy ways freshen a person up and make him forget his troubles. I have been here a month. I am cabining with a young fellow named " Sammy " Hillyer, about twenty-five, the only son of his mother — like me — and loves her dearly, and writes to her every week — part of which is like me. He is a timid body, and in the matter of intellect — well, he cannot be depended upon to set a river on fire; but no matter, he is well liked; he is good and fine, and it is meat and bread and rest and luxury to sit and talk with him and have a comradeship again. I wish " James Walker " could have it. He had friends; he liked company. That brings up that picture of him, the time that I saw him last. The pathos of it! It comes before me often and often. At that very time, poor thing, I was girding up my conscience to make him move on again!

Hillyer's heart is better than mine, better than anybody's in the community, I suppose, for he is the one friend of the black sheep of the camp — Flint Buckner — and the only man Flint ever talks with or allows to talk with him. He says he knows Flint's history, and that it is trouble that has made him what he is, and so one ought to be as charitable toward him as one can. Now none but a pretty large heart could find space to accommodate a lodger like Flint Buckner, from all I hear about him outside. I think that this one detail will give you a better idea of Sammy's character than any labored-out description I could furnish you of him. In one of our talks he said something about like this: " Flint is a kinsman of mine, and he pours out all his troubles to me — empties his breast from time to time, or I reckon it would burst. There couldn't be any unhappier man, Archy Stillman; his life has been made up of misery of mind — he isn't near as old as he looks. He has lost the feel of reposefulness and peace — oh, years and years ago! He doesn't know what good luck is — never has had any; often says he wishes he was in the other hell, he is so tired of this one."

CHAPTER IV

No real gentleman will tell the naked truth in the presence of ladies

IT was a crisp and spicy morning in early October. The lilacs and laburnums, lit with the glory-fires of autumn, hung burning and flashing in the upper air, a fairy bridge provided by kind Nature for the wingless wild things that have their homes in the tree-tops and would visit together; the larch and the pomegranate flung their purple and yellow flames in brilliant broad splashes along the slanting sweep of the woodland; the sensuous fragrance of innumerable deciduous flowers rose upon the swooning atmosphere; far in the empty sky a solitary œsophagus* slept upon motionless wing; every-

---

* [From the Springfield Republican April 12, 1902.]

To the Editor of the Republican: —

One of your citizens has asked me a question about the "œsopha-gus," and I wish to answer him through you. This in the hope that the answer will get around, and save me some penmanship, for I have already replied to the same question more than several times, and am not getting as much holiday as I ought to have.

I published a short story lately, and it was in that that I put the œsophagus. I will say privately that I expected it to bother some peo-ple--in fact, that was the intention, — but the harvest has been larger than I was calculating upon. The œsophagus has gathered in the

where brooded stillness, serenity, and the peace of God.

October is the time — 1900; Hope Canyon is the place, a silver-mining camp away down in the

---

guilty and the innocent alike, whereas I was only fishing for the inno-cent — the innocent and confiding. I knew a few of these would write and ask me ; that would give me but little trouble ; but I was not ex-pecting that the wise and the learned would call upon me for succor. However, that has happened, and it is time for me to speak up and stop the inquiries if I can, for letter-writing is not restful to me, and I am not having so much fun out of this thing as I counted on. That you may understand the situation, I will insert a couple of sample in-quiries. The first is from a public instructor in the Philippines :

SANTA CRUZ, Ilocos Sur, P. I.
February 13, 1902.
My Dear Sir: I have just been reading the first part of your latest story, entitled " A Double-barreled Detective Story," and am very much delighted with it. In Part IV, page 264, Harper's Magazine for Janu-ary, occurs this passage: " far in the empty sky a solitary ' œsophagus' slept, upon motionless wing; everywhere brooded stillness, serenity, and the peace of God." Now, there is one word I do not understand, namely, " œsophagus." My only work of reference is the " Standard Dictionary," but that fails to explain the meaning. If you can spare the time, I would be glad to have the meaning cleared up, as I consider the passage a very touching and beautiful one. It may seem foolish to you, but consider my lack of means away out in the northern part of Luzon.   Yours very truly.

Do you notice? Nothing in the paragraph disturbed him but that one word. It shows that that paragraph was most ably constructed for the deception it was intended to put upon the reader. It was my inten-tion that it should read plausibly, and it is now plain that it does; it was my intention that it should be emotional and touching, and you see, yourself, that it fetched this public instructor. Alas, if I had but left that one treacherous word out, I should have scored! scored every-where; and the paragraph would have slidden through every reader's sensibilities like oil, and left not a suspicion behind.

The other sample inquiry is from a professor in a New England uni-versity. It contains one naughty word (which I cannot bear to sup-

Esmeralda region. It is a secluded spot, high and remote; recent as to discovery; thought by its occupants to be rich in metal — a year or two's prospecting will decide that matter one way or the

---

press), but he is not in the theological department, so it is no harm:—

Dear Mr. Clemens: "Far in the empty sky a solitary œsophagus slept upon motionless wing."

It is not often I get a chance to read much periodical literature, but I have just gone through at this belated period, with much gratification and edification, your "Double-Barreled Detective Story."

But what in hell is an œsophagus? I keep one myself, but it never sleeps in the air or anywhere else. My profession is to deal with words, and œsophagus interested me the moment I lighted upon it. But as a companion of my youth used to say, "I'll be eternally, co-eternally cussed" if I can make it out. Is it a joke, or I an ignoramus?

Between you and me, I was almost ashamed of having fooled that man, but for pride's sake I was not going to say so. I wrote and told him it was a joke — and that is what I am now saying to my Springfield inquirer. And I told him to carefully read the whole paragraph, and he would find not a vestige of sense in any detail of it. This also I commend to my Springfield inquirer.

I have confessed. I am sorry — partially. I will not do so any more — for the present. Don't ask me any more questions; let the œsophagus have a rest — on his same old motionless wing.

MARK TWAIN.

New York City, April 10, 1902.

(Editorial.)

☞ The "Double-Barreled Detective Story," which appeared in Harper's Mag. for January and February last, is the most elaborate of burlesques on detective fiction, with striking melodramatic passages in which it is difficult to detect the deception, so ably is it done. But the illusion ought not to endure even the first incident in the February number. As for the paragraph which has so admirably illustrated the skill of Mr. Clemens's ensemble and the carelessness of readers, here it is:—

It was a crisp and spicy morning in early October. The lilacs and laburnums, lit with the glory-fires of autumn, hung burning and flashing in the upper air, a fairy bridge provided by kind nature for the wingless wild things that have their home in the tree-tops and would visit to-other. For inhabitants, the camp has about two hundred miners, one white woman and child, several Chinese washermen, five squaws, and a dozen vagrant buck Indians in rabbit-skin robes, battered plug hats, and tin-can necklaces. There are no mills as yet; no church, no newspaper. The camp has existed but two years; it has made no big strike; the world is ignorant of its name and place.

On both sides of the canyon the mountains rise wall-like, three thousand feet, and the long spiral of straggling huts down in its narrow bottom gets a kiss from the sun only once a day, when he sails over at noon. The village is a couple of miles long;

---

gether; the larch and the pomegranate flung their purple and yellow flames in brilliant broad splashes along the slanting sweep of the woodland; the sensuous fragrance of innumerable deciduous flowers rose upon the swooning atmosphere; far in the empty sky a solitary œsophagus slept upon motionless wing; everywhere brooded stillness, serenity, and the peace of God.

The success of Mark Twain's joke recalls to mind his story of the petrified man in the cavern, whom he described most punctiliously, first giving a picture of the scene, its impressive solitude, and all that; then going on to describe the majesty of the figure, casually mentioning that the thumb of his right hand rested against the side of his nose; then after further description observing that the fingers of the right hand were extended in a radiating fashion; and, recurring to the dignified attitude and position of the man, incidentally remarked that the thumb of the left hand was in contact with the little finger of the right — and so on. But it was so ingeniously written that Mark, relating the history years later in an article which appeared in that excellent magazine of the past, the Galaxy, declared that no one ever found out the joke, and, if we remember aright, that that astonishing old mockery was actually looked for in the region where he, as a Nevada newspaper editor, had located it. It is certain that Mark Twain's jumping frog has a good many more "pints" than any other frog.

the cabins stand well apart from each other. The
tavern is the only '' frame '' house — the only house,
one might say. It occupies a central position, and
is the evening resort of the population. They drink
there, and play seven-up and dominoes; also bil-
liards, for there is a table, crossed all over with torn
places repaired with court-plaster; there are some
cues, but no leathers; some chipped balls which
clatter when they run, and do not slow up gradually,
but stop suddenly and sit down; there is a part of a
cube of chalk, with a projecting jag of flint in it;
and the man who can score six on a single break
can set up the drinks at the bar's expense.

Flint Buckner's cabin was the last one of the village, going south; his silver claim was at the other
end of the village, northward, and a little beyond
the last hut in that direction. He was a sour
creature, unsociable, and had no companionships.
People who had tried to get acquainted with him
had regretted it and dropped him. His history was
not known. Some believed that Sammy Hillyer
knew it; others said no. If asked, Hillyer said no,
he was not acquainted with it. Flint had a meek
English youth of sixteen or seventeen with him,
whom he treated roughly, both in public and in
private; and of course this lad was applied to for
information, but with no success. Fetlock Jones —
name of the youth — said that Flint picked him up
on a prospecting tramp, and as he had neither home
nor friends in America, he had found it wise to stay

and take Buckner's hard usage for the sake of the salary, which was bacon and beans. Further than this he could offer no testimony.

Fetlock had been in this slavery for a month now, and under his meek exterior he was slowly consuming to a cinder with the insults and humiliations which his master had put upon him. For the meek suffer bitterly from these hurts; more bitterly, perhaps, than do the manlier sort, who can burst out and get relief with words or blows when the limit of endurance has been reached. Good-hearted people wanted to help Fetlock out of his trouble, and tried to get him to leave Buckner; but the boy showed fright at the thought, and said he "dasn't." Pat Riley urged him, and said:

"You leave the damned hunks and come with me; don't you be afraid. I'll take care of *him*."

The boy thanked him with tears in his eyes, but shuddered and said he "dasn't risk it"; he said Flint would catch him alone, some time, in the night, and then — "Oh, it makes me sick, Mr. Riley, to think of it."

Others said, "Run away from him; we'll stake you; skip out for the coast some night." But all these suggestions failed; he said Flint would hunt him down and fetch him back, just for meanness.

The people could not understand this. The boy's miseries went steadily on, week after week. It is quite likely that the people would have understood if they had known how he was employing his spare

31

time. He slept in an out-cabin near Flint's; and there, nights, he nursed his bruises and his humiliations, and studied and studied over a single problem — how he could murder Flint Buckner and not be found out. It was the only joy he had in life; these hours were the only ones in the twenty-four which he looked forward to with eagerness and spent in happiness.

He thought of poison. No — that would not serve; the inquest would reveal where it was procured and who had procured it. He thought of a shot in the back in a lonely place when Flint would be homeward bound at midnight — his unvarying hour for the trip. No — somebody might be near, and catch him. He thought of stabbing him in his sleep. No — he might strike an inefficient blow, and Flint would seize him. He examined a hundred different ways — none of them would answer; for in even the very obscurest and secretest of them there was always the fatal defect of a *risk*, a chance, a possibility that he might be found out. He would have none of that.

But he was patient, endlessly patient. There was no hurry, he said to himself. He would never leave Flint till he left him a corpse; there was no hurry — he would find the way. It was somewhere, and he would endure shame and pain and misery until he found it. Yes, somewhere there was a way which would leave not a trace, not even the faintest clew to the murderer — there was no hurry — he would find that way, and then — oh, then, it would just be good to be alive! Meantime he would diligently keep up his reputation for meekness; and also, as always theretofore, he would allow no one to hear him say a resentful or offensive thing about his oppressor.

Two days before the before-mentioned October morning Flint had bought some things, and he and Fetlock had brought them home to Flint's cabin: a fresh box of candles, which they put in the corner; a tin can of blasting-powder, which they placed upon the candle-box; a keg of blasting-powder, which they placed under Flint's bunk; a huge coil of fuse, which they hung on a peg. Fetlock reasoned that Flint's mining operations had outgrown the pick, and that blasting was about to begin now. He had seen blasting done, and he had a notion of the process, but he had never helped in it. His conjecture was right — blasting-time had come. In the morning the pair carried fuse, drills, and the powder-can to the shaft; it was now eight feet deep, and to get into it and out of it a short ladder was used. They descended, and by command Fetlock held the drill — without any instructions as to the right way to hold it — and Flint proceeded to strike. The sledge came down; the drill sprang out of Fetlock's hand, almost as a matter of course.

"You mangy son of a nigger, is that any way to hold a drill? Pick it up! Stand it up! There — hold fast. D—— you! *I'll* teach you!"

At the end of an hour the drilling was finished.

" Now, then, charge it."

The boy started to pour in the powder.

" Idiot! "

A heavy bat on the jaw laid the lad out.

" Get up! You can't lie sniveling there. Now, then, stick in the fuse *first*. *Now* put in the powder. Hold on, hold on! Are you going to fill the hole *all* up? Of all the sap-headed milksops I — Put in some dirt! Put in some gravel! Tamp it down! Hold on, hold on! Oh, great Scott! get out of the way! " He snatched the iron and tamped the charge himself, meantime cursing and blaspheming like a fiend. Then he fired the fuse, climbed out of the shaft, and ran fifty yards away, Fetlock following. They stood waiting a few minutes, then a great volume of smoke and rocks burst high into the air with a thunderous explosion; after a little there was a shower of descending stones; then all was serene again.

" I wish to God you'd been in it! " remarked the master.

They went down the shaft, cleaned it out, drilled another hole, and put in another charge.

" Look here! How much fuse are you proposing to waste? Don't you know how to time a fuse? "

" No, sir."

" You *don't!* Well, if you don't beat anything *I* ever saw! "

He climbed out of the shaft and spoke down:

"Well, idiot, are you going to be all day? Cut the fuse and light it!"

The trembling creature began,

"If you please, sir, I —"

"You talk back to *me?* Cut it and light it!"

The boy cut and lit.

"Ger-reat Scott! a one-minute fuse! I wish you were in —"

In his rage he snatched the ladder out of the shaft and ran. The boy was aghast.

"Oh, my God! Help! Help! Oh, save me!" he implored. "Oh what can I do! What *can* I do!"

He backed against the wall as tightly as he could; the sputtering fuse frightened the voice out of him; his breath stood still; he stood gazing and impotent; in two seconds, three seconds, four he would be flying toward the sky torn to fragments. Then he had an inspiration. He sprang at the fuse; severed the inch of it that was left above ground, and was saved.

He sank down limp and half lifeless with fright, his strength gone; but he muttered with a deep joy:

"He has learnt me! I knew there was a way, if I would wait."

After a matter of five minutes Buckner stole to the shaft, looking worried and uneasy, and peered down into it. He took in the situation; he saw what had happened. He lowered the ladder, and the boy dragged himself weakly up it. He was very white. His appearance added something to Buckner's un-

comfortable state, and he said, with a show of regret
and sympathy which sat upon him awkwardly from
lack of practice:

" It was an accident, you know.   Don't say anything about it to anybody; I was excited, and didn't
notice what I was doing.   You're not looking well;
you've worked enough for to-day; go down to my
cabin and eat what you want, and rest.   It's just an
accident, you know, on account of my being
excited."

" It scared me," said the lad, as he started away;
" but I learnt something, so I don't mind it."

" Damned easy to please!" muttered Buckner,
following him with his eye.   " I wonder if he'll tell?
Mightn't he? . . . I wish it *had* killed him."

The boy took no advantage of his holiday in the
matter of resting; he employed it in work, eager
and feverish and happy work.   A thick growth of
chaparral extended down the mountain-side clear to
Flint's cabin; the most of Fetlock's labor was done
in the dark intricacies of that stubborn growth; the
rest of it was done in his own shanty.   At last all
was complete, and he said:

" If he's got any suspicions that I'm going to tell
on him, he won't keep them long, to-morrow.   He
will see that I am the same milksop as I always was
— all day and the next.   And the day after to-morrow night there'll be an end of him; nobody will
ever guess who finished him up nor how it was done.
He dropped me the idea his own self, and that's odd."

CHAPTER V.

THE next day came and went.

It is now almost midnight, and in five minutes the new morning will begin. The scene is in the tavern billiard-room. Rough men in rough clothing, slouch hats, breeches stuffed into boot-tops, some with vests, none with coats, are grouped about the boiler-iron stove, which has ruddy cheeks and is distributing a grateful warmth; the billiard balls are clacking; there is no other sound—that is, within; the wind is fitfully moaning without. The men look bored; also expectant. A hulking broad-shouldered miner, of middle age, with grizzled whiskers, and an unfriendly eye set in an unsociable face, rises, slips a coil of fuse upon his arm, gathers up some other personal properties, and departs without word or greeting to anybody. It is Flint Buckner. As the door closes behind him a buzz of talk breaks out.

"The regularest man that ever was," said Jake Parker, the blacksmith: "you can tell when it's twelve just by him leaving, without looking at your Waterbury."

"And it's the only virtue he's got, as fur as I know," said Peter Hawes, miner.

"He's just a blight on this society," said Wells-Fargo's man, Ferguson. "If I was running this shop I'd make him say something, *some* time or other, or vamos the ranch." This with a suggestive glance at the barkeeper, who did not choose to see it, since the man under discussion was a good customer, and went home pretty well set up, every night, with refreshments furnished from the bar.

"Say," said Ham Sandwich, miner, "does any of you boys ever recollect of him asking you to take a drink?"

"*Him ?* Flint *Buckner ?* Oh, Laura!"

This sarcastic rejoinder came in a spontaneous general outburst in one form of words or another from the crowd. After a brief silence, Pat Riley, miner, said:

"He's the 15-puzzle, that cuss. And his boy's another one. *I* can't make them out."

"Nor anybody else," said Ham Sandwich; "and if they are 15-puzzles, how are you going to rank up that other one? When it comes to A 1 right-down solid mysteriousness, he lays over both of them. *Easy* — don't he?"

"You bet!"

Everybody said it. Every man but one. He was the new-comer — Peterson. He ordered the drinks all round, and asked who No. 3 might be. All answered at once, "Archy Stillman!"

"Is he a mystery?" asked Peterson.

"Is *he* a mystery? Is Archy *Stillman* a mystery?" said Wells-Fargo's man, Ferguson. "Why, the fourth dimension's foolishness to *him*."

For Ferguson was learned.

Peterson wanted to hear all about him; everybody wanted to tell him; everybody began. But Billy Stevens, the barkeeper, called the house to order, and said one at a time was best. He distributed the drinks, and appointed Ferguson to lead. Ferguson said:

"Well, he's a boy. And that is just about all we know about him. You can pump him till you are tired; it ain't any use; you won't get anything. At least about his intentions, or line of business, or where he's from, and such things as that. And as for getting at the nature and get-up of his main big chief mystery, why, he'll just change the subject, that's all. You can *guess* till you're black in the face — it's your privilege — but suppose you do, where do you arrive at? Nowhere, as near as I can make out."

"What *is* his big chief one?"

"Sight, maybe. Hearing, maybe. Instinct, maybe. Magic, maybe. Take your choice — grown-ups, twenty-five; children and servants, half price. Now I'll tell you what he can do. You can start here, and just disappear; you can go and hide wherever you want to, I don't care where it is, nor how far — and he'll go straight and put his finger on you."

"You don't mean it!"

"I just do, though. Weather's nothing to him —

elemental conditions is nothing to him — he don't
even take notice of them."

"Oh, come! Dark? Rain? Snow? Hey?"

"It's all the same to *him*. He don't give a
damn."

"Oh, *say* — including *fog*, per'aps?"

"*Fog!* he's got an eye 't can plunk through it
like a bullet."

"Now, boys, honor bright, what's he giving me?"

"It's a fact!" they all shouted. "Go on,
Wells-Fargo."

"Well, sir, you can leave him here, chatting with
the boys, and you can slip out and go to any cabin
in this camp and open a book — yes, sir, a dozen of
them — and take the page in your memory, and
he'll start out and go straight to that cabin and open
every one of them books at the right page, and call
it off, and never make a mistake."

"He must be the devil!"

"More than one has thought it. Now I'll tell
you a perfectly wonderful thing that he done. The
other night he — "

There was a sudden great murmur of sounds outside, the door flew open, and an excited crowd burst
in, with the camp's one white woman in the lead
and crying:

"My child! my child! she's lost and gone! For
the love of God help me to find Archy Stillman;
we've hunted everywhere!"

Said the barkeeper:

"Sit down, sit down, Mrs. Hogan, and don't worry. He asked for a bed three hours ago, tuckered out tramping the trails the way he's always doing, and went upstairs. Ham Sandwich, run up and roust him out; he's in No. 14."

The youth was soon downstairs and ready. He asked Mrs. Hogan for particulars.

"Bless you, dear, there ain't any; I wish there was. I put her to sleep at seven in the evening, and when I went in there an hour ago to go to bed myself, she was gone. I rushed for your cabin, dear, and you wasn't there, and I've hunted for you ever since, at every cabin down the gulch, and now I've come up again, and I'm that distracted and scared and heart-broke; but, thanks to God, I've found you at last, dear heart, and you'll find my child. Come on! come quick!"

"Move right along; I'm with you, madam. Go to your cabin first."

The whole company streamed out to join the hunt. All the southern half of the village was up, a hundred men strong, and waiting outside, a vague dark mass sprinkled with twinkling lanterns. The mass fell into columns by threes and fours to accommodate itself to the narrow road, and strode briskly along southward in the wake of the leaders. In a few minutes the Hogan cabin was reached.

"There's the bunk," said Mrs. Hogan; "there's where she was; it's where I laid her at seven o'clock; but where she is now, God only knows."

"Hand me a lantern," said Archy. He set it
on the hard earth floor and knelt by it, pretending
to examine the ground closely. "Here's her
track," he said, touching the ground here and there
and yonder with his finger. "Do you see?"

Several of the company dropped upon their knees
and did their best to see. One or two thought they
discerned something like a track; the others shook
their heads and confessed that the smooth hard
surface had no marks upon it which their eyes were
sharp enough to discover. One said, "Maybe a
child's foot could make a mark on it, but *I* don't
see how."

Young Stillman stepped outside, held the light to
the ground, turned leftward, and moved three steps,
closely examining; then said, "I've got the direction — come along; take the lantern, somebody."

He strode off swiftly southward, the files following, swaying and bending in and out with the deep
curves of the gorge. Thus a mile, and the mouth
of the gorge was reached; before them stretched
the sage-brush plain, dim, vast, and vague. Stillman called a halt, saying, "We mustn't start wrong,
now; we must take the direction again."

He took a lantern and examined the ground for a
matter of twenty yards; then said, "Come on; it's all
right," and gave up the lantern. In and out among
the sage-bushes he marched, a quarter of a mile, bearing gradually to the right; then took a new direction
and made another great semicircle; then changed

again and moved due west nearly half a mile — and stopped.

"She gave it up, here, poor little chap. Hold the lantern. You can see where she sat."

But this was in a slick alkali flat which was surfaced like steel, and no person in the party was quite hardy enough to claim an eyesight that could detect the track of a cushion on a veneer like that. The bereaved mother fell upon her knees and kissed the spot, lamenting.

"But where is she, then?" some one said. "She didn't stay here. We can see *that* much, anyway."

Stillman moved about in a circle around the place, with the lantern, pretending to hunt for tracks.

"Well!" he said presently, in an annoyed tone, "I don't understand it." He examined again. "No use. She was here — that's certain; she never *walked* away from here — and that's certain. It's a puzzle; I can't make it out."

The mother lost heart then.

"Oh, my God! oh, blessed Virgin! some flying beast has got her. I'll never see her again!"

"Ah, *don't* give up," said Archy. "We'll find her — don't give up."

"God bless you for the words, Archy Stillman!" and she seized his hand and kissed it fervently.

Peterson, the new-comer, whispered satirically in Ferguson's ear:

"Wonderful performance to find this place, wasn't it? Hardly worth while to come so far, though; any other supposititious place would have answered just as well — hey?''

Ferguson was not pleased with the innuendo. He said, with some warmth:

''Do you mean to insinuate that the child hasn't been here? I tell you the child *has* been here! Now if you want to get yourself into as tidy a little fuss as—''

''All right!'' sang out Stillman. ''Come, everybody, and look at this! It was right under our noses all the time, and we didn't see it.''

There was a general plunge for the ground at the place where the child was alleged to have rested, and many eyes tried hard and hopefully to see the thing that Archy's finger was resting upon. There was a pause, then a several-barreled sigh of disappointment. Pat Riley and Ham Sandwich said, in the one breath:

''What is it, Archy? There's nothing here.''

''Nothing? Do you call *that* nothing?'' and he swiftly traced upon the ground a form with his finger. ''There — don't you recognize it now? It's Injun Billy's track. He's got the child.''

''God be praised!'' from the mother.

''Take away the lantern. I've got the direction. Follow!''

He started on a run, racing in and out among the sage-bushes a matter of three hundred yards, and disappeared over a sand-wave; the others struggled after him, caught him up, and found him waiting.

Ten steps away was a little wickieup, a dim and formless shelter of rags and old horse-blankets, a dull light showing through its chinks.

"You lead, Mrs. Hogan," said the lad. "It's your privilege to be first."

All followed the sprint she made for the wickieup, and saw, with her, the picture its interior afforded. Injun Billy was sitting on the ground; the child was asleep beside him. The mother hugged it with a wild embrace, which included Archy Stillman, the grateful tears running down her face, and in a choked and broken voice she poured out a golden stream of that wealth of worshiping endearments which has its home in full richness nowhere but in the Irish heart.

"I find her bymeby it is ten o'clock," Billy explained. "She 'sleep out yonder, ve'y tired — face wet, been cryin', 'spose; fetch her home, feed her, she heap much hungry — go 'sleep 'gin."

In her limitless gratitude the happy mother waived rank and hugged him too, calling him "the angel of God in disguise." And he probably was in disguise if he was that kind of an official. He was dressed for the character.

At half-past one in the morning the procession burst into the village singing, "When Johnny Comes Marching Home," waving its lanterns, and swallowing the drinks that were brought out all along its course. It concentrated at the tavern, and made a night of what was left of the morning.

CHAPTER VI.

THE next afternoon the village was electrified with an immense sensation. A grave and dignified foreigner of distinguished bearing and appearance had arrived at the tavern, and entered this formidable name upon the register:

SHERLOCK HOLMES.

The news buzzed from cabin to cabin, from claim to claim; tools were dropped, and the town swarmed toward the centre of interest. A man passing out at the northern end of the village shouted it to Pat Riley, whose claim was the next one to Flint Buckner's. At that time Fetlock Jones seemed to turn sick. He muttered to himself:

"Uncle *Sherlock !* The mean luck of it! — that *he* should come just when . . . ." He dropped into a reverie, and presently said to himself: "But what's the use of being afraid of *him ?* Anybody that knows him the way I do knows he can't detect a crime except where he plans it all out beforehand and arranges the clews and hires some fellow to commit it according to instructions. . . . Now there ain't going to *be* any clews this time — so, what show has he got? None at all. No, sir; everything's ready. If I was to risk putting it off — . . No, I won't run any risk like that. Flint Buckner goes out of this world to-night, for sure." Then another trouble presented itself. " Uncle Sherlock 'll be wanting to talk home matters with me this evening, and how am I going to get rid of him? for I've *got* to be at my cabin a minute or two about eight o'clock." This was an awkward matter, and cost him much thought. But he found a way to beat the difficulty. " We'll go for a walk, and I'll leave him in the road a minute, so that he won't see what it is I do: the best way to throw a detective off the track, anyway, is to have him along when you are preparing the thing. Yes, that's the safest — I'll take him with me."

Meantime the road in front of the tavern was blocked with villagers waiting and hoping for a glimpse of the great man. But he kept his room, and did not appear. None but Ferguson, Jake Parker the blacksmith, and Ham Sandwich had any luck. These enthusiastic admirers of the great scientific detective hired the tavern's detained-baggage lockup, which looked into the detective's room across a little alleyway ten or twelve feet wide, ambushed themselves in it, and cut some peep-holes in the window-blind. Mr. Holmes's blinds were down; but by and by he raised them. It gave the spies a hair-lifting but pleasurable thrill to find themselves face to face with the Extraordinary Man who had

32

filled the world with the fame of his more than human ingenuities. There he sat — not a myth, not a shadow, but real, alive, compact of substance, and almost within touching distance with the hand.

"Look at that head!" said Ferguson, in an awed voice. "By gracious! *that's* a head!"

"You bet!" said the blacksmith, with deep reverence. "Look at his nose! look at his eyes! Intellect? Just a battery of it!"

"And that paleness," said Ham Sandwich. "Comes from thought — that's what it comes from. Hell! duffers like us don't know what real thought *is.*"

"No more we don't," said Ferguson. "What we take for thinking is just blubber-and-slush."

"Right you are, Wells-Fargo. And look at that frown — that's *deep* thinking — away down, down, forty fathom into the bowels of things. He's on the track of something."

"Well, he is, and don't you forget it. Say — look at that awful gravity — look at that pallid solemnness — there ain't any corpse can lay over it."

"No, sir, not for dollars! And it's his'n by hereditary rights, too; he's been dead four times a'ready, and there's history for it. Three times natural, once by accident. I've heard say he smells damp and cold, like a grave. And he — "

"'Sh! Watch him! There — he's got his thumb on the bump on the near corner of his forehead, and his forefinger on the off one. His think-works is just a-*grinding* now, you bet your other shirt.''

"That's so. And now he's gazing up toward heaven and stroking his mustache slow, and—"

" Now he has rose up standing, and is putting his clews together on his left fingers with his right finger. See? he touches the forefinger—now middle finger—now ring-finger—"

" Stuck!"

"Look at him scowl! He can't seem to make out *that* clew. So he—"

" See him smile!—like a tiger—and tally off the other fingers like nothing! He's got it, boys; he's got it sure!"

"Well, I should *say!* I'd hate to be in that man's place that he's after."

Mr. Holmes drew a table to the window, sat down with his back to the spies, and proceeded to write. The spies withdrew their eyes from the peep-holes, lit their pipes, and settled themselves for a comfortable smoke and talk. Ferguson said, with conviction:

" Boys, it's no use talking, he's a wonder! He's got the signs of it all over him."

"You hain't ever said a truer word than that, Wells-Fargo," said Jake Parker. "Say, wouldn't it 'a' been nuts if he'd a-been here last night?"

" Oh, by George, but wouldn't it!" said Ferguson. " Then we'd have seen *scientific* work. Intellect—just pure intellect—away up on the upper levels, dontchuknow. Archy is all right, and it don't

become anybody to belittle *him*, I can tell you.
But his gift is only just eyesight, sharp as an
owl's, as near as I can make it out just a grand
natural animal talent, no more, no less, and prime
as far as it goes, but no intellect in it, and for awful-
ness and marvelousness no more to be compared to
what this man does than — than — Why, let me
tell you what *he'd* have done. He'd have stepped
over to Hogan's and glanced — just *glanced*, that's
all — at the premises, and that's enough. See
everything? Yes, sir, to the last little *de*tail; and
he'd know more about that place than the Hogans
would know in seven years. Next, he would sit
down on the bunk, just as ca'm, and say to Mrs.
Hogan — *Say*, Ham, consider that you are Mrs.
Hogan. I'll ask the questions; you answer them."

" All right; go on."

" ' Madam, if you please — attention — do not let
your mind wander. Now, then — sex of the child? '

" ' Female, your Honor.'

" ' Um — female. Very good, very good. Age? '

" ' Turned six, your Honor.'

" ' Um — young, weak — two miles. Weariness
will overtake it then. It will sink down and sleep.
We shall find it two miles away, or less. Teeth? '

" ' Five, your Honor, and one a-coming.'

" ' Very good, very good, *very* good, indeed.
' You see, boys, *he* knows a clew when he sees it,
when it wouldn't mean a dern thing to anybody
else. ' Stockings, madam? Shoes? '

" ' Yes, your Honor — both.'

" ' Yarn, perhaps? Morocco?'

" ' Yarn, your Honor. And kip.'

" ' Um — kip. This complicates the matter. However, let it go — we shall manage. Religion?'

" ' Catholic, your Honor.'

" ' Very good. Snip me a bit from the bed blanket, please. Ah, thanks. Part wool — foreign make. Very well. A snip from some garment of the child's, please. Thanks. Cotton. Shows wear. An excellent clew, excellent. Pass me a pellet of the floor dirt, if you'll be so kind. Thanks, many thanks. Ah, admirable, admirable! *Now* we know where we are, I think.' You see, boys, he's got all the clews he wants now; he don't need anything more. Now, then, what does this Extraordinary Man do? He lays those snips and that dirt out on the table and leans over them on his elbows, and puts them together side by side and studies them — mumbles to himself, ' Female '; changes them around — mumbles, ' Six years old '; changes them this way and that — again mumbles: ' Five teeth — one a-coming — Catholic — yarn — cotton — kip — damn that kip.' Then he straightens up and gazes toward heaven, and plows his hands through his hair — plows and plows, muttering, ' Damn that kip!' Then he stands up and frowns, and begins to tally off his clews on his fingers — and gets stuck at the ring-finger. But only just a minute — then his face glares all up in a smile like a

house afire, and he straightens up stately and
majestic, and says to the crowd, ' Take a lantern, a
couple of you, and go down to Injun Billy's and
fetch the child — the rest of you go 'long home to
bed; good-night, madam; good-night, gents.' And
he bows like the Matterhorn, and pulls out for the
tavern.   That's *his* style, and the *Only* — scientific,
intellectual —all over in fifteen minutes — no poking around all over the sage-brush range an hour
and a half in a mass-meeting crowd for *him*, boys —
you hear *me !* "

"By Jackson, it's grand!" said Ham Sandwich.
"Wells-Fargo, you've got him down to a dot.
He ain't painted up any exacter to the life in the
books.   By George, I can just *see* him — can't you,
boys? "

"You bet you!   It's just a photograft, that's
what it is."

Ferguson was profoundly pleased with his success,
and grateful.   He sat silently enjoying his happiness
a little while, then he murmured, with a deep awe in
his voice,

"I wonder if God made him? "

There was no response for a moment; then Ham
Sandwich said, reverently,

"Not all at one time, I reckon."

CHAPTER VII.

AT eight o'clock that evening two persons were groping their way past Flint Buckner's cabin in the frosty gloom. They were Sherlock Holmes and his nephew.

"Stop here in the road a moment, uncle," said Fetlock, "while I run to my cabin; I won't be gone a minute."

He asked for something — the uncle furnished it — then he disappeared in the darkness, but soon returned, and the talking-walk was resumed. By nine o'clock they had wandered back to the tavern. They worked their way through the billiard-room, where a crowd had gathered in the hope of getting a glimpse of the Extraordinary Man. A royal cheer was raised. Mr. Holmes acknowledged the compliment with a series of courtly bows, and as he was passing out his nephew said to the assemblage,

"Uncle Sherlock's got some work to do, gentle- men, that 'll keep him till twelve or one; but he'll be down again then, or earlier if he can, and hopes some of you'll be left to take a drink with him."

"By George, he's just a duke, boys! Three cheers for Sherlock Holmes, the greatest man that ever lived!" shouted Ferguson. "Hip, hip, hip —"

"Hurrah! hurrah! hurrah! Tiger!"

The uproar shook the building, so hearty was the feeling the boys put into their welcome. Upstairs the uncle reproached the nephew gently, saying,

"What did you get me into that engagement for?"

"I reckon you don't want to be unpopular, do you, uncle? Well, then, don't you put on any exclusiveness in a mining-camp, that's all. The boys admire you; but if you was to leave without taking a drink with them, they'd set you down for a snob. And besides, you said you had home talk enough in stock to keep us up and at it half the night."

The boy was right, and wise — the uncle acknowledged it. The boy was wise in another detail which he did not mention,— except to himself: "Uncle and the others will come handy — in the way of nailing an *alibi* where it can't be budged."

He and his uncle talked diligently about three hours. Then, about midnight, Fetlock stepped downstairs and took a position in the dark a dozen steps from the tavern, and waited. Five minutes later Flint Buckner came rocking out of the billiard-room and almost brushed him as he passed.

"I've *got* him!" muttered the boy. He continued to himself, looking after the shadowy form: "Good-by — good-by for good, Flint Buckner; you called my mother a — well, never mind what: it's all right, now; you're taking your last walk, friend."

He went musing back into the tavern. "From now till one is an hour. We'll spend it with the boys: it's good for the *alibi*."

He brought Sherlock Holmes to the billiard-room, which was jammed with eager and admiring miners; the guest called the drinks, and the fun began. Everybody was happy; everybody was complimentary; the ice was soon broken, songs, anecdotes, and more drinks followed, and the pregnant minutes flew. At six minutes to one, when the jollity was at its highest —

Boom !

There was silence instantly. The deep sound came rolling and rumbling from peak to peak up the gorge, then died down, and ceased. The spell broke, then, and the men made a rush for the door, saying,

" Something's blown up ! "

Outside, a voice in the darkness said,

" It's away down the gorge; I saw the flash."

The crowd poured down the canyon — Holmes, Fetlock, Archy Stillman, everybody. They made the mile in a few minutes. By the light of a lantern they found the smooth and solid dirt floor of Flint Buckner's cabin; of the cabin itself not a vestige remained, not a rag nor a splinter. Nor any sign of Flint. Search parties sought here and there and yonder, and presently a cry went up.

" Here he is ! "

It was true. Fifty yards down the gulch they had

found him — that is, they had found a crushed and lifeless mass which represented him. Fetlock Jones hurried thither with the others and looked.

The inquest was a fifteen-minute affair. Ham Sandwich, foreman of the jury, handed up the verdict, which was phrased with a certain unstudied literary grace, and closed with this finding, to wit: that "deceased came to his death by his own act or some other person or persons unknown to this jury not leaving any family or similar effects behind but his cabin which was blown away and God have mercy on his soul amen."

Then the impatient jury rejoined the main crowd, for the storm-centre of interest was there — Sherlock Holmes. The miners stood silent and reverent in a half-circle, enclosing a large vacant space which included the front exposure of the site of the late premises. In this considerable space the Extraordinary Man was moving about, attended by his nephew with a lantern. With a tape he took measurements of the cabin site; of the distance from the wall of chaparral to the road; of the height of the chaparral bushes; also various other measurements. He gathered a rag here, a splinter there, and a pinch of earth yonder, inspected them profoundly, and preserved them. He took the "lay" of the place with a pocket compass, allowing two seconds for magnetic variation. He took the time (Pacific) by his watch, correcting it for local time. He paced off the distance from the cabin site to the corpse, and corrected that for tidal differentiation.   He took the altitude with a pocket-aneroid, and the temperature with a pocket-thermometer.   Finally he said, with a stately bow:

"It is finished.   Shall we return, gentlemen?"

He took up the line of march for the tavern, and the crowd fell into his wake, earnestly discussing and admiring the Extraordinary Man, and interlarding guesses as to the origin of the tragedy and who the author of it might be.

"My, but it's grand luck having him here — hey, boys?" said Ferguson.

"It's the biggest thing of the century," said Ham Sandwich.   "It'll go all over the world; you mark my words."

"*You* bet!" said Jake Parker the blacksmith. "It'll boom this camp.   Ain't it so, Wells-Fargo?"

"Well, as you want my opinion — if it's any sign of how *I* think about it, I can tell you this: yesterday I was holding the Straight Flush claim at two dollars a foot; I'd like to see the man that can get it at sixteen to-day."

"Right you are, Wells-Fargo!   It's the grandest luck a new camp ever struck.   Say, did you see him collar them little rags and dirt and things?   What an eye!   He just can't overlook a clew — 'tain't *in* him."

"That's so.   And they wouldn't mean a thing to anybody else; but to him, why, they're just a book — large print at that."

" Sure's you're born! Them odds and ends have got their little old secret, and they think there ain't anybody can pull it; but, land! when he sets his grip there they've got to squeal, and don't you forget it."

"Boys, I ain't sorry, now, that he wasn't here to roust out the child; this is a bigger thing, by a long sight. Yes, sir, and more tangled up and scientific and intellectual."

" I reckon we're all of us glad it's turned out this way. Glad? 'George! it ain't any name for it. Dontchuknow, Archy could 've *learnt* something if he'd had the nous to stand by and take notice of how that man works the system. But no; he went poking up into the chaparral and just missed the whole thing."

" It's true as gospel; I seen it myself. Well, Archy's young. He'll know better one of these days."

" Say, boys, who do you reckon done it? "

That was a difficult question, and brought out a world of unsatisfying conjecture. Various men were mentioned as possibilities, but one by one they were discarded as not being eligible. No one but young Hillyer had been intimate with Flint Buckner; no one had really had a quarrel with him; he had affronted every man who had tried to make up to him, although not quite offensively enough to require bloodshed. There was one name that was upon every tongue from the start, but it was the last to get utterance — Fetlock Jones's. It was Pat Riley that mentioned it.

"Oh, well," the boys said, " of course we've all thought of him, because he had a million rights to kill Flint Buckner, and it was just his plain duty to do it. But all the same there's two things we can't get around: for one thing, he hasn't got the sand; and for another, he wasn't anywhere near the place when it happened."

"I know it," said Pat. "He was there in the billiard-room with us when it happened."

"Yes, and was there all the time for an hour *before* it happened."

"It's so. And lucky for him, too. He'd have been suspected in a minute if it hadn't been for that."

CHAPTER VIII.

THE tavern dining-room had been cleared of all its furniture save one six-foot pine table and a chair. This table was against one end of the room; the chair was on it; Sherlock Holmes, stately, imposing, impressive, sat in the chair. The public stood. The room was full. The tobacco smoke was dense, the stillness profound.

The Extraordinary Man raised his hand to command additional silence; held it in the air a few moments; then, in brief, crisp terms he put forward question after question, and noted the answers with "Um-ums," nods of the head, and so on. By this process he learned all about Flint Buckner, his character, conduct, and habits, that the people were able to tell him. It thus transpired that the Extraordinary Man's nephew was the only person in the camp who had a killing-grudge against Flint Buckner. Mr. Holmes smiled compassionately upon the witness, and asked, languidly —

"Do any of you gentlemen chance to know where the lad Fetlock Jones was at the time of the explosion?"

A thunderous response followed —

" In the billiard-room of this house ! "

" Ah. And had he just come in ? "

" Been there all of an hour ! "

" Ah. It is about — about — well, about how far might it be to the scene of the explosion ? "

" All of a mile ! "

" Ah. It isn't *much* of an alibi, 'tis true, but — "

A storm-burst of laughter, mingled with shouts of " By jiminy, but he's chain-lightning ! " and " Ain't you sorry you spoke, Sandy ? " shut off the rest of the sentence, and the crushed witness drooped his blushing face in pathetic shame. The inquisitor resumed :

" The lad Jones's somewhat *distant* connection with the case " (*laughter*) " having been disposed of, let us now call the *eye*-witnesses of the tragedy, and listen to what they have to say."

He got out his fragmentary clews and arranged them on a sheet of cardboard on his knee. The house held its breath and watched.

" We have the longitude and the latitude, corrected for magnetic variation, and this gives us the exact location of the tragedy. We have the altitude, the temperature, and the degree of humidity prevailing — inestimably valuable, since they enable us to estimate with precision the degree of influence which they would exercise upon the mood and disposition of the assassin at that time of the night."

(*Buzz of admiration; muttered remark, " By George, but he's deep !"*) He fingered his clews.

"And now let us ask these mute witnesses to speak to us.

"Here we have an empty linen shotbag. What is its message? This: that robbery was the motive, not revenge. What is its further message? This: that the assassin was of inferior intelligence — shall we say light-witted, or perhaps approaching that? How do we know this? Because a person of sound intelligence would not have proposed to rob the man Buckner, who never had much money with him. But the assassin might have been a stranger? Let the bag speak again. I take from it this article. It is a bit of silver-bearing quartz. It is peculiar. Examine it, please — you — and you — and you. Now pass it back, please. There is but one lode on this coast which produces just that character and color of quartz; and that is a lode which crops out for nearly two miles on a stretch, and in my opinion is destined, at no distant day, to confer upon its locality a globe-girdling celebrity, and upon its two hundred owners riches beyond the dreams of avarice. Name that lode, please."

"The Consolidated Christian Science and Mary Ann!" was the prompt response.

A wild crash of hurrahs followed, and every man reached for his neighbor's hand and wrung it, with tears in his eyes; and Wells-Fargo Ferguson shouted, "The Straight Flush is on the lode, and up she goes to a hundred and fifty a foot — you hear *me !*"

When quiet fell, Mr. Holmes resumed:

"We perceive, then, that three facts are established, to wit: the assassin was approximately light-witted; he was not a stranger; his motive was robbery, not revenge. Let us proceed. I hold in my hand a small fragment of fuse, with the recent smell of fire upon it. What is its testimony? Taken with the corroborative evidence of the quartz, it reveals to us that the assassin was a miner. What does it tell us further? This, gentlemen: that the assassination was consummated by means of an explosive. What else does it say? This: that the explosive was located against the side of the cabin nearest the road — the front side — for within six feet of that spot I found it.

"I hold in my fingers a burnt Swedish match — the kind one rubs on a safety-box. I found it in the road, 622 feet from the abolished cabin. What does it say? This: that the train was fired from that point. What further does it tell us? This: that the assassin was left-handed. How do I know this? I should not be able to explain to you, gentlemen, how I know it, the signs being so subtle that only long experience and deep study can enable one to detect them. But the signs are here, and they are reinforced by a fact which you must have often noticed in the great detective narratives — that *all* assassins are left-handed."

"By Jackson, *that's* so!" said Ham Sandwich, bringing his great hand down with a resounding slap

33

upon his thigh; "blamed if I ever thought of it before."

"Nor I!" "Nor I!" cried several. "Oh, there can't anything escape *him*—look at his eye!"

"Gentlemen, distant as the murderer was from his doomed victim, he did not wholly escape injury. This fragment of wood which I now exhibit to you struck him. It drew blood. Wherever he is, he bears the telltale mark. I picked it up where he stood when he fired the fatal train." He looked out over the house from his high perch, and his countenance began to darken; he slowly raised his hand, and pointed—

"There stands the assassin!"

For a moment the house was paralyzed with amazement; then twenty voices burst out with:

"Sammy Hillyer? Oh, *hell*, no! *Him?* It's pure foolishness!"

"Take care, gentlemen—be not hasty. Observe—he has the blood-mark on his brow."

Hillyer turned white with fright. He was near to crying. He turned this way and that, appealing to every face for help and sympathy; and held out his supplicating hands toward Holmes and began to plead:

"*Don't*, oh, don't! I never did it; I give my word I never did it. The way I got this hurt on my forehead was—"

"Arrest him, constable!" cried Holmes. "I will swear out the warrant."

The constable moved reluctantly forward — hesitated — stopped.

Hillyer broke out with another appeal. "Oh, Archy, don't let them do it; it would kill mother! *You* know how I got the hurt. Tell them, and save me, Archy; save me!"

Stillman worked his way to the front, and said:

"Yes, I'll save you. Don't be afraid." Then he said to the house, "Never mind how he got the hurt; it hasn't anything to do with this case, and isn't of any consequence."

"God bless you, Archy, for a true friend!"

"Hurrah for Archy! Go in, boy, and play 'em a knock-down flush to their two pair 'n' a jack!" shouted the house, pride in their home talent and a patriotic sentiment of loyalty to it rising suddenly in the public heart and changing the whole attitude of the situation.

Young Stillman waited for the noise to cease; then he said,

"I will ask Tom Jeffries to stand by that door yonder, and Constable Harris to stand by the other one here, and not let anybody leave the room."

"Said and done. Go on, old man!"

"The criminal is present, I believe. I will show him to you before long, in case I am right in my guess. Now I will tell you all about the tragedy, from start to finish. The motive *wasn't* robbery; it was revenge. The murderer *wasn't* light-witted. He *didn't* stand 622 feet away. He *didn't* get hit

with a piece of wood.   He *didn't* place the explosive against the cabin.   He *didn't* bring a shot-bag
with him, and he *wasn't* left-handed.   With the exception of these errors, the distinguished guest's
statement of the case is substantially correct."

A comfortable laugh rippled over the house;
friend nodded to friend, as much as to say, "That's
the word, with the bark *on* it.   Good lad, good boy.
He ain't lowering his flag any!"

The guest's serenity was not disturbed.   Stillman
resumed:

"I also have some witnesses; and I will presently
tell you where you can find some more."   He held
up a piece of coarse wire; the crowd craned their
necks to see.   "It has a smooth coating of melted
tallow on it.   And here is a candle which is burned
half-way down.   The remaining half of it has marks
cut upon it an inch apart.   Soon I will tell you where
I found these things.   I will now put aside reasonings,
guesses, the impressive hitchings of odds and ends
of clews together, and the other showy theatricals of
the detective trade, and tell you in a plain, straightforward way just how this dismal thing happened."

He paused a moment, for effect — to allow silence
and suspense to intensify and concentrate the house's
interest; then he went on:

"The assassin studied out his plan with a good
deal of pains.   It was a good plan, very ingenious,
and showed an intelligent mind, not a feeble one.
It was a plan which was well calculated to ward off

all suspicion from its inventor.   In the first place, he marked a candle into spaces an inch apart, and lit it and timed it.   He found it took three hours to burn four inches of it.   I tried it myself for half an hour, awhile ago, upstairs here, while the inquiry into Flint Buckner's character and ways was being conducted in this room, and I arrived in that way at the rate of a candle's consumption when sheltered from the wind.   Having proved his trial-candle's rate, he blew it out — I have already shown it to you — and put his inch-marks on a fresh one.

"He put the fresh one into a tin candlestick. Then at the five-hour mark he bored a hole through the candle with a red-hot wire.   I have already shown you the wire, with a smooth coat of tallow on it — tallow that had been melted and had cooled.

"With labor — very hard labor, I should say — he struggled up through the stiff chaparral that clothes the steep hillside back of Flint Buckner's place, tugging an empty flour-barrel with him.   He placed it in that absolutely secure hiding-place, and in the bottom of it he set the candlestick.   Then he measured off about thirty-five feet of fuse — the barrel's distance from the back of the cabin.   He bored a hole in the side of the barrel — here is the large gimlet he did it with.   He went on and finished his work; and when it was done, one end of the fuse was in Buckner's cabin, and the other end, with a notch chipped in it to expose the powder, was in the hole in the candle — timed to blow the place

up at one o'clock this morning, provided the candle
was lit about eight o'clock yesterday evening —
which I am betting it was — and provided there was
an explosive in the cabin and connected with that
end of the fuse — which I am also betting there was,
though I can't prove it. Boys, the barrel is there in
the chaparral, the candle's remains are in it in the tin
stick; the burnt-out fuse is in the gimlet-hole, the
other end is down the hill where the late cabin
stood. I saw them all an hour or two ago, when
the Professor here was measuring off unimplicated
vacancies and collecting relics that hadn't anything
to do with the case."

He paused. The house drew a long, deep breath,
shook its strained cords and muscles free and burst
into cheers. "Dang him!" said Ham Sandwich,
"that's why he was snooping around in the chaparral,
instead of picking up points out of the P'fessor's
game. Looky here — *he* ain't no fool, boys."

"No, sir! Why, great Scott — "

But Stillman was resuming:

"While we were out yonder an hour or two ago,
the owner of the gimlet and the trial-candle took
them from a place where he had concealed them —
it was not a good place — and carried them to what
he probably thought was a better one, two hundred
yards up in the pine woods, and hid them there,
covering them over with pine needles. It was there
that I found them. The gimlet exactly fits the hole
in the barrel. And now — "

The Extraordinary Man interrupted him. He said, sarcastically:

"We have had a very pretty fairy-tale, gentlemen — very pretty indeed. Now I would like to ask this young man a question or two."

Some of the boys winced, and Ferguson said,

"I'm afraid Archy's going to catch it now."

The others lost their smiles and sobered down. Mr. Holmes said:

"Let us proceed to examine into this fairy-tale in a consecutive and orderly way — by geometrical progression, so to speak — linking detail to detail in a steadily advancing and remorselessly consistent and unassailable march upon this tinsel toy-fortress of error, the dream-fabric of a callow imagination. To begin with, young sir, I desire to ask you but three questions at present — *at present*. Did I understand you to say it was your opinion that the supposititious candle was lighted at about eight o'clock yesterday evening?"

"Yes, sir — about eight."

"Could you say exactly eight?"

"Well, no, I couldn't be that exact."

"Um. If a person had been passing along there just about that time, he would have been almost sure to encounter that assassin, do you think?"

"Yes, I should think so."

"Thank you, that is all. For the present. I say, all *for the present*."

"Dern him! he's laying for Archy," said Ferguson.

"It's so," said Ham Sandwich. "I don't like the look of it."

Stillman said, glancing at the guest,

"I was along there myself at half past eight — no, about nine."

"In-deed? This is interesting — this is very interesting. Perhaps you encountered the assassin?"

"No, I encountered no one."

"Ah. Then — if you will excuse the remark — I do not quite see the relevancy of the information."

"It has none. At present. I say it has none — at present."

He paused. Presently he resumed: "I did not encounter the assassin, but I am on his track, I am sure, for I believe he is in this room. I will ask you all to pass one by one in front of me — here, where there is a good light — so that I can see your feet."

A buzz of excitement swept the place, and the march began, the guest looking on with an iron attempt at gravity which was not an unqualified success. Stillman stooped, shaded his eyes with his hand, and gazed down intently at each pair of feet as it passed. Fifty men tramped monotonously by — with no result. Sixty. Seventy. The thing was beginning to look absurd. The guest remarked, with suave irony,

"Assassins appear to be scarce this evening."

The house saw the humor of it, and refreshed itself with a cordial laugh. Ten or twelve more candidates tramped by — no, *danced* by, with airy and

"STILLMAN ACCUSES SHERLOCK HOLMES"

ridiculous capers which convulsed the spectators — then suddenly Stillman put out his hand and said,

"This is the assassin!"

"Fetlock Jones, by the great Sanhedrim!" roared the crowd; and at once let fly a pyrotechnic explosion and dazzle and confusion of stirring remarks inspired by the situation.

At the height of the turmoil the guest stretched out his hand, commanding peace. The authority of a great name and a great personality laid its mysterious compulsion upon the house, and it obeyed. Out of the panting calm which succeeded, the guest spoke, saying, with dignity and feeling:

"*This* is serious. It strikes at an innocent life. Innocent beyond suspicion! Innocent beyond peradventure! Hear me *prove* it; observe how simple a fact can brush out of existence this witless lie. Listen. My friends, that lad was never out of my sight yesterday evening at *any* time!"

It made a deep impression. Men turned their eyes upon Stillman with grave inquiry in them. His face brightened, and he said,

"I *knew* there was another one!" He stepped briskly to the table and glanced at the guest's feet, then up at his face, and said: "You were *with* him! You were not fifty steps from him when he lit the candle that by and by fired the powder!" (*Sensation.*) "And what is more, you furnished the matches yourself!"

Plainly the guest seemed hit; it looked so to the

public. He opened his mouth to speak; the words did not come freely.

" This — er — this is insanity — this — "

Stillman pressed his evident advantage home. He held up a charred match.

" Here is one of them. I found it in the barrel — and there's *another* one there."

The guest found his voice at once.

" *Yes* — and put them there yourself ! "

It was recognized a good shot. Stillman retorted.

" It is *wax* — a breed unknown to this camp. I am ready to be searched for the box. Are you? "

The guest was staggered this time — the dullest eye could see it. He fumbled with his hands; once or twice his lips moved, but the words did not come. The house waited and watched, in tense suspense, the stillness adding effect to the situation. Presently Stillman said, gently,

" We are waiting for your decision."

There was silence again during several moments; then the guest answered, in a low voice,

" I refuse to be searched."

There was no noisy demonstration, but all about the house one voice after another muttered:

" That settles it ! He's Archy's meat."

What to do now? Nobody seemed to know. It was an embarrassing situation for the moment — merely, of course, because matters had taken such a sudden and unexpected turn that these unpracticed minds were not prepared for it, and had come to a standstill, like a stopped clock, under the shock. But after a little the machinery began to work again, tentatively, and by twos and threes the men put their heads together and privately buzzed over this and that and the other proposition. One of these propositions met with much favor; it was, to confer upon the assassin a vote of thanks for removing Flint Buckner, and let him go. But the cooler heads opposed it, pointing out that addled brains in the Eastern States would pronounce it a scandal, and make no end of foolish noise about it. Finally the cool heads got the upper hand, and obtained general consent to a proposition of their own; their leader then called the house to order and stated it — to this effect: that Fetlock Jones be jailed and put upon trial.

The motion was carried. Apparently there was nothing further to do now, and the people were glad, for, privately, they were impatient to get out and rush to the scene of the tragedy, and see whether that barrel and the other things were really there or not.

But no — the break-up got a check. The surprises were not over yet. For a while Fetlock Jones had been silently sobbing, unnoticed in the absorbing excitements which had been following one another so persistently for some time; but when his arrest and trial were decreed, he broke out despairingly, and said:

"No! it's no use. I don't want any jail, I don't want any trial; I've had all the hard luck I want, and all the miseries. Hang me now, and let me out! It would all come out, anyway — there couldn't anything save me. He has told it all, just as if he'd been with me and seen it — *I* don't know how he found out; and you'll find the barrel and things, and then I wouldn't have any chance any more. I killed him; and *you'd* have done it too, if he'd treated you like a dog, and you only a boy, and weak and poor, and not a friend to help you."

"And served him damned well right!" broke in Ham Sandwich. "Looky here, boys — "

From the constable: "Order! Order, gentlemen!"

A voice: "Did your uncle know what you was up to?"

"No, he didn't."

"Did he give you the matches, sure enough?"

"Yes, he did; but he didn't know what I wanted them for."

"When you was out on such a business as that, how did you venture to risk having him along — and him a *detective* ? How's that?"

The boy hesitated, fumbled with his buttons in an embarrassed way, then said, shyly,

"I know about detectives, on account of having them in the family; and if you don't want them to find out about a thing, it's best to have them around when you do it."

The cyclone of laughter which greeted this naïve discharge of wisdom did not modify the poor little waif's embarrassment in any large degree.

CHAPTER IX.

FROM a letter to Mrs. Stillman, dated merely "Tuesday."

Fetlock Jones was put under lock and key in an unoccupied log cabin, and left there to await his trial. Constable Harris provided him with a couple of days' rations, instructed him to keep a good guard over himself, and promised to look in on him as soon as further supplies should be due.

Next morning a score of us went with Hillyer, out of friendship, and helped him bury his late relative, the unlamented Buckner, and I acted as first assistant pall-bearer, Hillyer acting as chief. Just as we had finished our labors a ragged and melancholy stranger, carrying an old hand-bag, limped by with his head down, and I caught the scent I had chased around the globe! It was the odor of Paradise to my perishing hope!

In a moment I was at his side and had laid a gentle hand upon his shoulder. He slumped to the ground as if a stroke of lightning had withered him in his tracks; and as the boys came running he struggled to his knees and put up his pleading hands to me, and out of his chattering jaws he begged me to persecute him no more, and said,

"You have hunted me around the world, Sherlock Holmes, yet God is my witness I have never done any man harm!"

A glance at his wild eyes showed us that he was insane. That was my work, mother! The tidings of your death can some day repeat the misery I felt in that moment, but nothing else can ever do it. The boys lifted him up, and gathered about him, and were full of pity of him, and said the gentlest and touchingest things to him, and said cheer up and don't be troubled, he was among friends now, and they would take care of him, and protect him, and hang any man that laid a hand on him. They are just like so many mothers, the rough mining-camp boys are, when you wake up the south side of their hearts; yes, and just like so many reckless and unreasoning children when you wake up the opposite side of that muscle. They did everything they could think of to comfort him, but nothing succeeded until Wells-Fargo Ferguson, who is a clever strategist, said,

"If it's only Sherlock Holmes that's troubling 'you, you needn't worry any more."

"Why?" asked the forlorn lunatic, eagerly.

"Because he's dead again."

"Dead! Dead! Oh, don't trifle with a poor wreck like me. *Is* he dead? On honor, now — is he telling me true, boys?"

"True as you're standing there!" said Ham Sandwich, and they all backed up the statement in a body.

"They hung him in San Bernardino last week," added Ferguson, clinching the matter, "whilst he was searching around after you. Mistook him for another man. They're sorry, but they can't help it now."

"They're a-building him a monument," said Ham Sandwich, with the air of a person who had contributed to it, and knew.

"James Walker" drew a deep sigh — evidently a sigh of relief — and said nothing; but his eyes lost something of their wildness, his countenance cleared visibly, and its drawn look relaxed a little. We all went to our cabin, and the boys cooked him the best dinner the camp could furnish the materials for, and while they were about it Hillyer and I outfitted him from hat to shoe-leather with new clothes of ours, and made a comely and presentable old gentleman of him. "Old" is the right word, and a pity, too: old by the droop of him, and the frost upon his hair, and the marks which sorrow and distress have left upon his face; though he is only in his prime in the matter of years. While he ate, we smoked and chatted; and when he was finishing he found his voice at last, and of his own accord broke out with his personal history. I cannot furnish his exact words, but I will come as near it as I can.

THE "WRONG MAN'S" STORY.

It happened like this: I was in Denver. I had been there many years; sometimes I remember how many, sometimes I don't — but it isn't any matter. All of a sudden I got a notice to leave, or I would be exposed for a horrible crime committed long before — years and years before — in the East.

I knew about that crime, but I was not the criminal; it was a cousin of mine of the same name. What should I better do? My head was

all disordered by fear, and I didn't know. I was allowed very little
time — only one day, I think it was. I would be ruined if I was published, and the people would lynch me, and not believe what I said.
It is always the way with lynchings: when they find out it is a mistake
they are sorry, but it is too late,— the same as it was with Mr. Holmes,
you see. So I said I would sell out and get money to live on, and run
away until it blew over and I could come back with my proofs. Then
I escaped in the night and went a long way off in the mountains somewhere, and lived disguised and had a false name.

I got more and more troubled and worried, and my troubles made
me see spirits and hear voices, and I could not think straight and clear
on any subject, but got confused and involved and had to give it up,
because my head hurt so. It got to be worse and worse; more spirits
and more voices. They were about me all the time; at first only in the
night, then in the day too. They were always whispering around my
bed and plotting against me, and it broke my sleep and kept me fagged
out, because I got no good rest.

And then came the worst. One night the whispers said, " We'll
never manage, because we can't *see* him, and so can't point him out to
the people.''

They sighed; then one said: '' We must bring Sherlock Holmes.
He can be here in twelve days.''

They all agreed, and whispered and jibbered with joy. But my
heart broke; for I had read about that man, and knew what it would
be to have him upon my track, with his superhuman penetration and
tireless energies.

The spirits went away to fetch him, and I got up at once in the
middle of the night and fled away, carrying nothing but the hand-bag
that had my money in it — thirty thousand dollars; two-thirds of it are
in the bag there yet. It was forty days before that man caught up on
my track. I just escaped. From habit he had written his real name
on a tavern register, but had scratched it out and written " Dagget
Barclay '' in the place of it. But fear gives you a watchful eye and
keen, and I read the true name through the scratches, and fled like a
deer.

He has hunted me all over this world for three years and a half —
the Pacific States, Australasia, India — everywhere you can think of;
then back to Mexico and up to California again, giving me hardly any
rest; but that name on the registers always saved me, and what is left

of me is alive yet. And I am *so* tired! A cruel time he has given me, yet I give you my honor I have never harmed him nor any man.

That was the end of the story, and it stirred those boys to blood-heat, be sure of it. As for me—each word burnt a hole in me where it struck.

We voted that the old man should bunk with us, and be my guest and Hillyer's. I shall keep my own counsel, naturally; but as soon as he is well rested and nourished, I shall take him to Denver and rehabilitate his fortunes.

The boys gave the old fellow the bone-mashing good-fellowship handshake of the mines, and then scattered away to spread the news.

At dawn next morning Wells-Fargo Ferguson and Ham Sandwich called us softly out, and said, privately:

"That news about the way that old stranger has been treated has spread all around, and the camps are up. They are piling in from everywhere, and are going to lynch the P'fessor. Constable Harris is in a dead funk, and has telephoned the sheriff. Come along!"

We started on a run. The others were privileged to feel as they chose, but in my heart's privacy I hoped the sheriff would arrive in time; for I had small desire that Sherlock Holmes should hang for my deeds, as you can easily believe. I had heard a good deal about the sheriff, but for reassurance's sake I asked,

"Can he stop a mob?"

"Can *he* stop a mob! Can Jack *Fairfax* stop a mob! Well, I should smile! Ex-desperado — nineteen scalps on his string. Can *he!* Oh, I *say!*"

As we tore up the gulch, distant cries and shouts and yells rose faintly on the still air, and grew steadily in strength as we raced along. Roar after roar burst out, stronger and stronger, nearer and nearer; and at last, when we closed up upon the multitude massed in the open area in front of the tavern, the crash of sound was deafening. Some brutal roughs from Daly's gorge had Holmes in their grip, and he was the calmest man there; a contemptuous smile played about his lips, and if any fear of death was in his British heart, his iron personality was master of it and no sign of it was allowed to appear.

"Come to a vote, men!" This from one of the Daly gang, Shad-belly Higgins. "Quick! is it hang, or shoot?"

"Neither!" shouted one of his comrades. "He'd be alive again in a week; burning's the only permanency for *him*."

The gangs from all the outlying camps burst out in a thunder-crash of approval, and went struggling and surging toward the prisoner, and closed around him, shouting, "Fire! fire's the ticket!" They dragged him to the horse-post, backed him against it, chained him to it, and piled wood and pine cones around him waist-deep. Still the strong face did not blench, and still the scornful smile played about the thin lips.

"A match! fetch a match!"

Shadbelly struck it, shaded it with his hand, stooped, and held it under a pine cone. A deep silence fell upon the mob. The cone caught, a tiny flame flickered about it a moment or two. I seemed to catch the sound of distant hoofs — it grew more distinct — still more and more distinct, more and more definite, but the absorbed crowd did not appear to notice it. The match went out. The man struck another, stooped, and again the flame rose; this time it took hold and began to spread — here and there men turned away their faces. The executioner stood with the charred match in his fingers, watching his work. The hoof-beats turned a projecting crag, and now they came thundering down upon us. Almost the next moment there was a shout —

"The sheriff!"

And straightway he came tearing into the midst, stood his horse almost on his hind feet, and said,

"Fall back, you gutter-snipes!"

He was obeyed. By all but their leader. He stood his ground, and his hand went to his revolver. The sheriff covered him promptly, and said:

"Drop your hand, you parlor-desperado. Kick the fire away. Now unchain the stranger."

The parlor-desperado obeyed. Then the sheriff made a speech; sitting his horse at martial ease, and not warming his words with any touch of fire, but delivering them in a measured and deliberate way, and in a tone which harmonized with their character and made them impressively disrespectful.

"You're a nice lot — now ain't you? Just about eligible to travel with this bilk here — Shadbelly Higgins — this loud-mouthed sneak that shoots people in the back and calls himself a desperado. If there's anything I do particularly despise, it's a lynching mob; I've never seen one that had a man in it. It has to tally up a hundred against one before it can pump up pluck enough to tackle a sick tailor. It's made up of cowards, and so is the community that breeds it; and ninety-nine
34

times out of a hundred the sheriff's another one." He paused — apparently to turn that last idea over in his mind and taste the juice of it — then he went on: "The sheriff that lets a mob take a prisoner away from him is the lowest-down coward there is. By the statistics there was a hundred and eighty-two of them drawing sneak pay in America last year. By the way it's going, pretty soon there'll be a new disease in the doctor books — *sheriff complaint*." That idea pleased him — any one could see it. "People will say, 'Sheriff sick again?' 'Yes; got the same old thing.' And next there'll be a new title. People won't say, 'He's running for sheriff of Rapaho County,' for instance; they'll say, 'He's running for Coward of Rapaho.' Lord, the idea of a grown-up person being afraid of a lynch mob!"

He turned an eye on the captive, and said, "Stranger, who are you, and what have you been doing?"

"My name is Sherlock Holmes, and I have not been doing anything."

It was wonderful, the impression which the sound of that name made on the sheriff, notwithstanding he must have come posted. He spoke up with feeling, and said it was a blot on the country that a man whose marvelous exploits had filled the world with their fame and their ingenuity, and whose histories of them had won every reader's heart by the brilliancy and charm of their literary setting, should be visited under the Stars and Stripes by an outrage like this. He apologized in the name of the whole nation, and made Holmes a most handsome bow, and told Constable Harris to see him to his quarters, and hold himself personally responsible if he was molested again. Then he turned to the mob and said:

"Hunt your holes, you scum!" which they did; then he said: "Follow me, Shadbelly; I'll take care of your case myself. No — keep your pop-gun; whenever I see the day that I'll be afraid to have you behind me with that thing, it'll be time for me to join last year's hundred and eighty-two;" and he rode off in a walk, Shadbelly following.

When we were on our way back to our cabin, toward breakfast-time, we ran upon the news that Fetlock Jones had escaped from his lock-up in the night and is gone! Nobody is sorry. Let his uncle track him out if he likes; it is in his line; the camp is not interested.

CHAPTER X.

*T*EN *days later.*

"James Walker" is all right in body now, and his mind shows improvement too. I start with him for Denver to-morrow morning.

Next night.   Brief note, mailed at a way station.

As we were starting, this morning, Hillyer whispered to me: "Keep this news from Walker until you think it safe and not likely to disturb his mind and check his improvement: the ancient crime he spoke of was really committed — and by his cousin, as he said. *We buried the real criminal* the other day — the unhappiest man that has lived in a century — Flint Buckner. His real name was Jacob Fuller!" There, mother, by help of me, an unwitting mourner, your husband and my father is in his grave. Let him rest.

THE END.

AFTERWORD

Judith Yaross Lee

The publication of Mark Twain's *The $30,000 Bequest and Other Stories* in October of 1906 received much less attention than his birthday party ten months before. The book gives a nod to this irony through its frontispiece, a dignified photograph of the author "at his 70th Birthday," confirming Twain's stature as a celebrity in the modern American mold. A special supplement to the Christmas 1905 issue of *Harper's Weekly* covered the birthday dinner at Delmonico's. Photographs of Alice Duer Miller, Andrew Carnegie, and other distinguished guests seated at their tables filled nearly twenty pages; another ten documented the ceremony, reprinting greetings from President Theodore Roosevelt and recording the various testimonials, among them verses by William Dean Howells, Carolyn Wells, and John Kendrick Bangs, and toasts from fellow humorists Joel Chandler Harris and George Washington Cable.[1] Doubtless the *Harper's Weekly* supplement (an early version of our familiar Sunday magazine) gave a sales boost to both Twain and his publisher, Harper and Brothers, but such publicity did not have to be contrived. As suggested by the list under "Clemens, Samuel" in the 1906 index to the *New York Times*, hardly a month went by without at least one prominently placed article about him. The front page or the first column of the news briefs section recorded his public appearances, health, reputation, and witticisms. He was depicted writing in bed on January 17, being greeted by crowds at the Majestic Theater on March 4, and being feted by the Women's University Club on April 3. The September 20 report of his speech at the annual dinner of the Associated Press included a cartoon of the event as well as the text of his remarks. One article not indexed under his name nonetheless typifies his stature as a public figure. "TWAIN THE GREATEST," announces the headline; "In English Literature," the subhead explains. And the article, which reports that nine hundred Columbia University students attended a tea in his honor, concludes by quoting the opinion of the distinguished Professor Brander Matthews that "there is no man even in England who can be compared to Mark Twain as a master of the language."[2]

How could a volume containing thirty-eight tales and sketches, most of them minor and previously published, compete with the imposing presence of its author? Judging by the few advertisements for the book, *The $30,000 Bequest* — the last miscellany published during his lifetime — did not even try, and reviewers gave it only the briefest mention. The *Dial* and *Harper's Monthly* limited themselves to a sentence or two of announcement. The *Nation* offered a little commentary, observing that the volume included works copyrighted as early as 1872 and that "Mark Twain's longer discursive books are his best anthologies, but there is much of entertainment to be found in this collection."[3] The *New York Times*, which had inaugurated its *Saturday Review of Books* section ten years before, had the longest review, but its two hundred and fifty words barely sufficed for the obligatory praise of the author ("the head of the guild of American humor") and a survey of the book's contents. But the *Times* did go on to single out a few "capital bits of genuine American humor," including "A Telephonic Conversation," and to praise "A Double-Barrelled Detective Story" as "one of the elaborate literary hoaxes Mark has perpetuated from time to time."[4]

The lack of fanfare should not be misunderstood as scorn. Rather, a literary equivalent of market saturation was at work. Twain's best writing lay behind him, yet volumes continued to appear with factory regularity. As James Leonard has pointed out, fifteen legal editions of his collected works were published in the last dozen years of his life, and countless pirated editions of individual books took advantage of inadequate international copyright protection.[5] Perhaps most important, however, is the difficulty of characterizing a miscellany; its delightful serendipity also lends it a disappointing discontinuity, especially to readers who enjoy novels. Today's fans of *Tom Sawyer* and *Life on the Mississippi* will find it easy to overlook *The $30,000 Bequest* in favor of such lesser-known narratives as *Pudd'nhead Wilson* and *Following the Equator*. But in choosing depth over breadth, they will miss the long view of Twain's work that only *The $30,000 Bequest* provides. Its tales and sketches span the years from 1865 to 1905, almost the entire length of his career, and thus encapsulate key moments in Twain's personal and professional lives, which intertwined from the start.

Biographical details locate some of the sketches quite specifically in time. The two pieces on the Italian language grew out of his 1903-4 sojourn in Florence; both were published in magazines owned by Harper and Brothers, which bought exclusive rights to Twain's writing shortly before the Clemenses left for Italy in October 1903.[6] Topical sketches like these, which exploit a recent experience for its own humor and its opportunity for self-ridicule, were a mainstay of Twain's career. For example, more than thirty years earlier, in "Post-Mortem Poetry" (1870), he had lampooned the verses that families appended to newspaper death notices, especially those of children (a practice that continues in small-town papers today). With its contrast between the newspaper verses' sentimental clichés and his own saccharine literary criticism, this piece illustrates one of Twain's favorite comic techniques (the same ridicule of sentiment reappears in Emmeline Grangerford's poetry in *Huckleberry Finn*); Twain's wry comment here that a "child thus mourned could not die wholly discontented" (247) anticipates Tom Sawyer's satisfaction at his own funeral. But the exuberant mockery of mourning in "Post-Mortem Poetry" — so appropriate to Twain's life in June of 1870, five months into his marriage and about three months into his wife's first pregnancy — would soon evaporate. Just two years later, in June 1872, his nineteen-month-old son, Langdon, was lost to diphtheria, and a child's death was no longer a laughing matter. By 1897, in fact, he was himself composing the sentimental verses of "In Memoriam," which commemorates the death of his eldest daughter, Susy. "Eve's Diary" similarly records how intensely Twain felt the loss of his wife, Olivia Langdon Clemens, in 1904. When *The $30,000*

Bequest appeared late in 1906, only his daughters Clara and Jean remained of his immediate family, and the miscellaneous contents of the volume mark these changes in his life.

Two fables published in *The $30,000 Bequest* also express the abiding sadness of his last years. The crisis of "The Death Disk" (1901), in which a young girl inadvertently sentences her father to death, is particularly poignant in light of Twain's attachment to Susy, who was twenty-four years old when she died in 1896 but remained a child in his imagination. The seventeenth-century setting suggests Twain's desire to distance himself from the pain of her loss, while the little girl's power to rescind her father's death sentence hints of wish fulfillment. And as painful as this historical tale seems in the context of its author's life, "The Five Boons of Life" evinces true despair. In asserting that death is more precious than fame, love, riches, or pleasure, and that old age is a "wanton insult," the fable articulates Twain's misery in mid-1902, when the story came out in *Harper's Weekly*. Approaching his sixty-seventh birthday, Twain had already outlived his three brothers, his parents, and two of his children, and was witnessing a third child succumb to severe epilepsy while his wife, already in declining health, struggled to recover from nervous collapse.

Other works in *The $30,000 Bequest* lack biographical significance but illustrate important aspects of the writer's development. Consider, for example, the oldest sketch in the book. "Advice to Little Girls," one of several spoofs of children's literature that Twain wrote early in his career, is a slightly revised version of a parody first published in the San Francisco *Youth's Companion* in June of 1865[7] — just five months before he won national acclaim for "Jim Smiley and His Jumping Frog" (November 1865) and just two years after he adopted the pseudonym "Mark Twain." The sketch ridicules the heavy morality typical of nineteenth-century children's literature by presenting a series of paired statements; the first offers a traditional injunction, and the second recommends a more realistic, childlike act that actually subverts the rule: "If your mother tells you to do a thing, it is wrong to reply that you won't. It is better and more becoming to intimate that you will do as she bids you, and then afterwards act quietly in the matter according to the dictates of your best judgment" (245). Alternating serious and comic treatments of a subject, a device used in this simple sketch as a source of incongruity for humorous effect, ultimately became one of Twain's main tools for structuring long narratives. Indeed, such a structure underlies both *The Adventures of Tom Sawyer* (1876) and *Adventures of Huckleberry Finn* (1885), as Virginia Wexman has pointed out; the device also shapes *A Connecticut Yankee in King Arthur's Court* (1889). A slight piece of mainly historical interest, "Advice to Little Girls" reminds us that although Twain's place in American literature today rests on his novels, he built both his nineteenth-century reputation and his literary technique on comic journalism.

In contrast to the older works in *The $30,000 Bequest*, which document Twain's growth as a writer, the later pieces allow us to see variations on his favorite themes. One aspect of "Advice to Little Girls," and the theme of all his early little girl and boy stories — that virtuous behavior isn't a realistic expectation of children, for they don't see it as worth their effort — returns in a story from 1880, "Edward Mills and George Benton: A Tale." Like Jacob Blivens, Twain's hero in an 1870 send-up of Sunday school tracts, Edward Mills heeds his stepparents' advice — "Be pure, honest, sober, industrious, and considerate of others, and success in life is assured" — while his cousin and stepbrother, George Benton, completely flouts it. Their childhood relationship lasts as they grow up: Edward ekes out an existence of meager pleasures and small success; George drinks, gambles, and womanizes without a moment's guilt. Just as the child Edward dutifully deferred present pleasures for future ones, and gave up his toys (under pressure from their stepparents) to replace the ones George broke, so the adult Edward loses everything to his errant stepbrother. His betrothed, his inheritance, his business, even his life — are all sacrificed in one way or another to help George out of the various jams resulting from his indulgence in pleasure and whim. In the end, "Edward Mills and George Benton" jokes about the predictable unfairness of life with a pessimism more akin to the black humor of Nathanael West's 1934 *A Cool Million* (an Americanized parody of *Candide*) than to Twain's own early parodies, which laughed at faith in a benevolent Providence without questioning the very possibility of benevolence or Providence itself.

The gloomy humor arises as the story extends the contrast between Edward and George *ad absurdum*. (West used the same approach in his novel.) A sort of justice eventually prevails when George, convicted of the bank robbery that cost Edward his life, dies on the gallows. Yet female admirers give George a hero's headstone ("He has fought the good fight") while Edward's family continues to suffer from his willingness to play by the rules (the money raised to honor his bravery goes to establish a church rather than feed his children). With the message on Edward's headstone, Twain makes sure that we don't miss the moral of this black-humorous fable: "Be pure, honest, sober, industrious, considerate, and you will never — " (138). However funny this may be as a punch line, the word "never" gives the bleakest possible ending to a story in which good impulses pervert justice.

The question of justice and the running comparison between the stepbrothers anticipate the doubles who dominate two of Twain's better-known novels on social issues. The contrasting fates of Edward and George parallel the inequities exemplified by the look-alike heroes of *The Prince and the Pauper* (1881), which Twain was working on during the same period. (He had nearly finished the novel when "Edward Mills and George Benton" appeared in the August 1880 *Atlantic Monthly*.[8]) More ambitious and much more pessimistic is *The Tragedy of Pudd'nhead Wilson* (1894), which brings the nature-nurture question to the foreground by investigating the moral characters of physically identical boys born in a single household on the same day — one to a female slave and the other to her master's wife. Next to the profound social questions addressed by these novels, "Edward Mills and George Benton" seems superficial; its predictable plot and wooden characters suggest why Twain returned to these themes later. Yet the flatness of the short story makes sense within the conventions of fable and parody, and in the context of those genres "Edward Mills and George Benton" rewards attention as a look back at the broad comedy of Twain's youth and ahead toward the despairing humor of his later years.

Indeed, *The $30,000 Bequest* as a whole illustrates the contrast between Twain's early and late humor particularly well. His early work exploits opportunities for jokes in almost any subject, the more solemn the better.

"General Washington's Negro Body-Servant" (1868), for example, lampoons the extravagant and sentimental claims of newspaper obituaries; the sketch jokes about how a "cherished remnant of the revolution" dies repeatedly and with remarkable regularity, beginning in 1809 in Richmond, Virginia, and then in states from coast to coast until 1864, when he dies yet again in Detroit. Twain tops the humor of his mock-mournful "The faithful old servant is gone! We shall never see him more until he turns up again!" (209) by finding fault with a small detail, leaving the obvious impossibility unchallenged:

> One fault I find in all notices of his death which I have quoted, and this ought to be corrected. In them he uniformly and impartially died at the age of 95. This could not have been. He might have done that once, or maybe twice, but he could not have continued it indefinitely. Allowing that when he first died, he died at the age of 95, he was 151 years old when he died last, in 1864. But his age did not keep pace with his recollections. When he died the last time, he distinctly remembered the landing of the Pilgrims, which took place in 1620. He must have been about twenty years old when he witnessed that event, wherefore it is safe to assert that the body-servant of General Washington was in the neighborhood of two hundred and sixty or seventy years old when he departed his life finally. (210)

In a similar vein, "The Danger of Lying in Bed" (1871) builds an elaborate argument, complete with one set of statistics after another, for the claim that people need accident insurance for staying in bed, where most deaths occur, rather than for traveling, which by comparison is downright safe. These sketches capture for the reader of *The $30,000 Bequest* the exuberance and irreverence that first brought Twain fame as a writer from the Wild West.

They also reflect a career in flux. Both pieces appeared in the *Galaxy* magazine, founded in 1866 in New York City, which had not yet eclipsed Boston as a literary center but had begun striving for cultural recognition. Not until 1874 would Twain succeed in placing his first work in Boston's highbrow *Atlantic Monthly* (the piece was "A True Story, Repeated Word for Word as I Heard It"), but publishing even a playful sketch like "General Washington's Negro Body-Servant" in a national quality monthly shows the author moving to establish his place in America's literary establishment. The sketch also hints of Twain's efforts to differentiate himself from a rival lecturer of the 1867–68 season, P. T. Barnum, whose recent run for Congress had renewed discussion of his infamous exhibition (in 1835) of slave Joice Heth. Purportedly the 161-year-old nurse of George Washington, Joice Heth was probably the inspiration for Twain's "Negro Body-Servant." Debunking such extravagant claims enabled Twain to stake out the high moral ground as an entertainer who exposes — rather than exploits — humbug.

Twain published two pieces in the *Galaxy* before undertaking a regular monthly department for the magazine. His agreement with the editors allowed him to present any combination of long or short pieces under the heading "Memoranda." The department, which ran from May 1870 through April 1871, was the source of five pieces reprinted in *The $30,000 Bequest*: "Wit Inspirations of 'Two-Year-Olds,' " "An Entertaining Article," and "Portrait of King William III," in addition to "Post-Mortem Poetry" and "The Danger of Lying in Bed." The *Galaxy* not only offered a regular income in exchange for ten pages' worth of humor or commentary each month but also advanced his career in several other ways. First, its promotional materials and monthly issues repeatedly put his name before a national audience — an estimated 23,000 subscribers in 1871 — thus capitalizing on the success of his first book, *The Innocents Abroad* (1869), in the period shortly after its publication. In addition, the *Galaxy* fostered his reputation as an author rather than a mere journalist; it showcased his work alongside fiction by such famous writers as Anthony Trollope, and its publishers issued a pamphlet version of "A Burlesque Biography," *Mark Twain's (Burlesque) Autobiography and First Romance*, written during his courtship of Olivia as a comic response to her father's concern over Twain's rough background. Finally, and probably most important for the direction of his career, the need to churn out material for the *Galaxy* department soon gave Twain another incentive (beyond the obvious appeal of independence and status) to shift his attention from periodicals to novels. As Jeffrey Steinbrink has detailed in *Getting to Be Mark Twain*, he decided in a very brief period in March 1871 to give up the *Galaxy*, sell his share of the *Buffalo Express* (the newspaper that his late father-in-law had helped him buy), and dedicate himself to novel-writing. Despite its suddenness, the decision reflected a deliberate effort to shape a career outside the conventions of literary clowning. His *Galaxy* column for April 1871, for instance, pointed to the "grisly grotesqueness of the situation" wherein his contract with the magazine obliged him to write humor while "death has taken two members of my home circle and malignantly threatened two others." Although Twain scholars commonly point to his completion of *Roughing It* (1872) later that year as evidence that he made the right choice, *The $30,000 Bequest* provides documentation of its own. The miscellany includes just a few sketches from the period between 1872 and 1893, his most productive years as a novelist.

After *Pudd'nhead Wilson* appeared in 1894, Twain's imaginative writing split off into three strands. Much of his fiction remained fragmentary, like the pieces collected in *Mark Twain's Mysterious Stranger Manuscripts* and similar posthumous volumes. (These began with anthologies assembled by the first two editors of the Mark Twain Papers, Albert Bigelow Paine and Bernard DeVoto, and have continued in the volumes issued by the Mark Twain Project and the University of California at Berkeley.) A few works spun off from previous ones, like *Tom Sawyer Abroad* (1894) and *Tom Sawyer, Detective* (1896). Other stories remained novella-length, like "The $30,000 Bequest" (1904) and "A Double-Barrelled Detective Story" (1902), the two tales that frame this collection.

An ironic fable about the love for money, "The $30,000 Bequest" presents Twain in his role as a moralist, a stance he increasingly adopted in the years following *A Connecticut Yankee*. Thus the volume begins by announcing its literary seriousness, and follows up quickly with two fables on moral issues: "A Dog's Tale" (1903), on both the use of animals for scientific research and the parallels between a dog's life and a slave's, and "Was It Heaven? Or Hell?" (1902), on lying to spare an invalid from grief. A third story extends the serious mood. If "The Californian's Tale" (1893) had been composed early in Twain's career, the dialect and local color would probably have led to a tall yarn or a shaggy dog story at the expense of the naive narrator, apparently Twain himself. But in fact, the end of the story brings narrator and reader a different type of revelation: the title character, a miner, is mad, having lost his mind after his wife was captured by Indians almost twenty years before. By contrast with the heavy irony of the opening stories, the volume closes on a comic note, with "A Double-Barrelled Detective Story." In choosing this parody of Sherlock Holmes as the last piece in the book, Twain reminds us that he earned his fame in part because he understood how to balance his interests as a writer with the demands of his audience. That professionalism also shows in the arrangement of the remaining stories, with comic romps following somber works so that the book delights as well as instructs. In counterpoint to the moral tales that open the volume, the stories that close it — "Extracts from Adam's Diary" (1893), "The Death Disk" (1901), and "A Double-Barrelled Detective Story" — entertain more than teach.

"The $30,000 Bequest" concerns not only the problems of sudden wealth, but also a stranger's ability to poison social relationships. Twain had already treated these themes in "The Man That Corrupted Hadleyburg" (1899) and the "£1,000,000 Bank Note" (1893), but "The $30,000 Bequest" adds the question of dreams and their relation to reality. That theme had steadily increased in importance and complexity in Twain's work since the 1880s, when the runaway slave Jim called Huck Finn "trash" for persuading him that a real event was a dream. In contrast to that clear-cut distinction, *A Connecticut Yankee* never makes plain whether Hank Morgan dreamed his visit to medieval England or became deranged from his experiences there.

In "The $30,000 Bequest," reality and dream blur almost completely as Electra (Aleck) and Saladin (Sally) Foster get caught up in imaginary investments of their promised inheritance. When Aleck decides that the coal market has risen high enough, for example, she sells out for a huge profit; that night, Twain tells us, the couple "sat dazed and blissful . . . , trying to realize the immense fact, the overwhelming fact, that they were actually worth a hundred thousand dollars in clean, imaginary cash. Yet so it was" (22–23). The gender ambiguity in the Fosters' nicknames attributes equal responsibility to husband and wife, though Aleck manages the money. We see events through the eyes of both dreamers as we follow their conflation of trance and fact, "imaginary cash" and "so it was" — all the way through gradually more speculative investments, progressively grander homes, and increasingly ambitious matches for their daughters, until the crash of the stock market sends them into "mental night." But Twain does not settle for an ending that warns about counting one's profits before they come due. Rather, the conversion of their dreams to nightmares has two twists that keep the Fosters' story focused on the problems of money rather than the problems of dreaming. First, they discover that the promised bequest was fraudulent. It never existed as anything other than a temptation and a taunt, a mean-spirited dream of vengeance. And from that information, Sally reaches an ironic conclusion: the harm of the plan lay not in its falsehood but in its stinginess. "Without added expense" (49), the benefactor could have promised them much, much more, and through such wealth could have prevented their succumbing to the corruptions of financial speculation. This conclusion, clear-sighted in its economics but mad in both psychology and values, keeps the irony of the tale alive to the end. Sally's unwillingness to withdraw from his dream and rebuild his waking life shows the power of the imagination to create reality.

Twain played with the relation of the dream and waking worlds repeatedly in his later years. He left enough unpublished stories on the theme at his death to fill John S. Tuckey's collection *Which Was the Dream? and Other Symbolic Writings of the Later Years* (1967). Like *The Mysterious Stranger*, also posthumously published, these stories expand the exploration of dreams and reality to include what Susan K. Harris has called Twain's "creative solipsism" — "his sense that the mind of the creative artist is the God who creates and destroys the perceptible world but, alas, cannot destroy itself."[9] Though "The $30,000 Bequest" lacks such philosophical depth, Twain controls its narrative details and tempo so tightly that scholars have repeatedly cited it as the best of his late published works.[10]

Part of the story's power may derive from its personal significance for the author. Hamlin Hill has observed, for example, that selling "The $30,000 Bequest" relieved Twain's own financial difficulties — a deliciously ironic use of imagination in the service of reality. Hill also identifies some pointed parallels between Olivia Clemens and Electra Foster, the wife in the story. Both invest in coal. Both have strong Christian beliefs and feel hurt by their husbands' levity toward religion.[11] Both families lose their fortunes in pursuit of moneymaking dreams; in speculating on the wealth he would reap from the Paige Compositor, a typesetting machine on which he lost at least $300,000, Twain built castles in the air not very different from those of Aleck and Sally Foster. Considering the painful after-effects of Twain's dream — the failure of his publishing firm (which financed the Paige venture), his humiliation in declaring bankruptcy, his absence from the United States on a speaking tour when his daughter Susy died — Twain surely speaks for himself as well as the Fosters when their fantasies fizzle and he has Sally lament their abandonment of their "sweet and simple and happy life" (49).

"The Double-Barrelled Detective Story" closes *The $30,000 Bequest* on an appropriately complex note of humor and bitterness. To judge from the twenty-eight-line sonnet that William Dean Howells wrote for Twain's seventieth birthday celebration (and the similar one he'd composed three years before), the "double-barrelled" form was something of a joke among Twain and his circle.[12] The double barrels in Twain's story (first published serially in the January and February 1902 issues of *Harper's Monthly*) extend beyond plot and narrative structure to encompass sources and targets, as well. The novella opens with a parody of the melodramatic revenge tale: a pregnant woman, tortured and abandoned by her husband, Jacob Fuller, in reprisal for her father's objections to the marriage, retaliates years later by dogging him through her son Archy, who acquired the tracking skills of a bloodhound from the dogs Jacob set upon her. Archy's special gift does not, alas, prevent him from tracking the wrong man, a cousin of his father's also named Jacob Fuller. The story opens a second time three chapters later, now (as Howard Baetzhold has so skillfully shown) with a second parody, a deadpan spoof of Conan Doyle's *A Study in Scarlet*. Twain's imitation is so accurate that he and his editors gave *The $30,000 Bequest* a lengthy footnote (468–71) pointing the reader toward the joke without actually giving it away. The two detective stories intertwine as Sherlock Holmes, Archy, and cousin Jacob Fuller all converge on a Hope Canyon mining camp, where the famous detective's nephew Fetlock Jones has just murdered his master, Flint Buckner. Holmes gets his comeuppance when the amateur bloodhound, punningly named Archy *Stillman*, successfully tracks the killer. For his part, however, Archy finds not only that he has hounded the wrong Jacob Fuller but also that the right one is already dead — as Flint Buckner. The double-barrelled anticlimax is complete with this second comeuppance, the human bloodhound's discovery that the quest has become moot.

The pile-up of parodies leaves many readers perplexed, especially considering that the melodramatic opening chapter lacks any sign of burlesque. Indeed, William R. Macnaughton speculates that Twain, who had been researching a book on lynching when he began this story in 1901, may have originally intended the scene for some other purpose.[13] Still, as Hamlin Hill has observed, the novella engages major themes in Twain's fiction. Hill points to three — the language of the mining camp, the Southern ethos of revenge, and the lynch mob versus the spokesman for social order[14] — but others also surface, to varying degrees. "A Double-Barrelled Detective Story" raises questions of identity, doubles, and heredity familiar to readers of *Pudd'nhead Wilson*. And it ends ambiguously astride victory and failure, much as *A Connecticut Yankee* ends with Hank Morgan "getting up his last 'effect.'" In that sense, "A Double-Barrelled Detective Story" points up the increasing distance between humor and theme toward the end of Twain's career, and brings *The $30,000 Bequest* to a fitting close.

In addition to *The $30,000 Bequest*, 1906 saw the publication of two other books by Mark Twain: *What Is Man?* and *Eve's Diary*. A series of pessimistic philosophical dialogues between Young Man and Old Man, *What Is Man?* came out anonymously in a small private run of two hundred and fifty copies printed in August by the distinguished DeVinne Press. The book received very few reviews, probably because its ideas lacked the authority that Twain's name would have conferred, but as with *Personal Recollections of Joan of Arc* ten years earlier, he defended its anonymous publication on the ground that identifying the work as Mark Twain's would have raised expectations of humorous entertainment, thus detracting from his subject and disappointing his audience. Business concerns surely pressed as well. If he worried that fans disappointed with this book might shun the next, he had greater reason to fear his publisher's response: in 1906 he had an exclusive contract with Harper and Brothers for all his writings as Mark Twain. Certainly financial considerations prompted the publication of a lavishly illustrated edition of *Eve's Diary* in the summer of 1906, as a companion volume to *Extracts from Adam's Diary*, which Twain transformed in 1904 from a commercial promotion for Niagara Falls into a slender illustrated book. The reception of *Eve's Diary* gives credence to Twain's reading of his audience. Whereas today's scholars often focus on the narrative as evidence of Twain's sorrow over Livy's death, his contemporary readers treated it as a romp. Tongue in cheek, the *New York Times*'s "Saturday Review of Books" described it as a "new and unique translation from the original . . . vouched for by the unimpeachable Mark Twain." Harper and Brothers advertised it as a work of romantic irony, claiming, "Eve could hardly have understood how funny it would all sound to us."[15] When the diaries reappeared a few months later in *The $30,000 Bequest* alongside tales and sketches from his youth, the dark vision of Mark Twain's last years was tempered once again by the exuberance of his early work, and his career came to a formal close with a literary portrait of the Twain that readers knew and loved.

As important as what Twain included in *The $30,000 Bequest*, however, is what he left out. Nowhere in the volume are there tales of youthful heroes like Tom Sawyer and Huck Finn. Nowhere is there the piquant African-American dialect of Rachel in "A True Story" or Roxy in *Pudd'nhead Wilson*. Nowhere does the matter of Hannibal evoke idylls of youth or the mighty Mississippi. Though they form the background of "The Californian's Tale" and "A Double-Barrelled Detective Story," the rich materials that animated the novels of his middle years seem to have escaped either his grasp or his care near the end of his life. What remained to be collected in this last miscellany published during his lifetime were — quite literally — the remnants of youth and the products of old age. Yet far from being a sad collection of leftovers from the writer's trunk, *The $30,000 Bequest* testifies to Twain's enduring capacity to transform experience through his pen.

NOTES

1. "The Dinner at Delmonico's in Honor of Mark Twain's Seventieth Birthday," *Harper's Weekly* 49 (December 23, 1905): 1884–1912.

2. "Twain the Greatest," *New York Times*, February 21, 1906, p. 2, col. 6.

3. Books, *Nation* 83, no. 2154 (October 11, 1906): 304.

4. Books of the Week, Saturday Review of Books, *New York Times*, October 13, 1906, p. 670.

5. James Leonard, "Editions," *The Mark Twain Encyclopedia*, ed. J. R. LeMaster and James D. Wilson (New York: Garland, 1993).

6. The 1903 copyright agreements are included as Appendix E to *Mark Twain's Correspondence with Henry Huttleston Rogers, 1893–1909*, ed. Lewis Leary (Berkeley: University of California Press, 1969), 691–99. The volume also includes other contracts from the period.

7. Reprinted in *The Celebrated Jumping Frog of Calaveras County and Other Sketches* (New York: C. H. Webb, 1867); revised in 1872 and 1874, according to *Early Tales and Sketches, Volume 2 (1864–1865)*, ed. Edgar M. Branch and Robert H. Hirst (Berkeley: University of California Press, 1981), 243. Related stories include "Advice for Good Little Boys," "The Story of the Bad Little Boy," and "The Story of the Good Little Boy."

8. According to John Daniel Stahl in *The Mark Twain Encyclopedia*, Twain worked on *The Prince and the Pauper: A Tale for Young People of All Ages* from 1876 to 1881. Stahl believes that the novel "has been underrated in its reaction against the tenets of nineteenth-century genteel children's fiction," suggesting another link between *The Prince and the Pauper* and the humor in *The $30,000 Bequest*.

9. Susan K. Harris, "Dreams," *The Mark Twain Encyclopedia*.

10. See, for example, William R. Macnaughton, *Mark Twain's Last Years as a Writer* (Columbia: University of Missouri Press, 1979), 197; and Earl Briden, "'The $30,000 Bequest,'" *Mark Twain Encyclopedia*.

11. Hamlin Hill, *Mark Twain: God's Fool* (New York: Harper Colophon, 1975), 78–80.

12. Howells joked that his double-barrelled "Sonnet to Mark Twain" represented one of many modern improvements on Shakespeare. As transcribed in *Harper's Weekly*, the poem proved that Shakespeare's reputation was in no danger.

A traveller from the Old World just escaped
    Our customs with his life, had found his way
To a place up-town, where a Colossus shaped
    Itself, sky-scraper high, against the day.
A vast smile, dawning from its mighty lips,
    Like sunshine on its visage seemed to brood;
One eye winked in perpetual eclipse,
    In the other a huge tear of pity stood.

Wisdom in chunks about its temples shone;
    Its measureless bulk grotesque, exultant, rose;
And while Titanic puissance clothes it on,
    Patience with foreigners was in its pose.
So that, "What art thou?" the emboldened traveller spoke,
    And it replied, "I am the American joke."
I am the joke that laughs the proud to scorn;
    I mock at cruelty. I banish care.
I cheer the lowly, chipper the forlorn.
    I bid the oppressor and hypocrite beware
I tell the tale that makes men cry for joy;
    I bring the laugh that has no hate in it;
In the heart of age I wake the undying boy
    My big stick blossoms with a thornless wit,
The lame dance with delight in me: my mirth
    Reaches the deaf untrumpeted; the blind
My point can see. I jolly the whole earth,
    But most I love to jolly my own kind.
Joke of a people great, gay, bold, and free.
I type their master-mood. Mark Twain made me." (p. 1884)

13. Macnaughton 168.

14. Hill 31.

15. Review and advertisement, Saturday Review of Books, *New York Times*, June 16, 1906, pp. 386, 399.

Judith Yaross Lee

Despite its age, Henry Nash Smith's *Mark Twain: The Development of a Writer* (Cambridge: Harvard University Press, 1962) remains an excellent survey of the humorist's literary growth and a strong introduction to topics covered in more detail by later scholars. Scholarly introductions to the early stories are provided in the *Early Tales and Sketches* volumes of the Mark Twain Project at the University of California. An excellent recent analysis of Twain's early career is Jeffrey Steinbrink's *Getting to Be Mark Twain* (Berkeley: University of California Press, 1991); the later years are taken up in Hamlin Hill's *Mark Twain: God's Fool* (New York: Harper and Row, 1973) and William R. Macnaughton's *Mark Twain's Last Years as a Writer* (Columbia: University of Missouri Press, 1979). Virginia Wexman's important analysis of Twain's structural pairs appears in "The Role of Structure in *Tom Sawyer* and *Huckleberry Finn*," *American Literary Realism, 1870–1910* 6 (1973): 1–11. Susan Gillman's *Dark Twins: Imposture and Identity in Mark Twain's America* (Chicago: University of Chicago Press, 1989) interprets the significance of doubles and twins for the author's life and work.

James D. Wilson's *A Reader's Guide to the Short Stories of Mark Twain* (Boston: G. K. Hall, 1987) contains entries on the longest tales in *The $30,000 Bequest*; many of the shorter works are covered in *The Mark Twain Encyclopedia*, ed. J. R. LeMaster and James D. Wilson (New York: Garland, 1993). Twain's *Galaxy* writings are collected, with an introduction, in *Contributions to "The Galaxy," 1868–1871, by Mark Twain*, ed. Bruce R. McElderry, Jr. (Gainesville, Fla.: Scholars' Facsimiles and Reprints, 1961).

Discussions of the individual pieces in *The $30,000 Bequest* are limited. Ricki Morgan's "Mark Twain's Money Imagery in 'The £1,000,000 Bank-Note' and 'The $30,000 Bequest,'" *Mark Twain Journal* 19 (1977): 6–10, shows the careful control of word and idea behind both fables. Howard Baetzhold offers sympathetic readings of "A Double-Barrelled Detective Story" in both *Mark Twain and John Bull: The British Connection*

(Bloomington: Indiana University Press, 1970) and *The Mark Twain Encyclopedia.* Joseph B. McCullough traces the evolution of "Extracts from Adam's Diary" in "Mark Twain's First Chestnut: Revisions in 'Extracts from Adam's Diary,'" *Essays in Arts and Sciences* 23 (October 1994): 49–58.

A NOTE ON THE ILLUSTRATIONS

Ray Sapirstein

Although the spine of *The $30,000 Bequest and Other Stories* (1906) promised an illustrated volume, the work omitted nearly all the illustrations from stories that had originally appeared with them. Nevertheless, several unique and significant pictorial elements remained in this engaging compilation of diverse sketches and fragments.

The only fully illustrated piece in the book, "Italian Without a Master," retained its original images interspered within the short text. First published in the January 2, 1904, *Harper's Weekly*,[1] the illustrations are simpler and more informal than those that typify many of Twain's later books. The work of Albert Levering (1869–1929), they bridge several of the illustrative styles in Twain's books, integrating the burlesque of the cartoon with the stylized high-art print. In 1903, a year before illustrating "Italian Without a Master," Levering drew a comic strip for *Harper's Weekly* that satirized Twain's futile attempts to purchase Mary Baker Eddy's *Science and Health*,[2] and in 1909 he drew the cover and frontispiece for *Extract from Captain Stormfield's Visit to Heaven.*

The photomechanical reproductions of the newspaper clippings Twain translates in "Italian Without a Master" are also of interest. These cut-and-paste reproductions of the articles themselves, not reset in type, convey their reality and immediacy, convincingly testifying to their actual appearance in an Italian newspaper. Their inclusion is critical to the humor of the piece, allowing readers access to the real account as Twain embroiders his own interpretation. Twain had previously imagined this kind of collage in 1901, not for a comic article, but for a much more serious intent: a proposed but unrealized history of lynching, which was merely to assemble and reproduce newspaper accounts in a new context, with little editorial intervention.[3]

The most significant illustrations in *The $30,000 Bequest* are the rare published images Twain drew himself, including a self-portrait and a portrait of "William III., King of Prussia." In the comical article dedicated to his brilliant portrait of the kaiser (265), Twain lampoons artistic dilettantism and his own lack of artistic technique. As he did in *A Tramp Abroad*, he plays dumb to the portrait's technical inferiority, mimicking the pretension and formality of artists' statements and critical commendations. Though Twain sought to exaggerate his technical incapacity, the image is actually a successful simulation of the fine art of the grade school caricature, investing the figure with vacant stare, monkey suit, and cockeyed, bashful grin.

Twain's self-portrait (231) was originally published in *Harper's Weekly* with the article "Amended Obituaries" in 1902.[4] On the surface, Twain presented it as a joke, defying staid artistic realism in suggesting that a good portrait need not include a subject's mouth, and poking fun at art connoisseurship in defining the quality of the image by the ink he used to draw it, "warranted to be the kind used by the very best artists" (233). The image is not only playful, it is self-deprecating on two levels. In the caption Twain mocks his artistic ability, admitting, "I cannot make a good mouth, therefore leave it out." On a deeper level, without the pretense of humor, the image demonstrates Twain's capacity for serious artistic expression, and like the fatalism of the article itself, suggests profound unhappiness and self-criticism.

NOTES

1. Antonio Iliano, " 'Italian Without a Master': A Note for the Appreciation of Mark Twain's Undictionarial Translation as Exercise in Humor," *Mark Twain Journal* 17, no. 2 (Summer 1974): 17, n.1.

2. Albert Levering, "The Man Who Corrupted Eddyville, Being Some Account of the Troubles Which Beset Mark Twain During His Quest for Mrs. Eddy's Book," *Harper's Weekly*, February 7, 1903, p. 215. Thanks to Kent Rasmussen for bringing this item to my attention.

3. SLC to Frank Bliss, August 26, 1901. Samuel Clemens Letters, Harry Ransom Humanities Research Center, University of Texas at Austin.

4. Thomas Tenney, 1902 entry B16, *Mark Twain: A Reference Guide* (Boston: G. K. Hall and Company, 1977), p. 37. The article appeared in the November 15, 1902, issue of *Harper's Weekly*, p. 1704.

A NOTE ON THE TEXT

Robert H. Hirst

This text of *The $30,000 Bequest and Other Stories* is a photographic facsim-ile of a copy of the first American edition, all known copies of which are dated 1906 on the title page. The first edition was published in September 1906; two copies were deposited with the Copyright Office on September 27. The copy reproduced here is an example of Jacob Blanck's second state, with a boxed advertisement on the copyright page (*BAL* 3492). The original volume is in the collection of the Mark Twain House in Hartford, Connecticut (810/C625th/1906).

The Mark Twain House is a museum and research center dedicated to the study of Mark Twain, his works, and his times. The museum is located in the nineteen-room mansion in Hartford, Connecticut, built for and lived in by Samuel L. Clemens, his wife, and their three children, from 1874 to 1891. The Picturesque Gothic-style residence, with interior design by the firm of Louis Comfort Tiffany and Associated Artists, is one of the premier examples of domestic Victorian architecture in America. Clemens wrote *Adventures of Huckleberry Finn*, *The Adventures of Tom Sawyer*, *A Connecticut Yankee in King Arthur's Court*, *The Prince and the Pauper*, and *Life on the Mississippi* while living in Hartford.

The Mark Twain House is open year-round. In addition to tours of the house, the educational programs of the Mark Twain House include symposia, lectures, and teacher training seminars that focus on the contemporary relevance of Twain's legacy. Past programs have featured discussions of literary censorship with playwright Arthur Miller and writer William Styron; of the power of language with journalist Clarence Page, comedian Dick Gregory, and writer Gloria Naylor; and of the challenges of teaching *Adventures of Huckleberry Finn* amidst charges of racism.

CONTRIBUTORS

Frederick Busch is the author of twenty books, including a novel about Charles Dickens, *The Mutual Friend* (1978), *Rounds* (1979), *Take This Man* (1981), *Invisible Mending* (1984), *Sometimes I Live in the Country* (1986), *War Babies* (1989), *Harry and Catherine* (1990), *Closing Arguments* (1991), *Long Way from Home* (1993), *The Children in the Woods: New and Selected Stories* (1994), and *Girls* (1996). He lives in upstate New York with his wife, Judy, and is Edgar Fairchild Professor of Literature at Colgate University, where he teaches fiction and fiction writing and runs the Living Writers program.

Shelley Fisher Fishkin, professor of American Studies and English at the University of Texas at Austin, is the author of the award-winning books *Was Huck Black? Mark Twain and African-American Voices* (1993) and *From Fact to Fiction: Journalism and Imaginative Writing in America* (1985). Her most recent book is *Lighting Out for the Territory: Reflections on Mark Twain and American Culture* (1996). She holds a Ph.D. in American Studies from Yale University, has lectured on Mark Twain in Belgium, England, France, Israel, Italy, Mexico, the Netherlands, and Turkey, as well as throughout the United States, and is president-elect of the Mark Twain Circle of America.

Robert H. Hirst is the General Editor of the Mark Twain Project at The Bancroft Library, University of California in Berkeley. Apart from that, he has no other known eccentricities.

Judith Yaross Lee, associate professor in the School of Interpersonal Communication at Ohio University, earned her Ph.D. at the University of Chicago. She is the author of *Garrison Keillor: A Voice of America* (1991), and the co-editor (with Joseph W. Slade) of *Beyond the Two Cultures: Essays on Science, Technology, and Literature* (1990). Her studies of American popular culture have appeared in *Communication and Cyberspace, American Literature and Science, Literature and Technology,*

Studies in American Humor, American Heritage of Invention and Technology, Essays in Arts and Sciences, Eye on the Future, and other publications. She served as the first executive director of the Society for Literature and Science and as president of the American Humor Studies Association, and is currently book review editor of *American Periodicals.* A founding member of the Mark Twain Circle and a contributor to *The Mark Twain Encyclopedia* and other reference works, she lives in Athens, Ohio.

Ray Sapirstein is a doctoral student in the American Civilization Program at the University of Texas at Austin. He curated the 1993 exhibition *Another Side of Huckleberry Finn: Mark Twain and Images of African Americans* at the Harry Ransom Humanities Research Center at the University of Texas at Austin. He is currently completing a dissertation on the photographic illustrations in several volumes of Paul Laurence Dunbar's poetry.

ACKNOWLEDGMENTS

There are a number of people without whom The Oxford Mark Twain would not have happened. I am indebted to Laura Brown, senior vice president and trade publisher, Oxford University Press, for suggesting that I edit an "Oxford Mark Twain," and for being so enthusiastic when I proposed that it take the present form. Her guidance and vision have informed the entire undertaking.

Crucial as well, from the earliest to the final stages, was the help of John Boyer, executive director of the Mark Twain House, who recognized the importance of the project and gave it his wholehearted support.

My father, Milton Fisher, believed in this project from the start and helped nurture it every step of the way, as did my stepmother, Carol Plaine Fisher. Their encouragement and support made it all possible. The memory of my mother, Renée B. Fisher, sustained me throughout.

I am enormously grateful to all the contributors to The Oxford Mark Twain for the effort they put into their essays, and for having been such fine, collegial collaborators. Each came through, just as I'd hoped, with fresh insights and lively prose. It was a privilege and a pleasure to work with them, and I value the friendships that we forged in the process.

In addition to writing his fine afterword, Louis J. Budd provided invaluable advice and support, even going so far as to read each of the essays for accuracy. All of us involved in this project are greatly in his debt. Both his knowledge of Mark Twain's work and his generosity as a colleague are legendary and unsurpassed.

Elizabeth Maguire's commitment to The Oxford Mark Twain during her time as senior editor at Oxford was exemplary. When the project proved to be more ambitious and complicated than any of us had expected, Liz helped make it not only manageable, but fun. Assistant editor Elda Rotor's wonderful help in coordinating all aspects of The Oxford Mark Twain, along with literature editor T. Susan Chang's enthusiastic involvement with the project in its final stages, helped bring it all to fruition.

I am extremely grateful to Joy Johannessen for her astute and sensitive copyediting, and for having been such a pleasure to work with. And I appreciate the conscientiousness and good humor with which Kathy Kuhtz Campbell heroically supervised all aspects of the set's production. Oxford president Edward Barry, vice president and editorial director Helen McInnis, marketing director Amy Roberts, publicity director Susan Rotermund, art director David Tran, trade editorial, design and production manager Adam Bohannon, trade advertising and promotion manager Woody Gilmartin, director of manufacturing Benjamin Lee, and the entire staff at Oxford were as supportive a team as any editor could desire.

The staff of the Mark Twain House provided superb assistance as well. I would like to thank Marianne Curling, curator, Debra Petke, education director, Beverly Zell, curator of photography, Britt Gustafson, assistant director of education, Beth Ann McPherson, assistant curator, and Pam Collins, administrative assistant, for all their generous help, and for allowing us to reproduce books and photographs from the Mark Twain House collection. One could not ask for more congenial or helpful partners in publishing.

G. Thomas Tanselle, vice president of the John Simon Guggenheim Memorial Foundation, and an expert on the history of the book, offered essential advice about how to create as responsible a facsimile edition as possible. I appreciate his very knowledgeable counsel.

I am deeply indebted to Robert H. Hirst, general editor of the Mark Twain Project at The Bancroft Library in Berkeley, for bringing his outstanding knowledge of Twain editions to bear on the selection of the books photographed for the facsimiles, for giving generous assistance all along the way, and for providing his meticulous notes on the text. The set is the richer for his advice. I would also like to express my gratitude to the Mark Twain Project, not only for making texts and photographs from their collection available to us, but also for nurturing Mark Twain studies with a steady infusion of matchless, important publications.

I would like to thank Jeffrey Kaimowitz, curator of the Watkinson Library at Trinity College, Hartford (where the Mark Twain House collection is kept), along with his colleagues Peter Knapp and Alesandra M. Schmidt, for having been instrumental in Robert Hirst's search for first editions that could be safely reproduced. Victor Fischer, Harriet Elinor Smith, and especially Kenneth M. Sanderson, associate editors with the Mark Twain Project, reviewed the note on the text in each volume with cheerful vigilance. Thanks are also due to Mark Twain Project associate editor Michael Frank and administrative assistant Brenda J. Bailey for their help at various stages.

I am grateful to Helen K. Copley for granting permission to publish photographs in the Mark Twain Collection of the James S. Copley Library in La Jolla, California, and to Carol Beales and Ron Vanderhye of the Copley Library for making my research trip to their institution so productive and enjoyable.

Several contributors — David Bradley, Louis J. Budd, Beverly R. David, Robert Hirst, Fred Kaplan, James S. Leonard, Toni Morrison, Lillian S. Robinson, Jeffrey Rubin-Dorsky, Ray Sapirstein, and David L. Smith — were particularly helpful in the early stages of the project, brainstorming about the cast of writers and scholars who could make it work. Others who participated in that process were John Boyer, James Cox, Robert Crunden, Joel Dinerstein, William Goetzmann, Calvin and Maria Johnson, Jim Magnuson, Arnold Rampersad, Siva Vaidhyanathan, Steve and Louise Weinberg, and Richard Yarborough.

Kevin Bochynski, famous among Twain scholars as an "angel" who is gifted at finding methods of making their research run more smoothly, was helpful in more ways than I can count. He did an outstanding job in his official capacity as production consultant to The Oxford Mark Twain, supervising the photography of the facsimiles. I am also grateful to him for having put me in touch via e-mail with Kent Rasmussen, author of the magisterial *Mark Twain A to Z*, who was tremendously helpful as the project proceeded, sharing insights on obscure illustrators and other points, and generously being "on call" for all sorts of unforeseen contingencies.

I am indebted to Siva Vaidhyanathan of the American Studies Program of the University of Texas at Austin for having been such a superb research assistant. It would be hard to imagine The Oxford Mark Twain without the benefit of his insights and energy. A fine scholar and writer in his own right, he was crucial to making this project happen.

Georgia Barnhill, the Andrew W. Mellon Curator of Graphic Arts at the American Antiquarian Society in Worcester, Massachusetts, Tom Staley, director of the Harry Ransom Humanities Research Center at the University of Texas at Austin, and Joan Grant, director of collection services at the Elmer Holmes Bobst Library of New York University, granted us access to their collections and assisted us in the reproduction of several volumes of The Oxford Mark Twain. I would also like to thank Kenneth Craven, Sally Leach, and Richard Oram of the Harry Ransom Humanities Research Center for their help in making HRC materials available, and Jay and John Crowley, of Jay's Publishers Services in Rockland, Massachusetts, for their efforts to photograph the books carefully and attentively.

I would like to express my gratitude for the grant I was awarded by the University Research Institute of the University of Texas at Austin to defray some of the costs of researching The Oxford Mark Twain. I am also grateful to American Studies director Robert Abzug and the University of Texas for the computer that facilitated my work on this project (and to UT systems analyst Steve Alemán, who tried his best to repair the damage when it crashed). Thanks also to American Studies administrative assistant Janice Bradley and graduate coordinator Melanie Livingston for their always generous and thoughtful help.

The Oxford Mark Twain would not have happened without the unstinting, wholehearted support of my husband, Jim Fishkin, who went way beyond the proverbial call of duty more times than I'm sure he cares to remember as he shared me unselfishly with that other man in my life, Mark Twain. I am also grateful to my family — to my sons Joey and Bobby, who cheered me on all along the way, as did Fannie Fishkin, David Fishkin, Gennie Gordon, Mildred Hope Witkin, and Leonard, Gillis, and Moss

Plaine — and to honorary family member Margaret Osborne, who did the same.

My greatest debt is to the man who set all this in motion. Only a figure as rich and complicated as Mark Twain could have sustained such energy and interest on the part of so many people for so long. Never boring, never dull, Mark Twain repays our attention again and again and again. It is a privilege to be able to honor his memory with The Oxford Mark Twain.

Shelley Fisher Fishkin
Austin, Texas
April 1996